INTELLECTUAL TALENT

Previous volumes based on the annual Hyman Blumberg Symposia
on Research in Early Childhood Education
(available in both paperbound and clothbound editions)

Julian C. Stanley, general series editor

I. *Preschool Programs for the Disadvantaged: Five Experimental
    Approaches to Early Childhood Education*, pp. ix + 204, 1972.
    Edited by Julian C. Stanley.

II. *Compensatory Education for Children, Ages 2 to 8: Recent Studies
    of Educational Intervention*, pp. viii + 213, 1973.
    Edited by Julian C. Stanley.

III. *Mathematical Talent: Discovery, Description, and Development*,
    pp. xvii + 215, 1974.
    Edited by Julian C. Stanley, Daniel P. Keating, and Lynn H. Fox.

IV. *Social Development: Group and Family Influences*, in press, 1976.
    Edited by Roger A. Webb.

V. *Aspects of Reading Acquisition*, in press, 1976.
    Edited by John T. Guthrie.

The Blumberg Series is published by The Johns Hopkins University Press,
Baltimore, Maryland 21218.

INTELLECTUAL TALENT: RESEARCH AND DEVELOPMENT

Proceedings of the Sixth Annual
Hyman Blumberg Symposium
on Research in Early Childhood Education

EDITED BY DANIEL P. KEATING

THE JOHNS HOPKINS UNIVERSITY PRESS
BALTIMORE AND LONDON

Manufactured in the United States of America

The Johns Hopkins University Press, Baltimore, Maryland 21218
The Johns Hopkins University Press Ltd., London

Library of Congress Catalog Card Number 75-30554
ISBN 0-8018-1743-9 (clothbound edition)
ISBN 0-8018-1744-7 (paperbound edition)

Library of Congress Cataloging in Publication data
will be found on the last printed page of this book.

Many individuals have contributed greatly to the improvement of education for intellectually gifted students, but perhaps the most important are those teachers who seek out and nourish such talent. This volume is dedicated to three such teachers with whom SMPY had the good fortune to work during its initial phases: *Paul R. Binder, Doris K. Lidtke*, and *Joseph R. Wolfson.*

Acknowledgment

Figures 8.1, 8.2, and 11.1 were reproduced by special permission from the California Psychological Inventory by Harrison G. Gough, Ph.D. Copyright date 1956. Published by Consulting Psychologists Press, Inc., 577 College Avenue, P.O. Box 11636, Palo Alto, California 94306.

CONTENTS

Contributors   xv
Preface   xvii

I. Identification and Measurement of Intellectual Talent

1. Use of Tests to Discover Talent 3
   Julian C. Stanley

2. Discovering Quantitative Precocity 23
   Daniel P. Keating

3. Identification and Program Planning: Models and
   Methods 32
   Lynn H. Fox

4. Identifying Mathematical Talent on a Statewide Basis 55
   William C. George and Cecilia H. Solano

5. A Piagetian Approach to Intellectual Precocity 90
   Daniel P. Keating

II. Programs for Facilitation of Intellectual Talent

6. Curriculum Experimentation for the Mathematically
   Talented 103
   William C. George and Susanne A. Denham

7. Special Fast-Mathematics Classes Taught by
   College Professors to Fourth- through Twelfth-graders 132
   Julian C. Stanley

8. Verbally Gifted Youth: Selection and Description 160
   Peter V. McGinn

9. Sex Differences in Mathematical Precocity:
   Bridging the Gap 183
   Lynn H. Fox

10. Educators' Stereotypes of Mathematically Gifted Boys 215
    Richard J. Haier and Cecilia H. Solano

III. The Psychology of Intellectual Talent

11. A Summary Profile of the Nonintellectual Correlates of
Mathematical Precocity in Boys and Girls 225
Richard J. Haier and Susanne A. Denham

12. Career-related Interests of Adolescent Boys and Girls 242
Lynn H. Fox, Sara R. Pasternak, and Nancy L. Peiser

13. Creative Potential of Mathematically Precocious Boys............. 262
Daniel P. Keating

14. The Values of Gifted Youth.................................... 273
Lynn H. Fox

15. Random vs. Nonrandom Study of Values Profiles 285
Joan A. W. Linsenmeier

IV. Critique and Discussion

16. A Historical Step beyond Terman 295
Ellis Batten Page

17. SMPY in Social Perspective 308
Carl E. Bereiter

18. General Discussion 316

Index of Names 343

Tables

1.1   Success of the 10 SMPY early entrants at The Johns Hopkins
University during the fall semester of the academic year 1974–75
(all are males)   20

2.1   Grouped frequency distribution of SAT-M scores by grade and sex
for the 1972 (N = 396), 1973 (N = 667), and 1974 (N = 1519) Maryland
Mathematics Talent Searches   27

3.1   Means and standard deviations on the mathematics test (SAT-M)
for contestants in 1973, by grade and sex   36

3.2   Means and standard deviations on the verbal test (SAT-V) for
contestants in 1973, by grade and sex   36

3.3	Means and standard deviations on the mathematics test (SAT-M) for contestants in 1974, by grade and sex	37
3.4	A model for identification of seventh- and eighth-grade gifted boys and girls	46
4.1	Question—How did you find out about the Maryland Mathematics Talent Search?	65
4.2	Question—From whom did you receive the most encouragement to enter the Maryland Mathematics Talent Search?	65
	Supplemental material table 10.1 Distribution of SAT-M scores for the 26 January 1974 testing: I	84
	Supplemental material table 10.2 Distribution of all SAT-M scores for the 26 January 1974 testing: II	85
5.1	Means of four groups on Raven's Standard Progressive Matrices, with standard deviation and size of group	94
5.2	ANOVA of scores on formal operational tasks	96
6.1	Selection of Wolfson II class	106
6.2	Summary of cognitive test results for all students	108
6.3	Means and standard deviations of Holland scales and selected Basic Interest scales from the Strong–Campbell Interest Inventory	110
6.4	Rank order of the Holland scales from the Strong–Campbell Interest Inventory	111
6.5	Means and standard deviations of the six values from the Allport–Vernon–Lindzey Study of Values (SV)	113
6.6	Means and standard deviations of the six values from the Allport–Vernon–Lindzey Study of Values (SV) compared to norm group	114
6.7	Rank order of the six values for the Allport-Vernon–Lindzey Study of Values (SV)	116
6.8	Parents' level of education	117
6.9	Means and standard deviations of parental influence exerted on students during phases of class	118
6.10	Results of algebra II and algebra III tests	120
6.11	Product-moment correlations between test scores for various tests given to the Wolfson II class	121
6.A1	Update of Wolfson II from plane geometry	128
7.1	Tests information concerning the McCoart Saturday morning calculus class, September 1974 until May 1975	149
7.A1	Academic Promise Test (APT) and Raven's Standard Progressive Matrices (SPM) scores of 17 preselected boys and 23 preselected girls in the fourth through seventh grades of School R, 19–20 December 1973	155

7.A2   Differential Aptitude Test raw scores (RS) and percentile ranks (PR) of the 16 Wolfson I students on the 8 subtests of Form S, administered 12 May 1973   158

8.1   Comparison of SAT-V and SAT-M scores of Verbal Talent Search students with a norm group of college-bound juniors and seniors   163

8.2   Correlations between students' scores on SAT-V and demographic and biographic characteristics   164

8.3   Distribution of students' responses on selected biographic and demographic variables   165

8.4   Percentages of responses on selected biographic items   166

8.5   Comparison of average Study of Values scores of Verbal Talent Search boys with those of a norm group of high school boys reported by Allport, Vernon, and Lindzey (1970)   169

8.6   Comparison of average Study of Values scores of Verbal Talent Search girls with those of a norm group of high school girls reported by Allport, Vernon, and Lindzey (1970)   169

8.7   Average performance on seven tests by students with SAT-verbal scores greater than or equal to 570   171

8.8   Percent and mean strength of preferences on the Myers–Briggs Type Indicator by boys and girls in the 1973 summer program   175

8.9   Average scores of summer participants on Holland's Self-directed Search   176

8.10   Interrater correlations for rating of performance in summer program   177

8.11   Correlations between rating of performance in summer enrichment program and scores on eight tests of creativity and mental ability   178

8.A1   SAT-V scores of students at each level of parental education and occupation   182

9.1   Mean scores on SAT-M for students, by grade and sex, in the 1972, 1973, and 1974 talent searches   184

9.2   Scores on SAT-M for the three groups   190

9.3   Analysis of variance of SAT-M scores for the three groups   191

9.4   Tukey comparison of mean scores on the SAT-M for the three groups   191

9.5   Percent of mothers by level of education for the three groups   192

9.6   Percent of fathers by level of education for the three groups   193

9.7   Percent of fathers by Holland occupational type for the three groups   193

9.8   The number-correct score and percentile rank on ninth-grade national norms and the corrected-for-chance (C.C.) score on the algebra I pretest for the three groups   194

9.9   Analysis of variance of algebra I pretest scores for the
       three groups   195

9.10   Correlations between scores on SAT-M, SAT-V, and the
       algebra I test for each of the three groups and correlations
       between groups on the three tests   196

9.11   Mean scores on SAT-V and SAT-M for girls in each of the
       three accelerated mathematics programs   197

9.12   Acceptance and completion rates for girls in each of the
       three accelerated mathematics programs   198

9.13   Comparisons of girls who dropped out of the all-girl program
       with those who remained, on selected characteristics   198

9.14   Posttest algebra I test scores and percentile ranks on
       ninth-grade national norms for 18 girls who completed
       algebra I   199

9.15   Posttest algebra I scores and percentile ranks on eighth- and
       ninth-grade national norms for the three groups   200

9.16   Analysis of covariance of scores on posttest algebra I for the
       three groups   201

9.17   Tukey comparison of mean differences on posttest algebra I
       for the three groups   202

9.18   Flow chart of the all-girl algebra I class   205

9.19   Scores on cognitive tests for 18 girls who completed the special
       program, by degree of success in algebra II   206

9.20   Selected characteristics of girls who completed algebra I in the
       all-girl program, by degree of success in algebra II   208

10.1   Percent of educators with negative stereotypes   218

10.2   Unfavorable and favorable adjectives most frequently checked
       by educators holding *negative* stereotypes (percents checking) 219

10.3   Unfavorable and favorable adjectives most frequently checked
       by educators holding *positive* stereotypes (percents checking) 220

11.1   Means of the pooled MG boys group compared with the male
       EGR, EGG, HSG, and HSN groups on the CPI Scales   230

11.2   Means of MG girls group compared with female EGR, EGG, HSG,
       and HSN groups on the CPI scales   233

11.3   Comparison of the MG boys with a norm group on the Eysenck
       Personality Inventory   234

11.4   Percent of MG boys and girls scoring highest on each scale of the
       Study of Values   235

11.5   Percent of MG boys and girls scoring highest on each scale of the
       Vocational Preference Inventory   236

11.6 Standard score means and standard deviations of MG boys and creative and noncreative high school boys on the favorable and unfavorable ACL Scales 238

11.7 The percent of the most favorable and unfavorable adjectives selected by the MG boys compared with the frequency of those adjectives selected by a control sample 238

12.1 Scores on SAT-M and SAT-V for the matched pairs of boys and girls in the sample of gifted students 244

12.2 Scores on the 23 Strong–Campbell Basic Interest Scales for the sample of gifted students 246

12.3 Analysis of variance of preferences for the 23 Basic Interest Scales for the sample of gifted students 247

12.4 Scores on the 23 Strong–Campbell Basic Interest Scales for the sample of average ninth-grade students 250

12.5 Differences greater than five points on the 23 Strong–Campbell Basic Interest Scales between gifted and average samples by sex 251

12.6 Mean ratings of eight careers for the three gifted groups 254

12.7 Rank order of occupations for the three gifted groups 254

12.8 Analysis of variance of eight careers on the semantic differential for the three gifted groups 255

12.9 Tukey comparison of mean differences of ratings of careers among the three gifted groups 256

12.10 Tukey comparison of mean differences of ratings of each of the four male careers with each of the four female careers for the three gifted groups 257

12.11 Mean ratings of the four male and four female careers for the three gifted groups 257

13.1 Frequency of occurrence of the six SV values as highest, second highest, or lowest as percent of total 265

13.2 Mean scores of mathematically precocious boys on five measures related to creativity 267

13.3 Correlation matrix of five measures related to creativity for 57 mathematically precocious boys (base group) 269

13.4 Students at or above criterion, within-group and norm-group comparisons 269

13.5 Percent of students at or above within-group or norm-group criteria on one or more creativity-related measures (N = 57) 270

14.1 Means and standard deviations of scores on the Study of Values for 656 seventh- and eighth-grade students in the 1973 mathematics contest compared with those of high school students 275

14.2   Rank order of values for gifted seventh- and eighth-graders and high school students   276

14.3   Percent of students by their highest value on the Study of Values for 656 students in the 1973 mathematics contest   277

14.4   Means on the six values of the Allport–Vernon–Lindzey Study of Values for the three groups   278

14.5   ANOVA of preferences for six values on the Allport–Vernon–Lindzey Study of Values for the three groups   279

14.6   Tukey comparison of the mean scores on measures of theoretical and social values for the three groups   279

14.7   Means and standard deviations of SAT-M scores for 656 contestants in 1973 by highest value on the Study of Values   280

14.8   Percent of boys in the 1973 mathematics contest and winners from the 1972, 1973, and 1974 contests by highest value on the Study of Values   281

15.1   Distributions of scale scores for random profiles and actual subjects   289

15.2   Deviations of scores on actual profiles about means for edition 1 random profiles (percentages)   290

15.3   Distributions of profile standard deviations   290

16.1   Contribution of a "minority group" to extreme high scores of a population, given that minority group has 4 percent of total group and has a mean 0.6 σ above majority mean   305

Figures

2.1   Distribution of SAT-M scores from the first competition (1972)   25

2.2   Distribution of SAT-M scores from the second competition (1973)   26

4.1   Location of test centers in Maryland   58

5.1   Percent demonstrating formal operations on three tasks   95

6.1   Mean scores of boys for the six values from the Allport–Vernon–Lindzey Study of Values   115

6.2   Mean score of girls for the six values from the Allport–Vernon–Lindzey Study of Values   116

7.1   The Academic Promise Test numerical scores of the 40 students   137

8.1   Average CPI performance of 24 high SAT-V girls compared with
        adult norms and a random sample of eighth-graders tested by
        Lessinger and Martinson (1961)   173

8.2   Average CPI performance of 27 high SAT-V boys compared with
        adult norms and a random sample of eighth-graders tested by Lessinger
        and Martinson (1961)   174

11.1   Mathematically gifted (MG) boys and girls compared with eighth-
        grade random boys and girls from Lessinger and Martinson (1961)   231

15.1   Standard deviations of Study of Values profiles   291

Contributors

Carl E. Bereiter is a professor in the Department of Applied Psychology at the Ontario Institute for Studies in Education, Toronto, Ontario, Canada.

Susanne A. Denham, who received her M.A. degree in psychology from The Johns Hopkins University in 1974, is currently a consultant in educational and psychological testing for the Carroll County Board of Education, Westminster, Maryland.

Lynn H. Fox is director of the Intellectually Gifted Child Study Group and an assistant professor in the Evening College of The Johns Hopkins University, Baltimore, Maryland.

William C. George is the associate director of the Study of Mathematically Precocious Youth and a graduate student in the Evening College of The Johns Hopkins University, Baltimore, Maryland, from which he received a master's degree in 1975.

Richard J. Haier received his Ph.D. degree in psychology in 1975 from The Johns Hopkins University, Baltimore, Maryland. He is a researcher at the National Institute of Mental Health, Bethesda, Maryland.

Daniel P. Keating is an assistant professor in The Institute of Child Development, University of Minnesota, Minneapolis, Minnesota.

Joan A. W. Linsenmeier is a doctoral candidate in the Department of Psychology, Northwestern University, Evanston, Illinois.

Peter V. McGinn is a project associate of the Study of Verbally Gifted Youth and a doctoral candidate in the Department of Psychology, The Johns Hopkins University, Baltimore, Maryland.

Ellis B. Page is a professor of educational psychology at the University of Connecticut, Storrs, Connecticut.

Sara R. Pasternak, who received her B.A. degree in psychology from The Johns Hopkins University in 1974, is currently a psychological technician at the Adult Cortical Function Laboratory of The Johns Hopkins University Hospital and Medical School, Baltimore, Maryland.

Nancy L. Peiser, who received her B.A. degree in psychology from Goucher College in 1974, is currently a graduate student of dance at Southern Methodist University, Dallas, Texas, and an intern dance therapist.

Cecilia H. Solano is a project associate of the Study of Mathematically Precocious Youth, editor of its *Intellectually Talented Youth Bulletin*, and a doctoral candidate in the Department of Psychology at The Johns Hopkins University, Baltimore, Maryland.

Julian C. Stanley is director of the Study of Mathematically Precocious Youth and a professor of psychology at The Johns Hopkins University, Baltimore, Maryland.

Preface

Following a two-volume hiatus, the Blumberg series returns with this volume to the topic of intellectual talent. The current volume is based on the Sixth Annual Hyman Blumberg Symposium on Research in Early Childhood Education, which was held on October 4, 1974 at the Evergreen House of The Johns Hopkins University. Brief abstracts of fifteen papers were presented in the morning session, along with the two longer critiques by Ellis B. Page and Carl E. Bereiter. These comprise chapters 1 through 17 in this volume. The afternoon session was devoted to a general discussion, which is reported in full in chapter 18.

As noted above, the preceding volume in this series on the topic of intellectual talent was a result of the Third Annual Hyman Blumberg Symposium, which was published in 1974 as *Mathematical Talent: Discovery, Description, and Development*. That was also the first volume of *Studies of Intellectual Precocity* (Julian C. Stanley, Daniel P. Keating, and Lynn H. Fox, general editors); the current volume is the second in that series. Most of the reports in this volume again are from the Study of Mathematically Precocious Youth (SMPY), which is directed by Julian C. Stanley and funded by the Spencer Foundation of Chicago. The Spencer Foundation has also funded the Study of Verbally Gifted Youth (SVGY), directed by Robert T. Hogan and Catherine Garvey. In chapter 8 Peter V. McGinn reports on the results from that project. A National Science Foundation grant to the editor provided support for the research reported in chapter 5.

The four major sections of this volume help to organize the topics considered. Sections I–III are composed of five chapters each; the final section has three chapters. The first section concerns identification and measurement problems; the second section deals with educational research programs; the third section describes the psychological characteristics of these highly gifted youths; and the fourth section contains the critiques and the general discussion.

The editor of this volume wishes to thank Julian C. Stanley, not only for the opportunity to arrange and conduct this symposium but also for his professional and personal generosity. I thank also the authors of the various chapters, whose enthusiasm and willingness to work through several drafts is greatly appreciated.

As the acting director of SMPY during the first eight months of 1974, I wish to thank again the following groups and individuals: the educational institutions and teachers in the state of Maryland—elementary, secondary, and collegiate—without whose cooperation much of the research reported here would not have been possible; the College Entrance Examination Board and its Trial Administration Program, especially Sam A. McCandless and Michele Mayo Battermann, for their continuing assistance; The Johns Hopkins University, especially Vice President George S. Benton, University Registrar Robert E. Cyphers, and the Office of Admissions, whose generous support is much appreciated; and, far from least, the students with whom we have worked, whose enthusiasm and dedication make it all worthwhile.

A special note of thanks goes once again to the Amalgamated Clothing Workers of America for the $110,000 endowment that it funded at The Johns Hopkins University in 1969. Income from the endowment supports the Annual Hyman Blumberg Symposium, but the union has no responsibility for the contents of the symposia or the volumes resulting therefrom.

William B. Michael again provided a careful critique of an earlier draft of the manuscript, and the volume was much improved by his suggestions. The critiques by Ellis B. Page and Carl E. Bereiter, both formal and informal, were also of considerable assistance. None are of course responsible for any errors which remain.

The staff of SMPY has received much helpful advice about the teaching and learning of mathematics from many mathematicians, especially the following: Professors Frank Grosshaus, Roger A. Horn, Susan D. Horn, Jean-Pierre Meyer, and Joseph Shalika of The Johns Hopkins University; Professor Richard F. McCoart, Chairman of the Department of Mathematics at Loyola College in Baltimore; Professor Ann L. Wagner of Towson State College in Baltimore; and Professor George W. Booth of Brooklyn College, New York.

Virginia S. Grim, Joan A. Pierce, and Lois S. Sandhofer showed great patience and expertise in typing the various drafts of the manuscript. I especially wish to thank William C. George, who helped greatly in the organization and planning of the symposium and in the assembling of the manuscript.

DANIEL P. KEATING

Institute of Child Development
University of Minnesota

I

IDENTIFICATION AND MEASUREMENT OF INTELLECTUAL TALENT

1

USE OF TESTS TO DISCOVER TALENT[1]

Julian C. Stanley

ABSTRACT

Aptitude and achievement tests designed for much older students are invaluable for finding extremely high ability at younger ages. Results of the first three years of the Study of Mathematically Precocious Youth (SMPY) at The Johns Hopkins University are examined to show that considerable educational acceleration is not only feasible but also desirable for those young people who are eager to move ahead. Skipping school grades, taking college courses part-time, studying in special courses, and entering college early are inexpensive and supplemental to regular school practices. We do not advocate the usual in-grade, nonaccelerative "enrichment" procedures often recommended for intellectually gifted children. An heuristic overview is presented of the main assumptions and findings of the study thus far.

Once a year the Division of Evaluation and Measurement of the American Psychological Association allows an elder of its tribe to pontificate for fifty minutes on whatever topic he or she chooses. These presidential addresses tend to be hortatory, heuristic, summarizing, philosophical, or polemic, rather than primarily substantive and empirical. My first impulse was to overwhelm you with data from the five-year Study of Mathematically Precocious Youth (SMPY), funded by the Spencer Foundation, which my associates and I at Johns Hopkins have been conducting since September 1971. That would be

[1]Revised version of presidential address to Division 5 (Evaluation and Measurement) of the American Psychological Association on 27 August 1973 at its annual meeting in Montreal, Canada. I thank the Spencer Foundation for financial support that made this work possible and my associates Susanne A. Denham, Lynn H. Fox, William C. George, Linda K. Greenstein, Daniel P. Keating, and Cecilia H. Solano for their contributions to the study. Dr. Keating made numerous helpful suggestions concerning earlier drafts of this paper. Professor Ellis B. Page made important contributions to it. An earlier version appeared in the *Educational Psychologist* (see Stanley 1973). We thank APA Division 15 for permission to reproduce it in updated form.

redundant, however, because in 1974 The Johns Hopkins University Press published our *Mathematical talent: Discovery, description, and development* (Stanley, Keating, & Fox 1974), which reports on the first year or so. It is volume I of our *Studies of Intellectual Precocity.*[2]

Instead, I shall pursue a theme that, in my opinion, has been badly neglected: how tests can be valuable for quick, tentative identification of intellectually promising persons. High scores on standardized aptitude and achievement tests are probably the *best single* clue to high potential, often more valid than school grades or teachers' recommendations. Of course, identification in this way must be preliminary and supplemented by other evidence. There will be false positives, because not all high-scorers succeed in areas for which they seem to have talent. In my experience, however, the percent of false negatives on the basis of nontest information is usually greater; nontest procedures tend to miss many intellectually gifted persons. This is not an "either-or" matter; no wise measurement specialist would base judgments solely on test scores.

A corollary seems to be that the more one tests an intially highscoring individual, the greater the dependence one can put on the test-score data when planning radically accelerated educational programs, and the less direct use one needs to make of prior school information. By testing the promising examinees further for several full days with aptitude and achievement tests of *appropriate difficulty*, as well as personality and interest inventories, one can predict rather well which persons will succeed in courses and curricula far above the ones in which they are now placed.

The matter of "appropriate difficulty" of tests has also received less emphasis from measurement specialists than it merits. Recently, for instance, I was told of a sixth-grader who had a grade equivalent of eleven years zero months on a vocabulary test. This is remarkable, but it becomes more so when the fact that this student made a perfect score on the test is revealed. Because of lack of "ceiling" she was not adequately tested, and therefore should be examined further with a more appropriately difficult test, such as the verbal part of the Scholastic Aptitude Test (after she studies the practice booklet carefully). For further treatment of this topic see Keating (chapter 2 of this volume).

A third, closely related, point is that the higher the score the greater the potential of the scorer. Hollingworth and Cobb (1928) demonstrated this experimentally, and we have added much new evidence. Youngsters who score at the 99.0th percentile are extremely able of course, but not nearly as excellent learners as those who score much higher, e.g., the 99.9th percentile. Keating (see chapter 2 of this volume) and Fox (1974c) have treated the difficulty and validity points in considerable detail.

---

[2]In addition to the regular references, citations of chapters in that previous volume will be abbreviated throughout this book in the following manner: [I:1]. The I indicates the first volume of *Studies of Intellectual Precocity*; the 1 indicates chapter 1 of the volume [Editor].

Too often we have allowed both ourselves and the opponents of tests to believe that after a certain high score is reached more points do not make an appreciable difference in validity. This is an empirically testable assumption, of course. I do not know of any general evidence that it is true, and I do have considerable specific evidence that it is false. Very likely, the problem is that under the status quo of schools and similar organizations the extra validity is not used. If one already knows nearly everything in a course when it begins, or can learn almost instantaneously whatever little is new, ability beyond that is superfluous. What differences does it make in an eighth-grade general science class for a pupil to score at the 90th vs. the 99th percentile of college seniors on a college-level achievement test in general science? At either level, he or she will probably find practically no academic challenge in the class. But if the 90th percentile student is put into an appropriately taught class with those who scored at the 99th percentile, he may have difficulty keeping up. The fault is not in the validity of the test, but in the utter inadequacy of the general science course for both of these pupils. Such students need to be freed from their academic incarceration and given more suitably difficult subject matter.

In this preamble I have made three related assertions. To recapitulate, they are as follows:

1. Tests are a prime way—probably *the* prime way—for the preliminary identification of high-level developed aptitude or achievement.

2. It is even more important than generally realized for tests to have enough "ceiling" (and "floor," too) for each individual tested. This means bold use of tests designed for much older persons, as Hollingworth (1942) illustrated long ago.

3. The higher an examinee's scores are, the greater his or her potential tends to be. For *appropriate criteria*, validity does not drop at the upper part of the score range of a test *that is difficult enough* for the persons tested.

Out of these three points grows emphasis on the validity of the tests designed for older students when they are administered to brilliant younger ones. For example, highly precocious children can be tested well by tests designed for average and superior adolescents, and extremely able adolescents can be tested well by tests designed for average or superior adults. With all the fashionable speaking out against tests, against intelligence as a concept, and with all the efforts to distort the use of normative assumptions and to pretend (truthfully but misleadingly) that "everyone is an individual"—notwithstanding these trends, the fact remains: mental ability seems to be linear and additive, and the generalized concept of "mental age" is still an extraordinarily useful one. SMPY's programs are based on the recognition that, cognitively, the brilliant early adolescent is the match of a superior adult, and that the child continues growing mentally surely as long as he keeps growing physically. This means that high mental abilities, well beyond one's chronological age, imply higher final levels of ability—*higher*, not just earlier. High test scores at an early age do not, then, merely indicate "developmental" differences of rate or sequence. They presage long-range, lasting differences in ultimate ability.

EARLY BACKGROUND

Asking your indulgence for some reminiscing, I shall go back to my psychometric beginnings and illustrate how high test scores have alerted me to previously undiscovered talent—not always usable, of course. I was born shortly before World War I ended. That was thirteen years after the first form of the Binet–Simon intelligence test was published, two years after the appearance of Terman's original Stanford–Binet Intelligence Scale, and one year after the Army Alpha test was first employed. I entered the first grade in 1924 (there were few kindergartens then) and by skipping the fourth grade got into the first year of senior high school (grades 8–11) in 1930. While in the sixth or seventh grade I was told rather casually one spring day, by the special teacher for mathematics, that on what I would now call a standardized achievement-test battery my score in arithmetic was at the eleventh-grade level. This puzzled me a bit, because obviously I was not in that higher grade, but my curiosity wasn't great enough to impel me to ask the teacher about this phenomenon. I suspect that she, a fine mathematics teacher but probably completely untrained in testing, would not have been able to inform me further.

That seems to have been the only standardized test I took during those ten years of public school. In fact, because high school students who had grades of 90 percent or more in a subject during a given quarter were not required to take the final examination that quarter, I took few examinations of any kind other than weekly or mid-quarter quizzes. This pleased me then, but the inexorable examinations at college made the wisdom of those exemptions less clear later.

Standardized examinations were administered to all of us who entered the residential state junior colleges, but we received no information concerning the scores. Soon after graduation I tried to find out something about them, but apparently the answer sheets and score records had been discarded during the two-year period—unfortunately, not an uncommon way to treat test results, as if the mere taking of the tests conferred the benefits.

By August of the year that the Revised Stanford–Binet Intelligence Scales (Forms L and M) appeared (1937), I was through college and a barely nineteen-year-old senior high school teacher of science and mathematics in Atlanta. The next summer I attended a six-weeks session at the University of Georgia and took a standard course in tests and measurements, using Tiegs's (1931) book. The professor who taught that course administered to us quite a number of tests under standard conditions, among them the Otis Self-Administering Tests of Mental Ability, the Ohio State University Psychological Examination, and the Miller Group Mental Test. This experience whetted my interest in tests. For a year or two I went around administering the Otis to my students, members of my family, various girl friends, and some of my sister's boy friends. Also, I used a standardized chemistry test in the chemistry course I was teaching, but first I made sure that I had taught my class the specific point underlying every item! The ensuing scores were, to say the least, extremely high. One student scored 30 points above the 99th percentile. He wasn't *that* good, but the next fall he was the no. 1 student in chemistry at the Georgia Institute of Technology, so by inadvertently coaching for the test I had merely made an excellent examinee into a superb one.

During World War II, I saw many personnel records and informally compared Army General Classification Test (AGCT) scores with soldiers' educational and occupational backgrounds. It became obvious to me that some of the top scorers had missed the educational and vocational boats badly. For example, the highest-scoring enlisted man in our Corsican bomber command headquarters was a thirty-year-old high school graduate who in civilian life had been a postal clerk. On the AGCT he scored far above a Yale University Ph.D. and a New York lawyer in the group. It occurred to me vaguely that, to update Thomas Gray's immortal words, "Full many a brilliant person will not have his or her abilities recognized and nurtured." What if these persons' high scores had been known earlier and formed a basis for maximizing the utilization of their abilities? I resolved—rather dimly at the time, to be sure—to do something about this presumed wastage of talent.

LATER ILLUSTRATIONS

Four years of graduate study and teaching at Harvard University under the G.I. Bill brought contacts with Truman Kelley, Phillip Rulon, Walter Dearborn, Frederick Davis, and others that professionalized my interests in intellectual giftedness as revealed by tests. I left Harvard in 1949 to be the specialist in psychological statistics, measurement, experimental design, and research methodology at the George Peabody College for Teachers and part-time at Vanderbilt University across the street. As if this variegated assignment wasn't enough, I was also in charge of all testing at every level at Peabody: American Council on Education Psychological Examination and other instruments for incoming freshmen, Miller Analogies Test for graduate students, etc.

In addition, I was in charge of an IBM electric (not electronic) test-scoring machine that was used to score objective tests and examinations for any professors who requested that service. It was this temperamental, balky, clumsy machine that led to my first major postdoctoral discovery of academic talent, serendipitous rather than planned. A professor who tended to attract the most mediocre students to his classes had tested them with the American Council on Education Psychological Examination. As my two scorers expected, most of the scores ran quite low, but one student's stood out glaringly because hers were so much higher than the others', and practically perfect. The scorers suspected that this aberrant examinee may have had a scoring key. I glanced at her name and realized that she was a student in my large, very elementary statistics course. Apparently, she was exceptionally able, and bored. Having been graduated from college with high honors in English and mathematics at age eighteen and having taught for five years in high school, she was now working for a general master's degree in education with no definite goal in mind. The two scores alerted us to her potential, however. By the end of the year she had a master's degree in psychology and went on to obtain the Ph.D. degree in experimental psychology with top honors at a large university. Today she is an outstanding educational psychologist.

Over the years I continued this process, both serendipitously and deliberately. For example, in the summer of 1956 I tried out the recently published Terman Concept Mastery Test (CMT) of the Psychological Corporation on the eighty-three students in a large graduate educational psychology course at the University of Wisconsin. Total scores ranged from a shocking low of 11 points out of the possible 190 to a high of 169. Terman's "geniuses" who had earned Ph.D. degrees averaged 159 at age forty, so 169 was indeed very impressive. I talked with the young man and discovered that he had been graduated from a major university with high honors and election to Phi Beta Kappa. Then he had taken a master's degree in comparative literature but did not impress his hard-to-please major professor favorably enough to go on toward the doctorate. He was "retreading" to become a junior high school teacher of English. We helped him get university fellowships for three years and earn a Ph.D. degree in measurement. Nine years after taking the CMT test he was a full professor at a top-level university.

Though most of the high test-scorers went on to become quite successful, a few did not. One of the brightest I've found was an underachiever as an undergraduate and continued to be so in the doctoral program and thereafter, though in his first graduate year he did some astonishingly brilliant research. He has great mental ability, but seems chronically unable to use much of it effectively in a sustained manner.

Test scores can serve as useful antidotes to personality characteristics that make a person appear less bright than he or she really is. For example, a young man who scored 94 out of 100 points on the Miller Analogies Test and 49 out of 50 points on the Doppelt Mathematical Reasoning Test, even though he had little background in mathematics, was thought by a famed quantitative specialist to be rather mediocre intellectually because he was somewhat rigid and contentious. When encouraged to pursue a doctoral program, however, he quickly did important, original research that made his name widely known even before he received the Ph.D. degree. Nothing in his academic background or recommendations indicated how able he was. The test scores furnished the needed clue.

OUR FIRST "RADICAL ACCELERANT"

It would be possible to continue in this vein for the rest of this chapter, but instead I shall move on to more systematic use of test information in our Study of Mathematically Precocious Youth (SMPY). We have leaned heavily on test scores and with results so good they surprised even me. Leading up to the funding of the Study by the Spencer Foundation was my testing experience in early 1969 with Joseph Louis Bates,[3] a thirteen-year-old eighth-grader who during the preceding summer had taken a special computer course at Johns Hopkins. He was so startlingly precocious that the instructor of this course called him to my attention.

Joseph's scores on college-level and graduate-level tests, including College Board ones and the Doppelt Mathematical Reasoning Test, were so strikingly high that finally, for want of a better alternative, I had him admitted to Johns Hopkins in the fall of 1969, while he was still thirteen years old, to take honors calculus, *sophomore* general physics, and introduction to computer science. On that thirteen-semester-hour load of difficult courses he made a grade of A in both physics and computer science, ranking near the top of the large class in the latter, and a high B in honors calculus. His gradepoint average was 3.69, where 4.00 is straight A. Joseph went on to earn the B.A. degree in quantitative studies in May 1973 and the M.S. Engr. degree in computer science three months later. In the fall of 1973, while not yet eighteen years old, he began work toward the Ph.D. degree in computer science at Cornell University on a university fellowship.[4] Without that testing four years earlier he would probably have been a college freshman then. The thought of that stultifying possibility makes him, and his parents, pale.

ANOTHER SKIPS FOUR YEARS, A THIRD "ONLY" TWO

But one radical-accelerant swallow does not make an academic spring. For all we knew, Joseph was the only person in the country who could skip four years of high school profitably. The finding needed replication. By an improb-

---

[3]This is his real name, used by permission so that interested persons can follow his progress if they wish.

[4]Joseph has progressed excellently at Cornell. During his first year he passed all four written comprehensive examinations for the doctorate and two of the four oral ones. Also, he has served as a teaching assistant.

able coincidence this was obtained the next year (while Joseph was a sopho-more) because the parents of another precocious eighth-grader, Jonathan Middleton Edwards, happened to hear of Joseph. They urged me to admit their son in the fall of 1970, and eventually I did, after ascertaining that on test scores he was virtually Joseph's twin. (They were quite different in personality, however.) This young man was thirteen years old until November of his freshman year. His first-semester GPA was 3.75 and he has done well since then.

Then we skipped a year and in the fall of 1972 admitted, at the end of tenth grade, Jeffrey Nathan Rottman, who had written me about his academic dilemma. Jeff completed the freshman year with high As on all his 40 credits. He proved to be vastly overqualified even for Johns Hopkins. Clearly, he had been academically ready to enter college at least a year earlier. In the fall of 1973 he transferred to Princeton University, made a splendid record there in his sophomore year, and continued into his junior year as an eighteen-year-old mathematics major.

In the fall of 1973 two fourteen-year-olds entered Johns Hopkins, each with four or five college courses already completed while in high school. In September 1974, fourteen more students began several years early at Johns Hopkins or elsewhere. Each fall thereafter for several years we expect a dozen or more early entrants. Most of them will live at home, at least during the freshman year, and take, initially, whatever courses they can probably do best—typically, during the first semester, honors or advanced calculus, physics, and chemistry or computer science.

SMPY BEGINS

The experiences with the two thirteen-year-old boys emboldened me to apply to the newly created Spencer Foundation for, and get, a five-year grant, beginning 1 September 1971, to study extreme mathematical precocity syste-matically. We began with a nominations system, but it yielded too few seventh-, eighth-, and under-age ninth-graders at the high level we desired, roughly the upper one-half of one percent of the age group. Therefore, in March 1972 we launched a talent-search test competition, and conducted it again in January 1973 and 1974.

The first year we administered the College Entrance Examination Board's Scholastic Aptitude Test—Mathematical (SAT-M), and Mathematics I (i.e., lower level) Achievement Test to all mathematics competitors, and the Educational Testing Service's Sequential Test of Educational Progress (STEP) Science, Level I, Forms A and B, to all science competitors. Examinees were in the seventh or eighth grade, or, if in a higher grade, not yet fourteen years old. Two hundred fifty-eight boys and girls took the two mathematics tests only, 54 took the two science tests only, and 138 took both. They were meant to be drawn from the upper 5 percent of the age group, and probably most of those who came after seeing the practice materials were in the upper 2 or 3 percent. Many of the scores were gratifyingly high. For example, of the 396 who took the mathematics tests, 22 scored at least 660 on SAT-M, which is higher than the average Johns Hopkins University freshman scored when he was a high school junior or senior; one thirteen-year-old boy scored 790. In fact, 10 percent of all the 223 male mathematics entrants scored 660 or more. There was an unexpected sex difference: none of the 173 girls scored more than 600 on SAT-M, and 43 of the boys (19 percent) scored higher on that test than any girl did.

The results for science were similarly high. One seventh-grade boy scored 137 points out of a possible 150, which is the 99th percentile of college sophomores tested in the spring. Twenty-two of the 129 boys (17 percent) exceeded the top-scoring one of the 63 girls. We do not know *why* the top-scoring boys exceeded the top-scoring girls so greatly on both tests. Descriptively, this seems to mean that, while twelve thirteen-year-old girls are often extremely good mathematics or science students in their school grade (competing well with boys there), they are not learning outside of class enough of these subjects to score high on *college-level* tests. In a sense, they are as "smart" as the boys, but not as precocious in mathematics or science as the best boys. Astin (1974 [I:4]) and Fox (chapter 9 of this volume) have investigated sex differences in these subjects and tried systematically to eliminate or minimize them.

A LARGER COMPETITION THE SECOND YEAR

The competition in 1972 attracted entrants mainly from the greater Baltimore area. In 1973 we went farther afield, to the whole state, and especially to talent-rich Montgomery County north of the District of Columbia. Only the Scholastic Aptitude Test was used, but both parts (mathematical and verbal) were administered. We had decided from the first year's experience that it was better to locate the excellent mathematics reasoners in the general competition and to test them later for knowledge of general science. Scores ranged from 210 to 740 on verbal and 210 to 800 on mathematical. Thirty-seven of the 537 boys (7 percent) scored at least 660 on SAT-M, and 2 (one of them a seventh-grader) earned 800s. The reduction from 10 percent above 660 on SAT-M in 1972 to 7 percent in 1973 probably resulted partly from the fact that two competitions (verbal and mathematical) were run in 1973, but not in the preceding year. Five of the high-scorers on SAT-M came from the verbal competition.[5]

[5]The Study of Verbally Gifted Youth, funded by the Spencer Foundation for the period 1 September 1972–31 August 1977, is conducted at The Johns Hopkins University by Robert T. Hogan and Catherine J. Garvey. On 3 February 1973, 287 students were tested in the verbal

One of the 416 girls earned a score of 650 on SAT-M, so only 7 percent of the boys exceeded the top girl, vs. 19 percent in 1972. Better publicity, wider searching, and increased confidence in the testing situation seemed to produce more female mathematical talent, but even then 37 boys exceeded the top-scoring girl on this difficult test. In 1974 the percentage of nonoverlap dropped farther, to 1.7 percent. One girl scored 700, vs. 760 for the top boy.[6]

As might be expected, we have found our mathematics competition groups somewhat more precocious on the mathematical part of the SAT than on its verbal sections, but the difference is not dramatic. Few who score high on SAT-M fail to score high on SAT-V also, though usually not quite as high in terms of percentile rank of high school seniors. There is no *idiot savant* among the high SAT-M scorers. For example, the 35 top boys in 1972 averaged 660 (95th percentile of male high school seniors) on SAT-M and 546 (87th percentile of male high school seniors) on SAT-V when administered to them a month later. Only one verbal score was below 400, whereas 390 is the median of high school seniors. One was 740, compared with Johns Hopkins' average of about 610.

This brief background of material reported more fully elsewhere (Stanley, Keating, & Fox 1972; Keating & Stanley 1972; Stanley, Keating, & Fox 1974) is meant as further evidence concerning the first two of the three themes previously set forth. We discovered youths with great mathematical reasoning ability, studied them much more fully via several additional days of testing with high-level instruments, and then facilitated their educational development. Some of them skipped one or more grades in school, some entered college early, many took college courses for credit on a part-time basis, and quite a few had their mathematical development markedly accelerated in six special classes that we set up. Of course, a few chose not to do anything unusual at the time, but all of the highest-scorers received considerable educational counseling personally, by telephone, and via a monthly newsletter.

---

competition. Most of those who came on January 27 were more interested in mathematics than in the verbal area, whereas the opposite was true of the February 3 group. Nevertheless, of the 37 boys who scored at least 660 on SAT-M, 5 were tested in the so-called verbal competition. Similarly, the two highest verbal scores (710 and 740, earned by boys) occurred on January 27. But in every sex and grade category the January group scored higher on SAT-M than did the February group, and the opposite was true for SAT-V. The overall means were 516 vs. 442 for SAT-M, and 417 vs. 445 for SAT-V. The 74-point difference for M greatly exceeds the 28-point difference for V, so, apparently, the mathematically oriented youngsters knew their abilities rather well and were not handicapped verbally. A possible source of confounding should be noted, however: for motivational reasons, in January SAT-M was administered first, whereas in February SAT-V came first. See chapter 8 of this volume for a report on the verbal study.

[6]The 700 was not an extreme deviation from the rest of the girls. Two girls scored 690, two scored 680, two scored 660, and four scored 650, whereas the previous year only one girl had scored as high as 650.

SKIPPING GRADES

We judged that any of the high-scoring students were academically ready to skip one or more school grades. Much depends on how strongly the boy or girl wants to move ahead. Thus far, many of the boys—but few of the girls—have chosen this route. Two boys skipped from sixth to eighth to tenth grades. At age fourteen, the older of these entered Johns Hopkins as a full-time student at the end of the tenth grade. He had already taken six college courses: computer science in the Johns Hopkins day school at age thirteen, earning an A; set theory, economics, and political science at a local state college; and two semesters of chemistry. Also, he had earned four semester-hour credits in calculus and ten in physics by scoring well on Advanced Placement Program Examinations.

Another boy, the top scorer in the first mathematics competition, skipped the eighth and tenth grades. Several boys skipped the ninth grade of junior high school in order to get into a senior high school where courses are more appropriately difficult—often, to take twelfth-grade calculus. Two students discovered independently of the mathematics competitions went from the fourth to the seventh to the ninth grades. All who have skipped report good personal adjustment and no appreciable academic difficulties. At least three have won the mathematics contest in their high school while still ninth- or tenth-graders. Most of them plan to enter college early by completing high school in two years or simply leaving at the end of the tenth or eleventh grade.

BECOMING FULL-TIME FRESHMEN EARLY

Early entrance to college has already been discussed. As our high-scorers approach the tenth grade, we expect many of them to make plans to cut at least one year, and quite often two or more years, off their high school programs. Already a number of them are planning this with us and with school personnel. Most of the boys will come to Johns Hopkins for the first year, at least, because the university is prepared to admit them and provide financial aid, if needed. Some of the girls will probably attend nearby Goucher College, which has a long history of admitting some girls at the end of the eleventh grade. Our working hypothesis is that a youngster is ready to enter Johns Hopkins early when his College Board scores are in the upper fourth of its distribution, provided that he or she is *eager* to come. Parental zeal is not sufficient.

Several departments at Johns Hopkins offer master's degree programs that are concurrent with the bachelor's degree. That is, without taking an extra number of courses, but by including half a dozen graduate-level courses in the schedule, a student may receive the Bachelor of Arts or Bachelor of Engineering Science degrees along with the Master of Arts or Master of Science degrees in four years at no extra cost. These are not easy programs, of course, but our first radical accelerant, Joseph Bates, found the B.A.–M.S. route feasible. We expect that many of the other early entrants, particularly those who have financial problems, will also save another year or two in this manner.[7]

COLLEGE COURSES ON A PART-TIME BASIS

One of our most interesting innovations has been college courses for credit at a wide variety of institutions for these mathematically able youths while they were still in junior or senior high school. About fifty students thus far have taken from one to ten courses each, most of them with grades of A or B.

Their favorite course is introduction to computer science. Also popular are college algebra and trigonometry (a ten-year-old boy just out of the fourth grade made a B on it in The Johns Hopkins Evening College) and analytic geometry. Other courses taken include astronomy, chemistry, Russian, set theory, economics, political science, psychology, and calculus. As the study continues, the variety will increase.

OUR FIRST SATURDAY MORNING CLASS

In the summer of 1972, Lynn Fox, Daniel Keating, and I rather hastily set up a special course in mathematics, chiefly for students who had completed the sixth grade. We did this to check our notion that test scores are powerful indicants of readiness to move ahead fast in algebra, plane geometry, trigonometry, and analytic geometry. We had rather suddenly discovered a "reformed physicist" with zeal to produce mathematical prodigies. (This remarkable man, Joseph Wolfson, also worked well with difficult learners.) Our population consisted of thirty boys and girls who while in the sixth grade had scored at the 99th percentile on the Academic Promise Test Number subtest (APT-N) and also at the 99th percentile on either the APT Verbal (V) subtest *or* the APT Abstract Reasoning (AR) (nonverbal) subtest. We fudged a bit by inviting a boy who scored sixteen points above the minimum 99th percentile on

---

[7]The most radically accelerated person in our study is a boy residing in Brooklyn, New York, who in the fall of 1973 entered Brooklyn College as a full-time student (with advanced standing in mathematics) after the sixth grade, at age eleven and one-half years. During his first year he took 29 1/2 academic credits, including several advanced mathematics courses and made the grade of A on each of them. (He also made B in a 1-credit bowling course!) The next semester he made all A's.

N, even though he was a couple of points short of the 99th percentile on both V and AR. Also, we took into the group a boy who had completed the eighth grade and algebra I and was skipping to the tenth grade, because the college mathematics course he had planned to take was canceled. A third exception was a brilliant nine-year-old boy who had completed only the third grade.

Of the thirty who were invited to begin fast-paced study two hours each Saturday morning, starting in June 1972, twenty-one accepted. Nineteen of these freed themselves from summer vacations sufficiently to complete the first nine weeks, though not without absences; one attended only ten hours, i.e., just 56 percent of the class time. Then we administered Form A of the Educational Testing Service's Cooperative Test of Mathematics, algebra I, to these nineteen persons, eighteen of whom had studied algebra for a maximum of eighteen hours. All but four scored at the 60th-99th percentile of ninth-graders nationally who have studied algebra five days per week for a school year. A girl who had attended only twelve hours scored at the 97th percentile, as did the boy with the high APT-N score who had not quite qualified on V and NR. The nine-year-old boy scored at the 93rd percentile.

This seems a truly remarkable result for 18 or fewer hours of instruction, versus the 135–150 hours that are devoted to algebra I in the typical high school class. What had we known about these students in order to pick them so well?

1. The APT testing was done with the "ten top students" in each of forty Baltimore County elementary schools. Teachers had been asked to consult their test files and nominate the highest-scorers, but of course classroom excellence probably played a considerable part in the selection. Some "slippage" occurred because testing was conducted throughout the school year and no adjustment in scores was made for this.

2. We knew each student's sex and school attended, but made no use of these in deciding whom to invite.

3. We knew nothing at all about the invitee's school success, parents' education, socioeconomic status, or interest in mathematics, other than what was reflected in the teachers' nominations for testing and the students' choosing to enroll for the summer course. Most who did not enroll, however, seemed to have vacation or transportation problems, rather than motivational ones. The students and their parents knew little about us, except that we were based at the prestigious Johns Hopkins University in a department of psychology and at that time were operating under the title of "Study of Mathematically and Scientifically Precocious Youth."

We were relying largely on the APT scores, obtained by four undergraduates as a testing-course project. Later we noted that the APT-N is a composite of arithmetical reasoning and arithmetical fundamentals, whereas we desired mostly the former. This weakened our selection somewhat, so for choosing later special groups we have used the SAT-M instead.

RATE OF LEARNING

Thus we demonstrated anew the well-known but seldom-used fact that mathematically bright youngsters can learn algebra I better in far less than the usual time devoted to it. We also noticed that five of the six lowest-scorers on the algebra test had scored lower on a difficult verbal test than any of the other students except the nine-year-old. (The sixth was a bright troublemaker who did little homework and attended the least of anyone.) We immediately recalled McNemar's (1964) APA presidential address entitled "Lost: Our Intelligence? Why?" For highly able children approximately the same age, chiefly twelve years old, score on the School and College Ability Test (SCAT), Level 1C (appropriate for admitted college students), is a measure of developed verbal intelligence. Hence, it is a rough index of the learning rate for absorbing the course material fast and for answering forty different items on the algebra test in forty minutes. The APT-V did not show this up as well, but even there three of the bottom four algebra-scorers had the lowest APT-V scores of anyone in the group, and the fourth was the bright absentee mentioned above.

It appears that Abstract Reasoning, somewhat similar to what Raven's Progressive Matrices measure, cannot suitably substitute in this situation for a high verbal score. You will recall that we allowed it to do so. Fast learning seems to demand reasonably high verbal ability, measured on a difficult test.

But other qualities are important also; two boys of not extremely great general ability kept up the pace well for the entire thirteen months. One of them, at age thirteen, made A in the introduction to computer science course at Johns Hopkins and A in an analytic geometry course at a state college. The other skipped the eighth grade in order to take advanced subjects in a senior high school, also at age 13. See students 7 and 12 in table 7.A2.

THE HIGHLY SUCCESSFUL TEN VS. THE SUCCESSFUL SIX

The five lowest scorers on the algebra test dropped out of the Saturday morning class at the end of the summer, as did the close friend of one of these, who had herself scored a little higher. This left thirteen persons, to whom that fall (1972) we added two eighth-graders and a seventh-grader, none of whom had studied algebra in school but who on their own had learned a considerable amount of it. These sixteen (nine boys, seven girls) persisted into the summer of 1973. Ten of them kept up well with the fast pace maintained in geometry, algebra II, algebra III, trigonometry, and analytic geometry. The other six were assigned another instructor to help them in a self-paced fashion. They completed algebra II while seventh-graders, whereas that subject is rarely available until the ninth or tenth grade.

All seven of the boys from Mr. Wolfson's fast-paced section enrolled in high school or college calculus in the fall of 1973. None of its three girls did, but all of them enrolled for plane geometry. The least able of the seven boys became apprehensive and dropped back into a trigonometry and analytic geometry class.

Also, four of the nine boys skipped one grade, and three skipped two or more. Most of them will also take college courses part time and enter college early, thus illustrating the interactive effects of the various accelerating devices—particularly the special class.

Within the group of sixteen persons it is difficult to differentiate the highly successful ten from the "merely" successful six by test criteria. The girl and boy with the highest SAT-V scores for their sex among the ex-sixth-graders were in the six, but so were the boy with the lowest verbal ability and a girl with the lowest SAT-M score of the sixteen. Also, leading the six was a seventh-grader who entered the class in the fall without enough background in algebra I and could not catch up to the fast group, and a girl who had scored quite high on the algebra I test at the end of the summer.

IMPORTANCE OF ATTENDANCE, HOMEWORK, AND PARENTAL ATTITUDE

Obvious factors separating the two groups were class attendance and homework. The extremely bright boy attended poorly and did not bother to keep up with the work. He appeared preoccupied mainly with the church, scouting, and military history. His mother, who had not attended college, seemed to make little effort to get him to class well prepared. Contrasted with him, in the highly successful group there were three less able persons, a boy and two girls, whose intrinsic motivation seemed slight but whose parents insisted that they do homework regularly and carefully and attend class each week.

Even though both of her parents are college graduates, the bright girl in the less successful group never did homework well, if at all. Apparently, she is so apt that school work is easy for her. Therefore, she was an A student in her seventh-grade subjects, but given further competition she would not increase her efforts. Three different teachers, one of them female, were equally unsuccessful with her. Later, however, she forged ahead academically.

The Saturday morning class proved our point, that high-aptitude youngsters could learn *far* more mathematics quicker and better than they do in school. Not all such persons, identified mainly by a few test scores, will do well in a given special class, of course. We regret that the early dropouts from such a course will probably consist heavily of children from the lower socioeconomic levels in the group—especially, those whose mothers did not attend college. This is confounded somewhat by the tendency of such children not to score as well verbally as children of better-educated parents.

Just two of the six dropouts were female, but only one of the seven remaining girls stayed in the fast group until its last meeting, whereas seven of the nine boys did. None of the girls seemed to have as strong an interest in mathematics *per se* as most of the boys. The girls seemed to value the social experience of the class more than its theoretical orientation and (all but one) to shrink from mathematical competition with the boys.

MR. WOLFSON'S "SUPER-CLASS"

During the summer of 1973 Mr. Wolfson started another special class consisting of thirty-one persons, nearly all of whom had completed the eighth grade. In the 1973 competition, each of these had scored at least 400 on SAT-V and 500 on SAT-M, and later demonstrated good knowledge of algebra I on a standardized test. Thirty of these (twenty-two boys and eight girls) completed two 1-1/2-hour sessions per week for eight weeks, studying algebra II. Twenty-six of them, plus two others, continued into the fall, two hours per week with Mr. Wolfson in lieu of studying mathematics in school. Fourteen of these, plus two more who began June 1974, covered algebra II-III, plane geometry, trigonometry, and analytic geometry thoroughly by 2 August 1974. In the fall of 1974, when most of them became tenth-graders, the successful persisters were ready to enroll for honors advanced-placement calculus, a twelfth-grade subject.

This is an initially older group than the original Saturday morning class. It will be fascinating to see how they progress. Of course, some of them are already skipping grades, taking college courses part time, and planning to enter college early. For further information concerning these students, see chapters 6 and 7 of this volume.

Lynn H. Fox worked with an all-girl group of somewhat lower ability than Mr. Wolfson's. Her success with them during the summer of 1973 and the following school year was highly impressive. For later results, see chapter 9 of this book.

For the rationale of our special educational efforts and further details, see Fox (1974a,b [I:3,6]) and chapter 3 of this book.

As an unexpected by-product of our emphasis on academic acceleration Daniel P. Keating, one of the graduate students helping conduct the study, completed his own Ph.D. degree in psychology with distinction in the fall of 1973 at age twenty-four, just twenty-eight months after receiving the baccalaureate.

SUCCESS OF RECENT EARLY ENTRANTS

In September 1974 nine new students sponsored by SMPY began at Johns Hopkins, three of them with sophomore status, and two continued from previous years. One of the latter was a fifteen-year-old sophomore physics major, and the other was a seventeen-year-old fifth-year senior on leave at the Massachusetts Institute of Technology to complete the last two courses for his Hopkins B.A. degree in quantitative studies, while also studying in the artificial intelligence area. The grades of the ten registered at Johns Hopkins during the fall semester of 1974 were extremely impressive. There were no incompletes or missing grades, and only one course was taken on a pass-fail basis—one credit of scientific German by the sophomore, who also took sixteen other credits and made a perfect 4.00 term gradepoint average (GPA).

Course loads, GPAs, and other characteristics of these ten students are shown in table 1.1. GPAs ranged from three 4.00s to one 3.35, and the number of credits completed varied from 22.5 to 13. Seven of the ten students made the "dean's list" with a GPA of 3.50 or more and a course load of at least 14 credits; the one with a GPA of 3.69 was short one credit. No one made less than half As; the 3.35 occurred because that student made B in an 8-credit course. There was only one C, received in *advanced* calculus by a sixteen-year-old who had completed only the tenth grade; he made As in his other three subjects and a 3.50 GPA.

Ages of the students when they began at Johns Hopkins as full-time freshmen ranged from 14.75 to 17.25 years. Years of academic acceleration by grade-skipping, course-skipping, college courses taken early, and leaving high school before graduation ranged from 5 to 1.3. The youngest student was especially intrepid; he took advanced calculus (A), number theory (A), sophomore physics (B), and American government (B), a 15-credit course load on which his GPA was 3.47.

Mathematics courses taken by the ten were as follows: junior-year basic analysis (A), by the sixteen-year-old freshman who carried 22.5 credits (15 is considered a "full load"); 8-credit mathematical methods (A, B); advanced calculus (A, A, B, C); and calculus for physical science majors (A, A). One of the fifteen-year-olds did not take a mathematics course, because he had already completed five semesters of college mathematics before his fifteenth birthday —plus computer science at age twelve and four semesters of college chemistry before entering Johns Hopkins.

Obviously, these young men got off to a splendid start well ahead of their age group. They reported having a fine time at Johns Hopkins and being extremely glad not to be in high school courses that for them would be extremely boring.

To date, all of the SMPY early entrants to Johns Hopkins have been male. One young woman who skipped the eighth and twelfth grades was admitted for the fall of 1974 but took leave status in order to travel to Europe with her parents. She intends to begin as a history major in the fall of 1975. Another young woman who had entered kindergarten a year early and also managed to combine the eleventh and twelfth grades began in the fall of 1974 as a

Table 1.1.   Success of the 10 SMPY early entrants at The Johns Hopkins University during the fall semester of the academic year 1974-75 (all are males)

Semester GPA	Credits earned this semester	Credits earned to date	Lived in dormitory	Date of birth	School grades skipped	How identified initially	Probable major field
4.00	20	29	Yes	June 1957	12	Letter from maternal grandmother	Electrical engineering
4.00	17	56[a]	No	Nov. 1958	10, 11, 12	1972 contest	Physics
4.00	15	54	Yes	July 1959	2, 11, 12	Letter from mother and 1972–73 contests	Electrical engineering
3.73	22.5	31.5	No	Apr. 1958	8, 10	1972 contest (1st in mathematics)	Engineering science
3.70	16.5	26.5	No	July 1958	9, 12	1972 contest	Mathematics (?)
3.69	13	38	No	Aug. 1959	8, 11, 12	1972–73 contests (1st in science in 1972)	Computer science
3.59	17	23+	No	June 1958	8, 12	1972 contest	Pre-medicine (?)
3.50	16	27	Yes	Jan. 1958	11, 12	1972 contest	Mathematics
3.47	15	49	No	Dec. 1959	7, 9, 10, 12	Nominated by Md. Academy of Sciences, and 1973 contest	Mathematical sciences
3.35	17	17	No	May 1958	11, 12	1972 contest	Political science

[a]He had begun at age 14, in the fall of 1973. The other nine young men became full-time students at Johns Hopkins in the fall of 1974. During the second semester 7 of the 10 made the "dean's list" (GPA of at least 3.50 and 14 or more credits). Five made it both semesters, and only one made it neither semester.

premedical student at a nearby coeducational liberal arts college. We are confident that during the next few years a number of mathematically apt women will accelerate their academic progress substantially and that some of them will major in quantitative areas.

CONCLUSION

This chapter has been an attempt to illustrate the great value of standardized tests for locating talent that otherwise is likely to remain submerged and unidentified. The tests employed must be appropriate to the actual ability level of the persons tested. Often that will mean using college tests with children below the senior high school level. Only via such instruments can sufficient ceiling be obtained and the power of the examinee's mind be probed adequately.

The goals of our study are three-fold: discovery, description, and development. As we use the word "development" in this context, it means vigorous intervention in the educational process on behalf of the highly talented student. We try not to obstruct or frustrate the school system, but, instead, to augment its usual functions. Identification of talent, study of talent, and intervention to facilitate it are aided greatly by appropriately difficult tests of important aspects of mental development.

Critics of testing who allege that instruments such as the Scholastic Aptitude Test serve mainly to discriminate against low-scorers do not take into account fully enough the talent-finding aspect. This is particularly important in so-called disadvantaged groups, where persistent, careful testing is needed to discover general and special abilities that can be capitalized on in the educational process. It is equally important, or more so, for locating abilities that have developed to a high level early. If school personnel would study their test records and supplement them with additional harder tests, as needed, top-ability students could be found and provided for much better than is usually done at present. This calls more for dedication and daring than for money. In fact, the methods that we use and recommend for intellectually gifted youths can cut total educational costs greatly for parents and appreciably for school systems.

Those of us who are conducting the study have until at least August 1976 to strengthen our findings, provide workable prototypes, and promulgate them. We welcome comments, criticisms, and suggestions. Building on the pioneering work of the late Lewis M. Terman and his *Genetic Studies of Genius*, we feel keenly that much of the gifted-child research movement was buried with him in 1956. Great potential mental energy lies waiting to be made kinetic.

REFERENCES

Astin, H. S. 1974. Sex differences in mathematical and scientific precocity. In J. C. Stanley, D. P. Keating, and L. H. Fox (eds.), *Mathematical talent: Discovery, description, and development*. Baltimore, Md. 21218: The Johns Hopkins University Press, pp. 70–86.

Fox, L. H. 1974*a*. Facilitating educational development of mathematically precocious youth. In J. C. Stanley, D. P. Keating, and L. H. Fox (eds.), *Mathematical talent: Discovery, description, and development*. Baltimore, Md. 21218: The Johns Hopkins University Press, pp. 47–69.

———. 1974*b*. A mathematics program for fostering precocious achievement. In J. C. Stanley, D. P. Keating, and L. H. Fox (eds.), *Mathematical talent: Discovery, description, and development*. Baltimore, Md. 21218: The Johns Hopkins University Press, pp. 101–25.

Hollingworth, L. S. 1942. *Children above 180 I.Q. Stanford-Binet*. New York: World Book Co.

Hollingworth, L. S., and Cobb, M. V. 1928. Children clustering at 165 I.Q. and children clustering at 145 I.Q. compared for three years in achievement. *Twenty-seventh yearbook of the National Society for the Study of Education*, Part III: 3–33.

Keating, D. P., and Stanley, J. C. 1972. Extreme measures for the exceptionally gifted in mathematics and science. *Educational Researcher* 1(9):3–7.

McNemar, Q. 1964. Lost: Our intelligence? Why? *American Psychologist* 19: 871–82.

Stanley, J. C. 1973. Accelerating the educational progress of intellectually gifted youths. *Educational Psychologist* 10(3): 133–46.

Stanley, J. C., Keating, D. P., and Fox, L. H. 1972. Annual report to the Spencer Foundation on its five-year grant to The Johns Hopkins University covering the first year of the grant, 1 September 1971 through 31 August 1972, "Study of Mathematically and Scientifically Precocious Youth (SMSPY)," Baltimore, Md. 21218: The Johns Hopkins University, October.

———. (eds.). 1974. *Mathematical talent: Discovery, description, and development*. Baltimore, Md. 21218: The Johns Hopkins University Press.

Tiegs, E. W. 1931. *Tests and measurements for teachers*. Boston: Houghton Mifflin.

2
DISCOVERING QUANTITATIVE PRECOCITY[1]

Daniel P. Keating

ABSTRACT

To discover those few students who are operating at an exceptionally high level of ability in mathematics and quantitative sciences early in their academic careers (sixth through eighth grades), it is necessary to use more difficult tests than are normally administered in school testing programs. Tests at the age-in-grade level are not usually appropriate for several reasons. Often, they lack sufficient ceiling for adequate evaluation of these students. Second, the more difficult tests provide varied information for making the proper educational plans for these students not available from in-grade testing. The results of testing large numbers of gifted students with appropriately difficult tests on several occasions are reported. The level of mathematical ability in several cases is remarkable. The importance and implications of adequate testing for identifying the gifted and facilitating their educational development are discussed.

Identification of the gifted students in a school population is logically the first step in any educational program. The criterion that is set for inclusion in a "gifted" group usually depends on the aims and goals of the particular program. Among the criteria which have been used in the past are: above some specific IQ score, as in the Terman Gifted Study (1925, et seq.), which set a 140 IQ minimum; the top 10 percent on measures of general scholastic aptitude; or, more recently, above some criterion score on a test of "creativity" (more correctly, "ideational fluency," according to Wallach [1971]).

In the Study of Mathematically Precocious Youth (SMPY) at The Johns Hopkins University, the initial goal was to select the ablest mathematical reasoners of junior high school age from among an already able group (the top

---

[1]A brief report based on this article appeared in *Exceptional Children* 1975, 41(5): 435–36. The author wishes to thank Julian C. Stanley and Samuel A. Livingston for their helpful comments.

2-5 percent on tests of quantitative reasoning). The three mathematics competitions have been held for seventh-, eighth-, and accelerated ninth-graders, the first in March 1972, the second and third in January 1973 and 1974. No formal screening was done for the first competition, but it was recommended that the student have at least a 95th percentile (national norms) on whichever standardized test of arithmetic reasoning was used. The results of the first competition led to a restriction for the following years of a 98th or 99th percentile score (national norms for the applicant's school grade) on a standardized test of arithmetic reasoning (see chapter 4).

QUANTITATIVE PRECOCITY

It should be noted that we are interested in quantitative precocity, not just quantitative aptitude. Precocity, as the term is used here, means arriving at some stage of development earlier than expected, such that the individual's current state of development is more like that of someone much older. In this contest, "quantitative precocity" means having attained a stage of cognitive development in the quantitative area more like the developmental stage of someone several years older than the norm for age-mates.

The primary test for all competitions was the College Entrance Examination Board's (CEEB) Scholastic Aptitude Test—Mathematical (SAT-M), which is normally given to high school juniors or seniors seeking college admission. This test would be extremely difficult for most twelve- to fourteen-year-olds, of course, but it was chosen mainly for that reason. Before proceeding on to the detailed rationale for the use of such high-level tests for these groups, let us examine briefly the results of the testing competitions.

RESULTS OF TESTING

In the 1972 competition, 396 students took SAT-M. Detailed results have been reported elsewhere (Keating & Stanley 1972a, b; Keating 1974 [I:2][2]), but several major findings bear repetition. A score of 540 on SAT-M is about the 78th percentile of male high school seniors; 89 contestants, all seventh-, eighth-, or accelerated ninth-graders, scored that high or higher. A score of 620 is the 91st percentile, and forty-one contestants scored at least that high. The number scoring above such levels was even higher in 1973 and 1974. These are levels that the great majority of high school seniors never achieve. Consider also that

[2]In addition to the usual references, citations of chapters in volume I of *Studies of Intellectual Precocity* will be as follows: [I:2]. The I indicates volume I, and the 2 is the chapter number [Editor].

the average freshman at The Johns Hopkins University scores 656. The frequency distribution of scores for the first two competitions are shown in figures 2.1 and 2.2. The actual numbers scoring in each category are shown for all three years in table 2.1.

The results of the second and third competitions were consistent with the first year's findings. In all, 57 students in the second year and 111 in the third year earned scores of 640 or higher on SAT-M. One boy, an accelerated ninth-grader who was thirteen years zero months old at the time of the testing, earned an extrapolated score of 807 on SAT-M (i.e., one raw score point above the minimum required for a scaled score of 800). Another accelerated ninth-grade boy scored 770 on SAT-M and 710 on SAT-Verbal.

The level of mathematical reasoning ability evidenced by such scores is surprising to individuals accustomed to in-grade comparisons of gifted youngsters, even exceptionally gifted ones. When one is used to dealing with the full range of scholastic aptitude (as measured by standardized tests), from quite low to quite high, as is true of most school personnel, the feeling that anything above the 98th or 99th percentile "doesn't really make any difference" is understandable but unjustifiable. If the goal of the schools is to provide the best

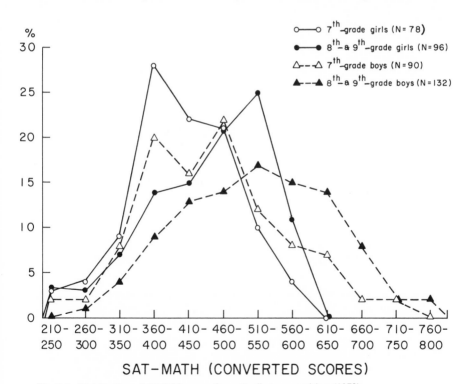

SAT−MATH (CONVERTED SCORES)

Fig. 2.1. Distribution of SAT-M scores from the first competition (1972)

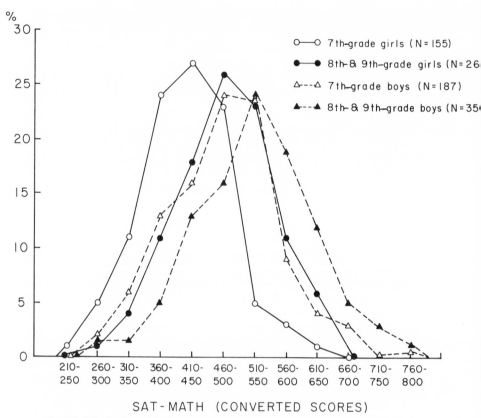

SAT-MATH (CONVERTED SCORES)

Fig. 2.2. Distribution of SAT-M scores from the second competition (1973)

possible educational alternatives to each individual, rather than to specifiable subgroups, then the distinctions, even at this high level, can be as important as in-grade testing.

VALUE OF ADEQUATELY DIFFICULT TESTS

There are several reasons for the use of high-level tests with gifted youngsters in educational as well as research settings. The first of these is that the 98th or 99th percentile students on in-grade tests are likely to be as different from each other as the group is different from 75th percentile youngsters. An example of this is available from another study of sixth-graders nominated as gifted who took the Psychological Corporation's Academic Promise Tests (APT) for 6th to 9th grade. A 99th percentile score on the numerical subscale for sixth-graders was 40 or greater on a sixty-item test. One student got 58 right, another 40. Both were 99th percentile on in-grade norms, but the same raw score difference of 18 between 40 and 22 was the difference between a 99th and a 65th percentile score.

Tests in-grade, however, rarely make these distinctions. In some cases the distinctions *could* be made on the basis of standardized tests in-grade, but more often such tests have too low a ceiling to separate these individuals accurately and reliably. The problem is especially acute if, as in some cases, the 98th and 99th percentile cutoff levels are only a few points below the ceiling of the test.

In such cases, errors of measurement are likely to lead to misclassification of a sizable number of high-scorers. This results from the lower reliability of the test for those scoring near the ceiling, since the effective test length for them is much shorter.

Consider a (hypothetical) sixty-item test of mathematical reasoning, which is standardized for a large group whose mean score on the test is 30. The reliability coefficient for the test is .81 and the standard error of measurement is 5.00. For an individual who scores at the ceiling, i.e., 60 out of 60 right, the 95 percent confidence interval around his estimated "true score" of 54.3 is 62.24 to 46.36 (Stanley 1971, p. 381). The "true score" of such an individual may, however, be far above that, but this test, because of lack of ceiling, can make no "true score" estimate higher than 62.24, even at a 95 percent confidence level.

Table 2.1. Grouped frequency distribution of SAT-M scores by grade and sex for the 1972 (N = 396), 1973 (N = 667), and 1974 (N = 1519) Maryland Mathematics Talent Searches

Score	1972				1973				1974			
	7G	8G	7B	8B	7G	8G	7B	8B	7G	8G	7B	8B
760–800	0	0	0	2	0	0	1	4	0	0	1	0
710–750	0	0	2	3	0	0	0	10	0	0	3	12
660–700	0	0	2	13	0	0	3	14	0	7	7	32
610–650	0	0	3	18	1	13	7	37	4	22	13	76
560–600	3	11	8	20	4	24	14	73	6	52	25	114
510–550	8	24	11	21	5	49	39	70	23	90	84	130
460–500	16	20	20	19	27	46	35	44	61	116	87	119
410–450	17	14	14	17	25	21	16	21	65	42	71	47
360–400	22	14	18	13	19	5	12	11	39	33	60	20
310–350	7	7	7	6	5	0	7	1	16	6	14	5
260–300	2	3	3	1	2	0	1	1	8	1	7	1
210–250	2	3	2	0	0	0	0	0	0	0	0	0
N	77	96	90	133	88	158	135	286	222	369	372	556
Mean	423	458	460	528	440	511	495	551	440	503	473	540
S.D.	75	88	104	105	66	63	85	85	68	72	85	82

Notes: 7G = seventh-grade girls; 8G = eighth-grade girls (including accelerated ninth-graders); 7B = seventh-grade boys; 8B = eighth-grade boys (includes accelerated ninth-graders).

The upper limit of the confidence interval at the 99 percent level is still only 63.74.

This usage of "true score" is slightly different from its strict meaning as the score one would hypothetically obtain after an infinite number of independent administrations of the test. The idea here is that the student is capable of performing far above the ceiling of the test.

If the reliability coefficient of the test were higher and the standard error of measurement lower, the confidence intervals would, of course, be even smaller. In the extreme case of perfect reliability, the one and only "true score" estimate would be 60. The point of the example is that for an individual whose "true score" lies above the ceiling of a particular test, that test is both practically and theoretically incapable of estimating his actual ability.

Thus, within the confines of classical test theory, there are two major problems with using most in-grade tests with exceptionally gifted students, both connected to lack of ceiling: (1) the tests can give no indication of how such students are different from each other; (2) the tests cannot give an accurate estimate of an individual's ability if his true level is above the ceiling of the test.

EDUCATIONAL PLANNING

Both of the above objections can be overcome by using adequately difficult tests. But before making this argument in detail, the question of the *purpose* of such accurate measurement should be addressed. The question of purpose is especially important in that some teachers and parents have suggested that using such difficult tests may, in fact, be harmful in some way to young children. Such testing may be traumatic for the average child, but these exceptionally able students seem to relish the challenge.

There would be no purpose to using these tests if we were to collect the scores, note them with some curiosity, and pass on to other endeavors. But such is not the case in SMPY. The purpose is to assist the student in planning his education, and these plans will be quite different for a student who scores 800 on SAT-M when thirteen years zero months old, and for another student of the same age who scores 540, even though both are at the 99th percentile on in-grade tests. Educational facilitation for the first student will certainly include released time and summer college courses while in high school, and probably early admission into college as well, while the second student would probably benefit from an accelerated high school curriculum (Fox 1974 [I:3]).

This raises the second major reason for using high-level tests with such students, and it is a primarily empirical rather than theoretical one: the more difficult tests have predictive validity for the kinds of challenging experiences that facilitating their education will present.

Testifying to the fact that these tests have good predictive validity is a series of (thus far) unbroken successes in placing young students found through these competitions in college courses on released time or during the summer. The mean GPA on 220 credits earned by thirty-five students who had taken courses on this basis by May 1974 was 3.77 (on a 4.0 scale). Prior to the official start of SMPY, two eighth-grade students were admitted to Johns Hopkins as full-time students before the age of fourteen. They had scores on CEEB aptitude and achievement tests superior to those of most entering freshmen, and their success at Hopkins has been discussed in case studies elsewhere (Keating & Stanley 1972a; Stanley 1974 [I:1]). A third student (who was not found through the testing competitions) was admitted in 1972 at age sixteen, after the tenth grade, on the basis of excellent scores on college-level tests and SMPY's recommendation. He compiled a 4.0 (straight A) average in his first year. Others have since followed their successful example (see chapter 1 in this volume).

MEANING OF TEST SCORES

The simplest way to discover quantitative precocity is to assess it directly. Thus, to find out which of a given group of able twelve- to fourteen-year-olds has attained a level of quantitative reasoning ability comparable with able high school seniors, one need only to give them the same test of mathematical reasoning one would give to a group of high school seniors. The excellent and frequently used test for this purpose is SAT-M.

This is not to imply that a score of 680 for a twelve- to fourteen-year-old on SAT-M necessarily means the same thing in terms of quantitative reasoning ability as the 680 earned by the high school senior. In fact, the younger student is probably being required to use more of his reasoning ability, since some of the formulas and identities that the older student has learned in high school are not available to the younger student, and he, consequently, must figure them out by using a higher-level process.

Before we elaborate this distinction, it should be noted that this element probably "biases" the predictive validity positively, if the criterion is "success in learning new material in introductory courses" (as reflected by the grade in the course), for almost certainly the reasoning element will be more important in such a situation than the "amount of knowledge previously accumulated."

The different meaning and interpretation of the test score depending on who the test-taker is raises an important point. As Anastasi (1974 [I:5]) has suggested, the test item is not an unchanging and objectively determinable "stimulus" across all groups. The sample of behavior that each item seems to evaluate is a complex interaction of the item and the individual, including his background and experience, and the way in which he reacts to the particular item.

An example serves to illustrate this point with regard to mathematics. One such item on a college-level test involved the division of one fraction by another. For the college population that the test was constructed for, the item was appropriately placed in the mathematical computation section. When the item was presented to an eleven-year-nine-month-old boy, however, it was a "different" item. He had not then learned the rule for division by a common fraction (i.e., invert and multiply), but got the item right nonetheless. It was clear from his explanation afterward that he had used insightful mathematical reasoning to complete the item correctly.

Such "clinical" item analyses need to be investigated by more conventional statistical methods. A full item-analysis of the SAT of the three testing competition groups is planned, and the results can be compared to item analyses of the SAT conducted by the Educational Testing Service (ETS) in its regular administrations. The comparisons, if the above discussion is accurate in its conclusions, should indicate future lines of investigation.

CONCLUSION

The techniques described here for the discovery of quantitative precocity are, of course, applicable in other areas. The general finding is that tests that are adequately scaled for a population defined by age and grade may not be the most useful for those near the top of the scale. This difficulty can be overcome by administering a higher-level test to a select subpopulation on the basis of the first (in-grade) test. (It should not be administered to the whole population, of course, because it would be both useless and discouraging for all but the top few.) This simple procedure, which is, as we have shown, both theoretically and practically justifiable, is often overlooked, even by those who most need the information to assist and counsel the student.

REFERENCES

Anastasi, A. 1974. Discovering and nurturing precocious talent in mathematics and physical sciences: Discussion. In J. C. Stanley, D. P. Keating, and L. H. Fox (eds.), *Mathematical talent: Discovery, description, and development.* Baltimore, Md.: The Johns Hopkins University Press.

Fox, L. H. 1974. Facilitating educational development of mathematically precocious youth. In J. C. Stanley, D. P. Keating, and L. H. Fox (eds.), *Mathematical talent: Discovery, description, and development.* Baltimore, Md.: The Johns Hopkins University Press.

Keating, D. P. 1974. The study of mathematically precocious youth. In J. C. Stanley, D. P. Keating, and L. H. Fox (eds.), *Mathematical talent: Discovery, description, and development.* Baltimore, Md.: The Johns Hopkins University Press.

Keating, D. P., and Stanley, J. C. 1972a. From eighth grade to selective college in one jump: Two case studies in radical acceleration. Paper presented at AERA Annual Meeting, Chicago.

———. 1972*b*. Extreme measures for the exceptionally gifted in mathematics and science. *Educational Researcher* 1(9): 3–7.

Stanley, J. C. 1971. Reliability. In Thorndike, R. L. (ed.), *Educational measurement.* Washington D.C.: American Council on Education.

———. 1974. Intellectual precocity. In J. C. Stanley, D. P. Keating, and L. H. Fox (eds.), *Mathematical talent: Discovery, description, and development.* Baltimore, Md.: The Johns Hopkins University Press.

Terman, L. M., et al. 1925–57. *Genetic studies of genius.* Vols. I–V. Stanford, California: Stanford University Press.

Wallach, M. A. 1971. *The intelligence/creativity distinction.* New York: General Learning Press.

IDENTIFICATION AND PROGRAM PLANNING: MODELS AND METHODS

Lynn H. Fox

ABSTRACT

There are two major aspects of program planning for the gifted—identification and the development of alternative educational strategies. In order to best match learner characteristics to specific educational strategies, it is important to assess patterns and levels of abilities and interests. A generalized model for selecting students for specific types of programs, such as special mathematics classes, is described. SMPY has experimented with a number of methods of acceleration for mathematically gifted junior-high-school-age youth, such as fast-paced school-systemwide classes and college courses. Models for alternative matriculation strategies for students who are mathematically gifted are presented. The reader is encouraged to consider how these models might be modified and expanded to meet the needs of students who are talented in other academic areas.

Educators are becoming increasingly aware of the fact that the American public school system has not effectively met the needs of all the nation's children. Over the past decade there have been numerous attempts to correct this situation. Most of these efforts, however, have been concerned only with the children labeled "mentally handicapped" or "educationally disadvantaged" (e.g., Stanley 1972, 1973). What has been overlooked too often is that our nation's brightest youngsters may also be "educationally disadvantaged," because schools fail to recognize their ability and to provide them with appropriate educational experiences. For a number of years there have been excellent programs, such as the Westinghouse Talent Search and the National Merit Scholarship Program, which have identified academically talented students throughout the country and encouraged them to pursue a college education. Unfortunately, these projects do not identify gifted students until after they have completed most of their public school education. If schools are to become more responsive to the needs of their ablest students, then large-scale efforts are needed to identify gifted students at the earliest grades and provide special educational opportunities for them.

The Study of Mathematically Precocious Youth (SMPY) has worked since September 1971 on problems of identifying intellectually gifted youth and developing various strategies to meet their educational needs. The purpose of this chapter is to discuss some methods of identifying gifted students and monitoring their progress through the junior and senior high school years. The first section explains the rationale for focusing on the large-scale identification of gifted students during the early adolescent years. The second section discusses some general considerations in the selection of appropriate tests. In the third section a specific model which school systems or states could employ to identify talented seventh- and eighth-graders is presented. The ultimate success of an educational program for the gifted is dependent upon comprehensive planning that takes individual differences into account and carefully evaluates and monitors an individual's or group's progress. Thus the fourth section describes ways in which long-range planning, including further testing and counseling of students, can be used to ensure the success of programs for the gifted.

The term *program* is used loosely in the ensuing discussions of educational strategies for the intellectually talented child. A *program for the gifted* in this chapter refers to a global approach to education that would encompass a variety of specific strategies. This would include the possibility of subject-matter acceleration, general grade-skipping, special classes, college credit by examination (e.g., the Advanced Placement Program), and college courses used alone or in combination for a particular student. Some examples of the types of strategies used by students identified by SMPY are discussed in the last section of this chapter. For a more detailed account of these various strategies for educational matriculation of the gifted in mathematics, the reader is referred to chapters 6 and 7 of this volume and Fox (1974*a,b* [I:3, 6]).[1]

IDENTIFICATION FOR PROGRAM PLANNING: WHY FOCUS ON THE EARLY ADOLESCENT YEARS?

The need for special efforts to identify talented students and design innovative educational programs for them is particularly acute during the junior high school years, for it is during those years that most schools are the least flexible in terms of individualized scheduling and self-paced instructional programs. It has been noted elsewhere (Fox 1974*a* [I:3]) that subject-matter acceleration

---

[1]In addition to the usual references, citations of chapters in volume I of *Studies of Intellectual Precocity* will be as follows [I:3,6]. The I indicates volume I, and the 3 and 6 are chapter numbers [Editor].

is an excellent educational procedure for the gifted. Yet this appears to be the most difficult thing to provide during the junior high school years.

In elementary school very bright children are often allowed to move ahead at their own pace in reading and arithmetic. Recent interest in the creation of open classrooms, team teaching, and small individualized learning centers in the elementary schools are potentially conducive to the fostering of individualized educational goals and programs. In these types of classroom environments, presumably a school could accommodate the educational needs of bright students independent of the number of such students in a given school or age group. Even the more traditional elementary school classroom can often allow for a wide range of individual differences in rates and levels of achievement. Thus, whether or not gifted children receive special attention during the elementary school years in a given school or school system has typically been more a function of the attitudes and philosophy of the teachers and school administrators than of the structure of the elementary school itself.

In most modern senior high schools, individualized scheduling of classes is possible. Usually in large schools there are a number of fairly advanced courses in each subject area from which to choose. Thus, theoretically at least, exceptionally able students can arrange individualized schedules that allow for subject area acceleration and perhaps let them complete high school a year early. In a few school systems it is now possible for students to arrange their high school schedule to include college courses taken for credit at a nearby college during the day, in the evening, during the summer, or by correspondence. (This has been done in a number of individual cases throughout the country. Maryland, for example, is one state that appears to encourage this actively at the present time.) Although few senior high schools are so individualized as to offer opportunities for students to complete a standard course in less than one year's time, there is still greater flexibility possible within the structure of such schools than is usually realized. If high schools are seriously interested in working with academically talented students there are usually many types of special arrangements that they can provide, such as subject-matter acceleration and credit by examination for independent study.

Junior high schools rarely provide the individualized scheduling approach of the high schools with a wide variety of options within subject areas, nor do they typically provide self-pacing programs within the courses they do offer. It is a rare junior high school that can provide adequate subject-matter acceleration for gifted students.

Thus it is at the end of the elementary school years that there is a real need to identify talented students and make special efforts to provide a bridging mechanism for them to span the years from elementary school to senior high school and college. In the area of mathematical talent this is a particularly crucial period. Mathematical reasoning ability is well developed in the upper few percent of youngsters by the end of the fifth or sixth grades. In terms of development of logical thought and reasoning ability, it appears that bright fifth-graders are more apt to be ready for the study of abstract mathematics and physical science materials than are average seventh-graders (see chapter 5 for a detailed discussion of this finding). Acceleration of mathematical achievement for the mathematically gifted is probably best accomplished by having them begin the study of algebra in the sixth or seventh grades.

The fact that many seventh- and eighth-graders are ready for the fast-paced study of mathematics has been well documented by SMPY. Details of the first talent search conducted by SMPY in the spring of 1972 are presented elsewhere (Keating 1974 [I:2]). In 1973 and 1974, SMPY held similar contests for junior high school students in the state of Maryland.

In 1973, 953 students who had scored at or above the 98th percentile on either the numerical or verbal subtests of the Iowa Tests of Basic Skills or another standardized in-grade test were tested on both parts (mathematical and verbal) of the College Entrance Examination Board's Scholastic Aptitude Test, with the cooperation of the Study of Verbally Gifted Youth.[2] The means and standard deviation on SAT-M and SAT-V by grade[3] and sex are presented in tables 3.1 and 3.2. The mean score (551) on SAT-M for the eighth-grade boys who were tested in January[4] was considerably higher than the mean for male high school seniors (510) who plan to attend college. Most, if not all, of the high school seniors had had considerably more mathematics instruction in school than the eighth-graders, who were typically enrolled in algebra I. Two boys, one seventh-grader and one ninth-grader, scored 800 on the SAT-M.

The results of the contest held in January 1974 further confirm the finding that a great number of boys and girls of junior high school age are extremely talented in mathematical reasoning, to the extent that they should receive more challenging experiences than are generally provided in their regular mathematics courses. Of the 1,519 students tested in 1974, 111 scored at or above 640 on SAT-M, which is at the 94th percentile of a random group of eleventh- and twelfth-graders. The means and standard deviations on SAT-M for the 1974 contestants by grade and sex are shown in table 3.3. Clearly there is enough evidence from these three years of testing to warrant some special program planning for mathematically talented students.

Details of the types of accelerated classes that have been initiated and studied by SMPY are reported by Fox (1974*b* [I:6]) and by George and

[2]The Study of Verbally Gifted Youth (SVGY) was begun in September 1972 at The Johns Hopkins University, under the direction of Dr. Robert T. Hogan, Dr. Catherine J. Garvey, and Dr. Roger A. Webb. Chapter 8 of this volume summarizes the work of this study during its first year.

[3]A few of the contestants in the talent searches were ninth-graders who had not reached their fourteenth birthday before the contest. Since the number of ninth-graders is small, their scores are combined with those of the eighth-graders.

[4]In 1973 two talent searches were sponsored jointly by SMPY and SVGY. Students primarily interested in mathematics were asked to take the test in January. Students who were primarily interested in the verbal areas were asked to take the test in February.

Table 3.1. Means and standard deviations on the mathematics test (SAT-M) for contestants in 1973, by grade and sex

	January group (math)			February group (verbal)			Combined groups		
	Number	Mean	Std. dev.	Number	Mean	Std. dev.	Number	Mean	Std. dev.
7th-grade girls	88	440.23	66.33	67	396.42	79.56	155	421.29	75.32
7th-grade boys	135	495.41	85.18	52	434.23	90.37	187	478.40	90.68
8th- and 9th-grade girls	158	510.82	62.60	103	445.63	78.11	261	485.10	76.02
8th- and 9th-grade boys	285	551.09	85.24	65	489.85	90.65	350	539.71	89.38
All girls	246	485.57	72.27	170	426.24	82.07	416	461.32	81.73
All boys	420	533.19	89.01	117	465.13	94.31	537	518.36	94.39
All 7th grade	223	473.63	82.67	119	412.94	86.16	342	452.51	88.64
All 8th and 9th grades	443	536.73	80.21	168	462.74	85.69	611	516.38	88.12
TOTAL	666	515.60	82.29	287	442.09	89.19	953	493.46	93.43

Table 3.2. Means and standard deviations on the verbal test (SAT-V) for contestants in 1973, by grade and sex

	January group (math)			February group (verbal)			Combined groups		
	Number	Mean	Std. dev.	Number	Mean	Std. dev.	Number	Mean	Std. dev.
7th-grade girls	88	373.86	73.63	67	392.99	86.34	155	382.13	79.67
7th-grade boys	135	384.74	71.39	52	410.19	76.94	187	391.82	73.66
8th-grade girls	158	441.96	82.90	103	475.73	90.32	261	455.29	87.31
8th-grade boys	285	431.02	89.94	65	476.15	90.15	350	439.40	91.55
All girls	246	417.60	86.02	170	443.12	97.36	416	428.03	91.58
All boys	420	416.14	87.07	117	446.84	90.39	537	422.83	88.63
All 7th grade	223	380.45	72.32	119	400.50	82.47	342	387.43	76.48
All 8th grade	443	434.92	87.56	168	475.89	89.98	611	446.19	90.04
TOTAL	666	416.68	86.62	287	444.63	94.44	953	425.01	89.92

Table 3.3. Means and standard deviations on the mathematics test (SAT-M) for contestants in 1974, by grade and sex

	Number	Mean	Standard deviation
7th-grade girls	222	439.51	67.60
7th-grade boys	372	473.12	84.93
8th-grade girls	355	499.72	70.93
8th-grade boys	533	535.18	80.10
9th- and 10th-grade girls	14	575.00	58.54
9th- and 10th-grade boys	23	648.26	65.83
All girls	591	478.88	76.62
All boys	928	513.10	89.70
All 7th grade	594	460.56	80.51
All 8th grade	888	521.00	78.47
All 9th and 10th grades	37	620.54	77.99
TOTAL	1,519	499.79	86.45

Denham in chapter 6 of this volume. Recent efforts to replicate this type of program in a public school in Baltimore City are described in chapter 7 of this volume. A number of school systems hope to experiment with their own adaptation of this type of approach to mathematics education for the very able student.

There are two crucial aspects of developing a program to guide gifted students through the secondary school years and into college (usually for such students, college entrance should be one or more years accelerated). The first is the early identification of talented students who need the types of special opportunities mentioned above. The second is the careful monitoring and evaluation of the students' progress through these critical years.

IDENTIFICATION: SELECTING THE METHODS

There are numerous considerations in selecting tests to identify intellectually gifted students. Of prime concern is how well the test will predict success in the type of program that is planned. In other words, is the test a valid measure for the purpose of identifying students who would most benefit from subject-matter acceleration, general acceleration, or special fast-paced classes? Closely related to this issue is the question of what aspects of ability and personality are related to high-level achievement in various situations. Of lesser, but substantial, concern are questions concerning the ease of administration, cost, and availability of the tests to be used.

General Intelligence Tests Versus Tests of Special Ability

In the 1920s the first monumental study of intellectually talented students by Lewis Terman (1925) used measures of global intelligence, such as the Stanford-Binet, to identify students who were extremely bright (IQ scores of 140 or above). The results of this first attempt to systematically study the characteristics of intelligent children and follow their development through adulthood were a major breakthrough toward our understanding of individual differences and intellectual ability (see Stanley 1974 [I:1]). The aim of the Terman study, however, was systematic study of the children rather than educational intervention. Subsequent research by SMPY has shown that program planning and educational facilitation of the gifted require a more comprehensive view of the cognitive abilities of a student, as well as some information about his or her interests (Stanley, Keating, & Fox 1974).

In the half-century since Terman's major longitudinal study of gifted children began, many educators have discussed the problem of operational definitions of intellectual giftedness and their implications for instituting identification procedures in the schools (e.g., Gowan 1971, Pegnato & Birch 1959; Witty 1967). Many have suggested solutions that involve the use of teacher nominations and measures of creativity to supplement intelligence test results (Gowan 1971; Torrance 1968). Few, however, have emphasized the importance of multiple ability testing.

Programs that seek to individualize instruction for gifted students will be better served by tests that provide information about a student's pattern of abilities, current level of achievement, and interests, rather than a merely global estimate of general intelligence. Neither individual nor group tests provide this type of information. Knowing that a student has an IQ of 160 is not adequate information for deciding whether or not the student is ready for a college course in science or mathematics. While it provides an estimate of higher learning potential, it tells little about actual level of achievement in a given subject area or about the relationship between the student's verbal and quantitative skills, nor does it indicate the student's special interests.

Assessing Patterns and Levels of Abilities

In order to assess most effectively a student's educational potential one should employ a variety of measures. Test batteries that show the relative strengths and weaknesses of a student on measures of both aptitude and achievement provide valuable information concerning appropriate educational placement. For example, a student who is unusually good at abstract reasoning problems and scores high on mathematical aptitude and knowledge, but relatively low on verbal measures, may have to proceed at a somewhat slower pace in mathematics than a student who scores extremely high on verbal as well as quantitative measures. Moderate acceleration in mathematics would seem more appropriate for the former, whereas skipping one or more entire grades might be feasible for the latter. No existing test battery will provide all the information useful in counseling gifted students. Thus, the ideal program for identifying gifted students will employ a variety of different tests at different levels.

When one tests very bright students it is particularly crucial to use tests that have enough ceiling to differentiate among them. Thus, in addition to patterns of abilities, one should be careful to assess accurately levels of abilities for bright students. Two students who in the seventh grade score at the 99th percentile on a number-ability subtest of a standardized in-grade test may still be very different in terms of mathematical aptitude and knowledge. One of these students may be so advanced in his ability and knowledge of mathematics that he is ready to study college calculus, whereas the other student may be very able but still lack the basic skills of plane and analytic geometry and algebra II. A single test, particularly a grade-level one, will fail to provide this type of information.

Thus, it is crucial to use tests of a higher level before making decisions as to educational placement. For the ablest adolescents precollege- and college-level tests would be more appropriate than in-grade tests for evaluating knowledge and aptitude. This point is elaborated upon in chapter 2.

Thus, the whole picture of the cognitive strengths and weaknesses of the student should be carefully assessed by using batteries of difficult tests. One might first begin by screening students on in-grade achievement tests, such as the Iowa Tests of Basic Skills. Students who score above the 95th percentile on mathematics or verbal subtests and 95th percentile overall on in-grade norms could be further tested on special tests of ability at a higher level, such as the Scholastic Aptitude Test (SAT), Preliminary Scholastic Aptitude Test (PSAT), Differential Aptitude Test (DAT), or School and College Ability Test (SCAT). These tests should then be followed by other tests of special abilities, such as Raven's Progressive Matrices, Bennett's Mechanical Comprehension Test, Sequential Tests of Educational Progress (STEP) Science, and College Entrance Examination Board (CEEB) achievement tests.

In addition to "ceiling," the "jingle-jangle" problems of tests need to be considered. The actual function of a test may be somewhat different from that which its name implies, and this should be carefully studied. To assess a student's degree of readiness to begin the study of algebra and other more abstract mathematical courses, one should not use a test that relies too heavily upon mathematical computation skills. One should be sure that a test purporting to assess mathematical aptitude and mathematical reasoning ability does not assess mainly computational skills. Readiness to study advanced courses may be somewhat independent of knowledge of specific skills. Some very bright students may be ready to study algebra before they have mastered all the rules of arithmetic operations. Indeed, very gifted students may grasp and enjoy the study of fractions, decimals, and percents more in the context of algebra operations and notation than in arithmetic classes. Similar distinctions should be made when analyzing the results of tests of verbal ability. One should determine whether or not they are measures of general vocabulary, reading level, or verbal reasoning.

Achievement Tests

Achievement tests, particularly those of a specific subject content and of a high level, are extremely important indicators for subject-matter placement. It is somewhat ludicrous to place an eighth-grader in algebra I, when in fact he has already mastered the principles of algebra I and algebra II. Yet this does occur and will continue to occur until more sophisticated testing is employed and the results used to make adequate adjustments in the student's educational program.

One seventh-grader scored 760 on SAT-M in a contest sponsored by SMPY in 1974. His school had not intended to place him in algebra I the next year. After learning of the results of the contest, they decided to test him on algebra I. He made a perfect score. Upon further testing by SMPY on CEEB achievement tests, he scored 800 (the highest score) on CEEB Mathematics Achievement II—a test that most high school seniors find difficult. The final outcome for this student was that he was allowed to take geometry the next year. (He studied algebra II and trigonometry during the summer.) Without the intervention of SMPY that student would have been placed in a mathematics course at least three years behind his ability and achievement level. This type of educational injustice to the gifted can and should be avoided.

Achievement tests sometimes serve another important function—that of indicators of interests. A student with high-level abilities in several fields may develop higher levels of achievement (perhaps by independent study) in one field, such as mathematics or science, than in others, such as languages. This selective acquisition of knowledge in a specific field is a strong indication of interest. For example, two students with very similar scores on SAT-M and SAT-V as eighth-graders may score quite differently on a test of general science knowledge, such as the college-level STEP science test or a test such as CEEB physics. The student who scores very high on such a test is probably more interested in science and mathematics than the student of similar aptitude who has a lower achievement score. Information about interests and career aspirations of students is quite useful in planning educational experiences for them.

Interests, Motivation, and Achievement

While achievement can be an indicator of interest, it is also true that more direct measures of interests and values can be useful predictors of future achievement. Students with similar patterns of cognitive abilities may indeed perform quite differently in different situations and, especially, in different subject-matter areas in school. Knowing a student's interests, as well as his or her level of ability, can make the educational planning process more efficient.

If a testing program or screening procedure to identify talent does not involve the type of self-selection and screening that operated in the SMPY talent searches, it might be wise to include some assessment of interests and values in conjunction with the cognitive testing.

Very bright students with strong quantitative abilities but little scientific or investigative interest may not find the atmosphere of a fast-paced mathematics program to their liking. Programs that ignore the affective components of achievement in their selection procedures are apt to find many students failing to perform well in the classes or be required to slow the pace of the class considerably in order to accommodate those who are not motivated to excel and not stimulated by the challenge of the pace and content. Students who lack the motivation should not be forced by well-intentioned parents and teachers to develop all their abilities at an equally fast pace and high level.

There is, of course, one caution. Students at ages eleven to fifteen, regardless of their intellectual abilities, may have somewhat poorly defined patterns of interests. Interests, particularly career interests, probably can fluctuate greatly during the period of adolescent development. A girl who, because of peer group pressures at age thirteen, may not aspire to an academic career, such as mathematician, could conceivably become more interested in this profession as a result of later experiences.

Thus, one should not require that a student have strong theoretical and investigative leanings in order to participate in a special program in mathematics or science. Information concerning values and interests should not be part of the selection criteria per se, but can be used for purposes of counseling and in the process of careful monitoring of program success. For example, students who are high on aesthetic and social values but low on scientific and investigative interests would probably be less successful working with self-paced geometry texts than in studying mathematics in a small informal class. On the other hand, a girl who is very social might be miserable if she were the only girl in a class of twenty theoretically oriented students. Boys and girls who score high on social values and interests and low on theoretical values and investigative interests are more likely to prefer modified programs of acceleration within subject matter in special classes to an overall grade acceleration, because they are less inclined to want to leave their social peer group. A more detailed discussion of the problems of social interests with respect to mathematics acceleration and fast-paced classes, for girls in particular, is presented in chapter 9.

Schools and school systems are likely to be limited by a number of factors in the number of options they can offer a given student in order to meet his unique needs. The size of the community, the amount of talent that exists in any school and age-grade level, the availability of teachers able to work effectively with very bright students, the geographic proximity of the junior and senior high school facilities, and the existence of a nearby university or community college will all determine the number and types of methods of facilitation that can be reasonably employed. What is suggested here is that the decision-making process for a given student may be simplified if one takes into account indicators of the student's personality, as well as his or her patterns of cognitive abilities.

Test Administration

In any testing program there are important considerations with regard to administering the test itself. Three points are particularly important when testing for the purpose of selecting students for a special program. First, tests of a restricted nature should be used, so that teachers and students do not have access to information about the content of the test in advance. If a test is to be used several different years in a row, it is probably wise to purchase alternate forms of the test, so that the test is somewhat different in specific content in successive years. This prevents leakage of information from one year to the next and avoids the accompanying problems if one needs to test the same students in both years.

Second, the testing should be done under controlled, standardized conditions. This includes testing all the students who are eligible at the same time of year, in similar of not identical testing facilities, with careful attention to exact instructions (especially with respect to cautions about guessing) and precise time limits. On the test for the final screening it would be desirable to test all eligible students at the same time and place.

Third, some tests, such as the SAT, provide practice booklets to be studied in advance. For seventh- and eighth-graders it would be particularly good to have them work with the practice booklets to gain insight into the nature of the test and specific item formats. This probably reduces some unnecessary test anxiety. If practice materials are available, *every* eligible student should be provided with them well in advance of the test and urged to study them carefully. It would even seem desirable to set up special coaching classes based on the practice booklets.

Untimed tests, such as Raven's Progressive Matrices, the Allport-Vernon-Lindzey *Study of Values*, and vocational interest inventories, are more difficult to administer in a standardized way. Special efforts should be made to ensure that the procedures used and explanations of the test given to the students are comparable in every test administration. It is probably wise to emphasize the fact that on "self-report inventories," such as tests of interests, there are no right or wrong answers, as junior high school students are often unfamiliar with these types of tests.

DEVELOPING A MODEL FOR EARLY IDENTIFICATION
OF THE GIFTED

Initial Screening

The first step in an identification program for the gifted in the junior high school years is to establish a master list or pool of all children in the school or school system who seem likely to be very gifted. Gowan (1971) terms this a "reservoir" of talent. There are two methods by which this can be done. The first is to scan carefully the latest test results from a standardized achievement test, such as the Iowa Tests of Basic Skills (ITBS). For economic and pragmatic reasons it is always good to take advantage of the existing test records. A master list of students' names and scores is usually available at the school system level. A single criterion or multiple criteria could be used to select students for further testing. One strategy would be to select all students who scored at the 95th percentile or above overall on national or local grade norms. In addition, one could add the names of students who scored below the 95th percentile overall, but who scored at the 98th percentile or above on either the total numerical or verbal subtest of the ITBS or other standardized test.

A second method, which could be used in conjunction with the first, if it is economically feasible, is teacher nomination. Gowan (1971) and others have suggested several types of nomination forms that could be used. This method is time consuming, expensive (if the school system is very large), and not as efficient as the first method. It should never be used as the only method of first screening. Terman (1925) and Pegnato and Birch (1959) found that most teachers are not good judges of intellectual giftedness. They are likely to identify average but dutiful old-in-grade students as gifted and to overlook the brightest child in the class. For political purposes, however, it may be wise to encourage teachers to make nominations. Children who are nominated by more than one teacher and by more than one criterion could then be added to the list of children to be tested further. To avoid testing too many children who are not likely candidates for special programs it might be wise to eliminate any students nominated by teachers who did not score at or above the 85th percentile overall on national norms of an in-grade test. Children who are only moderately above average may find the experience of taking difficult tests such as the SAT to involve considerable stress.

In identifying gifted children for special educational opportunities, it is probably best to err in the direction of over-selectivity. It is better to select children for special programs who have a high probability of success than to take children with marginal probabilities of success and expose them to a situation in which they are likely to fail. At present there are likely to be more children who are in desperate need of acceleration and special classes than can be handled with the limited resources now available. Thus, in the first attempts to break new ground in the area of educating the gifted, efforts should be concentrated where they are most needed. Enlarged programs to work with poorly motivated students and "underachievers" could be tried carefully later.

Assessing High-Level Potential—Second Screening

The second step of identification is to test the pool of the "potentially gifted" on difficult tests of aptitude and achievement in order to identify those who need immediate attention. There are several ways in which this stage can be handled. One is to have a large talent search conducted along the lines of a contest. Details of how this can be done are discussed by George and Solano in chapter 4.

A major advantage of a contest is that it allows for student self-selection. Students who are not eager to accelerate their educational progress can simply elect not to take the test. Self-selection among junior high school students is probably a desirable thing. SMPY has found that students who are not eager for special educational experiences will not typically benefit from them. Parents and schools should not try to force these opportunities.

There are numerous problems with the contest approach. First, it requires some time and effort for proper organization and can be fairly expensive. Unless the contest is given wide publicity, some eligible students will fail to learn about it. If the school system sponsors the contest in conjunction with an outside agency, such as a college, these problems could be minimal.

One method that would seem practical for schools and would avoid some of the problems inherent in a contest is utilization of existing precollege testing services. The Preliminary Scholastic Aptitude Tests (PSAT) administered, scored, and reported under the supervision of the Educational Testing Service (ETS) are given in high schools every fall on the last Saturday in October throughout the country. Although they are primarily taken by eleventh-graders, there is no reason why gifted seventh-, eighth-, and ninth-graders could not also be tested.

The Educational Testing Service has no special restrictions against these tests being given to younger students. School systems could easily use these available testing facilities for the purpose of identification of gifted junior high school students. The work involved for the school system would be minimal. Counselors at the junior high schools could notify eligible students (from the compiled pool) that they could take the test and then help them register for it. The cost to the students is about three dollars. If schools could afford it, they could pay the fees. Otherwise, students could pay the fee themselves, and perhaps groups, such as the PTA, could pay for any students who could not afford the fee. (The PSAT is suggested rather than SAT because it costs less and is given in the fall. The scores on the two tests are directly comparable.)

After the PSAT scores are reported to the schools, they could compile a list of students who had scored at various levels on the tests. For example, all students who scored at least 50 in the quantitative section and above 40 in the verbal section could be eligible for special accelerated classes in mathematics. This group could be tested further by the school system to decide what might be done for each individual.

Program Placement

At first glance the mechanics of placing a student in an appropriate special class appear complex. The strategy used is dependent upon the nature of the program offered and the number of students involved. Program placement can be greatly simplified by first specifying what educational experiences can be offered to a student and then selecting reasonable test score criteria to determine which alternatives can be offered to which students. The identification model as explained above and some suggested criteria and programs are shown in table 3.4.

Total Grade Skipping

If grade skipping is to be an alternative, then it is necessary to specify at what ability level students should be offered this opportunity. For example, seventh- and eighth-graders who score 50 or more on PSAT-V and PSAT-M might be offered the chance to skip a grade. Skipping should only be done by students who are eager to move ahead in all subjects. Some students may prefer subject-matter acceleration in mathematics and science rather than total grade acceleration.

Subject-matter Acceleration

Students who are very advanced in one subject area, such as mathematics, but who are not eager or able to skip an entire grade could be placed ahead by one or more years in just the one subject area. Thus, end-of-the-year sixth-graders who are known to be very talented in mathematics might be scheduled for regular algebra class when they are seventh-graders rather than waiting until the eighth or ninth grade to study algebra. A few very able students might even skip algebra I and begin with algebra II.

Subject-matter acceleration appears less desirable than homogeneously grouped classes for fast-paced instruction. The opportunity for interaction with peers of similar ability and interests is missing. Also, it is unlikely that the regular algebra class teachers will be able to teach such a class at as high a level or as great speed as special class teachers who are selected on the basis of mathematical expertise. The former, however, may be the best solution when there are too few students to justify a special class—even a county-wide class.

Table 3.4.   A model for identification of seventh- and eighth-grade gifted boys and girls

---

Step one—First screening

    A. Selection of students on the basis of available standardized in-grade test scores (such as the Iowa Tests of Basic Skills).

        1. 95th percentile overall; or

        2. 98th percentile on a verbal or numerical subtest; or

        3. combination of both criteria.

    B. Teacher nominations—include students nominated by more than one teacher who do not score below the 85th percentile overall on the achievement test used for selection in A. (Suggestions for teacher-nomination procedures can be found in Gowan [1971].)

Step two—Second screening

    A. Testing of the students selected in *Step one* on a more difficult test such as PSAT, SAT, DAT, or SCAT.

        1. Contest method; or

        2. regular PSAT administration.

    B. Criterion scores such as 40 on PSAT-V and 50 on PSAT-M could be used to select students for consideration for program placement.

Step three—Program placement

    A. *Mathematics*: Students who scored above 50 on PSAT-M and were interested in mathematics and science could be placed in a fast-paced mathematics class. Further testing could be done to determine which students were ready to begin with algebra II or geometry, and which ones needed to start with algebra I.

    B. *Science*: Students who scored above 40 on PSAT-V and 50 on PSAT-M could be tested on general science knowledge. Those who scored at or above the 75th percentile on 10th-grade norms and had a strong interest in science could begin to take chemistry, physics, and biology and skip general science courses. Probably, most should take AP level courses in these subjects.

    C. *Social Studies, English, and Languages*: Students who scored 50 or more on PSAT-V who had strong interests in these areas could be placed in accelerated classes or given special advanced classes in creative writing, sociology, anthropology, political theory, foreign languages, and other subjects. This could be accomplished in a variety of ways. Two periods a week for twelve-week periods could be devoted to special topics in English or social studies or both. The courses could be conducted like college seminars. Students who score above 60 on PSAT-V could probably be skipped one or more grades if special courses were not offered in their junior high schools.

    D. *College courses*: Students who scored very high on the PSAT (at least 50 on PSAT-V and above 60 on PSAT-M) might be ready to take some college courses in conjunction with skipping a grade in order to enter high school early. Students who scored at least 640 on SAT-M in the 1974 Talent Search conducted by SMPY were offered the opportunity to take a variety of courses in mathematics and science. These students earned grades of A or B in college courses taken as seventh- or eighth-graders. Clearly this can be done. Whether or not it is a practical alternative depends upon the cooperation of nearby colleges. Some colleges are eager to work with gifted high school students and can assist the schools in planning for the individual course needs of students.

Fast-paced Classes

SMPY has found that students who score at least 500 on SAT-M and 400 on SAT-V (this would be similar to 50 on PSAT-M and 40 on PSAT-V) can do well in a fast-paced mathematics class in which three or more years of mathematics are studied in one two-hour meeting a week for a year (see chapters 6 and 7 for details). Students of somewhat lower ability can do one and a half or two years of work in one. The pace of the class and the criteria used for selection will be a function of a number of factors. School-system-wide classes could be highly selective and move at a very fast pace. School-based programs would probably be less selective and slower (see chapter 7 for details).

The success of fast-paced classes depends upon a number of factors. First, the teacher must be very well trained in mathematics at a high level in order to be able to challenge and instruct the very gifted children. Second, good study habits are necessary for success in such a class. Teachers, counselors, or parents may need to work with individual students who have poor study skills. Third, students should never be pushed into attending a class. This type of class is intended for the highly motivated child who is eager to learn at a fast pace.

Advanced Placement Courses

Advanced placement (AP) courses are available in most large high schools for at least some course areas. Students who take such a course may then take a standardized examination. Students who score high on these tests can then earn college credits or be exempted from introductory college courses, or both, at colleges and schools that recognize and cooperate with the Advanced Placement Program. (Details of this program can be obtained from Educational Testing Service, Princeton, New Jersey.)

Unfortunately, high schools typically offer very few of these AP courses in a given year and may restrict participation to seniors. If school systems would conduct special county-wide AP courses and allow gifted ninth-, tenth-, and eleventh-graders to participate, it could be a highly effective program for the gifted. A brief report on such a course in calculus, sponsored by SMPY, is included in chapter 7 of this volume.

College Courses

If college courses taken in the summer or in an evening school class are to be offered as an option, more testing would be desirable to best determine what level course the student should take. SMPY has found that very few students who have not taken high school chemistry are ready for college chemistry, but those who are eager to try such a course could be tested on a CEEB chemistry test, or other standardized high school chemistry test, before making any decisions as to their readiness for a college course. SMPY has found that students who score 640 or more on SAT-M have been very successful in college computer science courses and college mathematics courses. The appropriate mathematics course for a given student depends upon his knowledge of mathematics, as determined by achievement tests in algebra I, II, trigonometry, plane and analytic geometry, and the level of the college courses offered. A very bright student who scores 700 on SAT-M may not be ready for college calculus if he has not mastered most of the precalculus material.

Interests and Maturity

If possible, students should be interviewed or tested on interests before offering them any of the alternatives. The more a counselor knows about the student's interests the better he can help the student select the appropriate program from the available alternatives. Students who have theoretical values and mathematical and scientific career-related interests may be more successful in fast-paced mathematics classes and college courses than students who have other interests and values. Early college admission appears to have the most general appeal for all students.

Students who are immature or who have a history of emotional or social adjustment problems in school should be carefully interviewed. It is possible that their behavior problems are a result of their frustration from being continually bored in school, and that special classes will alleviate the problem. On the other hand, children who have serious emotional problems may be unable to respond to intellectual challenges in a positive way. The experience of acceleration or college courses could be more then they can handle. Great caution should be used in these cases. Fortunately, such cases appear infrequently among mathematically precocious students. SMPY has found that selection of students on difficult precollege level tests in a contest tends to attract students who appear to be unusually mature. Although they may be bored in school they appear to have learned to cope to some extent by studying on their own outside of school subjects that interest them. Students who score well above grade level on tests of mathematical reasoning have personality profiles on the California Psychological Inventory (CPI) which are more typical of older students than do their more average grade-age peers (Weiss, Haier, & Keating 1974 [I:7]; Haier & Denham, chapter 11 in this volume).

TOWARD A MODEL FOR LONG-RANGE EDUCATIONAL PLANNING AND COUNSELING

The initial identification of gifted students is actually the easiest step to plan and conduct. More difficult to implement is a process by which the student and the schools work out long-range educational plans and then monitor the student's progress at each stage of the program. Theoretically, there are almost an infinite number of possible variations by which one could progress from seventh grade to college. The task of the school is to maximize the possibilities for meeting the needs of individuals without becoming inundated with administrative problems. Fortunately, the number of possibilities can be somewhat organized into a manageable number of general strategies that can each be moderately flexible. The nature of the strategies will be dependent upon a number of factors, such as the following: the physical aspects of locations of students, junior high schools, senior high schools, and colleges; the number of students involved; the various talents of the students; the students' personalities; and the parents' and students' goals.

Although each school system will need to generate its own programs, some general guidelines can be provided. Some problems are apt to be almost universal and can be solved. A few general strategies and solutions that have been tried with success by SMPY relative to the mathematically talented student will be presented. Individuals can then decide how these can be translated to meet their own situational demands and extended to cover the area of verbal precocity.

Plan I: Seventh Grade to College in Five Years

This plan is ideal for seventh-grade students who scored at least 40 on PSAT-V and 42 on PSAT-M in the fall of the seventh grade and have strong interests in mathematics and science.

A. *Acceleration.* Students could accelerate their progress through high school by one year. This could be done by formal grade promotion during the course of the five years or by simply allowing the student to fulfill all graduation requirements by the end of the fifth year.

B. *Mathematics.* Fast-paced mathematics classes (as described in chapters 6, 7, and 9) could be organized from the second half of the seventh grade through the fifth year. An example of this would be as follows:
   Year 1: Begin algebra I in January
   Year 2: Algebra II and college algebra
   Year 3: Plane geometry
   Year 4: Trigonometry and analytic geometry
   Year 5: Calculus (advanced placement course)

C. *Science.* Advanced placement (AP) courses in biology, chemistry, and physics could be taken in years three, four, and five, respectively.

D. *Optional Opportunities.* During the fourth and fifth years some students might begin taking college courses in the summer, evenings, or on released time from school, in such subjects as computer science, psychology, astronomy, English composition, or foreign languages. A student's readiness for these experiences could be determined by retesting on the PSAT in the fall of year four.

Plan II: Seventh Grade to College in Four Years

This plan would be suitable for seventh-grade students who scored at least 40 on PSAT-V and at least 50 on PSAT-M in the fall of the seventh grade and had strong interests in mathematics and science.

A. *Acceleration.* Students could be allowed to complete six years of high school in four by taking fast-paced mathematics classes (as described in chapter 6) and beginning their program of senior high school level science, social studies, and English courses a year or more early. In a school system with a three-year middle-school or junior high school program this could be done by completing the three years in two and then moving to senior high school and completing those three years in two.

B. *Mathematics.* Fast-paced classes could be designed for those students in the following sequence:
  Year 1: Begin algebra I in second half of the year.
  Year 2: Algebra II, college algebra, and plane geometry
  Year 3: Trigonometry, analytic geometry
  Year 4: Calculus (advanced placement course)

C. *Science.* Students could take biology, chemistry, and physics in years two, three, and four, respectively. Advanced placement courses would be desirable.

D. *Optional Opportunities.* Students who were qualified based on scores on PSAT taken in years two, three, or four (e.g., 60 on PSAT-M and 50 on PSAT-V) could take college courses in computer science, and other subjects in summers, evenings, or on released time from school. Students who did not desire to enter college full time at the end of the fourth year could arrange a schedule in the fifth year, which combined high school and college courses.

Plan III: Radical Acceleration Alternative

This plan could be used for eighth-grade students who scored 64 or above on PSAT-M and 60 or above on PSAT-V, who showed signs of great interest in mathematics and science and a strong desire for acceleration.

A. *Acceleration.* Students could be placed in the tenth grade at a senior high school the following year in all subjects except mathematics.

B. *Mathematics.* Mathematics could be taken in college courses through all precalculus courses during summer and evenings before, during, and after the tenth grade. An advanced placement calculus course (BC level) could be taken in the eleventh grade.

C. *Science.* Science courses could be arranged to allow the student to take both chemistry and physics during the tenth grade and advanced biology in the eleventh grade.

D. *English.* A college course in English composition and one in literature could be taken in lieu of twelfth-grade English in the summer after the eleventh grade.

E. *Early College Entrance.* Acceptance to college and high school graduation after the eleventh grade with advanced standing in some subject areas such as mathematics and science. Some students could enter college at the end of the tenth grade, if they took calculus and one science course in college during the summer or evening.

Plan IV: Subject-matter Acceleration Only

This plan could be used for students who are very good in mathematics but not interested in or ready for more total grade-skipping or fast-paced classes. Students would need to be identified by the end of the sixth grade. Therefore, tests such as the SCAT or DAT would be better than the PSAT or SAT for identification.

A. *Acceleration.* Students would be accelerated only in mathematics.

B. *Mathematics.* Students could take the regular nonaccelerated school classes in mathematics, but begin one year ahead of the typical schedule. They might wish to take two regular mathematics classes in one year. An example of this would be as follows:

1: Algebra I
2: Algebra II
3: Plane geometry
4: Trigonometry and analytic geometry
5: Calculus
6: College algebra, computer science, and/or statistics.

MONITORING THE STUDENT'S PROGRESS

The student's progress through any of the suggested programs can and should be assessed by the periodic use of standardized tests and by success in these courses.

Special Classes

When the teacher of a fast-paced accelerated mathematics class feels the students have completed the study of a subject such as second-year algebra, an algebra II test such as that in the Cooperative Mathematics Series published by Educational Testing Service can be administered. (Similar tests are available for science courses.) Students who score at or above the 75th percentile on national norms on this test can then proceed with the next course. Students who do not reach that level of mastery could return to a slower paced algebra II class to finish the algebra II and not continue with the accelerated program. SMPY has found that students who have a high score on tests such as the SAT have little difficulty mastering the material for most courses in less than half a year, meeting two hours a week, unless they are poorly motivated, in which case they should not strive for acceleration.

Advanced Placement Courses

The Educational Testing Service offers examinations in a variety of courses in May of each year. Students who score three to five on a five-point scale are considered to have mastered the material at a high level. Colleges and universities have varied policies with respect to these examinations. Some give college credit and allow the student to waive the first basic course in that field and begin with a second-level course. Other colleges give college credits, but do not waive basic course requirements, and vice versa.

Readiness for College Full Time

Students who have participated in any of the program alternatives can be evaluated for readiness for full-time college entrance by the same processes of examination used for all college-bound high school seniors. They should take the SAT and CEEB achievement tests and the appropriate Advanced Placement Program examinations and apply for college admission in the regular way.

SUMMARY

It is important that gifted students be identified sometime between the beginning of the fifth grade and the end of the eighth grade in order that they and the schools can develop an appropriate course of study to aid each such student in the transition from junior and senior high school to college. The degree of acceleration involved will be a function of the ability and motivation of the student and the program options available.

Efforts to identify intellectually able students at the junior high school level will be most effective if they involve difficult tests which assess breadth of special abilities rather than merely global measures of intelligence. A suggested identification plan that would involve minimal cost to schools in time and money was outlined in table 3.4. This method takes advantage of existing achievement testing programs at the school level and precollege aptitude testing at the national level.

Formulas for inclusion in various types of programs were presented based on three years of research by SMPY. Some examples of the types of long-range-planning models that could be used by school systems were discussed. These included different degrees of acceleration and amount of use of outside support agencies, such as colleges and the Advanced Placement Program course guides.

The models for identification and long-range programs discussed in this chapter were based on strategies used by students identified as mathematically talented by SMPY. More research is needed to determine what types of programs would best meet the needs of gifted students who are not especially talented or interested in mathematics and science. It is possible that programs for the gifted in more verbal subject areas will involve less acceleration and special classes of a radically different type than those used in mathematics by SMPY.

Although planning will take time and effort, there is no reason to delay programs to identify and help academically talented youth. The methods and technology exist now. Early identification is possible. The time has come to provide suitable program options for intellectually talented junior and senior high school students.

REFERENCES

Fox, L. H. 1974a. Facilitating the educational development of mathematically precocious youth. In J. C. Stanley, D. P. Keating, and L. H. Fox (eds.), *Mathematical talent: Discovery, description, and development.* Baltimore, Md. 21218: The Johns Hopkins University Press, pp. 47–69.

———. 1974b. A mathematics program for fostering precocious achievement. In J. C. Stanley, D. P. Keating, and L. H. Fox (eds.), *Mathematical talent: Discovery, description, and development.* Baltimore, Md. 21218: The Johns Hopkins University Press, pp. 101–25.

Fox, L. H., and Denham, S. A. 1974. Values and career interests of mathematically and scientifically precocious youth. In J. C. Stanley, D. P. Keating, and L. H. Fox (eds.), *Mathematical talent: Discovery, description, and development.* Baltimore, Md. 21218: The Johns Hopkins University Press, pp. 140–75.

Gowan, J. C. 1971. Identifying gifted students for a program. In J. C. Gowan and E. P. Torrance (eds.), *Educating the ablest.* Itaska, Illinois 60143: F. E. Peacock Publishers, pp. 153–55.

Keating, D. P. 1974. Precocious cognitive development at the level of formal operations. *Dissertation Abstracts International* 34 (11B): 5655.

Pegnato, C. C., and Birch, J. W. 1959. Locating gifted children in junior high school. *Exceptional Children* 25:300–04.

Stanley, J. C. (ed.) 1972. *Preschool programs for the disadvantaged: Five experimental approaches to early childhood education.* Baltimore, Md. 21218: The Johns Hopkins University Press.

———— (ed.). 1973. *Compensatory education for children ages two to eight: Recent studies of educational intervention.* Baltimore, Md. 21218: The Johns Hopkins University Press.

————. 1974. Intellectual precocity. In J. C. Stanley, D. P. Keating, and L. H. Fox (eds.), *Mathematical talent: Discovery, description, and development.* Baltimore, Md. 21218: The Johns Hopkins University Press, pp. 1–22.

Terman, L. M. 1925. Mental and physical traits of a thousand gifted children. *Genetic studies of genius*, vol. I. Stanford, California: Stanford University Press.

Torrance, E. P. 1968. Creativity and its educational implications for the gifted. *The Gifted Child Quarterly* 12:67–78.

Weiss, D., Haier, R. J., and Keating, D. P. 1974. Personality characteristics of mathematically precocious boys. In J. C. Stanley, D. P. Keating, and L. H. Fox (eds.), *Mathematical talent: Discovery, description, and development.* Baltimore, Md. 21218: The Johns Hopkins University Press, pp. 126–39.

Witty, P. A. 1967. The gifted child in 1967. *The Gifted Child Quarterly* 11:255–62.

4
IDENTIFYING MATHEMATICAL TALENT ON A STATEWIDE BASIS[1]

William C. George and Cecilia H. Solano

ABSTRACT

This paper shows that mathematical talent can be identified on a large-scale basis in an economical and systematic fashion. The 1974 Maryland Mathematics Talent Search is used as the model. Eligibility criterion, test selection, mail-out procedures, publicity, test administration, personnel, reporting of test results, cost analysis, and community involvement are discussed in detail. Fifteen hundred and nineteen students from all twenty-three counties of Maryland and Baltimore City took the Scholastic Aptitude Test-Mathematical (SAT-M). The cost per student was $3.40 for the Talent Search vs. the $8.00 charge for the SATs during a regular administration. In final analysis, 1,300 students were identified as capable of greatly accelerating their mathematical programs before the end of high school. One hundred and eleven contestants scored 640 or more on the SAT-M, which is the 95th percentile of a random sample of male high school juniors. Forty-one of these talented youths received one-course scholarships from twelve different local colleges.

In recent years the Study of Mathematically Precocious Youth (SMPY) has been concerned with the identification, description, and facilitation of mathematically highly able youngsters. The identification of such youths on a large-scale basis has therefore been a major concern. Initial studies led SMPY to believe that a great deal of mathematical talent existed untapped in junior high school students in the state of Maryland. That there is such a resource of unfacilitated talent is supported by Keating and Stanley (1972) and Stanley, Keating, and Fox (1974). These studies show that students with high mathemati-

[1]The authors would like to thank Dr. Julian C. Stanley for his helpful comments and encouragement in earlier drafts of this chapter.

cal aptitude are found in school classrooms, performing at levels far below their capabilities. Often students such as those identified through SMPY already know the material being introduced or understand it immediately. Little enthusiasm or motivation can be expected from those gifted students who must continually wait for their less able fellow students to catch up.

In the first two years of SMPY, 1972 and 1973, many mathematically able students in the Baltimore metropolitan area were tested. In the second year the area canvassed was expanded to include students in the Washington-metropolitan-area counties of Maryland as well. Only those students who were in the top 2 percent of their school grade on national norms in arithmetic reasoning, total arithmetic, quantitative aptitude, or an equivalent were allowed to participate in the second contest. In the 1972 testing, 396 students participated in the contest by taking the Scholastic Aptitude Test-Mathematical (SAT-M) and the College Entrance Examination Board Mathematics Level I Achievement Test (CEEB MI). In the second year of the mathematics talent search, 953 pupils took both the SAT-M and the Scholastic Aptitude Test-Verbal (SAT-V) in contests conducted by SMPY and the Study of Verbally Gifted Youth (SVGY). (A qualified student entered only one of the two contests.) These talent searches found an unexpectedly high degree of mathematical ability in seventh-, eighth-, and underage ninth-grade junior high school students. In the first year, twenty-five students in the talent search scored at least 640 on the SAT-M, which is the 95th percentile for male high school juniors. In the second year two boys scored 800, the highest score attainable, and fifty-seven students (three of them girls) scored at least 640 on the SAT-M. Such scores are truly remarkable.

The goals of SMPY for the third talent search (January 1974) were to identify a large pool of mathematical talent, report the findings to the school systems involved, study the highest scoring students further, and assist them in their educational progress. It was hoped that the school systems would then work in conjunction with their gifted students to develop these mathematical potentials to the fullest. The school systems would be encouraged to use grade-skipping, fast-paced mathematics classes, and other curricular innovations (Fox 1974a[I:3]; chapters 6 and 7 in this volume).[2] The purpose of this paper is to show that mathematical talent can be identified on a large-scale basis in an economical and systematic fashion. Although an undertaking of this size presents difficulties, the importance of such an effort makes the endeavor worthwhile.

RECRUITING INSTITUTIONAL SUPPORT

The first step in this process was the recruiting of institutional support. SMPY felt that in order to ensure a complete coverage of the state of Maryland for its

---

[2]In addition to the usual references, citations of chapters in volume I of *Studies of Intellectual Precocity* will be as follows: [I:3]. The I indicates volume I, and the 3 is the chapter number [Editor].

1974 Mathematics Talent Search, the support of other colleges and universities was needed. First, having test centers conveniently located throughout the state would facilitate reaching pupils who otherwise might not make the long trip to a single, central test site. Second, the desire for institutional support was a result of SMPY's previous successful experience with highly able mathematically talented students who had taken college courses. The Johns Hopkins University was aware of this talent due to the previous success of the early entrants in 1969 and 1970 (Stanley 1974[I:1]) and established an early admission program for students recommended by SMPY.

In addition, approximately twenty-five other junior high school students had already taken college courses on a part-time basis through The Johns Hopkins University Evening College, the College in Escrow Program at Towson State College, Goucher College, American University, and Montgomery Junior College. Some of the courses taken included computer science, algebra and trigonometry, analytic geometry, calculus, astronomy, chemistry, Russian, and economics. This very talented group of youngsters had a combined 3.82 grade point average out of a possible 4.00, for a total of 174 college credits. The remarkable achievement of these twenty-five other students indicated the need for institutional support.

These institutions of higher education, however, are located in the Baltimore and Washington, D.C. area. Enlisting the support of colleges and universities throughout the state would provide opportunities for gifted students in other areas to take college courses while still in junior high school. The colleges and universities involved would profit by attracting students from this talent pool to their institutions a year or two early, while helping academically gifted students move ahead more rapidly.

Consequently, a letter (see Supplemental Material 1, p. 69) was sent in the latter part of the summer of 1973 to sixteen institutions of higher education in the state of Maryland and in Washington, D.C. An invitation was extended to these universities and colleges to send representatives to a conference to learn how they could help mathematically gifted youths in their geographical areas. Each institution was asked to provide a one-course scholarship. In addition, some colleges were asked to provide space in their institution for a testing center in the 1974 Mathematics Talent Search. The response was excellent; twelve institutions[3] (75 percent) sent representatives to the conference.

The outcome of the meeting was encouraging. Four institutions[4] committed their schools as testing centers. These four institutions were advantageously located over the state (see figure 4.1), with one being on the Eastern Shore, one in

---

[3]The twelve institutions represented were The American University, Catonsville Community College, Frostburg State College, George Washington University, Georgetown University, Goucher College, The Johns Hopkins University, Loyola College, Salisbury State College, Towson State College, University of Maryland—Baltimore County, and University of Maryland—College Park.

[4]The four test centers were located at Frostburg State College, The Johns Hopkins University, Salisbury State College, and University of Maryland—College Park.

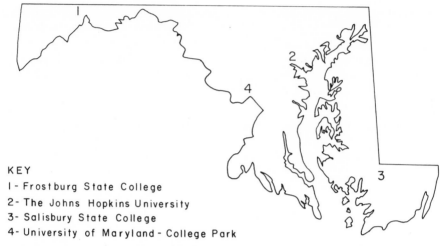

KEY

I - Frostburg State College
2 - The Johns Hopkins University
3 - Salisbury State College
4 - University of Maryland - College Park

Fig. 4.1. Location of test centers in Maryland.

Western Maryland, one in the Washington, D.C. metropolitan area, and one in the Baltimore metropolitan area. The test dates were also confirmed, with the testing centers choosing one of two different dates, which were a week apart. In addition, many of the other colleges attending the conference felt that they would be able to offer one or more one-course scholarships.

PRELIMINARY CONCERNS OF THE TALENT SEARCH

The next point to be determined was the establishment of the criteria for eligibility. The 1974 Maryland Mathematics Talent Search was opened to any student enrolled in the seventh or eighth grades of any public or private school in the state of Maryland or to any student who resided in Maryland but attended as a day student a school outside of Maryland. In addition, any person in a higher grade was also eligible if not yet fourteen years old by 31 December 1973. Each applicant also had to have scored in the upper 2 percent of his school grade on national norms in arithmetic reasoning, total arithmetic, or quantitative aptitude as measured by the most recently administered standardized test, such as the Iowa Tests of Basic Skills (ITBS) or the School and College Ability Tests (SCAT). A student could not qualify on the basis of a general intelligence test, such as the Stanford–Binet or the Otis (see Supplemental Material 2, p. 70).

The decision was made to continue the use of the SAT-M for the talent search, since it had sufficient ceiling to differentiate among the ability levels of students who were uniformly in the top 2 percent of their grade on national norms (see chapter 2 in this volume). Even with this college level test, two students the previous year had earned the top reported score of 800. Since this initial testing was for screening purposes, it was decided that no other tests would be administered at that time. Further follow-up testing would be administered to the highest scoring 100 or so persons. Those students would then be tested on verbal ability, abstract reasoning, mathematics achievement, and other things.

Prizes for the top students were to be one-course tuition waivers to a local college awarded by region. The only stipulation was that a student would be offered a scholarship only from the region in which he chose to be tested. This was done to eliminate the possibility that students from the large metropolitan areas would drive to the eastern or western test sites, which had fewer enrollments, to avoid the stiffer competition in their home regions. Cash prizes and books were awarded to those individuals who SMPY decided were worthy of scholarships, but due to the limited number of tuition prizes, could not be awarded them.

INITIAL MAILING PROCEDURE

Having established the eligibility criteria and handled the preliminary concerns, the next step was to mail out applications. The mail-out procedure was designed to cover every public, private, and parochial school at the middle or junior high school level in the state of Maryland. At least ten applications were sent initially to the mathematics chairperson of each school, with a letter (see Supplemental Material 3, p. 73) requesting cooperation in identifying the highest mathematically able students in their school. Copies of this letter and the application were also sent to the guidance department chairperson and the school principal. If SMPY knew of any eligible students in a given school, their names were included in the information packet sent to the counselor. A request was made for the distribution of the enclosed applications to all eligible students.

Senior high schools that had ninth grades were also contacted. The mathematics department chairperson and the principal of high schools having a ninth grade also received letters explaining the talent search and were requested to help identify the students in their school who were eligible by age, even though they were accelerated by one year or more. In addition to this broad approach, SMPY knew of many students who had participated in previous contests and were still eligible; these students were contacted directly (see Supplemental Material 4, p. 74). Each school system was sent a packet of the talent search materials and a copy of the application, so that all levels of the state school system would be aware of the contest. A special note of thanks is extended to those city and county school system administrators who wrote letters asking their schools to cooperate with the talent search.

This phase of the mail-out was designed to give the students seven weeks before the deadline to enroll for the contest. To do this, the student needed to send in a completed application, with certification of his eligibility. His parents, teacher, counselor, or other qualified school administrator had to certify that he was in the upper 2 percent of his school grade in arithmetical ability on national norms. Finally, the student sent SMPY 50¢ postage to cover the cost of mailing, first, the preparation materials for the talent search and, later, his test results. Postage received in this manner substantially reduced the mailing costs of the talent search.

PUBLICIZING THE TALENT SEARCH

Another important contributor to the success of such an undertaking is publicity. The necessary, and much appreciated, cooperation of the schools has already been mentioned. In addition, SMPY used many other available means of publicity. Newspapers in each area of the state were sent releases slanted toward the appropriate test center (see Supplemental Material 5, p. 74). To provide maximum coverage, radio and television were also enlisted to give the 1974 Maryland Mathematics Talent Search free sixty-second public announcement time on the air (see Supplemental Material 6, p. 76). Posters announcing the contest were sent to all of the public libraries in the state of Maryland. This portion of the publicity campaign was timed for approximately three weeks before the closing date for receipt of applications. Publicity such as this is vital for reaching people when participation is voluntary, because some schools make little or no effort to inform eligible students.

The mass mailing and the follow-up publicity produced 2,000 applications to process, many telephone calls, and much correspondence. Immediate feedback is essential, and specific individuals need to be trained to respond to questions, especially regarding the eligibility criteria. Two cooperating persons (George and Solano) were delegated to answer all questions regarding the competition, return all phone calls, and process all talent-search-related mail. In a period of eight weeks, over 500 telephone calls and letters came through the SMPY office regarding the 1974 Maryland Mathematics Talent Search. Many of these calls were requests from schools and individuals for more applications, for further explanations of acceptable mathematics aptitude scores, for clarification of the age requirements, for acceptable test norms, and so forth. By limiting the individuals responsible for answering such questions, few, if any, contradictory answers were given. Prompt, direct replies made this part of the public relations for the talent search run smoothly.

PROCESSING APPLICATIONS

Processing of the applications was made as routine as possible; the system was set up before any applications were sent out. A form letter was prepared ahead of time for students found to be ineligible (see Supplemental Material 7, p. 76). The same procedure was used for students who had incomplete applications. A letter (see Supplemental Material 8, p. 77) explaining why the application was incomplete was filled in and returned immediately. SMPY did not want to reject applicants for the contest because of their carelessness in filling out the application; promptness was therefore a necessity. The third procedure dealt with reviewing an application that was complete to verify the applicant's eligibility; this occurred in 95 percent of the cases. The other 5 percent of the cases were incomplete or ineligible.

If an application was in the proper form, it was initialed, given a number, and filed numerically by the center to which the student had applied. Another member of the staff then processed the return materials, which included the following: test center room assignment, map of the test site, SAT-M practice booklet, sheet of procedures to follow, and questionnaire (see Supplemental Material 9, p. 78).

The questionnaire was designed to be useful for later follow-up research, counseling activities, and attitude studies. It requested such information as the student's name, address, telephone number, birthdate, school name and address, sibling data, parental occupation and educational level, self-perceptions, and college considerations.

After a double check, the return materials were sent out, in most cases on the same day the application was received. The speed of processing enabled students to know as soon as possible whether or not they were eligible.

This procedure also allowed those students who were eligible the maximum time possible to study the SAT-M practice booklet and decide whether they still wished to participate in the contest.

Giving the applicants a chance to try the type of items they were to be tested on provided a further screening mechanism. Students who were eligible but did not do well on the practice booklet tended to eliminate themselves from the contest. Some 400 of the final 1,900 applicants dropped out at this point. This meant that those students who did participate were more likely to be highly able, well motivated in mathematics, and not disappointed on the day of the contest.

PREPARATIONS FOR THE TEST ADMINISTRATION

The deadline for receipt of the applications was five weeks before the contest itself. This time interval was needed to prepare for the testing after the exact number of applicants was known.

While the processing of the applications was being completed, another aspect of the testing was already under consideration. The first concern in the actual testing was to have qualified administrators and proctors. Only persons with previous testing experience were asked to administer the SAT-M for the talent search. To achieve the most standardized procedure possible over many rooms at several test sites, there were meetings with the chief testers in which the exact testing schedule was discussed and proctors assigned. Each chief tester was responsible for his particular proctors. One person was assigned the responsibility for overseeing each test center and the chief testers. This person handled emergencies that arose in any of the testing rooms. Detailed instructions, with a list of points to remember in case of emergency, were also available for each chief tester. Phone locations and extra dimes for telephone calls were just some of the backup procedures that helped make the testing run more smoothly. A monetary payment for main testers and proctors seemed to induce them to take their jobs more seriously.

Another service-oriented feature that is useful when testing on a large scale is a coffee room for the parents who have brought their children to the test site. There, in the vicinity of the test site, waiting parents can be comfortable and meet each other. Thus, parents can be kept out of the testing rooms, allowing the testers and proctors to do a more effective job without creating hard feelings.

On the day of the testing it is essential that all operations go smoothly. The months of advance planning, including student preparation, room reservations, and training testers will be wasted if the testing itself is confused. Preparation of the test materials for that day should be done carefully in advance. All testing personnel should be familiar with their assigned places and duties. Sickness, weather conditions, and other emergencies should be planned for. With this in mind a large-scale program should come off well. In the 1974 Talent Search, no major problems occurred when 1,519 students from Baltimore City and all twenty-three counties of Maryland arrived at the four test centers located in four different regions of the state.

SELECTING A SCORING METHOD

Long before the completion of the actual testing in 1974, SMPY had to decide on the proper scoring procedure for the tests. Cost and speed were major considerations. The first decision involved machine scoring versus hand scoring. This problem will arise in any large testing program. For SMPY, it was less expensive and faster to hand score 1,519 tests than to pay for machine scoring. A major problem with hand scoring, especially with tests having a correction factor or other scoring complication, is the possibility of error. To minimize this source of error as much as possible, teams of four people both scored the answer sheet and checked the scoring. Having the tests scored by machine, at $2 per test, would have cost SMPY $3,038. However, by hand scoring and paying scorers $4 an hour, the cost was approximately $850. Each alternative has its advantages and disadvantages.

REPORTING THE TEST RESULTS

Upon completion of the scoring, it is important to give the students who took the test as much feedback as possible. With this information, very talented students may realize they have not been performing in school to their fullest potential. Well-motivated students may press for more advanced material in their classroom or for other procedures to increase their learning of mathematics. Scores of those students who do well should also be presented to the school systems. If parents and schools work cooperatively, programs can be established to develop the abilities of mathematically talented students. Distributions of the scores and their meaning were mailed in duplicate to the talent search participants (see Supplemental Material 10, p. 82). Parents were encouraged to report these test scores to the student's school, in the hope that it would help the student, parent, and counselor decide on his or her optimum program. Following up the reporting of scores to the individual, each school system received a list of those students who scored at least 420, the 50th percentile of a random sample of males taking the Scholastic Aptitude Test-Mathematics in their senior year of high school; 1,312 students out of the 1,519 scored that high.

In hopes of preparing the way for the counties and the city to facilitate the students identified on the lists, SMPY sent a letter out to the school systems, offering to help in setting up programs for mathematically gifted junior high school students that had been tried and proved to be highly successful at Johns Hopkins (see Supplemental Material 11, p. 86). This letter pointed out that this was SMPY's third year for such a talent search and that it was statewide. School systems were encouraged to accommodate their gifted students in economically feasible and manageable ways, such as fast-paced mathematics classes (see Fox 1974*b* [I:6], and chapters 6 and 7 in this volume).

THE AWARDS CEREMONY

As noted above, the 1974 Maryland Mathematics Talent Search was highly successful. Of the 1,519 contestants, 111 students scored 640 or greater on the SAT-M, which is the 95th percentile of a random sample of male high school juniors taking the SAT-M. This group was declared the talent search winners group for 1974. In order to acknowledge these students properly it was decided to have an awards ceremony for them (see Supplemental Materials 12, p. 87, and 13, p. 88). On the day of the ceremony approximately 500 to 600 people came to see their sons and daughters honored. From the stage that day SMPY awarded forty-one one-course scholarships from twelve different area colleges.[5] This was

[5]The twelve colleges were The American University, Catholic University, Frostburg State College, Goucher College, Georgetown University, The Johns Hopkins University, Loyola College,

an important step in recognizing the potential and talent of mathematically able youth.

The importance of the awards ceremony was three-fold. First, those students who had participated in the talent search and had scored 640 or more were recognized. Second, by offering scholarships the colleges and universities were publicly recognizing the existence of highly mathematically able students and showing their willingness to help stimulate such abilities. The third emphasis of the awards ceremony was informational. An address centering on the need to motivate talented students was made to the parents. In this way SMPY attempted to help the students and their families understand the alternatives (see Fox 1974*a* [I:3]) and possibilities that could be opened to highly able students. SMPY hoped that the boys and girls honored on this day were challenged to try some of these alternatives, which include special fast-mathematics classes, college courses, subject-matter acceleration, and grade skipping (including entering college before graduating from high school).

EVALUATION

Publicity Campaign

The goal of systematically identifying a large group of mathematically talented young people was thus accomplished. In order to ascertain how the information regarding the talent search reached the contestants and what motivated them to participate, two questions were analyzed from the questionnaire. They were:

1. Where did you find out about the Mathematics Talent Search?
2. From whom did you receive the most encouragement to enter the Mathematics Talent Search?

The first question (see table 4.1) gave SMPY a partial evaluation of the differential effectiveness of its publicity techniques. It was only somewhat useful for differentiating, since the students were asked to list all people who had contacted them about the contest. This question did show that school cooperation was of great value, particularly the mathematics teacher. The systematic mail-out to every school had been extremely important. After mathematics teachers, the order of most frequent notification was from guidance counselors, letters from SMPY, friends, the news media, parents, and, finally, a variety of other sources. The important sources after the school were friends and the news media. SMPY knows of at least ten newspapers throughout the state that publicized the contest. There were also at least two radio stations and one television network that gave a short message on the contest. The importance of good coverage cannot be overlooked when planning to test on a large-scale basis.

Salisbury State College, Towson State College, University of Maryland—Baltimore County, University of Maryland—College Park, and Western Maryland College.

Table 4.1.   Question–How did you find out about the Maryland Mathematics Talent Search?

Form of publicity	Number (N = 1519)	Percent of mentions
Mathematics teacher	960	43
Guidance counselor	453	20
Letter to student	405	18
Friend	131	6
News media	117	5
Parents	116	5
Others	36	2

The cost of publicity was minimal when the returns that it produced are considered.

The second question (see table 4.2) pertained to the student's self-perception of who encouraged him the most. Interestingly enough, over half of the students felt that their parents offered them the most encouragement to participate in the talent search. The other real source of encouragement in the eyes of the students was their mathematics teachers. Almost 500 of the students felt that their mathematics instructors were instrumental in their participating in the contest. This is also another indication that the statewide mail-out campaign was presented properly to the schools, as well as to the parents and students themselves.

Cost

In evaluating the cost of the 1974 Maryland Mathematics Talent Search, two questions arise: (1) Could it be done more economically? (2) Is the cost too burdensome to be worthwhile for a school system or other institutions to attempt? The answer to both questions is a qualified "no." Systematic identification on a large-scale basis is both economical and worthwhile.

For the 1974 Maryland Mathematics Talent Search the cost per student was approximately $3.40. This included the initial mail-out, publicity, notification of

Table 4.2.   Question–From whom did you receive the most encouragement to enter the Maryland Mathematics Talent Search?

Person	Number (N = 1519)	Percent of mentions
Parents	875	48
Mathematics teacher	491	27
Guidance counselor	153	8
Myself	142	8
Friends	72	4
Others	97	5

acceptance, practice material, purchasing of tests and answer sheets, scoring, reporting of scores, and testing personnel. The cost of taking the SATs during a regular administration is at least $8.00. The cost per student will vary depending upon the size of the talent pool. The larger the contest, the more inexpensive the search can be per person. The total cost of the 1974 Maryland Mathematics Talent Search was $5,164 (see Supplemental Material 14, p. 89). The study had reduced the cost by asking the student to send postage money or stamps to cover the cost of return mailing. Even if SMPY had absorbed this cost the total cost per student would have been no more than $3.74 per person.

For a school system this is a small sum to pay for the amount of information it can obtain regarding its mathematically ablest students. From this minimal initial cost of identification of gifted youth, the system will benefit by being better able to meet the needs of these students through such means as subject-matter acceleration, special fast-paced mathematics classes, or even grade-level acceleration. Such an identification program is invaluable to the school system and, more importantly, to the student.

SUMMARY

In the final analysis, SMPY identified through the 1974 Maryland Mathematics Talent Search over 1,000 students capable of accelerating their mathematics program in some significant way before the end of their high school years. Many of these students will be ready to enter college a year or two early. Other students, with the help of stimulating college courses and advanced placement examinations, will earn many credits toward their college degree, while being challenged to learn and study to their fullest potential. Early identification of talent through tests with enough ceiling will help school systems differentiate among students who are in the top 1 or 2 percent on their age-grade tests. Identifying the talented is both economical and manageable. It is to be hoped that school systems, colleges, and universities will set up similar identification programs.

The Scholastic Aptitude Test is not the only acceptable selection instrument. Appropriately difficult levels of tests, such as the Preliminary Scholastic Aptitude Test (PSAT) or the School and College Ability Tests (SCAT), are also quite useful. The chief point to note is that for the top 2 percentile seventh- and eighth-graders taking the test, the ability level that the test measures should be at the twelfth grade or college freshman level. This will allow for differentiation of abilities. Previous test scores can be used as a preliminary screening device similar to the talent search's use of prior test results. If these tests were available to the school systems, then these initially selected students could be retested during the school day on a routine basis.

Since the number tested per school system would not be large, reporting should be relatively quick and simple. Then programs suitable to each individual student's needs could be established. If there was not enough talent in one school, students within a region of the school system could meet together on released time or outside regular school hours to study mathematics at a fast pace, as previously mentioned (Fox 1974*b* [I:6], and chapters 3, 6, and 7 in this volume.)

Within a school system mailing could be simplified. Materials could be distributed through the students to go home. Questions could be answered through telephone conversations, letters, or personal interviews. Actually, the cost for a school system should be considerably cheaper. Many of the materials and facilities are generally available already.

SMPY has worked out in three successive years one form of large-scale identification that is successful. Modifications to such a program will probably be feasible for various institutions and school systems. Some colleges and universities are becoming interested in the mathematically gifted, as evidenced by their cooperation and support in providing SMPY with testing centers and one-course tuition waivers. The Montgomery County (Maryland) public school system has set up two fast-paced classes which started in the fall of 1974 for approximately sixty of its mathematically ablest students identified through the talent search. In the spring of 1975, Montgomery County used the appropriately difficult level of the SCAT in place of the SAT to identify their mathematically talented students who qualified for an additional three fast-paced mathematics classes established for fall 1975. Another county, Charles, established its fast-mathematics program in November 1974 (two classes). This county used the PSAT as its screening device to identify those individuals who were qualified to participate in an additional fast-paced mathematics class which began in February 1975. Several private schools have set up their own identification and facilitation programs as a result of the 1974 Maryland Mathematics Talent Search. A city school began its program in January 1974 (see chapter 7 in this volume). A middle-school instituted two fast-mathematics classes into its curriculum in October 1974. It is to be hoped that other schools and school systems—public, parochial, and private—will be able to use SMPY's identification procedures or some variation of them to identify and facilitate their gifted students, not only in mathematics but also in other subject-matter areas.

REFERENCES

Fox, L. H. 1974*a*. Facilitating educational development of mathematically precocious youth. In J. C. Stanley, D. P. Keating, and L. H. Fox (eds.), *Mathematical talent: Discovery, description, and development*. Baltimore: The Johns Hopkins University Press, pp. 47-69.

———. 1974*b*. A mathematics program for fostering precocious achievement. In J. C. Stanley, D. P. Keating, and L. H. Fox (eds.), *Mathematical talent: Discovery, description, and development*. Baltimore: The Johns Hopkins University Press, pp. 101-25.

Keating, D. P., and Stanley, J. C. 1972. Extreme measures for the exceptionally gifted in mathematics and science. *Educational Researcher* 1(9): 3–7.

Stanley, J. C. 1974. Intellectual precocity. In J. C. Stanley, D. P. Keating, and L. H. Fox (eds.), *Mathematical talent: Discovery, description, and development.* Baltimore: The Johns Hopkins University Press, pp. 1–22.

Stanley, J. C., Keating, D. P., and Fox, L. H. (eds.). 1974. *Mathematical talent: Discovery, description, and development.* Baltimore: The Johns Hopkins University Press.

LIST OF SUPPLEMENTAL MATERIALS
PERTAINING TO CHAPTER 4

1. Letter to institutions of higher education, inviting them to participate in a conference on the mathematically talented.
2. Application Form for the 1974 Maryland Mathematics Talent Search.
3. Cover letter to junior high school mathematics chairpersons.
4. Cover letter to known eligible students for the talent search.
5. Newspaper press release from The Johns Hopkins' Office of Public Information (OPI).
6. Radio and television release from OPI.
7. Cover letter to students applying, informing them that they are ineligible for the talent search.
8. Cover letter to students sending in incomplete applications.
9. Talent search questionnaire.
10. Cover letter and distribution sheet explaining to each individual participating in the talent search his/her score on the SAT-M.
11. Cover letter to mathematics supervisor of each county and city school system in Maryland.
12. Letter to talent search scholarship winners.
13. Letter to talent search nonscholarship winners.
14. Cost analysis of the 1974 Talent Search.

SUPPLEMENTAL MATERIAL 1

THE JOHNS HOPKINS UNIVERSITY • BALTIMORE, MARYLAND 21218

DEPARTMENT OF PSYCHOLOGY
Study of Mathematically
Precocious Youth (SMPY)

Area 301—366-3300
Extensions 538 and 1410

31 August 1973

Dear _____

In March of 1972 and January of 1973 we conducted an all-state search among seventh-, eighth-, and under-age ninth-graders for exceptionally high mathematical reasoning ability. There were 396 entrants the first year and 666 the second. These represented approximately the upper 2 percent of the age group. Our main instrument was the Scholastic Aptitude Test, Mathematical, of the College Entrance Examination Board. In 1972, twenty-two of the entrants scored 660 or more (Johns Hopkins' average freshman scored 656 when he or she was in the eleventh or twelfth grade). In 1973, thirty-seven scored 660 or more. The highest SAT-M score in 1972 was 790. In 1973 there were two 800s. In fact, a *seventh*-grader tested in the latter year scored 800 on each of the College Board's three mathematics tests: SAT-M, Mathematics I achievement, and Mathematics II achievement. During the coming school year he will be taking honors advanced placement calculus with twelfth-graders.

In the 1974 testing (probably to be held on January 26) we would like even better coverage of the entire state of Maryland. Every seventh-, eighth-, or under-age ninth- grader (or higher) who resides in the state *or* attends a school in the state will be eligible, if he or she has recently ranked in the upper 2 percent of the grade on national norms in an arithmetical or mathematical reasoning test.

In order to facilitate the testing of youngsters, we are hoping to set up several testing centers throughout the state, rather than (as in past years) doing all of the testing on the Johns Hopkins campus. Tentatively, we have chosen the University of Maryland at College Park, Frostburg State College, Salisbury State College, and The Johns Hopkins University as the testing sites.

We would like to meet for lunch at 11:30 a.m. on Saturday, September 15, in the lounge of The Johns Hopkins Club on the Homewood campus of The Johns Hopkins University to discuss this. We invite you or your designated representative to be our guest then until 3:00 p.m.

Enclosed is some material concerning our program of identification, study, and facilitation of these brilliant youths. If you have any questions about the meeting or would like any other materials, please write us or telephone 301-366-3300, ext. 1410 (Mrs. Denham, Mrs. Fox, Mr. George, or Mr. Keating), or ext. 538 (me). We feel that there are great mutual benefits in such cooperation.

This year we would like to give as the top prizes tuition scholarships for appropriate computer science and mathematics courses that the winner could take at a college near him or her. Already, many of our winners, one only ten years old, have taken courses at Johns Hopkins, Towson State College, Goucher College, Montgomery County Community College, and Washington area colleges with excellent grades—mostly As, and nothing lower than B. For example, a boy at age twelve took introduction to computer science in the JHU day school and earned a grade of A. That summer he took college algebra and trigonometry at the JHU Evening College and, even though he had completed only algebra I in the eighth grade, made a B. He then took fundamentals of mathematics two semesters during the academic year at a local liberal arts college and was its best student (while enrolled in grade 9). This summer he took eight credits of chemistry there and made As. Now, at age fourteen years and two months, he is going into the tenth grade and will also take calculus as a part-time student at the college. By May of 1974 he will still be fourteen years old but will have 30 college credits, a whole year's worth, with superb grades. He is no average boy, of course (though we have half a dozen as able as he), but he is especially ambitious and well-rounded. He is a good musician (playing seven instruments), a fine athlete, and unusually handsome.

Would you be willing to inquire tentatively about the possibility of your college's offering several (at least one, and preferably three or more) course-tuition waivers to be used as prizes for the very ablest of the contestants? This is a fine way to attract high talent to your institution. We can discuss this further at the meeting.

We would like to have you come yourself, if feasible, unless you feel that someone else at your institution would be more appropriate. If you would like to attend and feel that someone else should also come, please let us know. We would appreciate hearing from you on the enclosed card by Monday, September 10, if possible, so that we can plan the luncheon and meeting.

Sincerely yours,

JULIAN C. STANLEY
Professor of Psychology
Director of the Study

Enclosures: *NYT* article
K & S article
Fox AAAS #3 paper
Preface and Table of Contents of *MT:D*[3]
Map of the campus, with Club circled
Stamped, addressed postal card

SUPPLEMENTAL MATERIAL 2

MARYLAND MATHEMATICS TALENT SEARCH CONDUCTED BY
THE STUDY OF MATHEMATICALLY PRECOCIOUS YOUTH (SMPY)
OF THE JOHNS HOPKINS UNIVERSITY

What: The Scholastic *Aptitude* Test, Mathematical, of the College Entrance Examination
Board.
Place and date:

Region	College	Location	Date
1	Frostburg State College	Frostburg, Md.	19 Jan. 1974
2	The Johns Hopkins University Homewood Campus	Baltimore, Md.	26 Jan. 1974
3	Salisbury State College	Salisbury, Md.	26 Jan. 1974
4	University of Maryland	College Park, Md.	26 Jan. 1974

Time: 1:00–3:00 p.m. for both test dates.
Prizes: Tuition waivers by local colleges for one course per person will be offered to the top scorers within each of the above four regions. These course scholarships (worth as much as $300 each) will be good through approximately August 1975, but only if used by the student participating in the contest and winning in that particular region. Courses such as introduction to computer science, college algebra and trigonometry, analytic geometry, and

astronomy may be taken for credit, which generally can be applied later to one's regular college program. A number of other, lesser prizes—$10 and/or mathematics books—may also be given. Awards will be made in the latter part of March. Each entrant will be told his or her score, together with an explanation of its meaning, as soon as the scores become available. School systems will be told who their high-scoring students are. Considerable educational guidance and facilitation will be offered to those who score well on this test of mathematical reasoning ability.

Who is Eligible: Any person enrolled in the *seventh or eighth* grade of any school, public or private, in the state of Maryland or who resides in the state of Maryland but attends as a *day* student a school outside the state. Also, any person in a higher grade who is not yet, on 31 December 1973, fourteen years old. (Most such students will have skipped a grade in school or entered early.) In addition, each applicant *must* have scored in the upper 2 percent of his school grade on *national* norms in arithmetic reasoning, total arithmetic, or quantitative aptitude, as measured by a recently administered standardized test, such as the Iowa or SCAT. This means scoring at the 98th or 99th percentile. Seventh- or eighth-graders scoring lower than that usually find the Scholastic Aptitude Test too difficult, because it was constructed for testing above-average high school juniors and seniors. (You can *not* qualify by means of IQ tests, such as the California Test of Mental Maturity, the Stanford–Binet, or the Wechsler.)

NO WAIVERS OF GRADE, AGE, RESIDENTIAL, OR TEST-SCORE REQUIRE-MENTS CAN BE MADE. For example, if you live in the District of Columbia and do not attend school in Maryland, you are ineligible. But if you live in Maryland and attend as a *day* student a school in D.C. or another place, you are eligible. For example, a Washington resident attending the Canterbury School in Accokeek, Maryland is eligible, as is a Maryland resident attending the Sidwell Friends School in D.C. A Maryland resident at boarding school in another state is *not* eligible, but someone in a Maryland boarding school is.

If you will be fourteen years old on 31 December 1973 or earlier, *and* will be in the ninth grade or higher by the time the test is administered, you are ineligible (but note that there is no age limitation if you are a seventh- or eighth-grader). If your score on a recent test of *mathematical* aptitude is less than the 98th percentile of national norms for your grade, you are ineligible. Sometimes it is difficult to locate *national* norms for a test. If so, suggest to your guidance counselor that he or she confer with the director of testing of your school system.

How and When to Apply: Fill out the enclosed application blank and return it to Mr. William C. George, SMPY, Department of Psychology, The Johns Hopkins University, Baltimore, Maryland 21218, *before* Friday, 14 December 1973—the earlier the better. Along with the application, please return the two mailing labels, each showing your printed mailing address, and six 8¢ stamps (or 50¢ in coins) to defray mailing costs. You will then be sent a practice booklet for the Scholastic Aptitude Test, which will enable you to know what the test is like before taking it, and a background questionnaire to fill out. Also, you will receive further information concerning the test site.

Please *print* or type the information requested on the enclosed application form and *send it to us as soon as possible.* Do not wait for your friends or schoolmates to send theirs. The sooner we get your *fully* completed application, the quicker you will receive a practice booklet to study and improve your chances in the Maryland Mathematics Talent Search.

Further Information: This is the third, and last, Maryland Mathematics Talent Search that The Johns Hopkins University will conduct. There *may* be regional contests in 1975.

If you have any questions about procedures, write to Mr. George or telephone him or others on the SMPY staff at (301) 366–3300, exts. 538 or 1410.

DEADLINE FOR RECEIPT OF APPLICATION: FRIDAY, 14 DECEMBER 1973.

MARYLAND MATHEMATICS TALENT SEARCH CONDUCTED BY THE STUDY OF
MATHEMATICALLY PRECOCIOUS YOUTH (SMPY) OF THE JOHNS HOPKINS
UNIVERSITY

NAME＿＿＿＿＿＿＿＿＿＿＿＿＿＿＿＿＿＿＿＿＿＿SEX: M   F
(PRINT)   first   middle   last   (circle one)

BIRTHDATE＿＿＿＿＿＿＿＿ Full name of ＿＿＿＿＿＿＿＿＿＿＿＿＿
                month   day   year

                                school attended ＿＿＿＿＿＿＿＿＿＿＿＿＿

                                ＿＿＿＿＿＿＿＿＿＿＿＿＿＿＿＿＿＿＿

PRESENT SCHOOL   Full address ＿＿＿＿＿＿＿＿＿＿＿＿＿＿＿
GRADE __7
        —8   of school   ＿＿＿＿＿＿＿＿＿＿＿＿＿＿＿
        —9
        —Other (＿＿＿)   ＿＿＿＿＿＿＿＿＿＿＿＿＿＿＿＿＿
                                                            zip code

Type: Public   Private   Parochial. If parochial, the religious denomination:
                 (circle one)

＿＿＿＿＿＿＿＿＿＿＿＿＿＿＿＿＿＿＿＿＿＿＿＿＿＿＿＿＿＿＿＿＿＿

Home address ＿＿＿＿＿＿＿＿＿＿＿＿＿＿＿＿＿＿＿＿＿＿＿＿＿
                    street   city   state   zip code

Check the (one) regional center which you will attend. Give this careful consideration *now*,
because it will be difficult to change your assignment later.
    __Region 1: Frostburg State College   (Sat. afternoon, Jan. 19)
    __Region 2: Johns Hopkins University   (Sat. afternoon, Jan. 26)
    __Region 3: Salisbury State College   (Sat. afternoon, Jan. 26)
    __Region 4: University of Maryland—College Park   (Sat. afternoon, Jan. 26)

I hereby certify that this student scored at the (circle one)   98th   99th   percentile of national
norms on the mathematics or quantitative-aptitude part of the ＿＿＿＿＿＿＿＿＿＿＿＿
＿＿＿＿＿＿＿＿＿＿＿＿taken in＿＿＿＿＿＿＿(year).   test name: ITBS, SCAT, etc.

＿＿＿＿＿＿＿＿＿＿Signature ＿＿＿＿＿＿＿＿＿＿＿＿＿＿＿＿＿＿＿＿
month   day   (circle one)   Parent   Teacher   Principal   Counselor

Comments or explanations ＿＿＿＿＿＿＿＿＿＿＿＿＿＿＿＿＿＿＿＿＿

＿＿＿＿＿＿＿＿＿＿＿＿＿＿＿＿＿＿＿＿＿＿＿＿＿＿＿＿＿＿＿＿＿＿

    Please enclose six 8¢ postage stamps *or* 50¢ in coins and the two mailing labels, each contain-
ing your full *printed* mailing address. We cannot process your application without these items.
We reserve the right to reject applications if all information is not completed.
    If you need further information, telephone Mr. George, Mrs. Denham, Mrs. Fox, Mr. Keating,
Miss Solano, or Professor Stanley at (301) 366–3300, ext. 538 or (if no answer) ext. 1410.

Mailing Address: Mr. William C. George, SMPY, Department of Psychology, The John Hopkins University, Baltimore, Maryland 21218

DEADLINE FOR RECEIPT OF APPLICATION: FRIDAY, 14 DECEMBER 1973.

SUPPLEMENTAL MATERIAL 3

THE JOHNS HOPKINS UNIVERSITY

Baltimore, Maryland 21218

Department of Psychology
Study of Mathematically Precocious Youth

18 October 1973

SUBJECT: 1974 Maryland Mathematics Talent Search

TO: Chairmen of Mathematics Departments in Junior High Schools

FROM: Dr. Julian Stanley, Professor of Psychology and Director of the Talent Search, The Johns Hopkins University

The enclosed copies of an announcement concerning the forthcoming Maryland Mathematics Talent Search will probably be of interest to your mathematically ablest students, particularly those who reason exceptionally well mathematically. We would greatly appreciate your distributing them to such persons.

In 1972, 396 highly able seventh-, eighth-, and under-age ninth-graders participated in the mathematics contest. Last year 667 students entered the second competition. Of these contestants, 59 scored between 660–800 on the Scholastic Aptitude Test—Mathematics (SAT-M). The mean score for our contestants was 515, which exceeds the score of 75 percent of high school seniors.

We have helped a number of these students to obtain high intellectual stimulation via college courses taken for credit at Johns Hopkins, Towson State College, American University, and elsewhere at night, during the summer, or on released time from their schools. The basic course in computer science is a special favorite (15 As and 3 Bs thus far). Other courses taken were college algebra and trigonometry (7 As and 2 Bs), analytic geometry (4 As and 1 B), mathematics theory (1 A, 1 B), descriptive astronomy (1 A, 1 B), chemistry (2 As, 2 Bs), Russian (2 As), and economics (A). For this very talented group of students a 3.82 grade-point average out of a possible 4.00 has been obtained for 174 credits of college courses.

This year, besides offering college course scholarships as prizes, there will be some cash and book awards. Also, winners and near-winners will be invited to become associated with our Study of Mathematically Precocious Youth, thereby providing them, without cost, continuing educational guidance and facilitation.

Thank you for helping us find mathematically highly talented youngsters. If you should need any more applications or information please call Mr. George (366–3300, ext. 538).

cc: Principal
　　Guidance Department chairman
Enclosures: Applications for the 1974 Maryland Mathematics Talent Search

SUPPLEMENTAL MATERIAL 4

THE JOHNS HOPKINS UNIVERSITY

Baltimore, Maryland 21218

Department of Psychology
Study of Mathematically Precocious Youth

16 October 1973

SUBJECT: Mathematics Talent Search in the state of Maryland
TO: Those persons whom we already know to be eligible
FROM: Dr. Julian Stanley, Professor of Psychology and Director of the study;
           Mrs. Lynn Fox, Mr. Daniel Keating, Mrs. Susanne Denham, and Miss Cecilia
           Solano, project associates; and Mr. William George, project coordinator

We specially invite you to enter the mathematics talent search this year, as indicated on the enclosed sheets. You need not secure certification of your mathematics aptitude; ignore that part of the application. Return the completed application before December 14. Hope to see you there!

Enclosure: 1 copy of the talent search announcement. (Be sure to tell your eligible friends.
           They must, however, have their mathematics aptitude certified.)
CS/ls

SUPPLEMENTAL MATERIAL 5

Office of Public Information
The Johns Hopkins University
Baltimore, Maryland 21218
Telephone: (301) 366–3300, ext. 704

FOR IMMEDIATE USE

The Johns Hopkins University has announced testing dates for a program that seeks to identify seventh- and eighth-grade Maryland youngsters who have exceptional ability in mathematical areas.

To be conducted under the university's Study of Mathematically Precocious Youth, this test will make gifted boys and girls eligible for tuition waivers by colleges in their areas, cash prizes, books, extensive educational counseling, and possible participation in an accelerated academic program at Johns Hopkins.

According to Julian C. Stanley, professor of psychology at the university and director of the project, the gifted students identified by the test will become affiliated with a program that aims to help such boys and girls obtain doctoral degrees in their early 20s, so that they may have the maximum number of their most productive years free for creative research.

In addition, Dr. Stanley says, the study is developing a model program for selecting and assisting precocious students all over the country.

The test will be given at several centers throughout the state. On January 19, 1974, it will be given at Frostburg State College in Western Maryland. On January 26, it will be given at Johns Hopkins in Baltimore, Salisbury State College on the Eastern Shore, and the University of Maryland at College Park.

Any person enrolled in the seventh or eighth grades of any school (public or private) in the state of Maryland, or who resides in Maryland but attends as a day student a school outside the state, is eligible to take the test. Also eligible is any person in a higher grade who will have not reached age fourteen by December 31, 1973. In addition, each applicant must have scored in the upper 2 percent of his high school grade on national norms in arithmetic reasoning, total arithmetic, or quantitative aptitude, as measured by a recently administered standardized test, such as the Iowa Test of Basic Skills (ITBS) or the School and College Ability Test (SCAT). This means scoring in the 98th or 99th percentile.

In order to obtain application forms, qualified students or their parents should contact William C. George, project coordinator for the project, at the Department of Psychology, The Johns Hopkins University, Baltimore, Md. 21218. The telephone is (301) 366-3300, ext. 538. Completed applications must be returned no later than Friday, December 14.

Commenting on the kinds of children involved in the project, which is now in its third year, Dr. Stanley says: "Contrary to popular opinion, the precocious child is not immature, shy, and retiring. Instead, he or she is a young person who has developed intellectual abilities and personal characteristics more advanced than one would expect within his age group. Our gifted students have high mathematical aptitude because they have had the ability and the inclination to study the subject on their own at an early age."

The project is currently facilitating the educational progress of over 100 students from the Baltimore area, Dr. Stanley adds, most of whom were first identified in the seventh or eighth grades.

The Study of Mathematically Precocious Youth is sponsored by a five-year grant totaling $266,000 from the Spencer Foundation of Chicago, a national organization that supports research in a number of areas of education.

The general goal of his project, Dr. Stanley says, is to identify a number of promising students each year, study their abilities, enable them to make the best use of their talents, and assist them as much as possible through college and graduate school. The project includes work with gifted youngsters both individually and in small groups.

There is presently a Saturday algebra class for junior high school children averaging fourteen years of age, and there are a number of twelve- to 14-year-olds taking advanced courses or full-time programs at area colleges. Other students are being accelerated at their own schools. Participants are identified by means of the mathematics talent search.

The oldest participant in the project—age eighteen—is currently enrolled as a full-time graduate student in computer science at Cornell University, working toward his Ph.D. degree; he completed the M.S. degree at Johns Hopkins while still seventeen years old. Another participant is a sixteen-year-old senior at Johns Hopkins who entered college at age thirteen, after having completed the eighth grade; he is expected to earn a bachelor's degree in philosophy by the time he is seventeen, Dr. Stanley says. Also, two new youngsters who are presently at Johns Hopkins entered this fall at the age of fourteen.

It is expected that half a dozen or more young men and women will enter Johns Hopkins next fall as full-time students at age fourteen or fifteen, some of them with sophomore standing.

*   *   *

(For further information call John Schmidt, [301] 366-3300, ext. 704.)

Release 5472
11-16-73

SUPPLEMENTAL MATERIAL 6

Office of Public Information
The Johns Hopkins University
Baltimore, Maryland 21218
Telephone: (301) 366-3300, ext. 704

FOR IMMEDIATE USE

(60 seconds)

THE 1974 MARYLAND MATHEMATICS TALENT SEARCH FOR SEVENTH- AND EIGHTH-GRADERS WILL BE HELD DURING JANUARY AT VARIOUS LOCATIONS AROUND THE STATE. THE TESTING CENTER FOR THE BALTIMORE METROPOLITAN AREA IS THE JOHNS HOPKINS UNIVERSITY. APPLICATIONS ARE AVAILABLE TO ELIGIBLE STUDENTS FROM MATHEMATICS TEACHERS, COUNSELORS, OR PRINCIPALS AT LOCAL SCHOOLS. THE DEADLINE FOR APPLICATIONS IS DECEMBER 14. NONE CAN BE ACCEPTED AFTER THAT DATE. TUITION SCHOLARSHIPS FOR ONE COLLEGE COURSE, CASH PRIZES, AND BOOKS WILL BE AWARDED TO THE HIGHEST SCORING STUDENTS IN EACH REGION. IF YOU WOULD LIKE TO PARTICIPATE AND THINK YOU ARE ELIGIBLE, CONTACT YOUR MATHEMATICS TEACHER OR GUIDANCE COUNSELOR AS SOON AS POSSIBLE.

*　　　*　　　*

SOURCE: Professor Julian C. Stanley
Study of Mathematically
Precocious Youth
Department of Psychology
The Johns Hopkins University
Baltimore, Maryland 21218

Release 5484
11–26–73

SUPPLEMENTAL MATERIAL 7

THE JOHNS HOPKINS UNIVERSITY

Baltimore, Maryland 21218

Department of Psychology
Study of Mathematically Precocious Youth

SUBJECT: 1974 Maryland Mathematics Talent Search
TO:　　　Ineligible students
FROM:　　Dr. Julian C. Stanley, Professor of Psychology and director of the study

Dear_____

We appreciate your application to our mathematics talent search; however, we find that you are ineligible to take the January college level test for the following reason(s):

_____ 1. *Grade:* You must be in the seventh or eighth grade, or in a higher grade *only* if you will not yet be fourteen years old on December 31, 1973.

_____ 2. *Location of school:* Your school must be located within Maryland, although you may live out of the state, or you may live in Maryland but attend as a DAY student a school outside Maryland.

_____ 3. You must have scored in the upper 2 percent of your school grade on national norms in arithmetic reasoning, total arithmetic, or quantitative aptitude, as measured by the most recent standardized test, such as Iowa or SCAT. This means the 98th or 99th percentile.

_____ 4. Other:

We realize that our strict requirements, needed because the test is optimally difficult for only certain students, make it necessary to turn away a number of very able persons. We greatly regret that you are one of those.

Best wishes for success in your future education!

JULIAN C. STANLEY
Professor of Psychology
Director of the Study

JCS:ls

SUPPLEMENTAL MATERIAL 8

THE JOHNS HOPKINS UNIVERSITY

Baltimore, Maryland 21218

Department of Psychology
Study of Mathematically Precocious Youth

SUBJECT: 1974 Maryland Mathematics Talent Search
TO: Students with incomplete applications
FROM: Cecilia Solano, project associate, and
             William George, project coordinator

Dear_____

In reviewing your application for the mathematics talent search we found the following item(s) to be missing:

_____ 1. *Postage:* To keep ahead of our mailing costs we need either six eight-cent stamps or fifty cents.

_____ 2. *Test location and date:* You failed to specify the date and test site to which you wish to be assigned.

_____ 3. *Certification:* You failed to give adequate certification indicating that you scored at either the 98th or 99th percentile of the national norms for your school grade on a recently administered standardized test in arithmetic reasoning, total arithmetic, or quantitative aptitude.

_____ 4. *Other:*

Without the above checked items we cannot consider your application complete. Please send in the stamps or the completed application as soon as possible so that we can enroll you for the test. The deadline for receipt of the completed application here is December 14, 1973. Please don't miss it!

Mailing address: Mr. William C. George
SMPY, Department of Psychology
The Johns Hopkins University
Baltimore, Maryland 21218

SUPPLEMENTAL MATERIAL 9

Questionnaire for Maryland Mathematics Talent Search

This is your *ticket of admission* to the testing. Please fill all of it out carefully and be *sure* to bring it with you to the test center. See page 4 for test site information.

NAME_____ Sex: M_____ F_____
(PRINT)   last   first   middle

1. Name of school that you attend_____ grade _____

   name of county_____ Public_____ Private_____ Parochial_____
                                               (check one.)

2. Full address of school _____

3. Your home address _____
                                                                 zip code

4. Home phone number (including area code)_____

5. Date of birth_____month_____day_____year

6. How many older brother do you have? _____ Their birthdates _____

   How many older sisters do you have? _____ Their birthdates_____

   How many younger brothers do you have? _____ Their birthdates _____

   How many younger sisters do you have? _____ Their birthdates _____

7. Is your father alive? _____yes _____no

   His full name _____

   a. Check the highest educational level he *completed*:

   Less than high school _____ high school graduate _____

   Some college _____ college graduate _____ more than college _____

   b. College(s) attended, if any, location, and degrees received (both undergraduate and advanced, and date of receipt) _____

   _____

c. His occupation (or if he is deceased, his main occupation when alive). Please be quite specific. _____

_____

8. Is your mother alive? _____ yes _____ no

Her full name _____

a. Check the highest educational level she *completed*:

Less than high school _____ high school graduate _____

Some college _____ college graduate _____ more than college _____

b. College(s) attended, if any, location, and degrees received (both undergraduate and advanced, and date of receipt) _____

_____

c. Her occupation (or if she is deceased, her main occupation when alive). Please be quite specific. _____

Former occupations other than homemaker _____

_____

9. Any comments you care to make to clarify questions no. 7 or 8:

_____

_____

10. What mathematics courses are you taking this year?

_____ general 7th grade _____ general 8th grade _____ algebra I _____ algebra II

_____ geometry _____ Other: specify _____

11. Circle the words which *best* describe each of the following:

a. Your liking for school

Very strong   Fairly strong   Slight liking   Positive dislike

b. Your liking for arithmetic and mathematics

Very strong   Fairly strong   Slight liking   Positive dislike

12. Check the *one* statement that best describes how well you are doing in your mathematics class this year.

a. _____ Better than all of your classmates

b. _____ Better than all but one or two other classmates

c. _____ About as well as most of your classmates

d. _____ Less well than the majority of your classmates

13. This school year, how are you learning most of your arithmetic and mathematics? Check only one.

a. _____ In regular classwork with other students

b. _____ In school, but working on your own with some help or direction from your teacher

c. _____ On your own outside of school, helped by a tutor or parent

d. _____ On your own outside of school with little help from anyone

14. If you are working on your own in arithmetic or mathematics, rank the main types of work you are doing (1 = highest rank):

a. _____ Working with a textbook mostly on your own

b. _____ Working with a textbook aided by someone

c. _____ Working on mathematics puzzles in books or magazines

d. _____ Working on assignments made by your teacher, other than just extra problems in the class arithmetic book

15. Please list the three specific occupations that, at the present time, appeal to you most for your life work. List them in order of preference, *1* being the most preferred.

1. _____

2. _____

3. _____

16. How *important* do you think mathematics will be for the job you will someday have? (circle one)

Very   Fairly   Slightly   Not at all

17. If you have been considering college, which ones have you thought about applying for?

1. _____ 3. _____

2. _____ 4. _____

18. What is your main reason for wanting to participate in the Mathematics Talent Search? ____

_____

_____

19. Where did you find out about the Mathematics Talent Search: Check all that apply:

_____ parent   _____ guidance counselor

_____ mathematics teacher   _____ friend

_____ library poster   _____ newspaper

_____radio or TV   _____letter from Mathematics
                                                Talent Search

_____Other: Specify _____

20. From whom did you receive the *most* encouragement to enter the Mathematics Talent

Search? _____

_____

21. Comments of any sort: _____

_____

_____

_____

Maryland Mathematics Talent Search

Room Registration Form

PRINT NAME: _____

Test site to which you are assigned:

_____ Frostburg State College   (January 19)

_____ Johns Hopkins University   (January 26)

_____ Salisbury State College   (January 26)

_____ University of Maryland—College Park   (January 26)

You are assigned to the following building and room. Study the enclosed map and locate the
building (circled in red) to which you have been assigned. _____

Please arrive on time! Plan to reach the test center not later than 12:30 p.m. on January 26,
if you are being tested at *Johns Hopkins University, University of Maryland at College Park*, or
Salisbury State, or at 12:30 p.m. on January 19 if you are being tested at *Frostburg State College*.
We ask you to arrive early so you can locate the building and be in your seat by 12:45 p.m. The
test is timed and therefore all students in a room must start at the same time. The test will start
promptly at 1:00 p.m. There will be signs in the parking lots and on the campus to help you locate
your assigned building. The test should be over at 3:00 p.m.

Parents are welcome to stay at the test site during the tests but will not be allowed in the testing
room. Parking space will be available and is shown on your map. Lounging space will be available
for parents from 12:30 p.m. until 3:00 p.m. at the various test sites. The building is circled on the
map and the room is indicated as well. Further information will be given concerning this on the
various test days.

SUPPLEMENTAL MATERIAL 10

THE JOHNS HOPKINS UNIVERSITY
Baltimore, Maryland 21218

Department of Psychology
Study of Mathematically Precocious Youth

SUBJECT: Scholastic Aptitude Test (SAT) Mathematics Talent Search
TO: Each of the 1,519 persons tested on 19 and 26 January 1974
FROM: Dr. Daniel P. Keating, acting director of the study; Lynn H. Fox, associate director; Susanne A. Denham, assistant director; Cecilia H. Solano, project associate; and William C. George, coordinator of projects

On January 19 and 26 you took the Scholastic Aptitude Test—mathematical sections only. In this memorandum we explain what that test measures and report your scores to you.

The SAT was first developed in 1926 for the College Entrance Examination Board by an experimental psychologist at Princeton University. In the nearly fifty years since then various forms of it have been administered to *millions* of eleventh- and twelfth-graders applying for admission to the nation's colleges. As the "scholastic aptitude" name suggests, the test is meant to help predict academic success in college.

SAT-M is a sixty-item 75-minute test of mathematical reasoning ability. It depends somewhat on special experiences (that is, mathematical ones) in school and out. It also depends on one's verbal and nonverbal reasoning ability and intellectual flexibility (to move rapidly from one type of problem to another.)

Because SAT-M is designed chiefly for above average eleventh- and twelfth-graders, it is quite difficult for all but the ablest seventh-, eighth-, and young ninth-graders. Especially, it requires information and skills seldom taught in junior high schools. In order to score high on SAT-M, one must have learned a great deal mathematically on his or her own—at home, by independent study, and/or by special instruction.

The scores on SAT-M range from a chance score of 275 to the highest score reported, 800. The *average* male high school *senior* would score 422 on SAT-M. The average female high school senior would score 382 on SAT-M. Three-fourths of high school senior boys would score less than 517 on SAT-M. For girls this figure is 461.

THE SCORES

Now please see Supplemental Material tables 10.1 and 10.2 for information about the distribution of SAT-M scores. Your score is circled there. Note the percentage of high school juniors of your sex whose SAT-M score you exceeded. Remember that the talent search contestants on those dates represented the ablest 1 or 2 percent of junior high school students in the state, so do not be surprised or disappointed if you did not exceed most (or even many) of them! Just to be in the group at all is a mark of distinction. Don't feel that you are inferior or have "failed" if you did not exceed most of them.

WHAT DO YOUR SAT SCORES MEAN?

Mathematical reasoning ability of the kinds tested by SAT-M helps you learn such subjects as arithmetic, algebra, geometry, trigonometry, calculus, statistics, probability theory, computer science, mathematical economics, mathematical psychology, mathematical sociology, and the physical sciences, such as chemistry and physics.

If you are already highly developed mathematically, you can—and probably want to—move ahead faster in those areas than your less highly developed classmates do. In the Study of Mathematically Precocious Youth we have already helped many high school youths progress faster by taking more advanced courses in high school, studying mathematics on their own, skipping a school grade, taking college courses for credit, or (for five of them) entering college full-time long before graduating from high school. One or more of these procedures for accelerating your school progress may be feasible and desirable.

No prescription or general plan can be given, however. You are a unique *individual* whose mental, physical, emotional, and socioeconomic characteristics must be taken fully into account in any plan to supplement your regular education. Such a plan can be devised by you and your parents in collaboration with your teachers, guidance counselor, and school principal. Those of you who want further suggestions may write to Mrs. Lynn H. Fox, Department of Psychology, The Johns Hopkins University, Baltimore, Maryland 21218, for a copy of her paper entitled "Facilitating educational development of mathematically and scientifically precocious youth."

We are enclosing an extra copy of this report, which you may want to give to your school principal. Also, we shall tell county school system curriculum coordinators about those of you who scored above the average high school *senior* of your sex on SAT-M, so that they can consider supplementing the education of such persons.

THE WINNERS

The list of winners this year is too long to include in this communication. We have arranged for over forty one-course tuition scholarships to be given to the high-scorers from various centers from over twelve local colleges. Since the scores varied somewhat from center to center, there is no absolute "cut-off" for scholarship winners. Those individuals who are to receive the scholarship prizes are to be contacted separately. If you wish to know who the winners were at your center, you may write and request a copy of the winners list, which will also be released to the press.

Everyone, however, who scored 640 or higher will receive a prize of some kind. An award presentation ceremony will be held on March 23, 1974 at 3:30 p.m. in Shriver Hall Auditorium on The Johns Hopkins University campus. The meeting is open to the public, but all who scored 640 or more are especially urged to attend.

NEXT YEAR

There are currently no plans for SMPY to sponsor a statewide mathematics talent search in 1975. There *may* be some limited testing of high-scoring seventh-graders from this year's contest; if so, those individuals will be contacted directly in advance of such testing. If there are any changes in this plan, they will be widely publicized through the press and other media as well as through the schools.

Sincerely,

DANIEL P. KEATING
Acting Director of the Study

DPK:vsg

Enclosure

Supplemental Material Table 10.1: Distribution of SAT-M scores for the 19 and 26 January 1974 testing

Score	Frequency	Percentage of *male* 11th-graders who scored lower	Score	Frequency	Percentage of *male* 11th-graders who scored lower
800		99+	490	74	72
790		99+	480	68	70
780		99+	470	52	68
770		99+	460	114	66
760	1	99+	450	53	64
750	4	99+	440	50	61
740	2	99	430	53	59
730	7	99	420	33	57
720		99	410	36	54
710	2	98	400	34	52
700	8	98	390	46	50
690	8	98	380	19	47
680	10	97	370	20	45
670	9	97	360	33	42
660	11	96	350	13	39
650	15	96	340	10	35
640	34	95	330	8	31
630	21	94	320	3	28
620	15	93	310	7	25
610	30	92	300	7	22
600	25	91	290	3	18
590	35	89	280	2	14
580	45	88	270	3	11
570	49	87	260	2	8
560	43	86	250		5
550	86	84	240		4
540	51	82	230		3
530	56	80	220		2
520	60	78	210		1
510	74	76	200		
500	75	74			

Supplemental Material Table 10.2: Distribution of all SAT-M scores for the 19 and 26 January 1974 testing

Score	Frequency	Percentage of female 11th-graders who scored lower	Score	Frequency	Percentage of female 11th-graders who scored lower
800		99+	490	74	83
790		99+	480	68	81
780		99+	470	52	79
770		99+	460	114	77
760	1	99+	450	53	75
750	4	99+	440	50	73
740	2	99	430	53	70
730	7	99	420	33	68
720		99	410	36	65
710	2	99	400	34	63
700	8	99	390	46	61
690	8	99	380	19	58
680	10	99	370	20	55
670	9	98	360	33	53
660	11	98	350	13	50
650	15	98	340	10	46
640	34	98	330	8	42
630	21	97	320	3	39
620	15	97	310	7	35
610	30	96	300	7	31
600	25	96	290	3	27
590	35	95	280	2	22
580	45	94	270	3	18
570	49	93	260	2	13
560	43	92	250		9
550	86	91	240		7
540	51	90	230		6
530	56	89	220		4
520	60	87	210		3
510	74	86	200		
500	75	85			

SUPPLEMENTAL MATERIAL 11

THE JOHNS HOPKINS UNIVERSITY • BALTIMORE, MARYLAND 21218

DEPARTMENT OF PSYCHOLOGY
Study of Mathematically
Precocious Youth (SMPY)

Area 301—366-3300
Extensions 538 and 1410

January 14, 1974

Dear_____

As you are well aware, the education of gifted children is an important area of concern for educators, parents, and the students themselves. For over two years the Study of Mathematically Precocious Youth has been helping junior high school age young people highly gifted in quantitative abilities to make the best use of their considerable potential. Several programs that we have instituted have been highly successful educationally and extremely popular with the students. We are hopeful that these programs will in the future be widely adopted by school systems such as your own, and we wish at this time to offer to help in establishing in_____ County a prototype of one of these programs.

This year for the third time we are holding a statewide mathematics talent search for seventh- and eighth-grade students; please see the enclosure. You may recall that last year the names of all the students in your county who participated in the contest and scored 420 or more on the Scholastic Aptitude Test—mathematical were sent to the mathematics supervisor. In the Baltimore metropolitan area, fifty-three highly able students were invited to participate in fast-paced mathematics programs conducted by Joseph Wolfson, whose Saturday morning classes for younger students are described in the enclosed paper. (The paper will appear as chapter 6 in *Mathematical Talent: Discovery, Description, and Development*, edited by Julian Stanley, Daniel Keating, and Lynn Fox, which is scheduled to be published by The Johns Hopkins University Press in fall 1974.)

As you can tell somewhat from a perusal of the enclosed program evaluation, the steps in instituting such a program for highly mathematically gifted students are quite simple: identification of the students able to benefit from such a mathematics class, which will already have been done through the Maryland Mathematics Talent Search; designation of a teacher with proven talent in working with gifted students; finding a convenient place and time for the students to meet once a week for two hours; and arrangement for the modest funding necessary.

The commitments from the school system would be first, to make the minor scheduling adjustments needed to accommodate the students in the program, and second to agree to find the financial support necessary. For a full-scale program involving a full-time teacher and sixty to seventy-five students, an annual budget would be $12,000—$15,000, depending on the teacher's salary. A much more limited program conducted once a week on Saturdays for the mathematically ablest fifteen to twenty students could be run for less than $2,500 per year. We would be pleased to help in the planning of such a program, and we will, of course, have located the students.

The benefits of this both to the students and to the school system would be multiple. The students would get interesting and challenging work at a high level and would avoid the frustrations of a slow-paced (for them) program. It is quite likely that such a program would soon be widely recognized as one of the most innovative and effective in the country. The pilot programs conducted by SMPY have already received such recognition.

At this point you must have many questions about the program and the possibilities we have suggested. Dr. Keating would be pleased to meet with interested parties in your school system at their convenience. We hope that you will consider this possibility and contact us for further information.

Sincerely,

LYNN H. FOX
Associate Director of the Study

DANIEL P. KEATING
Acting Director of the Study

SUSANNE A. DENHAM
Assistant Director of the Study

WILLIAM C. GEORGE
Coordinator of Projects

CECILIA H. SOLANO
Project Associate

DPK/ls

cc:

Enclosures

SUPPLEMENTAL MATERIAL 12

THE JOHNS HOPKINS UNIVERSITY ● BALTIMORE, MARYLAND 21218

DEPARTMENT OF PSYCHOLOGY
Study of Mathematically
Precocious Youth (SMPY)

Area 301—366-3300
Extensions 538 and 1410

March 4, 1974

It is indeed a pleasure for us to inform you that you are one of the one-course tuition scholarship award winners. Your score of _____ was at the _____ percentile of the 1,519 students tested, and you ranked _____ among the students at your chosen center.

The courses in general which we would recommend are computer science, college algebra and trigonometry, or a science course in which you may be especially interested. Later we will be in touch with you regarding specific details. The final course selection will be a joint decision by you, the school, and SMPY. The school awarding you the scholarship is _____ .

We congratulate you on your accomplishment, and look forward to meeting you at the awards ceremony on March 23, 1974 at Shriver Auditorium, on The Johns Hopkins University Homewood campus from 3:30 to approximately 5:00 p.m. Please feel free to invite family and friends, since space at the awards presentation will not be a problem.

Sincerely yours,

LYNN H. FOX
Associate Director of the Study

DANIEL P. KEATING
Acting Director of the Study

SUSANNE A. DENHAM
Assistant Director of the Study

CECILIA H. SOLANO
Project Associate

WILLIAM C. GEORGE
Coordinator of Projects

DPK:vsg

SUPPLEMENTAL MATERIAL 13

THE JOHNS HOPKINS UNIVERSITY • BALTIMORE, MARYLAND 21218

DEPARTMENT OF PSYCHOLOGY
Study of Mathematically
Precocious Youth (SMPY)

Area 301—366-3300
Extensions 538 and 1410

March 4, 1974

Congratulations! Your score of _____ makes you eligible for a (nonscholarship) prize at the awards ceremony on March 23, 1974 at Shriver Hall on the Johns Hopkins University Homewood campus, from 3:30 p.m. to approximately 5:00 p.m. Please feel free to invite family and friends, since space at the awards presentation will not be a problem.

Everyone who scored 640 or higher will receive a prize of some kind. All those people are also qualified to take a college course in the summer or in the evenings, but unfortunately we do not have enough scholarships for all 111 individuals who scored that high. We would encourage them, however, to pursue this possibility with their school principal or counselor. A copy of this letter is enclosed so that you may give one to your school principal.

We commend you on your accomplishment and look forward to meeting you at the awards ceremony.

Sincerely yours,

LYNN H. FOX
Associate Director of the Study

DANIEL P. KEATING
Acting Director of the Study

SUSANNE A. DENHAM
Assistant Director of the Study

CECILIA H. SOLANO
Project Associate

WILLIAM C. GEORGE
Coordinator of Projects

DPK:vsg
Enclosure

SUPPLEMENTAL MATERIAL 14

Cost Analysis of the 1974 Maryland Mathematics Talent Search

Item	Cost
Luncheon—seminar	60.00
Paper, stencils, envelopes for entire contest	500.00
Postage, initial mail-out	500.00
Cost of SAT booklets	1,519.00
Cost of SAT answer sheets and keys	152.00
Proctors	500.00
Main testers	340.00
Travel expenses to three test centers	70.00
Coffee, cookies, and supervision of coffee room	50.00
Scoring costs	850.00
Personnel costs—secretarial staff, clerical help	500.00
Electrical set-up, janitorial services, lighting for awards ceremony	153.00
TOTAL	$5,164.00*

*This breaks down to a cost of $3.40 per person.

5
A PIAGETIAN APPROACH TO INTELLECTUAL PRECOCITY[1]

Daniel P. Keating

ABSTRACT

Two traditions currently exert the major influence on theories of intelligence: the psychometric and the Piagetian. Theoretical and experimental comparisons have been drawn, but concentrate mainly on infancy and childhood. In this study, early adolescents (5th- and 7th-graders) classified by psychometric testing as bright and average were evaluated on Piagetian tasks of formal operations in order to examine the relationship between brightness and precocity. The bright group evidenced formal operations far more frequently than the average groups of the same age. Thus the major finding was that brightness psychometrically defined implies cognitive developmental precocity within the stage theory of Piaget.

The two traditions that currently exert the major influence on theories of intelligence are the psychometric and the Piagetian. The basis of the psychometric tradition is the measurement of individual differences in mental abilities or traits through the evaluation of a representative sample of behavioral products in a standardized situation. It has given rise to a diversity of theories, all of which, however, share a belief that the test scores are meaningful numbers that can be manipulated mathematically to gain psychological insights. They share also an underlying assumption that variability exists in all traits, the scores on which when measured are assumed to be distributed approximately normally (Elkind 1970). Comparisons on the basis of precocity and retardation in performance in

[1]This research was supported by grant GS-39775 to the author from the National Science Foundation. I thank Professors Julian C. Stanley, Roger A. Webb, and John T. Guthrie for their helpful comments at several stages of the research. I thank also William C. George for his help in subject selection and assignment, Dr. John McCauley of the Baltimore County School System for supplying information on the subject pool, Dr. Francois Stoll for advice on the use of Piaget's *methode clinique*, and, especially, Rosalind Schaefer for serving as research assistant. A brief report of this research appeared in *Child Development* 46 (1975): 276–80. I thank the Society for Research in Child Development for permission to include substantial portions of that earlier article.

the standardized situations (i.e., the tests) characterize much of the history of psychometrics (Goodenough 1949).

In contrast to this, Piaget's is a unified theory whose goal is the identification of the universal structures of human thought and of the operational transformations that bring them about (Piaget 1950, 1970). The approach is principally developmental, and the methodology is essentially clinical in that it seeks behavioral *signs* of underlying cognitive processes. Less attention is paid to individual differences in precocity and retardation.

Comparisons have been drawn, both theoretically (Elkind 1970) and experimentally (De Vries 1973, 1974). Relatively more attention has been accorded infancy and childhood than adolescence. In the present study the relationship between psychometrically defined brightness and cognitive developmental precocity within Piaget's stage theory was examined in early adolescents.

The purpose of the comparison was to investigate several related questions. The first and most important had to do with the relationship of brightness with precocity. Since Binet's original insight, which linked the two, and the subsequent empirical confirmation of the relationship (especially Terman 1916, 1925-59), there has been little direct investigation.

The use of psychometric tests to identify precocious students for educational programs (Keating 1975 and chapter 2 of this volume), sparked the second question. It has been suggested that the high-scorers on psychometric tests are not necessarily precocious, but just "good test-takers." Evaluation of the cognitive developmental level of psychometrically defined bright and average students through a separate methodology would seem to resolve this question.

The third question was whether similar aspects of "intelligent behavior" are being tapped by the differing methodologies of the two traditions. If the same or essentially similar aspects are observed by the two methods, then similar results in terms of individual differences would be expected. Even if, as frequently suggested, the psychometric evaluation looks at products and the clinical Piagetian evaluation at processes, it is to be expected that a close relationship exists between product and process of the same global behavior. They are of course not identical (Kagan & Kogan 1970), and thus group rather than individual differences were looked at for the purpose of this study.

METHOD

Subjects

The subjects were middle-class, 5th- and 7th-grade boys,[2] most of whom were white, from the Baltimore County school system. They were tested in the summer

---

[2] A parallel study, using a sample of girls, has been completed, and the major findings reported here were replicated. There was some evidence, however, that the bright girls were less precocious than the bright boys. For details, see Keating and Schaefer (1975).

following the completion of those grades. A computer print-out of the students in those grades who scored at the 98th and 99th percentiles, and those between the 45th and 55th percentiles of Baltimore County norms (somewhat stricter than national norms) on the arithmetic section of the Iowa Tests of Basic Skills (ITBS) was obtained. The arithmetic subtest was used, because it seemed to reflect operational reasoning ability better. From this list 50 students were randomly selected from each of the four groups: 7th-grade bright (7B); 7th-grade average (7A); 5th-grade bright (5B); and 5th-grade average (5A). All 200 students were offered a small fee to be tested for possible participation in the study.

In the 7B group 31 students came; in the 7A group, 19; in 5B, 37; and in 5A, 22 came to the test. From these 109 individuals, 13 in each group were selected for the Piagetian evaluation by choosing the highest in the bright groups on the screening test and the middle of the average groups. The mean ages of the groups within each grade were comparable, both for those selected and unselected for follow-up, with no significant differences between the bright and average groups. The seventh-graders averaged thirteen years, zero months, and the fifth-graders eleven years, one month, with standard deviations of about 4.5 months.

Procedure

The 200 invited students were randomly assigned to a morning and an afternoon session on the same day. The 109 who came took the sixty-item Raven's (1960) Standard Progressive Matrices (SPM), i.e., Sets A-E. This was intially designed as a nonverbal measure of general intelligence, specifically Spearman's "g"; although no longer regarded as a pure "g" measure, it is an excellent test of abstract reasoning ability. Piaget has recognized it as an outstanding example of a test of multiplicative classification (Inhelder & Piaget 1964, p. 281). The directions for group administration stated in the manual were used unaltered. Although obtained primarily for screening purposes, the SPM results generated the specific hypotheses for the psychometric-Piagetian comparison (see below).

The subjects selected for the Piagetian evaluation were quasi-randomly assigned (dependent only on availability) to individual sessions during a single three-week period to eliminate the possibility of differential developmental maturation. One advanced concrete operational task (conservation of volume) and three formal operational tasks from Inhelder and Piaget (1958) were used in the evaluation. The formal operational tasks were: displacement, in which the subject had to elucidate the reason for the sinking and floating of a variety of common objects; equilibrium in the balance, in which the subject had to discover the proportionality of distance from the fulcrum and weight; and period of a pendulum, in which the subject had to eliminate the distractor variables of height of drop, weight of object, and force of drop to isolate the controlling variable of length of the string.

The scoring system was adapted from Inhelder and Piaget (1958). A score of 1 was assigned to a clearly concrete operational response; a score of 2 to a response that indicated the breakdown of a concrete operational structure, but with no discernible inclination toward a formal operational response (i.e., recognizing the inconsistency, but not knowing in which direction to proceed to resolve it); a score of 3 to a response which indicated definite transition toward formal operations; and a score of 4 to a definite formal operational response. For the purpose of the analysis, scores of either 3 or 4 were considered "formal operational," since they correspond roughly to Inhelder and Piaget's 3AB and 3B categories.

The experimenter and an additional rater, who was in the room during the Piagetian evaluation, each scored the session independently to check for inter-rater agreement. Both the experimenter and the rater were blind as the group membership of each subject until all subjects had been evaluated. Conflicts were resolved by consensus after listening to an audio tape that was made at each session.

Design

In order to generate meaningful specific hypotheses in terms of the order of the groups under both conditions (psychometric and Piagetian), the SPM results were used to determine the "psychometric order" of the groups. The prediction was that the groups would be arranged in terms of Piagetian cognitive developmental level in the same order as in the psychometric evaluation.

RESULTS

Order of Groups on SPM

The results from testing the original 109 students are shown in table 5.1. It is clear that 7B and 5B were at the top of the four groups, with no significant differences between them. The unexpected discovery of no difference between 7B and 5B may have been the result of these two groups having already reached the asymptote of their ability on this particular test, a "personal ceiling" rather than the absolute ceiling of the test. This explanation is moderately supported by the fact that their mean score is at about the 80th percentile of an adult population. Considering the possibility of positive errors of measurement for the bright groups on the initial test (the ITBS), one would perhaps not anticipate much growth on this test over the next several years for these samples. The 7B and 5B groups were followed by the 7A group, which scored significantly lower than both 7B ($p<.001$) and 5B ($.02<p<.05$), using Scheffé's multiple comparison method for the latter comparison, in McNemar (1969). As expected, the 5A group scored lowest, and significantly lower than the 7A group ($.01<p<.02$).

Thus the "psychometric order" of the groups, and hence the prediction for the Piagetian evaluation, was

$$7B = 5B > 7A > 5A.$$

Obviously the most powerful test of the precocity hypothesis was the 5B, 7A comparison, since the latter group averaged two years older than the former, and on age comparisons alone would be expected to be developmentally advanced.

Table 5.1. Means of four groups on Raven's Standard Progressive Matrices, with standard deviation and size of group

		Average	Bright
7th	N	19	31
	$\overline{X}$	43.58	48.42
Grade	S.D.	4.81	4.25
5th	N	22	37
	$\overline{X}$	37.77	47.73
Grade	S.D.	6.58	4.53

Note: Highest possible score on SPM = 60

Order of Groups on Piagetian Evaluation

Before considering the data from the Piagetian evaluation, it is worthwhile to look at the inter-rater agreement to see if the data are meaningful. The correlation for inter-rater agreement over all four groups was .94, ranging for each group from a low of .92 to a high of .98. The percentages of inter-rater agreement were 83 percent for exact agreement, 16 percent for a one-point difference, and 1 percent for a two-point difference. These figures were based on the 156 formal operational ratings (52 subjects $\times$ 3 tasks), since the concrete task yielded no variation.

All the subjects in this study showed evidence of advanced concrete operations by passing the conservation-of-volume task. This was somewhat surprising only for the 5A group, but it must be remembered that all of the A students were actually somewhat above average on national norms. These results were thus not considered further in the analysis

The results in terms of percent in each group showing evidence of formal operations (defined as a score of 3 or 4) are shown in figure 5.1. The first set of columns shows the percent of students in each group who evidenced formal operational thinking in all three tasks. This was, of course, the most stringent criterion, and by it the order of the groups was

$$7B > 5B > 7A > 5A.$$

The next three sets of columns show the percent in each group scoring a 3 or a 4 on each task individually.

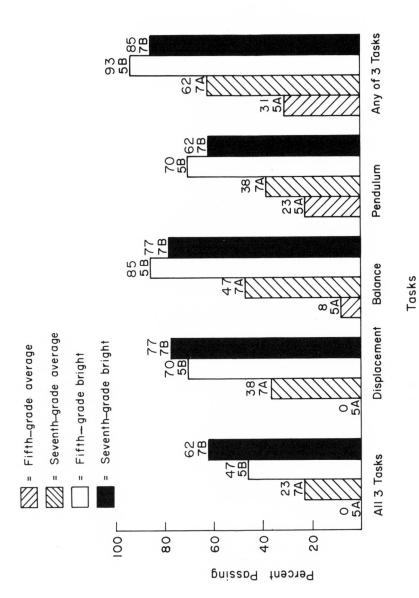

Fig. 5.1.   Percent demonstrating formal operations on three tasks

The final set of columns shows the percent in each group demonstrating formal operational thinking on any of the three tasks. By this most lenient criterion, one concludes in Piagetian terms of 75 percent passing that the 7B and 5B groups were formal operational, the 7A group was transitional, and the 5A group was advanced concrete operational. In terms of total score on formal operations (i.e., by adding the 1 to 4 score on all three tasks together for each subject), the order of the groups was

$$7B = 5B > 7A > 5A.$$

There was no significant difference on total score between 7B and 5B, but both were marginally better than the 7A group ($.05 < p < .10$). The 7A group outscored 5A significantly ($.02 < p < .05$). If a one-tailed t-test of significance is made for the crucial 5B, 7A comparison, which is reasonable since the prediction was stated a priori, 5B was significantly better than 7A ($p < .05$).

The formal operations scores were also examined by analysis of variance as shown in table 5.2. The main effect for psychometric level was highly significant ($p < .001$). The main effect for age (grade) was only marginally significant ($.05 < p < .10$), and this was almost certainly due to the transitional nature of the 7A group. There was not a significant main effect for tasks, and there were no significant interactions. In the analogous situation in the concrete operational period there exists a clear developmental trend in the difficulty of the tasks, from conservation of number to weight to volume, and so on, which is not found here for formal operations.

Finally, internal homogeneity reliability estimates were obtained for the Piagetian tasks within groups, which showed that there was no inherent unreliability for the Piagetian evaluation except within the 5A group. In that group there was not enough variation to generate a meaningful reliability estimate; the obtained figure was $r = -.08$. For the other three groups, the r's ranged from .55 to .92. By means of the ANOVA formula for estimating

Table 5.2. ANOVA of scores on formal operational tasks

Source of variance	df	SS	MS	F
Psychometric level (P)	1	61.603	61.603	30.119*
Age-grade (G)	1	6.603	6.603	3.234[†]
PG	1	3.653	3.653	1.794
S/PG	48	97.744	2.036	
Tasks (T)	2	2.186	1.093	1.465
PT	2	2.070	1.035	1.387
GT	2	2.993	1.497	2.007
PGT	2	.443	.222	.298
ST/PG	96	71.641	.746	

*$p < .001$
[†]$.05 < p < .10$

homogeneity (Stanley 1971, p. 399) it was possible to obtain a pooled within-groups estimate, and that figure was .63. This quite respectable, considering that the "test" contained only three "items" (the three tasks) and that each group was severely restricted in range in two psychometric tests.

In comparison with typical psychometric evaluation, then, the Piagetian evaluation was not unreliable, but it was inefficient in terms of amount of time and effort per subject required. This is not a criticism, however, of the Piagetian evaluation, which was designed for for a different purpose, to generate a different kind of information. A more detailed discussion of the psychometric properties of Piagetian tasks can be found in Keating (1974).

DISCUSSION

The major hypothesis of this investigation was that brightness as measured by psychometric testing implies developmental precocity in reasoning. This precocious reasoning was to be confirmed by comparisons of bright and average groups both on further psychometric testing and, more importantly, on measures of cognitive developmental level, which have been used by Piagetian researchers. This hypothesis was confirmed, as the results presented above indicated.

This confirmation extended to the somewhat unexpected result regarding the 5B and 7A groups. Even though they averaged two full years younger, the 5B students were at a more advanced cognitive developmental level than the 7A students, as witnessed by their superior performance on both the psychometric test of abstract reasoning ability, the SPM, and, especially, on the Piagetian evaluation of cognitive development.

The absence of a main effect for tasks suggests that development within the formal operational period is not entirely analogous with that in the concrete operational period, and thus further suggests the possibility of overall developmental maturation, which is subsequently reflected in a significant change in cognitive strategies. That is, instead of a series of structural stage changes in the developing adolescent, there may be instead a global structural change, which is then exhibited in different areas in no particular order. Piaget (1972) has proposed that such findings are likely.

As for the questions raised initially with respect to this investigation, several comments are appropriate. The first is that when students are selected for high scores on psychometric tests, those selected are indeed precocious in cognitive development, and not just "good test-takers." This is especially true when a test with sufficient ceiling for the ablest in a group is used.

Second, this research again confirms the empirical relationship of brightness and precocity and does so across differing traditions. Although it can offer no explanation of this relationship, it does allow for speculation on the topic. It seems that brightness leads to precocity, perhaps in the following fashion.

Since, according to Piaget, cognitive development proceeds as an interaction of the organism and the environment, the brighter individual would be at an advantage in moving through the successive stages more quickly. This would be so because the bright child would be involved in more varied and interesting interactions with the environment, generating a greater quantity of useful information, and would also be more able to make effective use of the information generated. That is, the "self" enriches the cognitively relevant environment.

This would suggest that where the development is more closely tied to physiological maturation, as would seem to be the case at the "period" changes (two years, six to seven years, and twelve to fifteen years old), precocity would be less pronounced than when the development is more closely tied to environmental interaction, as would be the case within stages. Webb (1974) has also suggested such a possibility, and with very bright children younger than those in this study he has found evidence of rapid acceleration in concrete operations, but no evidence of formal operations, except in those children whose ages approached the youngest in this study. Lovell (1968) obtained similar findings. Precocity across stages is clearly present, but perhaps not as pronounced as that within stages.

DeVries (1973) argues that two intelligences are represented by the psychometric and the Piagetian traditions. She draws this conclusion from her research, in which mental age was insufficient in some cases to predict operational level accurately. But these failures of prediction occurred across developmental periods (i.e., preoperational to concrete operational). If in addition to the psychometric level we know the chronological age of the child and adjust predictions respecting within vs. across stage development appropriately, it seems likely both from this research and DeVries's, Webb's, and Lovell's results that prediction of operational level would be significantly improved. Thus we need not posit two intelligences, but only recognize two perspectives on the same intelligence.

In conclusion, what is clearly required, if a fuller understanding of cognitive development and human intelligence is to be gained, is movement toward a synthesis of the differential tradition rooted most deeply in psychometrics and the generalizing tradition represented by Piaget. One major area for investigation, suggested by the discussion, is a better characterization of the somewhat vague "organism-environment" interaction, and an attempt at discerning individual differences in such interactions, which are related to intelligence.

REFERENCES

DeVries, R. 1973. The two intelligences of bright, average, and retarded children. Biennial Meeting of the Society for Research in Child Development, Philadelphia, March.

———. 1974. Relationships among Piagetian, IQ, and achievement assessments. *Child Development* 45: 746–56.

Elkind, D. 1970. *Children and adolescents: Interpretive essays on Jean Piaget.* New York: Oxford University Press.

Goodenough, F. L. 1949. *Mental testing: Its history, principles, and applications.* New York: Rinehard & Co.

Inhelder, B., and Piaget, J. 1958. *The growth of logical thinking from childhood to adolescence.* New York: Basic Books.

———. 1964. *The early growth of logic in the child.* New York: Norton.

Kagan, J., and Kogan, N. 1970. Individual variation in cognitive processes. In P. H. Mussen (ed.), *Carmichael's manual of child psychology* (3rd edition). New York: John Wiley & Sons.

Keating, D. P. 1974. Precocious cognitive development at the level of formal operations. *Dissertation Abstracts International*, 34(11B): 5655.

———. 1975. Testing those in the top percentiles. *Exceptional Children* 41(6): 435–36.

Keating, D. P., and Schaefer, R. A. 1975. Ability and sex differences in the acquisition of formal operations. *Developmental Psychology* 11(4): 531–32.

Lovell, L. 1968. Some recent studies in cognitive and language development. *Merrill-Palmer Quarterly of Behavior and Development* 14: 123–38.

McNemar, Q. 1969. *Psychological statistics* (4th edition). New York: John Wiley & Sons.

Piaget, J. 1950. *Psychology of intelligence.* London: Routledge & Kegan Paul.

———. 1970. *Structuralism.* New York: Basic Books.

———. 1972. Intellectual evolution from adolescence to adulthood. *Human Development* 15: 1–12.

Raven, J. C. 1960. *Guide to the Standard Progressive Matrices.* London: H. K. Lewis & Co.

Stanley, J. C. 1971. Reliability. In R. L. Thorndike (ed.), *Educational measurement* (2nd edition). Washington, D.C.: American Council on Education.

Terman, L. M. 1916. *The measurement of intelligence.* Boston: Houghton.

Terman, L. M., et al. 1925–59. *Genetic studies of genius.* Five volumes. Stanford, California: Stanford University Press.

Webb, R. A. 1974. Concrete and formal operations in very bright 6- to 11-year-olds. *Human Development* 17: 292–300.

II
PROGRAMS FOR
FACILITATION OF
INTELLECTUAL TALENT

6
CURRICULUM EXPERIMENTATION FOR THE MATHEMATICALLY TALENTED[1]

William C. George and Susanne A. Denham

ABSTRACT

Fast-paced mathematics classes were established to meet the needs of highly gifted junior high school students. Thirty-three students participated in the program. In 108 hours of instruction twenty-eight class members learned algebra II and plane geometry at a high level of achievement. Twenty-three persons completed algebra III. In addition, thirteen boys successfully completed the four and one-half years of precalculus mathematics. These students self-paced themselves through their homework and preparation for class. Class success was based on: (1) identification of qualified students through appropriately difficult tests of mathematical and nonverbal reasoning; (2) a dynamic teacher who introduced challenging material at a rapid-fire pace; and (3) voluntary participation by students. It appears that once these considerations are met the academic and social aspects of such a program will proceed "naturally," as evidenced by these two classes.

One of the most successful innovations begun by the Study of Mathematically Precocious Youth (SMPY) is its program of special fast-paced mathematics classes. The first of these was described in detail by Fox (1974*b*[I:6]) in volume I of this series.[2] In the summer of 1973, another such class was instituted, taught at The Johns Hopkins University by the same teacher, Joseph Wolfson. This chapter presents the results of this second class to date and

[1]The authors would like to thank Dr. Julian C. Stanley for his helpful comments and encouragement in earlier drafts of this chapter.

[2]In addition to the usual references, citations of chapters in volume I of *Studies of Intellectual Precocity* will be as follows: [I:6]. The I indicates volume I, and the 6 indicates the chapter number [Editor].

guidelines for the institution of such programs in school systems.[3] Thus, our purpose is to describe the workings of a fast-paced mathematics curriculum for young persons, in the hope that the principles and practices developed will be implemented by others.

These programs were begun as experiments in fitting a curriculum to the needs of young students who reason extremely well mathematically. If students with ability *and* interest in mathematics were given the *opportunity* to learn as fast as they could, we reasoned, their achievements and satisfaction would probably be apparent (Fox 1974*b* [I:6]). Moreover, we wanted to show that accounting for individual differences in education, specifically of the gifted, would not be costly or administratively unmanageable. It was our hope that after the demonstration of the program's feasibility more fast-paced mathematics models could be established along similar lines in public school systems.

THE FIRST MODEL PROGRAM

The first class, begun in June 1972, has since been concluded. It met, and in some cases exceeded, our expectations. We invited twenty-nine top ex-sixth-graders, one ex-eighth-grader, and one ex-third-grader from the Baltimore area; twenty-one of these accepted our invitation to take the course.[4] Nineteen of them persisted through the nine initial two-hour-per-week summer class meetings. One of these then left the program voluntarily; five others were asked to return to their school mathematics class. Three persons (one ex-seventh-grade girl, one ex-eighth-grade girl, and one ex-eighth-grade boy) were added to the class in September. All sixteen of these persons (nine boys and seven girls) completed algebra I and algebra II. Ten of the sixteen students completed algebra III and trigonometry. Nine of the ten continued through analytic geometry; eight of these nine also finished plane geometry during the summer of 1973, demonstrating that up to four and one-half years of precalculus mathematics can be learned well by some mathematically highly talented young students studying two hours on Saturday mornings for about thirteen months. During the June 1972–September 1973 period, seven of the nine boys in the class skipped one or more grades. By fall of 1974, all seven enrolled in calculus or precalculus courses in high school. Five girls and one boy began independent work in plane geometry, one girl took a correspondence course in geometry, and a boy and a girl took a senior high plane geometry course. Several also enrolled for credit in mathematics-related college courses.

---

[3]Appendix 6.A1 updates the fast-mathematics class progress through geometry, trigonometry, analytic geometry, and their course placement in the various school systems.

[4]Selection of the sixth-graders was based on scores on the numerical, abstract reasoning, and/or verbal scales of The Psychological Corporation's Academic Promise Test; the eighth- and the third-graders were previously known to us.

As is evident, the first attempt at such a special class was highly successful. In less than fourteen months, meeting one two-hour period per week, the eight top students completed material that would have taken five periods per week for four and one-half years in the regular school curriculum sequence. This gave them an invaluable head start toward higher learning and satisfied their desire to meet the challenge of mathematics, as well as saving both their parents and the school system much money (for further details on this class, see Fox 1974*b*[I:6]).

Spurred on by this success, the staff of SMPY made plans to begin a similar class in the summer of 1973. This time, however, somewhat different selection procedures were employed. In January 1973 the second SMPY Talent Search was conducted (in conjunction with the Study of Verbally Gifted Youth's Talent Search—see chapter 8). Nine hundred and fifty-three Maryland seventh-, eighth-, and under-age ninth-grade students who scored in the upper 2 percent on standardized mathematical or verbal reasoning aptitude tests were administered the Scholastic Aptitude Test (SAT), including both the mathematics and the verbal sections; 666 were in the mathematics talent search. From the results of this testing, it was decided that Baltimore County and Howard County students who had obtained at least a score of 500 on SAT-M *and* 400 on SAT-V would be eligible for a class to be conducted at The Johns Hopkins University. Scores on both SAT sections were used as criteria, since we had learned from the first special class that a certain minimum degree of verbal mastery was probably necessary to learn mathematics at a rapid-fire pace (Anastasi 1974 [I:5]; Fox 1974*b* [I:6]).

Thus, eighty-five students (not including seventeen eligible students who had already participated in the first class or were participating in other special projects) were notified by mail of the opportunity to take part in a new fast-paced mathematics class. Steps 1 to 3 of table 6.1 summarize the details of the selection process. In order to qualify, the forty-one students who expressed interest in the class were administered the eighty items in both forms of the Educational Testing Service's Cooperative Mathematics algebra I test. As can be seen in table 6.1, the response rate for girls (35.3 percent) was much less than for boys (56.9 percent). Of the forty-one students, only one boy did not qualify for entrance into the class; nine others, however, decided against coming, leaving thirty-one persons (twenty-eight ex-eighth-graders, two ex-seventh-graders, and one ex-sixth-grader)[5] enrolled in the second class.

In June 1973 these thirty-one students began attending algebra II classes conducted by Joseph Wolfson. Of the girls, 91.7 percent (all but one) had taken algebra I already; of the boys, 75.8 percent had completed an algebra I course. Those students who had not had algebra I had been enrolled in courses diversely labeled as pre-algebra, general mathematics, and SSMCIS.[6]

[5]The sixth-grader had not yet taken the SAT but was known to be highly talented; SMPY had previously arranged private tutoring for him.
[6]SSMCIS (Secondary School Mathematics Curriculum Improvement Study).

Table 6.1. Selection of Wolfson II class

Step in selection	Criteria	Total number	Girls	Boys	Howard County		Baltimore County		Percent proceeding to next step		
					Girls	Boys	Girls	Boys	Total	Girls	Boys
1. Initial invitation to join class	SAT-M ≥ 500 SAT-V ≥ 400	85	34	51	10	16	24	35	48.2	35.3	56.9
2. Algebra I tests taken	Alg. I ≥ 48	41	12	29	4	7	8	22	75.6	75.0	75.9
3. Entered class	Voluntary	31	9	22	3	6	6	16	83.9	55.6	95.4
4. Class after summer departures and additions[a]	Voluntary	28	5	23	2	6	3	17	100.0	100.0	100.0
5. Breaking into sections	Alg. III ≥ 26										
a. Section A (faster paced)		23	3	20	1	5	2	15			
b. Section B		5	2	3	1	1	1	2			

[a]Four girls and one boy dropped out of the special mathematics class in August 1973. Two boys (one ninth-grader and one sixth-grader) were added to the class in September. The percent proceeding from step 3 to step 4 was calculated on totals before addition of two boys.

FURTHER ASSESSMENT OF PARTICIPANTS

To learn more about each student so that appropriate counseling could be given, SMPY personnel administered a battery of cognitive and vocational interests tests. This included the Raven's Progressive Matrices, Standard and Advanced (SPM [Raven 1960] and APM [Raven 1965]); Sequential Tests of Educational Progress, Science (Sci., Form 1A); Revised Minnesota Paper Formboard Test (RMPFBT, Forms MA and MB); Bennett's Mechanical Comprehension Test (MCT, Forms AA and CC); revised scales from Holland's Vocational Preference Inventory (VPI [Holland 1965]); the Strong–Campbell Interest Inventory (SCII [Campbell 1974]); and the Allport–Vernon–Lindzey Study of Values (AVL). Table 6.2 shows, as of January 1974, means and standard deviations, along with percentile ranks, for appropriate norm groups for each cognitive test for the total group; for females and for males; for those who continued with the special class (Group C); and for those five students who chose to return to the regular mathematics program of the school (Group NC) at the end of the summer. As can be seen from the percentile ranks, these students score quite high on tests that are designed primarily for older persons. Their mathematical aptitude and concomitant skill in nonverbal reasoning are especially impressive for persons their age.

COGNITIVE TESTS

Sex Differences on Cognitive Tests

Significance tests were computed between test score means of boys vs. girls (see table 6.2 for those means which showed a significant difference). Girls scored significantly lower than boys on the SAT-M and on the MCT(AA).

From these differences it appears that from the outset boys had more mathematical reasoning ability than girls, as evidenced by their SAT-M score, even though a greater percentage of girls than boys had taken algebra I already. It seems that boys acquire some of their mathematical skills from sources outside the classroom (Keating 1974 [I:2]; Astin 1974[I:4]). Neither sex showed much variability in scores on the Raven's tests of nonverbal reasoning.

Cognitive Differences between Group C and Group NC

At the .05 level, there were no statistically significant differences in scores of mathematical ability between the 28 persons (twenty-three boys and five girls) choosing to continue (Group C) and the five (one boy and four girls) deciding not to continue (Group NC). The trend of the score differences, however, was consistent with the sex composition of the groups. There was little difference between the algebra I scores and the nonverbal reasoning scores of the Raven's for these two groups. This seems to indicate that, within a homogeneous high-

Table 6.2. Summary of cognitive test results for all students

	Total group (N=33)[a]				Boys (N=24)			Girls (N=9)			Group NC (N=5)			Group C (N=28)		
	N	Mean	S.D.	Percentile rank[b]	N	Mean	S.D.	N	Mean	S.D.	N	Mean	S.D.	N	Mean	S.D.
SAT-M[c]	33	580.9	49.5	86	24	593.3*	49.0	9	547.8	34.6	5	554.0	27.0	28	585.7	51.4
SAT-V	31	496.1	69.2	79	22	490.4	77.4	9	510.0	43.9	5	498.0	43.2	26	495.8	73.8
RPM SPM[d]	32	55.9	2.2	96	24	55.5	2.3	8	56.9	1.7	4	56.5	1.3	28	55.8	2.3
RPM APM	32	29.4	3.9	95+	24	28.9	4.2	8	30.8	1.9	4	29.0	4.1	28	29.4	3.9
Sci. IA[e]	30	46.7	7.7	78	22	47.7	7.1	8	44.0	9.2	4	45.8	10.0	26	46.8	7.6
MRPFBT MA[f]	32	46.8	7.6	34	23	46.7	8.3	9	47.0	6.0	5	50.4	5.9	27	46.1	7.8
MRPFBT MB	32	50.1	7.9	50	23	51.1	8.1	9	47.4	7.0	5	47.2	9.5	27	50.6	7.7
CMT I[g]	29	18.9	10.0	–	21	19.4	10.7	8	16.8	8.0	4	16.0	6.5	25	19.3	10.4
CMT II	29	29.4	6.6	–	21	30.0	7.1	8	27.8	4.9	4	30.8	4.4	25	29.2	6.9
MCT AA[h]	29	41.0	9.7	22	21	43.6†	9.5	8	34.3	6.4	4	35.3	2.5	25	42.0	9.9
MCT CC	28	32.4	10.9	33	21	33.8	10.8	7	26.7	9.2	3	25.0	10.5	25	33.2	10.6
Algebra IA + IB[i]	31	65.6	7.7	95	22	67.0	7.7	9	62.1	7.1	5	65.4	11.1	26	65.6	7.2

[a] This number includes all departures and additions to class as of January 1974.
[b] Percentile ranks are shown for: 12th-grade males (SAT-M, SAT-V), 20-year-olds (SPM and APM), college sophomores in spring (Science IA), engineering freshmen (RMPFBT and MCT), and eighth graders national (algebra I); relevant norms are unavailable for CMT.
[c] Highest possible score on SAT-M and SAT-V, which test mathematical and verbal reasoning, respectively, is 800.
[d] Highest possible score on SPM, which tests nonverbal reasoning, is 60; for APM, it is 36.
[e] Highest possible score on Science IA is 75; this test is designed to measure college students' knowledge of general science.
[f] Highest possible score on either RMPFBT form, which measures spatial relations ability, is 64.
[g] Highest possible score on CMT I, vocabulary is 115; for CMT II, verbal analogies, it is 75.
[h] Highest possible score on both forms of MCT, which tests mechanical comprehension, is 60.
[i] Highest possible score of algebra IA + IB combined is 80.
* .005 < p < .01
† .01 < p < .05

ability group, mathematical skill alone will not predict success or insure continued interest in a fast-paced mathematics program. Those in Group NC left for various reasons, not necessarily because they lacked algebra II proficiency. One girl, who left in the middle of the summer, had the lowest combined SAT-M + V score (M-510, V-430) in the program, but she had high expectations for success in mathematics. One boy did better than all of the other students who took the two algebra I tests (total score 40 + 40). His total SAT-M + V score (M-570, V-530) ranked in the upper one-third of the class. After he ranked in the middle of the group on the first algebra II test, given in August 1973, he dropped out.

It was hoped that the battery of tests given to these students would help shed light on the abilities necessary for success in such a fast–paced class. The relationship between these test scores and success on standardized mathematics tests will be discussed later in this chapter.

INTEREST INVENTORIES

Sex Differences on the SCII and VPI

Results from the Strong–Campbell Interest Inventory are also of interest. Table 6.3 shows the means and standard deviations for Holland's six interest orientations (Holland 1973) and four pertinent Basic Interest Scales. As can be seen from these tables, the students, boys in particular, are investigative in outlook. By investigative, Holland means inquisitive and scientifically oriented. (For more information on the interests and values of gifted youth, see Fox & Denham 1974 [I:8], and chapters 12 and 14 in this volume.) The total group also shows peaks on the science and mathematics basic interest scales. These findings make intuitive sense, but it is gratifying to see that the students are exhibiting on standardized tests interests congruent with our day-to-day observations.

Some differences between the sexes did emerge. One encouraging sign, however, is of a difference which did *not* occur. Boys were not significantly higher than girls on the investigative Holland Scales. This finding may bode well for the progress of these girls. Girls may not choose the investigative scales first, but they still score highly on this scale (nearly as high as on the social scale), indicating their high interest orientation in this area. The boys were, however, far less social and artistic than the girls (a mean difference of 9.6 and 13.7 points); these findings agree with previous interest patterns noted in similar groups. The girls were significantly lower than the boys on science and mathematics basic interest scales ($p < .01$). Perhaps, then, their desire to learn in these fields is less all-consuming than that of the boys; or their environment may not have encouraged them to perceive these fields as particularly useful for their future occupations (Anastasi 1974 [I:5]). Furthermore,

Table 6.3. Means and standard deviations of Holland Scales and selected basic interest scales from the Strong–Campbell Interest Inventory[a]

Scales[b]	Total group[c] (N=31)		Boys (N=22)		Girls (N=9)		Group NC (N=5)		Group C (N=26)	
	Mean	S.D.	Mean	S.D.	Mean	S.D.	Mean	S.D.	Mean	S.D.
Holland:										
Investigative	54.9	7.1	56.2	5.4	51.8	9.7	47.2*	10.9	56.4	5.3
Realistic	49.7	8.8	50.0	8.6	49.2	9.8	42.2*	8.9	51.2	8.4
Conventional	48.3	9.0	48.3	8.8	48.3	10.0	52.2	12.4	47.5	8.4
Enterprising	45.7	8.5	45.7	8.6	45.7	8.5	45.2	9.5	45.8	8.6
Artistic	43.2	10.4	40.4*	9.7	50.0	9.3	48.2	6.8	43.2	5.0
Social	42.7	10.9	38.7†	9.2	52.4	8.4	53.2*	10.0	40.6	10.2
Basic Interest:										
Mathematics	58.0	5.6	59.4*	4.4	54.3	6.6	56.2	7.4	58.3	5.3
Science	57.3	8.4	59.9*	5.9	51.1	10.5	46.2†	10.6	59.5	6.2
Social service	43.1	11.4	38.3†	7.8	54.9	10.5	49.4	11.9	41.9	11.4
Writing	42.4	10.8	41.0	10.3	46.1	12.0	46.0	11.9	41.8	11.0

[a] Mean scores are based on scales where a score of 60 or more is considered "high." Of course, these mean scores do not reflect the actual magnitude of some individual scores.

[b] Holland Scales are based on Holland's (1973) theory, while interest scales are empirically devised.

[c] The N=31 because two students in Group C were not administered the SCII.

*.001 < p < .01
†p < .001

the girls were significantly higher than the boys on the social service interest scale (p < .001). The magnitude of this difference (16.6) may well be of practical educational significance. Their highest interests, in social services and mathematics, may, in combination with their accompanying social-investigative orientation, lead them into the teaching field (probably in the social sciences), into medicine, into psychology, or similar careers. On the other hand, the boys were far more scientifically oriented, pointing to possible careers as scientists, mathematicians, or computer designers. In addition, table 6.3 shows that the boys differed greatly on the six Holland Scales, whereas the girls were similar on all the Holland Scales except the enterprising scale, which was considerably lower. This seems to indicate that boys are more definite in their likes and dislikes.

This distinction between investigative and social orientations is more pronounced when looking at rank order on the Holland Scales. Table 6.4 shows these rank orderings. Boys are more inclined to choose investigative (I) and realistic (R) scales; the social (S) scale is last in the order of importance for them. Conversely, the Strong–Campbell Basic Interest Scales indicate that the girls are most strongly oriented toward social activities. The interesting difference is that the close second choice of the girls is the investigative scale. This means that these girls are still more research-science-theory oriented than the general female population. Such a strong S-I value profile, along with considerable interest in mathematics, is encouraging when one considers how few women are actually in mathematics-science fields.

Holland's six VPI Occupational Scales, equivalent to the Strong–Campbell Holland Scales, were administered in the one-page form to the students. The girls had the investigative scale (I) on the VPI as first choice 25 percent of the time, versus the 17 percent expected by chance. The boys selected I as first

Table 6.4. Rank order of the Holland Scales from the Strong–Campbell Interest Inventory

Total group (N=31)	Boys (N=22)	Girls (N=9)	Group NC (N=5)[a]	Group C (N=26)[b]
I	I	S	S	I
R	R	I	C	R
C	C	A	A	C
E	E	R	I	E
A	A	C	E	A
S	S	E	R	S

Key:

I = Investigative   E = Enterprising
S = Social   C = Conventional
A = Artistic   R = Realistic

[a]1 boy and 4 girls.
[b]21 boys and 5 girls.

choice 64 percent of the time. An earlier finding (Fox & Denham 1974[I:8]) was, however, corroborated: girls who were predominantly investigatively oriented did well in the class, while those who were artistically or socially inclined via these scales either did not continue in the fall (Group NC) or remained low in the class. On the other hand, almost equal numbers of highly investigative boys were successful and unsuccessful in algebra II and algebra III. Thus, it again appears that interest patterns must be taken into account in the organization of such classes, *especially* for female students (also noted by Fox 1974*a*).

Differences between the sexes and between Group C and Group NC on both the SCII and the VPI clearly indicate that an investigative orientation toward pursuing goals and choosing activities is helpful if one is to survive in an investigative environment. This finding would have been predicted by Holland's (1973) theory.

This conclusion has far-reaching implications. Placing a socially (but *not* investigatively) oriented student in a highly investigative environment may not allow for the effective use of an individual's talents. It is worth considering whether social classroom environments should be constructed for the benefit of social, people-oriented types, and investigative environments should be engineered for those students who can benefit from them most. This would imply considerable segregation by sex (see chapter 12).

Differences between Group C and Group NC on the SCII

Group NC, when compared with students who stayed in the program (Group C), were significantly lower (see table 6.3) on investigative and realistic orientation and scientific interest (p < .01). On the other hand, they were significantly higher (p < .01) on the Holland social scale. All of the students in Group NC except one were girls; apparently their lack of investigative orientation and scientific interests was such that they were poorly motivated to keep up with the work. Table 6.4 shows that Group NC ranked the investigative scale in the lower half; thus, social (S), conventional (C), and artistic (A) values predominated. For Group C the I–R profile is strong, with the A–S values ranking at the bottom. Social values are not the important attributes for success in this fast-paced class. It is, again, an inquisitive mind with a strong interest in mathematics that seems to be necessary to keep up. Those individuals whose values are investigative appear to have a better "fit" with this type of learning environment.

VALUES

The Allport–Vernon–Lindzey Study of Values (SV) was also administered to the group. This measure yields scores on six scales that are somewhat comparable to the Holland Scales. This test was designed primarily for use with college students and graduates. The SV consists of two sets of questions asking the individual to choose preferences in relatively familiar situations. The six scales reflect relative value levels rather than absolute value levels. The average score for any individual's six values is 40. The six value scales are classified by Edward Spranger (1966) in the following manner: (1) the (T)heoretical individual is interested in scientific, intellectual, and philosophical pursuits; (2) the (E)conomic individual is interested in production, consumption, and wealth; (3) the (A)esthetic individual is noted for valuing grace, symmetry, and other artistic qualities; (4) the (S)ocial individual is interested in mankind and its welfare; (5) the (P)olitical individual is concerned with power; and (6) the (R)eligious individual is basically concerned with the mystic. Mean scores and standard deviations for the total class, boys, and girls, those who continued and those who did not, are given in table 6.5.

Table 6.5 shows that the boys have strong theoretical values. There is little differentiation in their point total between economic and political values. Both values are far higher for boys than for girls in the program. The boys have a higher social value (people-oriented) and aesthetic value (sense of balance, symmetry) on the SV than on the comparable Holland Scales.

Girls maintain a strong social value as their first choice. The aesthetic scale ranked higher than the theoretical scale on the SV. Girls were significantly lower on the theoretical value scale (p < .001) than the boys. On the SCII girls were not as investigative as boys but this difference was not significant. Girls placed investigative on the Holland Scale closely behind social; however, between the social and theoretical scales on SV there is a spread of 9.1 points. This difference between these two values is greater than the entire spread of points for all six Holland Scales on the SCII. Boys are significantly lower (p < .05) on the *religious* value. On the SV, these highly selected girls (by cognitive test scores) look much more conventional than they do on the Holland Scales.

Table 6.5.   Means and standard deviations of the six values from the Allport–Vernon–Lindzey Study of Values (SV)

Values	Total group (N=33)		Boys (N=24)		Girls (N=9)		Group NC (N=5)		Group C (N=28)	
	Mean	S.D.	Mean	S.D.	Mean	S.D.	Mean	S.D.	Mean	S.D.
Theoretical	46.2*	8.0	49.1[†]	6.7	38.3	5.4	40.4[‡]	8.3	47.2	7.6
Economic	40.5	9.2	43.4[†]	8.7	32.8	5.7	33.6[‡]	8.8	41.7	8.9
Aesthetic	35.6	9.5	32.6[†]	8.5	43.6	7.3	41.6	9.4	34.5	9.2
Social	41.1	7.8	38.7[†]	6.7	47.4	7.2	44.6	9.8	40.5	7.4
Political	41.8	5.8	43.3*	5.0	37.7	5.8	36.8[‡]	8.0	42.7	4.9
Religious	33.9	11.9	31.6[‡]	12.4	40.2	8.2	43.0[‡]	5.1	32.3	12.1

*.001 < p < .01
[†]p < .001
[‡].01 < p < .05

The boys and girls in the Wolfson II class were noticeably different on some scales than the comparable high school norm groups as shown by table 6.6 and figures 6.1 and 6.2. For example, the boys were significantly higher (p < .001) on the theoretical (investigative, truth-seeking) value than a large population of high school boys (see table 6.6). They were, on the other hand, significantly lower (p < .001) than the norm group of boys on the religious (mystic) value. This combination of placing high priority on theoretical activities and less on religious aspects of life is found elsewhere in this study of gifted boys (Fox & Denham 1974 [I:8]) and creative persons (Hall & MacKinnon 1969; Helson & Crutchfield 1968).

The girls in the class were more aesthetic (beauty-seeking, artistic; p < .01) and social (people-oriented; p < .05) than the norm population of high school girls. The norm group, on the other hand, was more economically oriented (concerned with production, consumption, and wealth; p < .01) than the girls in the fast-paced mathematics program.

Sex Differences on the SV

These girls and boys fit the general pattern of differential value orientation reported elsewhere (Allport, Vernon, & Lindzey 1970; Moshin 1950). That is, the boys are higher on theoretical, economic, and political (power-oriented) tendencies, while the girls favor aesthetic, social, and religious attitudes and pursuits more than the boys. The above finding is seen more explicitly when looking at the rank ordering of the SV values listed in table 6.7.

Table 6.6. Means and standard deviations of the six values from the Allport–Vernon–Lindzey Study of Values (SV) compared to norm group

	Boys				Girls			
	Class (N = 24)		High school (N = 5320)[a]		Class (N = 9)		High school (N = 7296)[a]	
Values	Mean	S.D.	Mean	S.D.	Mean	S.D.	Mean	S.D.
Theoretical	49.1*	6.7	43.3	6.4	38.3	5.4	37.0	6.9
Economic	43.4	8.7	42.8	6.9	32.8[†]	5.7	38.2	6.3
Aesthetic	32.6	8.5	35.1	7.7	43.6[†]	7.3	38.2	7.1
Social	38.7	6.7	37.0	6.2	47.4[‡]	7.2	43.3	6.9
Political	43.3	5.0	43.2	5.9	37.7	5.8	39.0	5.9
Religious	31.6*	12.4	37.9	8.3	40.2	8.2	43.7	8.1

[a]High school population is based on 5,320 boys and 7,296 girls in grades 10–12. These Ns are found in the 1970 Allport–Vernon–Lindzey *Manual for the Study of Values*.

*p < .001
[†].001 < p < .01
[‡].01 < p < .05

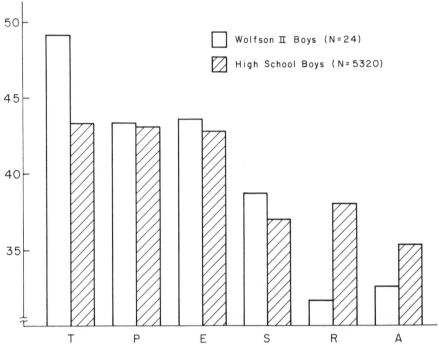

Fig. 6.1. Mean scores of boys for the six values from the Allport–Vernon–Lindzey Study of Values.

The strong social-aesthetic value setting for girls supports the Holland VPI and the SCII interest scales. The boys rank theoretical qualities first and place social-aesthetic tendencies on the lower end of the scale. This seems to indicate an important difference. Boys, being more investigative and research minded, seem to be willing to work independently and on their own time. This is necessary for such a fast–paced mathematics class. Girls, even when strongly interested in mathematics, probably need the social environment of working as a group to maintain their success in a class. Again this lends credibility to the possibility of exploring interest-centered classes in addition to classes divided by sex, e.g., students all high on theoretical and low on social, or all high on social and low on theoretical.

Value Differences between Groups C and NC

Group C was significantly higher than Group NC on the theoretical, political, and economic values, but far lower on the religious value, as seen by table 6.7. Their social and aesthetic values were not as strong as political and economic tendencies. Group NC, in contrast, tends to be strongly social with a high religious orientation. Economic values are last in their value-ranking, as

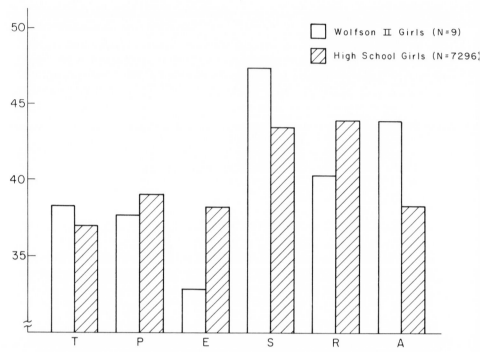

Fig. 6.2. Mean scores of girls for the six values from the Allport–Vernon–Lindzey Study of Values.

Table 6.7.   Rank order of the six values for the Allport–Vernon–Lindzey Study of Values (SV)

Total group (N=33)	Boys (N=24)	Girls (N=9)	Group NC (N=5)[a]	Group C (N=28)[b]
T	T	S	S	T
P	E	A	R	P
S	P	R	A	E
E	S	T	T	S
A	A	P	P	A
R	R	E	E	R

Key:

T = Theoretical   S = Social
E = Economic   P = Political
A = Aesthetic   R = Religious

[a] 1 boy and 4 girls.
[b] 23 boys and 5 girls.

they were for the nine girls. This seems to indicate that those who chose not to continue in the fast-paced mathematics class were not as independently and theoretically oriented as those who did continue. Another factor that may be suggested by the data is that the strong social interest indicated in the SCII scales, as well as the SV, may not be met by this type of class, even though the students express strong liking for mathematics. As in the previous analyses, however, the C-NC differences are almost wholly confounded with sex differences.

SUCCESS IN THE PROGRAM

Parental Variables

In addition it was hypothesized that parents might greatly affect their child's success or nonsuccess. Parents who are more highly educated might value education more and be more facilitative of their child's progress. Table 6.8 shows that the modal educational level for fathers of Group C was a master's degree, while Group NC's fathers' modal educational level was high school graduation. The bachelor's degree was the modal level of education for the mothers of those students who mastered the material the best (Group C). For the mothers of those students who chose to return to the regular classroom pace (Group NC), the modal educational level was high school graduation. Thus, it does appear that the majority of those students who chose to terminate their

Table 6.8. Parents' level of education

| | Group C (N=26) | | | | Group NC (N=5) | | | |
| | Father | | Mother | | Father | | Mother | |
Level of education	Number	Percent of group	Number	Percent of group	Number	Percent of group	Number	Percent of group
1	1	4	–	–	–	–	1	20
2	3	12	7	27	3	60	2	40
3	3	12	1	4	–	–	–	–
4	4	15	13	50	1	20	–	–
5	8	30	5	19	1	20	1	20
6	7	27	–	–	–	–	1	20

1 = less than high school
2 = high school
3 = some college, including A.A. degree
4 = bachelor's degree
5 = master's degree
6 = Doctor of philosophy or medical doctor

participation in the class did come from less well-educated parents. This difference is probably sex-related to some extent. Five of the boys' parents in Group C had less than a high school education. None of these boys discontinued, however, while each girl whose parents had at best a high school education did not continue at this rigorous fast pace.

Self-report measures were also evaluated. From table 6.9 it is apparent that, as perceived by the students, parents of girls in Group C had more influence (though not necessarily significantly) on their children with respect to the class. The parental influence, however, is found to be unrelated ($r = -.12$) to success in the class (a score of 28 on form A or 29 on form B of the algebra III test, which was the median of the class). Possibly, the best students need the least "prodding."

So far we have described the philosophy behind such a special class, explained the selection procedure, and given detailed cognitive and interest profiles of the class. At this point, however, we must recount some aspects of the class that one must understand before undertaking such a project.

Teacher's Style and Ability

The teacher's style and ability are vital to the success of such a program. It is clear that without these prerequisites, the class cannot be the absorbing challenge that it has been for our students. The teacher we have employed so successfully in both our special classes does not rely on the usual pedagogical tools. He is a fast pace-stimulator who races through the material at the pace of the quickest students, not the slowest. The other students are forced to stretch their minds and catch up—between classes, if necessary. With their talent, they can generally do so and enjoy it. It seems likely that college teachers would adapt more readily to this approach than secondary teachers who have been

Table 6.9.   Means and standard deviations of parental influence exerted on students during phases of class[a]

Phase	Group NC (N=4)[b]		Group C (N=26)		Group C			
					Boys (N=21)		Girls (N=5)	
	Mean	S.D.	Mean	S.D.	Mean	S.D.	Mean	S.D.
Joining class	3.0	0.71	3.5	1.47	3.5	1.53	3.8	1.17
Staying in class	3.0	1.58	2.9	1.54	2.8	1.66	3.6	0.49
Monitoring class	2.0*	0.71	3.0	1.00	2.9	1.04	3.6	0.49

[a] 5-point scale, where 5 = strongest influence
[b] 1 boy and 3 girls
*$p < .05$

taught to teach to the slower members of the class. It is important to remember that the students self-pace themselves through their homework (Stanley 1973) and preparation for the class. By keeping up with their extensive assignments the students go over what they missed in class and study the finer points of the problem.

In addition to the fast pace set by the teacher, his style is qualitatively different from that of many mathematics teachers. The students work collectively and individually at the blackboard, with the teacher urging and congratulating, helping out a discouraged student here and there, but generally leaving them to master the work fast. Individuality is important and is encouraged.

During "lecture" periods the teacher is quite elaborative, explaining the more elegant tools of algebra with considerable finesse. His dramatic style is truly a "tour de force," worthy of emulation. The students are excited, effusive, but under his control. He is receptive to new ideas and novel approaches to solutions. Yet, no problem is allowed to dominate discussion for long. Spontaneous verbal interjections are not, however, suppressed.

In short, besides a keen mind and excellent knowledge of mathematics, the teacher of such a class must have a personality that is attractive to the students and is interwoven with a keen sense of humor. Also, genuine respect for one's students and their feelings is a must. These factors help establish a positive atmosphere in a fast-paced program. Each student must be imbued with enthusiasm, and the student must feel that the problems are elegant and meaningful.

The material covered in this unique manner included all of algebra II and a large chunk of algebra III, taught during one two-hour period per week from June to December 1973. Results of standardized tests on this subject matter, given in August, November, and December 1973, are summarized in table 6.10. As is obvious from the percentile ranks shown there, the students had mastered algebra II by November. Sex differences were marked on the August algebra II test, the only test of those reported that was taken by the three girls who subsequently dropped out at the end of the summer (one other girl quit early), and were also pronounced on the algebra III test.

Prerequisites for the Success of the Class and Its Members

One question that crops up after we know who was successful in the class and who was not is this: What tests in our test battery are most predictive of this success?[7] The most predictive of these tests could then be used profitably in future screening sessions held by individual counselors, schools, and school

---

[7]By success we mean those people who were in the upper half of the distribution for a given cognitive or mathematical achievement test. This is not to imply that those whose scores are in the lower half of the distribution are doing poorly. When they are compared to a random school population taking the same courses their scores in many instances will put them in the top, and at a younger age.

Table 6.10.   Results of algebra II and algebra III tests[a]

Test	Total group				Boys			Girls		
	N	Mean	S.D.	Percentile rank[b]	N	Mean	S.D.	N	Mean	S.D.
First algebra II (8/73)	30	27.2	4.4	80	22	28.1*	4.4	8	23.6	4.3
Second algebra II (11/73)	28	34.0	3.5	97	23	34.4[†]	2.8	5	31.0	4.2
Algebra III (12/73)	28	28.7	4.8	81	23	29.8*	4.0	5	24.6	4.6

[a]Standardized tests used are Cooperative Achievement Mathematics Tests.
[b]Percentile ranks are shown for national high school norms (first and second algebra II tests) and college liberal arts norms (algebra III test).
*.001 < p < .01
[†].01 < p < .05

systems. Table 6.11 shows product moment correlation coefficients between various cognitive and achievement tests taken by the students.

It is apparent from table 6.11 that success in learning the algebra II sequence of mathematics in this class was predicted best by the SAT-M (p < .05). Success in the more inclusive, high-powered algebra III segment of the program was predicted more closely by the algebra II (p < .01) and APM scores (p < .05). Thus, we see that for algebra success, abstract reasoning tests seem to have predictive validity. A large measure of nonverbal skill is necessary in order for students to tackle abstract material quickly and thoroughly. A firm understanding of algebra I and algebra II concepts, in addition to abstract reasoning ability, seem to be important factors for a student to understand algebra III's extension of the abstract material presented previously. This information, however, suggests only the tentative nature of the conclusions regarding the predictors of success in such a class.

Before starting such a class, then, it is important to assess thoroughly the ability of the students in abstract reasoning, as well as their grounding in the prerequisites for the planned coursework. In addition, the coursework, like that described above, should be sufficiently challenging.

If individual school systems are going to develop similar classes, it is important, also, to assess the students' own feelings about their experiences in this fast-paced class. Prior to the inception of the class, which has been discussed previously, the students noted that they did enjoy mathematics. The majority of the potential pupils rated their liking for mathematics as "very high." Thus, one important prerequisite for success was present before the beginning of the class. Again, it is clear that investigative interests are linked to success in an investigative environment. The required interest level can be obtained through voluntary participation.

Table 6.11. Product-moment correlations between test scores for various tests[a] given to the Wolfson II class

	SPM (N=32)	APM (N=32)	SAT-M (N=33)	SAT-V (N=31)	Alg. 1A + 1B (N=31)	Alg. II(1) (N=31)	Alg. II(2) (N=28)	Alg. III (N=28)
SPM	—							
APM	.54*	—						
SAT-M	-.30	.33	—					
SAT-V	-.12	.06	.25	—				
Algebra IA + IB	.04	-.21	-.06	.18	—			
Algebra II(1)	-.18	.14	.07	.09	.39†	—		
Algebra II(2)	.24	.31	.43†	.00	.15	.39†	—	
Algebra III	.22	.42†	.35	-.18	.30	.31	.66*	—

[a]See table 6.2 for explanation of cognitive tests given in this table.
*p < .01
†.01 < p < .05

In August 1973, after eight weeks of classes, the students were asked to make several judgments on different aspects of the class. Compared with their regular mathematics classes, the majority of the students found the new class more productive, more fun, and more competitive (in order of decreasing frequency of response). Clearly, the class was a success from the point of view of the students. This finding should encourage educators interested in beginning such a class; for students of high caliber such an experience is rewarding.[8]

What particular aspects of the class are most appreciated? In the same set of August responses, the students rated the teacher's style highest, with the challenge of mathematics and their own feeling of accomplishment rated next highest, respectively. Another important factor was that they were encouraged to work on their own and think for themselves. Social aspects of the class were not rated as important for these students in Group C as opposed to Group NC. These ratings are very revealing: as we have mentioned before, the style of teaching in such a class emerges as very important. It seems that the ability of the teacher to motivate the students and make the curriculum alive and worthwhile is an essential part of the success of the class. Of course, Mr. Wolfson may be less effective with girls than an equally skilled, socially oriented woman might be.

In December 1973 the students were asked to give information on their individual educational progress, again via questionnaire. The answers given then were illuminating. Over half were interested in gaining information and advice on taking further advanced coursework and possibly in going to college a year or two early. Five had already taken college courses, and two boys were taking calculus or precalculus courses in school in addition to the Saturday class.[9]

The successful academic progress of these students is obvious. Moreover, their zest for learning is apparent during class. As one college student observer[10] put it:

The first ten to fifteen minutes were devoted to settling down. Kids shuffled to seats, greeted one another, and collected homework papers. After that short adjustment period they were ready to concentrate on the day's work. The teacher allowed a high degree of openness in his classroom. Kids got up to leave the room for snacks and were allowed open-ended discussion of problems. The lesson was referred to as "fun" by one student—the other student attitudes seemed to concur with this view. In this student-centered class the children were attentive and interested, volunteering to go to the board

---

[8]It is interesting to note that dropouts did not respond like nondropouts in this August questionnaire.

[9]Three of the eight girls, as opposed to only two of nineteen boys, wanted no information or advice on such educational advancement.

[10]Members of a class on gifted children from a nearby college observed the special class on two Saturdays during January 1974. Contributions quoted here are from Linda Bergman.

to demonstrate a point as needed. Several times solutions to problems were tried in several ways. It was good to see the teacher encourage this type of thinking. Other times he let the class know they were jumping too far ahead in course content by putting off their advanced questions. It was impressive to see these children in action. Their high motivation was displayed by choosing this productive way to spend a Saturday morning.

Further testimony to the academic success of the class members can be noted: one member was the winner of the ninth-grade section of a local countywide mathematics contest during the 1973-74 school year. Other local colleges have shown interest in this program. For instance, six members of the mathematics class took a college course in computer science for credit during the spring 1974 semester, with no one earning a final course grade less than B. This is just another example of the ability of these students to grasp higher-level curriculum challenges.

Even within a highly select group such as this, there is a great deal of differentiation (Stanley 1974 [I:1]). At the end of the algebra III segment of the class it was decided to split the class into two sections. The majority had been able to keep up with the fast pace. Some of the students, however, needed more detail than the current teaching style was giving them. Therefore, when plane geometry was started, a second class section (N = 5) was begun, in hopes that these talented youths could keep up with the rest of the class.

In the new section they were given more individual attention and a more detailed approach. Homework and self-pacing were still the key factors in this teaching style. One college student observer[11] described the new class thus: The teacher

seemed to have an uncanny control of the class and kept things moving at a fast clip by the attention she gave to the subject, drawing the pupils with her. She continually rewarded responses positively. She zeroed in for details. Some of her statements were as follows: "Oh, that's terrific," "Do this for emphasis—this is important," "OK, how do I get from here to the conclusion?" She pretends to struggle with the problems with them, they get anxious and start thinking and produce the answers. When one girl worked out a solution another girl clapped spontaneously—that's how involved they were. The teacher enforced thinking and good working habits while problem solving. Some typical statements were: "Think about your general line of attack," "Good habit to specify what you are given." I feel she is skill building very effectively. Once she stopped writing on the board and gave attention to a boy who softly asked a question. Her teaching approach is not without humor, either. After a lengthy explanation and precise instruction, she said, turning toward the class, "You have to put it down this way—I'd zap you if you didn't." And zap them she did, for each one of those students walked out of there feeling sharper—and that is what really counts!

[11]Contributions quoted here are from Paul Meyers.

In both sections of the class the concern is with the students. Both teaching styles have an important common feature: feedback. Questions are frequently asked and answers sought in order that the teacher may be sure that the class is following the materials. In both sections, the teachers use the blackboard and seek ingenious responses. The key to success here is to challenge the students to learn mathematics well, and in each section the approach is being fulfilled.

What of the social growth of these students for the duration of this special class? Anecdotal material gives evidence of this growth. Another college student observer[12] noted,

The physical appearance of the children as a class seemed similar to any regular class of this age with a few exceptions. No children were overly large or too maturely developed, but two boys stood out for their extreme smallness. They appeared to be younger than the majority of their classmates. Both were also valuable to the class progression. One responded maturely in his actions despite his size, contributing intelligent solutions and posing good questions. The other appeared to derive pleasure in producing witty remarks to make the others laugh. However, in this classroom situation, among their intellectual peers, both of these two boys were accepted and appreciated for their contributions.

At the board, age and sex appeared to make very little difference. Members of the class frequently discussed the problems and asked the person next to them to explain the problem if they did not grasp the concept the first time. Quite frequently the two smallest boys in the class had the two tallest youths as their blackboard partners. All attacked the problems with enthusiasm. Size or age did not seem to affect the enthusiasm of the individual or the verbal exchange. Various age groups worked together toward goals or interests they had in common. This is an impressive observation when considering the age span of five years in the class. Their interest was in mathematics, and the common goal was to master its intricacies.

While the students continuing through the summer and into the fall (Group C) did not rate social aspects of the class as important to them, it was obvious that they did get along well. As mentioned above, the youngest boys, whose size difference when compared with the older students was quite visible, fraternized freely and without reservation with the others. In general, however, the girls clustered together in the front of the room; they did not seem to shun the male members of the class, though. One of the girls, however, was always in the middle of the boys. She worked with them, discussing the problems and posing questions quite frequently. All in all, the classroom seemed to differ little socially from a regular junior high school class, except perhaps for the obvious zest, freedom, and enthusiasm of the students.

[12]Contributions quoted here are from Barbara McCloskey.

SUMMARY: ELEMENTS OF A SUCCESSFUL PROGRAM

A retrospective look at the present special class reveals that in order to conduct such a class, careful attention must be paid to: (1) the identification of qualified, mathematically oriented students through appropriately difficult tests of mathematical and nonverbal reasoning and prerequisite achievement; (2) the selection of a dynamic, bright assertive teacher who can create an atmosphere of fun and productivity while introducing challenging materials; and (3) *voluntary* participation by the students. It appears that once these considerations are met, the academic and social aspects of such a class will proceed "naturally," at least from the experience with these two groups. Some students will, however, need a somewhat slower and more detailed pace. These students will also thrive if given careful and prompt consideration.

If the above points are followed, then such a class would probably be successful, as these most certainly have been. Further specific guidelines, however, would probably be beneficial for individual school systems embarking upon such a course of action. As has been noted here many times before, the choice of an appropriate teacher is of paramount importance.[13] This fact cannot be overemphasized.

Second, over and above the relatively simple task of identifying apt students through tests,[14] the scheduling adjustments for the students to participate in a fast-paced class must be made. This point has been viewed by some counselors and administrators as a great inconvenience. If seen in perspective, though, it need not be such a problem. Arranging a time and place for students to meet once or twice a week for class, and providing study periods during the rest of the week can be handled without much stress; flexibility is necessary, of course. If courses to be held during school hours were arranged at the beginning of an academic year, all students involved could be scheduled similarly, with their schedules planned around the special mathematics course. Other unusual courses taken by the students would, of necessity, have to be held during other periods. These scheduling hurdles have been surmounted without snags by the majority of our students' counselors. Ideally, a mathematically highly talented student could progress through special classes in high school mathematics and then advance into college courses on released time from his high school or at night, or by correspondence, after he has completed his high school work (also see chapter 3).

[13]Mr. Joseph R. Wolfson graduated Phi Beta Kappa from Johns Hopkins University earning his B.A. in physics and mathematics. In addition he received his M.S. from the University of Chicago.

[14]There has recently been a general retreat from testing in the schools. We feel it important to reiterate here that high-level, appropriately difficult tests are vital tools for the identification of students for such special programs. Moreover, standardized tests can accurately and convincingly show these students' progress in such programs.

Assuming that these three points (identification, teacher, and scheduling) are attended to, at least on paper, by school administrators, there remains an important problem to solve: funding. The felicitous solution to this possible roadblock is that, as we estimate it, the cost of such programs need not be exorbitant. For a large systemwide group of 60 to 100 pupils, a full-time teacher would travel daily to one or two junior high schools, each of which would have around twenty special mathematics pupils. Music and art teachers do this; teachers of the mathematically gifted could also do it. The cost per year for such a large, full-scale program would be somewhere in the range of $13,000 to $16,000, depending on the teacher's salary, books, and clerical fees. A class of the fifteen to thirty most mathematically able students in the school system could meet on Saturdays in a central location and cost the system less than $2,000 for the instructor (at $50 per two-hour meeting). Mr. Wolfson's two Saturday programs were funded almost totally through parent contributions of three dollars per week.

The benefits of such a program far outweigh the costs, even monetarily. Obviously, talented students' time would be used more wisely, without the boredom that so often occurs in the regular classroom situation. Furthermore, the amount of money cited above would probably cover three years' worth of mathematical education in one year, for many students. Thus the costs of the program would be amply justified, especially when one considers the impact it will have on students who will find mathematics more meaningful and challenging. The ablest and best-motivated of these will go on to careers in which their fine knowledge of mathematics will be highly useful.

Also, an attentive and interested student in the right educational environment will have more to contribute to his class and feel more satisfied as an individual. This consideration is especially important when the goal of education is to improve the individual and help him find a satisfactory place in society.

REFERENCES

Allport, G., Vernon, P. E., and Lindzey, G. 1970. *Manual for the study of values* (3rd ed.). Boston: Houghton Mifflin.

Anastasi, A. 1974. Commentary on the precocity project. In J. C. Stanley, D. P. Keating, and L. H. Fox (eds.), *Mathematical talent: Discovery, description, and development*. Baltimore: The Johns Hopkins University Press, pp. 87–100.

Astin, H. S. 1974. Sex differences in mathematical and scientific precocity. In J. C. Stanley, D. P. Keating, and L. H. Fox (eds.), *Mathematical talent: Discovery, description, and development*. Baltimore: The Johns Hopkins University Press, pp. 70–86.

Campbell, D. P. 1974. Assessing vocational interests: a manual for the Strong–Campbell interest inventory (unpublished paper).

Fox, L. H. 1974a. Facilitating the development of mathematical talent in young women. Doctoral dissertation in psychology, The Johns Hopkins University.

———. 1974*b*. A mathematics program for fostering precocious achievement. In J. C. Stanley, D. P. Keating, and L. H. Fox (eds.), *Mathematical talent: Discovery, description, and development.* Baltimore: The Johns Hopkins University Press, pp. 101–25.

Fox, L. H., and Denham, S. A. 1974. Values and career interests of mathematically and scientifically precocious youth. In J. C. Stanley, D. P. Keating, and L. H. Fox (eds.), *Mathematical talent: Discovery, description, and development.* Baltimore: The Johns Hopkins University Press, pp. 140–75.

Hall, W. B., and Mackinnon, D. W. 1969. Personality inventory correlates of creativity among architects. *Journal of Applied Psychology* 53(4): 322–26.

Helson, R., and Crutchfield, R. S. 1970. Mathematicians: The creative researcher and the average Ph.D. *Journal of Consulting and Clinical Psychology* 34(2): 250–57.

Holland, J. L. 1965. *The vocational preference inventory.* Palo Alto, Calif.: Consulting Psychologists Press.

———. 1973. *Making vocational choices: A theory of careers.* Englewood Cliffs, N.J.: Prentice-Hall.

Keating, D. P. 1974. The study of mathematically precocious youth. In J. C. Stanley, D. P. Keating, and L. H. Fox (eds.), *Mathematical talent: Discovery, description, and development.* Baltimore: The Johns Hopkins University Press, pp. 23–46.

Moshin, S. M. 1950. A study of relationship of evaluative attitudes to sex differences, intellectual level, expressed occupational interest and hobbies. *Indian Journal of Psychology* 25: 59–70.

Raven, J. C. 1960. *Guide to the standard progressive matrices.* London: H. K. Lewis & Co.

———. 1965. *Advanced progressive matrices.* London: H. K. Lewis and Co.

Spranger, E. 1966. *Types of men: The psychology and ethics of personality.* New York: Johnson Reprint. Translation of *Lebensformen*; originally published in 1928 in German.

Stanley, J. C. 1973. Accelerating the educational progress of intellectually gifted youths. *Educational Psychologist* 10(3): 133–46.

———. 1974. Intellectual precocity. In J. C. Stanley, D. P. Keating, and L. H. Fox (eds.), *Mathematical talent: Discovery, description, and development.* Baltimore: The Johns Hopkins University Press, pp. 1–22.

Appendix 6.1

UPDATE ON THIS FAST-MATHEMATICS CLASS

The success of fast-paced mathematics programs is demonstrated by the continued success of the Wolfson II class. Table 6.A1 shows the progress of the program from plane geometry to the completion of the precalculus curriculum sequence.

As mentioned in chapter 6, the class was divided into sections, the faster-paced taught by Mr. Wolfson and the slower-paced taught by Miss Shuppert. These sections met once a week on Saturdays for nineteen two-hour periods from 26 January 1974 until the Educational Testing Service Cooperative

Appendix Table 6.A1.   Update of Wolfson II from plane geometry

Step in update	Criteria	Total number			Howard County		Baltimore County		Percent proceeding to next step		
			Girls	Boys	Girls	Boys	Girls	Boys	Total	Girls	Boys
1. Students taking plane geometry	Algebra III ⩾ 26										
a. Section A (faster paced)		23	3	20	1	5	2	15	100	100	100
b. Section B		5	2	3	1	1	1	2	100	100	100
2. Successful completion of plane geometry	Plane geometry ⩾ 52										
a. Section A		23	3	20	1	5	2	15	78	67	80
b. Section B		5	2	3	1	1	1	2	40	0	67
3. Invited to take trigonometry[a]	Plane geometry ⩾ 59	22	2	20	0	7	2	13	77	50	80
4. Entered trigonometry class	Voluntary	17	1	16	0	5	1	11	100	100	100
5. Successful completion of trigonometry	Trigonometry ⩾ 20	17	1	16	0	5	1	11	94	0	100
6. Continued on to analytic geometry	Voluntary	16	0	16	0	5	0	11	100	0	100
7. Successful completion of analytic geometry	Analytic geometry ⩾ 23	16	0	16	0	5	0	11	81	0	81
8. Taking calculus during 1974–75 school year[b]	Voluntary	14	0	14	0	5	0	9	64	0	64
9. In McCoart Saturday morning college calculus class	Voluntary	9	0	9	0	4	0	5	89	0	89
10. In McCoart class until Christmas of 1974[c]	Voluntary	8	0	8	0	3	0	5			

[a] Two new boys (a seventh-grader and a ninth-grader) were invited to join the new consolidated class in June 1974. The percent proceeding from step 2 to step 3 was calculated before addition of two boys.

[b] This includes the regular high school program and/or college courses taken in lieu of high school calculus. The percent proceeding from step 7 to step 8 was calculated before the addition of one boy who chose to continue his mathematics program in college after completing geometry in June 1974.

[c] The eight students completed Dr. McCoart's class in May 1975. On 13 May 1975, all eight took the APP calculus BC level examination. Three boys

Mathematics Test in geometry was administered on 1 June 1974 and 22 June 1974. The classes covered about the same material, but in a different manner. The smaller class (N = 5) was much more personalistic and group-oriented. Mathematics games were used to keep incentive high and make fast-mathematics learning a stimulating experience. The fast-paced group (N = 23) was more individualistic, and new solutions were suggested in a much more theoretical manner. Both teachers, however, insisted on self-instruction through a properly paced homework process. Before-class preparation was a necessity. Neither class was slowed by those students who chose not to read and complete their homework.

The results of the class were indicative of the students' willingness to learn in this style. All twenty-eight students scored at the 85th percentile or higher on the national high school norms as measured by this eighty-minute, eighty-item test. This means that in only 38 hours of instruction they exceeded the total score earned by 85 percent or more of the students who had studied for 170 or more forty-five- to fifty-minute school periods.

Twenty members from the two groups were invited to continue through much of the summer of 1974 and complete their precalculus sequence by taking trigonometry and analytic geometry. In addition, two other highly talented boys were asked to join the class. The first, a seventh-grader, had learned algebra I, algebra II, algebra III, and plane geometry since December 1973, with the assistance of a tutor. The other boy, a member of the original Wolfson class (student five in Fox 1974b[I:6]), had just completed plane geometry in his high school. These two boys, along with fifteen members (one girl, fourteen boys) of the invited group completed trigonometry in sixteen hours. The mean score for the group on the forty-item, forty-minute ETS Cooperative Mathematics Test in trigonometry was 28. This is the 96th percentile of national high school norms. No student scored below the 76th percentile of national norms.

At this point, for various reasons, the last remaining girl in the class decided to leave the fast-mathematics instruction program before completing analytic geometry. In the fall of 1974 she returned to the regular classroom and took the usual trigonometry and analytic geometry course that her high school offered.

THE SIXTEEN WHO COMPLETED THE PRECALCULUS SEQUENCE

Sixteen boys continued the rapid-fire pace and completed analytic geometry in fourteen hours of instruction. No one scored below the 75th percentile of national high school norms. In seven two-hour classes these students learned analytic geometry better than at least three-quarters of the high school population which takes analytic geometry five days a week for ninety periods. The mean score of this group on the Cooperative Mathematics Test in analytic geometry, 29, is the 95th percentile of national high school norms.

Of the sixteen boys who completed analytic geometry in August 1974, fourteen had finished all the precalculus mathematics curriculum in 108 hours. The fast-paced approach has repeatedly demonstrated its success. In September 1974 thirteen boys joined their regular high school calculus class. The other three boys, at the strong encouragement of their schools, chose to join the regular trigonometry and analytic geometry class. As of January 1975, no student has reported encountering difficulty in the high school classroom. Two of these boys are eleventh-graders, accelerated one and two years. They plan to enter a college or university in the fall of 1975. Ten of the boys are tenth-graders, including one who is accelerated. Many of these students have expressed interest in beginning college a year early, in 1976–77. One of the two ninth-graders skipped one grade and the other skipped three grades to reach the advanced courses at private schools in the Baltimore area. The ninth-grader, who is eleven, has previously earned two A's for college credit in coursework relating to computer science.

In September 1974, nine of these highly able mathematical reasoners began a college calculus class taught for two hours each Saturday morning by Dr. Richard McCoart. The purpose of this program was to help prepare these young men for the College Entrance Examination Board's Advanced Placement Program (APP) examination in calculus at the higher (i.e., BC) level. APP exams are offered each May. Quite a few high school programs are capable of preparing their students fairly well for the AB level, but few have the student talent or instructional staff needed for the BC level. By earning a 4 or 5 on the calculus BC level test each student can receive a year of college credits in mathematics, with the opportunity to take more advanced mathematics courses in college. Many colleges will give a year of college credits for a 3, as well. A 4 or 5 on the AB level will insure a student of at least 4 credits or one semester of calculus. Students who were in the Wolfson II class and are presently in the high school program only have been encouraged to take at least the AB level examination in May 1975.

COURSE PLACEMENT FOR THE REMAINING FOURTEEN

Taking calculus for college credit is the alternate route two students chose to solve possible scheduling problems created by limited course offerings in the junior high schools. The first, as a ninth-grader in junior high school, registered for calculus at the local community college in the fall of 1974, after completing analytic geometry the previous summer. The second student chose to continue his mathematics program in college, after completing plane geometry in June 1974. Having successfully completed a computer science course in the spring 1974 semester, as an eighth-grader (1974–75) he took a precalculus college course during the summer of 1974. The following semester he completed calculus I and then registered for calculus II in the spring 1975 semester.

The remaining twelve students (seven boys, five girls) completed algebra II, plane geometry, and, in seven cases, algebra III in a total of thirty-nine two-hour meetings. Three of the tenth-grade boys decided on doubling up on their mathematics during the 1974-75 school year to complete the precalculus sequence. At least one of these is planning to enter college in 1976–77. Eight of the remaining nine students (four boys, five girls) are taking trigonometry and analytic geometry. The final student is entering a major university in 1976–77 and took Math Analysis I at the local community college in lieu of high school mathematics during the spring semester of 1975. The final evaluation of success will have to wait until these students have completed the rest of their high school mathematics program.

The results of SMPY's curriculum experimentation programs encouraged Montgomery County and Charles County to each establish two fast-mathematics classes on a countywide basis for their highly talented mathematical reasoners in the fall of 1974. In spring 1975, Charles County established another fast-paced mathematics class whose participants the county itself identified. Montgomery County also completed its testing of candidates for three additional classes begun in fall 1975. In addition, there are at least six other in-school classes based on the accelerative mathematics model operating in the Baltimore-Washington area. For further information regarding the in-school model, see chapter 7 in this volume.

7
SPECIAL FAST-MATHEMATICS CLASSES TAUGHT BY COLLEGE PROFESSORS TO FOURTH-THROUGH TWELFTH-GRADERS[1]

Julian C. Stanley

ABSTRACT

We tried having high-school algebra taught quickly to mathematically apt fourth- through seventh-graders. Principles and techniques were derived from three classes previously conducted at The Johns Hopkins University with somewhat abler youths. Twelve boys and twelve girls were taught within their school, by mathematics professors of their own sex, one two-hour session each week, for a total of thirty-seven hours. Twenty-one students finished. On a standardized algebra I test eighteen of them scored between the 49th and 99.4th percentile of national eighth-grade norms. Five beat every eighth-grade algebra student in the school. Quality of instruction was crucially important. Homogeneous grouping can be highly effective. Experimentation with the ensuing second-year algebra class was done during the 1974–75 school year. Progress of a college-level fast-calculus class is discussed. Material concerning the Wolfson I class (Fox 1974 [I:6]), especially their scores on the Differential Aptitude Test, is presented in an appendix.

This is the report of an initially successful attempt to develop within a single school a program for teaching algebra to mathematically apt students earlier and faster than usual. In the Study of Mathematically Precocious Youth (SMPY) we had tried such programs outside of school hours—typically, two hours each Saturday morning—with three different rather highly selected groups of junior

[1] I thank William C. George and Leon L. Lerner for providing some of the data used in this paper and Daniel P. Keating, Harris J. Silverstone, and Michael Beer for helpful comments.

132

high school boys and girls. For detailed reports about these, see Fox (1974 [I:6])[2] and Appendix 2 of this chapter, Fox (chapter 9 of this volume), and George and Denham (chapter 6 of this volume).

All three of these earlier efforts drew from the most mathematically talented in a large population of students, nearly all of whom were seventh-, eighth-, or ninth-graders. The primary criterion was upper 1 percent mathematical reasoning ability in two of the programs and, approximately, the upper 2 to 3 percent in the third. Other criteria, especially verbal and nonverbal reasoning ability, were also used.

All three previous programs were completely under the control and supervision of SMPY. None was conducted on school time. Arrangements for credit and accelerated placement in mathematics were worked out with the public schools in which the students were enrolled, but those schools did not prescribe the curriculum, furnish the teacher, supervise the instruction, or prompt the students to work harder. Two programs enrolled both boys and girls in the same classes, whereas the other (Fox, chapter 9 of this volume) was an exploratory study confined to girls.

NEED TO TRY THE PROGRAM WITHIN A SINGLE LARGE SCHOOL

SMPY's role is to try out programs in semilaboratory settings, improve them, and then see whether the principles and practices developed can be used under more typical school conditions. The most direct transfer would be from programs on The Johns Hopkins University campus to a city or county school system that would operate special fast-mathematics classes on Saturdays, in the late afternoon, or evenings; these would draw from the entire county, or a sizable portion of it, rather than from just one school. Our programs have involved more than one county or city school system. Other things being equal, the larger the educational unit the more high-level talent is likely to be found and the greater is the need for special classes.

In the fall of 1974 the Montgomery County (Maryland) public school system, situated north of the District of Columbia, set up two such classes on a countywide basis; these were taught by Joseph Wolfson. He pioneered with us the first two coeducational classes, which we call Wolfson I and Wolfson II. Wolfson I was completed in August 1973 and Wolfson II in August 1974. See Fox (1974 [I:6]) and George and Denham (chapter 6 of this volume).

It also seemed desirable to try out modified Wolfson and Fox techniques in a single school. Fortunately, late in 1973 an opportunity to do this arose. We were

---

[2]The citation in brackets indicates that the reference is to a chapter in the previous volume on SMPY. I signifies volume I of the *Studies of Intellectual Precocity*; 6 signifies chapter 6 of that book. This convention is used throughout [Editor].

approached by Leon L. Lerner, the seventh-grade guidance counselor of a kindergarten through ninth-grade public school and executive director of the B'nai B'rith Career and Counseling Services in Baltimore. Having known of SMPY for some time, he suggested that we collaborate to set up special first-year algebra classes in that school, two hours per week for the last half of the school year. We offered to help select the most mathematically talented students in the fourth through seventh grades, organize the classes, and find teachers for them.

From Fox's work, it seemed to us that there should be two separate classes, one for boys and the other for girls, each with approximately twenty students initially. The least able enrollees should be mathematically talented enough to learn algebra fast and not get far behind the rest of the students in the class. The classes would be continued for at least one and one-half years (i.e., through June 1975) under the school's sponsorship and control.

Approval for the program was given by the school principal and faculty. The Parent-Teacher Association (PTA) was involved in the planning for the classes. This was desirable from the standpoint of general parental approval and also, as will be noted below, when deciding how to finance the classes. SMPY staff members and Mr. Lerner met several times with parents of children considered for the program.

THE SELECTION PROCESS

Characteristics of the School

School R, as we shall designate it, is located in an affluent residential community within a large city and near several elite private schools. It draws from the vicinity students for its kindergarten through sixth grade. Many of the youths in that area who come from upper-socioeconomic-level homes attend private schools, however.

Entering its seventh grade in the fall of 1973 were students from approximately sixty-three different elementary schools in the city. (This number varies radically from year to year, depending partly on pressures for racial integration.) The abler of these students stay only two years, however. At the end of the eighth grade the more capable students transfer to the ninth-grade "A(dvanced)" college preparatory curriculum in one of several public or private schools.

Enrollments in the fourth through eighth grades of School R during the academic year 1973–74 were as follows: fourth, 67; fifth, 63; sixth, 68; seventh, 370; and eighth, 360.

According to Mr. Lerner, approximately 70 percent of its students are black. About 5 to 10 percent of the students are Oriental, Mexican-American, or other foreign-language backgrounds. Only a few are Jewish.

The students in this school seem, on the average, somewhat abler academically than are students in the typical school of Baltimore City, but probably there is appreciably less high-level intellectual talent in grades four to seven of this school than in several schools in the nearby county.

A more direct comparison can be made via results of SMPY's January 1974 Maryland mathematics talent search. Of the fourteen students from School R who entered that contest, ten scored on the College Entrance Examination Board's Scholastic Aptitude Test, mathematical part, as high as the average male high school senior does. Of the fourteen public middle and junior high schools in the city which participated in that contest, only two had more high scorers than that. Of the twenty-five junior high schools in the adjacent county that participated, nine had more. Because participation in the contest was voluntary, however, these comparisons can be only suggestive. The number of students from a given school who took the test depended heavily on recruiting within the school by guidance counselors and mathematics teachers. We do know that School R's counselors tried to enroll all eligible students.

Through the seventh grade, students in School R usually study general mathematics or a variant thereof. The better students are permitted to take introductory algebra as eighth-graders. Other students who want to take algebra must wait until the ninth grade. As noted above, by ninth grade many of the academically ablest students in the school have left to enter senior high school.

Identifying the Population

It was decided to locate all boys and girls in the fourth through seventh grades who had scored quite high on the Iowa Tests of Basic Skills (ITBS) achievement battery's arithmetic reasoning section and who also had high total scores. A sliding scale was used. Seventh-graders had to score at least the 98th percentile on mathematics and the 95th percentile overall. Sixth-graders needed 99 and 97. For fifth-graders the required percentiles were 99 and 98. For fourth-graders they were 99 and 99.

This prescreening by Mr. Lerner from the students' records yielded twenty-three girls and seventeen boys to be examined further by SMPY with more difficult tests. They were in the following grades: girls—seven 4th, three 5th, five 6th, and eight 7th; boys—five 4th, two 5th, three 6th, and seven 7th.

Selecting the Students

On 19 December 1973 all but four of the above students took the 1962 version of the Psychological Corporation's Academic Promise Test (APT), which is designed for grades 6–9. It was administered by the writer and William C. George. The next day Mr. George administered the sixty-item Raven's Standard Progressive Matrices (SPM). Testing of the absentees was done by Mr. Lerner.

APT consists of four subtests, each of which has sixty items. They are Numerical (N), Verbal (V), Abstract Reasoning (AR), and Language Usage (LU). From previous experience, we knew that those subtests were predictive of success in such a class in the order listed: N most, V next, and AR next. Therefore, in choosing members for the two classes (one for boys, the other for girls) most weight was given to N and to the V + AR + LU sum. An examinee's AR score could be compared for consistency with his or her SPM score.

The scores and other information are listed in the first appendix to this chapter, which is table 7.A1. A number of facts can be gleaned from that large table, where the rows are in descending order of the forty N scores ranging from 54 to 5. The highest N score was earned by a seventh-grade girl, but eight of the top ten N scores were obtained by boys. One of these boys, who ranked fourth on N and seventh on APT–total, was a fifth-grader. Two others were sixth-graders. Most of the low scorers on N were fourth- or fifth-grade girls. The seventh-grader scoring lowest on N (27) was a boy who ranked 27th out of 40. Only one of the students scored far lower (APT-total 64) than would be predicted from the prescreening scores.

Grade and sex differences for APT-N are set forth graphically in figure 7.1. There the scale of the abscissa is the same as the scale of the ordinate, i.e., the 5–54 score range. The two rectangles for each grade are centered over the mean score for that grade. (Near the middle of each rectangle is indicated the mean for that grade-sex group.) The means of the grades were as follows: 18.2 for the 4th, 27.4 for the fifth, 37.6 for the sixth, and 40.8 for the seventh. The figure shows quickly that the sixth- and seventh-graders differed far less from each other than from the other two grades, which were about as different from each other as the fifth grade was from the sixth grade. The small sixth- vs. seventh-grade difference might represent some aspects of instruction in arithmetic, but more likely it is due to higher preselection criteria for the former grade than for the latter and some loss of high talent to private schools after the sixth grade.

The figure also indicates that the girls lagged behind the boys by about one grade. Fifth-grade girls, whose mean score was 21.0, were a little below fourth-grade boys (23.2). Sixth-grade girls (36.2) were about the same as fifth-grade boys (37.0). Seventh-grade girls (39.2) were about the same as sixth-grade boys (40.0). Sex differences in means within the two lower grades were large: 8.6 points for the fourth and 16 for the fifth. They were much less in the sixth and seventh grades, 3.8 and 3.4 respectively.

Inspection of the birth dates in the table reveals that not a single one of these forty highly able students is accelerated in grade placement even one day by local standards (i.e., must become five years old during the calendar year in order to enter kindergarten in September). Three girls—two seventh-graders and one fourth-grader—are a year behind schedule, however. One of the seventh grad-ers, of Chinese background, was born in July 1960, so by the above criterion she was more than five months older than the entering minimum. The other girls have October and November birthdays, so they may have been kept out of school an extra year because of their presumed "immaturity." Perhaps, instead, they began their schooling in another school district that had an earlier

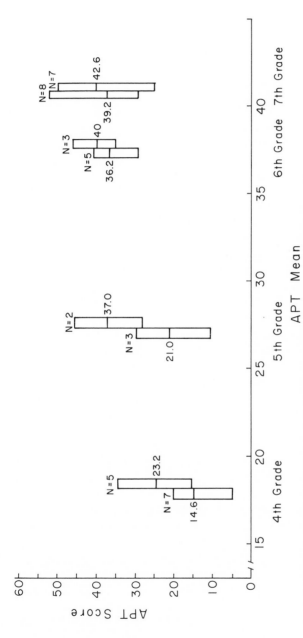

Fig. 7.1. The Academic Promise Test numerical scores of the 40 students, by grade and sex. (*Left* rectangle for each grade represents range of scores for females, with mean also shown. *Right* rectangles represent males. Each APT subtest has 60 items.)

entrance criterion, such as August 31 or September 30. But in any event it seems to the writer unfortunate that there was no acceleration in school grade but some retardation among the ablest students in a large public school.

Beside the girl of Oriental ancestry, the forty include four with Spanish surnames, one of them of Philippine background, and two Blacks. Also, quite a few of the names seem Germanic.

Of the twenty-three girls tested, twelve were chosen for the girls' class (see the eleventh column of table 7.A1). Seven of these were seventh-graders and five were sixth-graders.[3] No fourth- or fifth-grade girl scored high enough to be considered ready for the class. All but one of the girls in the class had APT-total scores ranging from the 99th percentile to the 95th percentile of seventh-graders; hers (rank 16.5 in table 7.A1) was the 85th percentile.

Of the seventeen boys tested, twelve were chosen. Half of these were seventh-graders. There were three sixth-graders, two fifth-graders, and one fourth-grader. One of the male fifth-graders scored two points lower on N and 24 points lower on T than the lowest N girl accepted, but the other boys chosen were comparable to the girls.[4]

Because considerable attrition must be expected from one year to the next, each class should have had at least twenty students, so that the number the second year would be sufficient with which to continue. As noted above, there did not prove to be enough talented youths in the fourth through seventh grades of School R to do this separately by sex, as the work by Fox (chapter 9 of this volume) indicates is probably desirable. This is a severe limitation to conducting fast-mathematics classes within a single school during school hours. Only large schools in high-ability areas (usually upper-middle-class suburbs) are likely to have sufficient students with highly enough developed mathematical reasoning ability to create effective fast-mathematics classes meeting one two-hour period per week and enrolling at least twenty boys and twenty girls.

An alternative possibility is to put the boys and girls together in one class and have it taught by a woman skilled in capitalizing on the socialization needs of the girls. Another is to offer one regular section of algebra I to especially well-qualified boys and girls a year earlier than usual—e.g., in the seventh grade, if algebra is ordinarily begun in the eighth. This means that the typical junior high school, with grades 7 to 9 and algebra I and II not usually available until the eighth and ninth grades (if then), would need to add plane geometry to its curriculum for this accelerated group—i.e., algebra I in the seventh grade,

---

[3]Before the course began, one of these, a sixth-grade girl from another school, had joined the group. See rank 11 in table 7.A1.

[4]One of the boys (rank 16.5 in table 7.A1) earned the extremely low score of 17 on AR, even though his scores on the other three subtests were good. No other one of the forty examinees scored lower than 25 on AR, and that was the lowest-scoring fourth-grader (rank 40). He did a great deal better on SPM, but his pattern of errors was peculiar; he missed a number of easy items and few difficult ones. This boy, alone among the students, proved totally unwilling to do *any* homework and therefore finally dropped out of the class.

algebra II in the eighth, and geometry in the ninth. It would not seem wise to leave these able accelerants with no mathematics in their last year of junior high school. (Some might prefer to skip the ninth grade, though, and thereby move into senior high school a year early if it begins with the tenth grade.)

The twenty-four students chosen for these two classes represented a wide range of family backgrounds and education, as diverse as police sergeant, carry-out shop operator, and university professor. Education of parents ranged from second grade to Ph.D.s. On the average, this group of students is from a somewhat lower socioeconomic level than the students in the Wolfson I and II classes were. That accords with known differences between this city and its adjacent counties, and with the fact that students in the School R classes are less able, on the average, than were Wolfson's students. Yet even the lowest of them in the class are within the upper few percent of the age group in mathematical ability.

SETTING UP THE CLASSES

A female teacher was needed for the girls and a male teacher for the boys. We knew from experience with the Wolfson and Fox classes that these teachers should meet several criteria:

1. They must know mathematics well at a level far above that at which they would teach.

2. They must be bright and alert.

3. They must want to teach elementary algebra *fast* and well to mathematically apt youths. They must not be easily slowed down or distracted from this central concern. Above all, they must *not* adjust their pace to the slower members of the class. Instead, they must require these students to fill in gaps in their comprehension of the material between classes by doing a great deal of carefully designed homework.

4. They must hold the students to high standards of homework and class performance.

Those four specifications pointed toward college teachers of algebra and higher mathematics courses, or persons who had extensive graduate work in a related area (such as Mr. Wolfson, who studied physics). Previous experience teaching students of junior high school age was not essential, nor perhaps even desirable, we had found.

For the boys' class we were exceedingly fortunate to get Professor Richard F. McCoart, chairman of the Department of Mathematics at Loyola College in Baltimore, a well-trained teacher of calculus and other mathematics courses. He knew of our study and had already volunteered to teach a course such as this.

For the girls we were also exceedingly fortunate to get Ann L. Wagner, an assistant professor of mathematics at Towson State College, near Baltimore. She is an experienced teacher. The first prodigy in our study had audited her precalculus and calculus courses during the school year 1968–69. Miss Wagner proved to have the warm, friendly manner that seems important for teaching mathematics to sixth- and seventh-grade girls, as well as the necessary expertise in mathematics.

Next we decided on the textbook. The simplest alternative was to choose the book used in the regular eighth-grade algebra classes at School R, because it would make transition to that class the following fall easier for those who had not done well enough in the fast class to continue in it. Also, the book could be supplied free to each student. Mr. Wolfson had decided that getting through algebra I quickly and into a comprehensive algebra II textbook was important, so for a knowledgeable teacher the vintage of the book was not seen to be crucial. The one used was Smith, Lankford, and Payne (1962).

The special classes met for one two-hour period per week, without a formal intermission. This amount of time was chosen deliberately for the convenience of the teacher and because mathematically apt, interested youths appear to benefit from massing of instruction. They have longer attention spans than average children. Also, in the school context, this one period per week facilitates scheduling of time and room.

We have often considered whether two separate fifty-minute periods per week would distribute learning and homework assignments better. Perhaps so, but because the special class is meant only for students who can more readily learn to work well on their own between classes the two-hour period seemed more efficient.

It might be well to stress here that for the students chosen these special classes are a privilege, not a right. We know from logic and experience that not all of the starters (or their parents) will appreciate the opportunities they afford, so built into the plan are provisions for moving low-achieving students into more suitable classes as early in the course as they become definitely recognized. All students remained in their regular arithmetic or general mathematics class five periods per week for the rest of the school year.

Dr. McCoart met his group for the first time on Friday, 18 January 1974, and each Friday thereafter (with two exceptions) through June 7, when during the second hour the standardized test to be described later was administered. Miss Wagner's class began on January 25, and the test for her group came on June 5. The next week in June each teacher reviewed the test results for one hour and then met with the students' parents.

Thus Dr. McCoart taught his boys for 37 hours before the test. Miss Wagner also taught her girls for 37 hours. The classes were conducted independently of each other. It was not crucial that the boys or girls learn the first year of algebra well in this short period of time, because from the beginning it was planned that they would resume studying algebra I in the special class(es) during the fall of 1974 before progressing to algebra II.

Each teacher was paid a set fee per week. The school asked the parents of each child in the special classes to pay $2.00 per week, if able. The Parent-Teacher Association agreed to furnish the rest. In our own programs we have paid instructors from $25 to $75 per two-hour session, depending on the size of the class, the level of subject matter, and the experience of the teacher with that kind of group. Fees students pay have been set at enough per week to meet all or most such costs. The remainder, if any, has come out of our research funds.

CONDUCTING THE CLASSES

Drs. Fox, Keating, and Stanley visited some of the classes and helped the two instructors get acquainted with their bright young students. Dr. McCoart had no teaching experience below the college level, but he quickly proved to be an enthusiastic, ingenious teacher. Miss Wagner molded her girls into a smoothly interacting, well-socialized group.

Attendance was splendid. During the semester the teachers at School R went on strike along with other city teachers. Because Dr. McCoart and Miss Wagner were ad hoc teachers in this school, they continued to come each week. Their students crossed picket lines in order to continue learning algebra.

A boy and a girl dropped out of the classes quickly, and one more boy did so after about fifteen weeks. Test scores of the former two, both sixth-graders, were rather low in the classes' distribution (see footnote p of table 7.A1). The other student, a seventh-grader, finally quit after persistently not doing *any* homework (see footnote 4 in the text). These dropouts left ten boys and eleven girls who continued until the final meetings.

Dr. McCoart and Miss Wagner moved through the algebra textbook fast, operated at a more abstract level than could be done in a usual class, and assigned considerable homework. Dr. McCoart's manner was more intensively forceful and aggressive, whereas Miss Wagner's emphasized group cohesiveness and working together. The latter was intentional, because Dr. Fox had found that girls exposed to a highly theoretical, individualistic, competitive teaching approach tended to do poorly and quit.

It was obvious to persons, such as the writer, who audited some of the two-hour sessions that these were splendid teachers. They kept the attention and good will of the youths. The next section shows that they were indeed successful.

EVALUATING PROGRESS

Results of the first standardized algebra test administered to the ten boys and eleven girls by the writer are shown in the next-to-last column of table 7.A1. The boys ranged in percentile rank on national eighth-grade norms from 99.4 (the brilliant fifth-grader) to 18 (the fourth-grader). No sixth- or seventh-grade boy was below the 68th percentile. No one of the five students who had scored 33 or lower on APT-N exceeded the 49th percentile, whereas all but two of those sixteen whose N score was at least 36 achieved or exceeded the 68th percentile.

In summary, only three of the twenty-one scored lower than 49 percent of eighth-graders who have studied algebra for a school year, approximately 175 fifty-minute periods that total some 146 hours. Two of those (ranks 20.5 and 26 in table 7.A1) were very young, being in only the fourth and fifth grades. An equally young fifth-grader (rank 4) was, however, the best algebra student of the entire group. A high score on APT-N seems especially important for students younger than most in the class. Otherwise, they will probably need far too much tutoring and other special attention.

The teachers agreed substantially with the results of the standardized test, which was independent of their own evaluations, except that the lowest-scoring girl (rank 24) was judged to be a better student than her score indicated, and a sixth-grade boy (rank 9.5) was judged to be less able than his 68th percentile score suggested. The girl had scored relatively low (30) on APT-N. Both of her parents are college graduates, and her father is an engineer. Perhaps she got more help at home than most of the girls, and this made her homework and class responses seem to show more achievement than she could demonstrate on a test containing forty multiple-choice items to be answered without assistance in forty minutes. When retested in the fall with another form of the test she improved greatly, scoring at the 95th percentile.

The above boy's "surprisingly high" algebra score tied him for sixth place with two of the other nine boys, whereas he ranked 7.5 among them on APT-N. He had the lowest APT-verbal score of any boy in the class except one of the fifth-graders, whom he tied. This verbal deficit may have caused him to appear less quick-minded in the class than on the test. His mathematics aptitude is considerably higher than his rate of learning. We have encountered several boys like this, who learn mathematics well if given enough time and exposure. They have good mathematical reasoning ability but less high IQs.

Fortunately, it was possible to compare the algebra test scores of these twenty-one fourth- through seventh-graders with those of the eighth-graders who took algebra every day in regular classes, both sections of which were taught by the same new, inexperienced teacher. (Remember, though, that both Dr. McCoart and Miss Wagner had not previously taught students this young, either.) These were the ablest 18 percent of the eighth-grade students.

At the invitation of the eighth-grade counselor, Mr. George and the writer tested the sixty-six eighth-graders on 11 June 1974, several days after testing the special-class students. Most of the special-class students achieved better after thirty-seven hours of instruction than the regular-class, older ones did near the end of a school year. Five of the 21 (24 percent) scored higher than *any* of the sixty-six. Twenty-three of the sixty-six (35 percent) scored lower than *any* of the twenty-one. These are startling figures, because the eighth-graders themselves were a selected group that included virtually all of the ablest students in that grade. Less able students wait until the ninth grade, if at all, to begin algebra. *These great contrasts in favor of students in the special classes, who were younger and were taught only thirty-seven hours, are the most salient findings of the within-school study.*

The most important factors that produce results such as the above, which were also found at least that strong in our previous fast-mathematics classes, seem to be as follows: a teacher who knows mathematics well, is enthusiastic, has high standards, and moves the group fast; students who have considerable mathematical and verbal aptitude, as determined by standardized tests, and are fairly homogeneous in these respects but not necessarily alike in grade placement or chronological age; interest in learning mathematics quickly and well, which (especially among girls) does not always accompany aptitude; facilitative parents who value the unusual educational opportunity the special class represents and therefore encourage their children to do well; and helpful school personnel who do not try to obstruct the program because they feel threatened by it.

BACKGROUND CHARACTERISTICS

We got a rough assessment of interest in mathematics and several other aspects by means of a questionnaire filled out early in the course by the girls, because our previous experience had indicated that some of them would probably not be greatly interested. One girl left the class even before it began, so the questionnaire was not offered her. The other eleven provided information that can be summarized as follows:

Both of the parents of five of the girls were at least college graduates. Only one parent (a mother) did not complete high school. Five of the mothers work outside the home. Three of the fathers (and one of the mothers) are teachers, two are engineers, and one is a lawyer. Other fathers hold positions such as department head in a large steel plant, deputy chief of maintenance at an airport, owner of a carry-out shop, and police sergeant.

None of the girls was an only child. Their number of siblings ranged from one to four. Six of the girls had no older siblings, but only two of them had no younger siblings. Two had no brothers and two no sisters. Three of the eleven families matched the stereotype—"if you have daughters first, keep on having children until a son is born and then stop." All in all, these sibling relationships seem fairly typical of the types of communities from which the girls came, with perhaps somewhat more tendency for them to be the oldest child. Only one was the youngest child in the family, being four grades lower in school than the closest one of her two brothers and two sisters. In fact, she was the only one of these eleven girls who had both older brothers and older sisters.

This analysis of siblings is based on only eleven students, so it must be considered highly tentative. Astin (1974 [I:4], p. 81) made similar comparisons for six girls in the first Wolfson fast-mathematics class and provided the following statistics: "None of the 17 children [including 11 boys] were *only* children. Six of the boys were first-borns, but none of the girls. Boys tended to be among the oldest in relatively small families, whereas girls tended to be the youngest in relatively large families. No girls came from two-child families, but four of the boys belonged to such families."

Like Astin's, this sample contained no only children. More than half of the girls were first-borns, however. Two of these eleven girls came from two-child families. Many or all of these discrepancies may be due to sampling fluctuations between small groups drawn from essentially the same population. Some of it may reflect the suburban, extremely high ability nature of Astin's girls vs. the urban, less high ability nature of the School R ones. Parents who persist in a somewhat deteriorating city environment may differ in their child bearing and rearing practices from those who move into the surrounding county. Also, the "creaming off" of able children into private schools within Baltimore is probably much more prevalent than in the surrounding counties. The city parents with small families are more likely to send their children (perhaps especially their older sons) to private schools than are those with larger families.

On the questionnaire the girls were asked a number of questions concerning their interest in the course and in mathematics. Eight of these were quantified and a score produced for each girl. The coefficient of correlation between these scores and the algebra scores, with APT-N score partialled out, was .30. Inspection of the interest scores reveals that the highest scorer performed disappointingly on the algebra test, but one of the lowest scorers also ranked low in the group. The interest items, being in self-report form, may have been quite susceptible to social desirability bias and other atmosphere effects at the start of the course.

It would, of course, be interesting to have similar questionnaire information for the boys, but that was not collected at the start of the class. The self-report items would not have the same meaning if completed later.

CHANGES IN FALL OF 1974

All of the girls were invited to continue in the fall with more algebra I and then go on with algebra II. All of the boys except the fourth-grader (rank 20.5 in table 7.A1) and one of the fifth-graders (rank 26) were also invited. Continuation in the fall of 1974 is discussed in the next section of this chapter.

The new class in beginning algebra was recruited from incoming seventh-graders—those who entered School R from elementary schools—and those persons on the table 7.A1 list from ranks 24–39 who when retested were found to have improved their N and V scores sufficiently. The criteria for this were scores of at least 36 on APT-N and 36 on APT-V. Those whose V scores were already high in December 1973 had a fair chance to meet these criteria, because the nonclass group got special instruction in arithmetic during the spring of 1974. Unfortunately, it did not seem to increase most of the APT-N scores much.

Two other accelerated algebra classes were set up in a "middle" school (grades 6 to 8) near School R.

THE CONTINUING GROUP

As noted above, ten boys and eleven girls remained in the class from its inception in January 1974 until school ended in June. Of these, five boys and nine girls continued in it on September 12. This 33 percent attrition over the summer seems high, but is probably typical of public schools in a city, but outside its center. Because there were not enough students to have separate-sex classes, Miss Ann Wagner took over the whole group.

The five boys who dropped out are accounted for as follows: the brilliant fifth-grader who had ranked fourth on APT-N and first on the standardized algebra test moved away, the rank 7.5 sixth-grader went on a one-semester trip to Europe with his parents, the rank 9.5 sixth-grader transferred to a nearby private school, the rank 20.5 fourth-grader went on a long trip with his parents (but would have been dropped from the class anyway, because he did not seem ready to keep up with its pace), and the rank 26 fifth-grader was asked to drop out because although conscientious and apparently attentive he was lagging behind the group.

Of the two girls who dropped out, one (the rank 11 sixth-grader) attended another school and did not want to make the continued effort to come for the class, and the other (the rank 12 sixth-grader) transferred to a nearby private school.

These departures left the class composed of five eighth-grade boys, seven eighth-grade girls, and two seventh-grade girls. A glance at the last column of table 7.A1 reveals that one of the seventh-graders (rank 24) did quite well on the algebra retest, whereas the other (rank 20.5) scored at the very bottom of the class (33rd percentile). The former's father is an engineer and helps her with homework. That probably partly explains her rise from the 39th percentile, lowest of all the eleven girls, on the first test to 95th on the second. Doing homework carefully, with encouragement and preferably some assistance at home, seems highly important, especially for girls.

On the retest the boys had percentile ranks in nearly the same order as on the first test, but averaging 0.23 standard deviations higher. One gained 0.55 s.d., two 0.48, and one 0.00, and one lost 0.36. These do not seem substantial enough gains for the amount of instructional time involved since the previous test, about twenty-four hours. Too-low ceiling was not a problem except for the top-scorer, who missed only one of the forty items. The other boys scored 31, 28, 28, and 27. It seems that direct review of algebra I is not as productive as going on into a good algebra II textbook.

The girls gained more than the boys (average of 0.42 s.d.), but their changes were far more variable: 1.92, 1.91, 0.69, 0.67, three 0.00's, –0.41, and –1.03 standard deviations. On the retest, the boys averaged 1.33 s.d. above the mean of the national eighth-grade norms, whereas the girls averaged 0.91. Three girls scored considerably lower than any boy, but four girls scored higher than any boy except the top one. At least one of the girls seemed unlikely to be able to learn algebra II fast enough to keep up with the rest of the class. In March of 1975 she finally dropped out.

It is difficult to ascertain what varied factors operated to make the boys achieve better than several of the girls, even though they had a teacher of the opposite sex from their former one, whereas the girls kept the same female teacher from one year to the next. Ranks on APT-N in table 7.A1 may give clues to the difficulties that some of the girls had. The five boys' ranks were 2, 3, 5.5, 7.5, and 9.5. The nine girls' ranks were 1, 5.5, 13.5, 13.5, 15, 16.5, 20.5, 20.5, and 24.

Seven of the nine girls had scored 4 to 13 points lower on APT-N than any of the five boys. This difference in numerical aptitude may be more important than even the sex of the teacher and coeducational nature of the class. But, clearly, most of the girls did well, and four of them improved spectacularly from test to retest.

It will be interesting to see how those students who continue in the class until algebra II is completed (probably by the end of the 1974–75 school year) do on a standardized test. The girls have the advantage of numbers and a familiar female teacher who seems especially good in creating the social atmosphere that Fox (chapter 9 of this volume) believes is needed by most girls in their mathematics classes. The boys have an edge in age (all eighth-graders) and numerical aptitude, but they may not be as well motivated by the class atmosphere as most of the girls.[5]

PREPPING FOR THE APP CALCULUS EXAMINATION

On 7 September 1974 Dr. McCoart began a new class, rather unlike any we had offered before. It involved a population of students different from that discussed in the first part of this chapter. Meeting two hours each Saturday morning at nearby Loyola College, where he is head of the Mathematics

[5]Note added at galley proof stage: See footnote q of table 7.A1 for the algebra II test results.

Department, it was meant to supplement high school calculus courses so that students would score 4 or 5 on the level BC (i.e., the higher level) calculus examination of the College Entrance Examination Board's Advanced Placement Program (APP) on 13 May 1975. This college-level calculus course would carry no direct credit. The student's sole reward for taking it would be, we hoped, a better score on the APP exam and therefore a full year of college credit in calculus. The 4 or 5 on a 5-point scale was set as the goal, because Johns Hopkins requires at least a 4 to provide 8 credits of calculus I and II and permission to begin with advanced calculus. Many other universities will accept a 3, and indeed even at Johns Hopkins a 3 on level BC gives 4 credits and exemption from calculus I.

Without supplementation, the typical high school calculus course does not prepare most able students for doing well on the BC level examination. At best, they are likely to be ready only for the easier level, AB, which usually provides less credit than BC. For example, one of our most brilliant boys took AB and made a 5, but at Johns Hopkins this automatically earned him only 4 credits and the waiver of calculus I. (He went into advanced calculus, anyway, and earned a grade of A.)

Fifteen boys—and, regretfully, no girls—signed up for the course. Three of them were regular-age twelfth-graders, being three of the four ablest calculus students at a large suburban high school; the fourth decided that probably he would not need the supplementation, thereby giving us a strong "control group" of size 1.

One of the other boys, a tenth-grader who had skipped the eighth grade, had been an outstanding student in our first Wolfson I fast-mathematics class. In the fall of 1973 as a thirteen-year-old ninth-grader he took calculus, a twelfth-grade subject, at a large suburban high school and ranked in the upper two-fifths of an excellent class.

Another tenth-grader, who had also skipped the eighth grade, had been a less successful student in Wolfson I, but went into the latter part of Wolfson II and did well.

A third student, an eleven-year-old ninth-grader taking level AB calculus in the eleventh grade of a private school and chemistry in the tenth, had done well in Wolfson I at ages nine and ten.

Another student, a tenth-grader who had skipped the ninth grade, had as an eighth-grader scored high (SAT-M 700, SAT-V 590) in our January 1974 mathematics-reasoning contest. He had not been in any of our special classes and therefore had less mathematics background than anyone else in the class.

The other eight students who began were graduates of the Wolfson II algebra I–III, plane geometry, trigonometry, and analytic geometry speeded-up program (see chapter 6 of this volume). Ages of the fifteen students ranged from eleven years (two) to eighteen. Grade placement ranged from ninth (three) to twelfth (three).

Thirteen of these students continued in the class after Christmas of 1974. The eleven-year-old mentioned above fell behind and dropped out because he would be taking level BC calculus in the twelfth grade of his high school. He and his father felt that, despite this boy's extremely high Stanford–Binet IQ (212) and SAT-M ability (730 at age ten), he had enough work in school to keep him busy—being accelerated three years in basic grade placement and more in two subjects.

The other dropout just before Christmas was the boy mentioned above who had done poorly in Wolfson I but better in Wolfson II after taking two mathematics courses in high school as an accelerated ninth-grader. He seemed to find getting around to doing his homework difficult, presumably because of lack of motivation and organization. His mathematical and verbal abilities are unusually high, even for the SMPY group (SAT-V 720 and SAT-M 680 at age thirteen), but some of his other cognitive scores, such as for nonverbal reasoning, mechanical comprehension, and spatial relationships, are less outstanding. His chief academic interest seems to be military history, so perhaps he is simply not "cut out" to choose a field in which high-level mathematical achievement is essential. One wonders, however, how much better he might do in the fast-mathematics classes—and like them more—if his homework time were more carefully organized.

The Standardized Test

As table 7.1 indicates, the thirteen boys who continued in the class from its inception until 1 February 1975 (a total of thirty-four class hours) learned differential and integral calculus extremely well. Only one of them, a regular twelfth-grader, scored on a difficult speeded standardized test below the 88th percentile of the exceptionally able group of high school students—mostly seniors—across the country who elected a calculus course and pursued it five days per week for approximately 180 45 to 50 minute periods.

Six of the students scored higher than 99 percent of that norm group, and only two scored less well than 94 percent; they exceeded 88 percent and 76 percent, respectively. Even the eleven-year-old in the special class outscored 94 percent of the elite norm groups. Two years earlier he had been a fourth-grader!

By comparison with college students who have completed two semesters of introductory calculus the scores of this group are even more impressive. Only two boys scored below the 99.1th percentile of the national college norms; they were at the 98th and 94th percentiles.

Only ten of the thirteen boys are actually accelerated in their mathematical placement. The other three are regular-age high school seniors who have not skipped a grade. They are in the class as "pacers." One of these earned the highest score on the test, 57 out of the possible 60 points. Another scored 56, being tied by two of the accelerated boys (no one of whom is older than the typical tenth-

Table 7.1. Test information concerning the McCoart Saturday morning calculus class, September 1974 until May 1975[d]

Coop. Math. Test, Calculus,
Form B, taken 1 Feb. 1975[a]

Number right		Percentile rank of total score[b]		Present school grade	Grade(s) skipped	Percentage scores on prior tests				Later
Part I	Part II	High school	National college			1	2	3	4	5
29	28	99.8	99.97	12		84	52	56	54	84
28	28	99.5	99.95	12		82	72	88	80	93
29	27	99.5	99.95	11	9	71	−	−	78	81
29	27	99.5	99.95	10		88	69	77	71	72
28	26	99	99.9	10		43	24	76	54	85
26	28	99	99.9	10		60	52	77	70	70
28	24	97	99.5	10		55	42	67	56	58
26	25	97	99.5	10	9	45	49	88	47	92
27	23	94	99.1	10	8	67	73	78	66	93
27	23	94	99.1	9	8	54	56	80	77	74
26	24	94	99.1	9	5, 7, 8	48	45	42	48	69
24	23	88	98	10		59	17	78	53	73
25	17	76	94[c]	12		88	59	92	−	82

[a]This 60-item, 5-option, multiple-choice standardized test consists of two 30-item 40-minute subtests. It was published by the Educational Testing Service, Princeton, New Jersey 08540, copyright 1963.

[b]The total score is the number of the 60 items marked correctly—i.e., the sum of the Part I and Part II scores. You will note that the high school norms are more stringent than the national college norms; students who take calculus in high school tend to be mathematically abler and better motivated than those who defer it until college. Norms are from pages 51 and 53 of the *Cooperative Mathematics Tests Handbook*, ETS, 1964. Of course, norms may have shifted somewhat—though probably not radically—during the dozen years or so since these were developed.

[c]95th percentile of the college liberal arts group. The score of the middle person in this class (52) exceeded that of all but 3 in 1,000 students in liberal arts curricula who have completed two semesters of college calculus.

[d]Form A of the same test was administered to the thirteen students in early May of 1975. National college percentile ranks on it were as follows, reading from the top to the bottom of the table: 99.5, 99.5, 99.1, 99.1, 99.6, 99.1, 99.1, 99.9 (perfect score), 99.5, 99.1, 99.5, 99.1, and 99.1. Thus before taking the national Advanced Placement Program calculus test not one of these students scored lower on Coop. A than 99.1% of college calculus students do after studying the subject for two semesters. (There was one other monthly class test, the sixth. Scores on it were 87, 77, 79, 43, 77, 60, 56, 68, 72, 72, 39, 81, and 88.) All thirteen boys took the APP Level BC calculus test on May 13, 1975. They earned nine 5's (extremely well qualified), three 4's (well qualified), and one 3 (qualified). The 11-year-old scored 4, as did the barely 14-year-old. The only 3 was obtained by one of the best students in the class, who had made a perfect score (60 out of 60) on Form A of the standardized calculus test. His father had been taken to the hospital the preceding evening with what seemed to be a heart attack, and this may have hurt his concentration on the examination. He was, however, one of the youngest students in the class and had the least mathematics background, not having studied any analytic geometry before the class began. By all criteria the course was a resounding success. In just 30 two-hour supplemental meetings with Dr. McCoart these able young men learned college calculus I and II splendidly, and a great deal of calculus III also.

grader). The third twelfth-grader ranked thirteenth in the group, with a score of 42. It seems likely that he had not worked much in the course for two months before the test, because he started off splendidly and then fell behind.[6]

From the results of this standardized testing, it seems quite likely that all of the present group who continue in the course will be splendidly prepared to make 5s or at least 4s on the level BC APP calculus test that they take in mid-May 1975. Meanwhile, they will be getting a high-level version of calculus III, including some coverage of differential equations. By the summer of 1975 nearly all of them should be ready for a strong course in advanced calculus or linear algebra.

The present eleventh-grader (who skipped the ninth grade) plans to become a full-time student at Johns Hopkins in the fall of 1975. Some of the tenth-graders, and perhaps one of the ninth-graders, will probably enter in the fall of 1976. As noted several times in this volume, success in SMPY's special fast-mathematics classes leads to much general acceleration.

This book went to press before results of the May 1975 APP testing were known, so the outcome of that interesting experiment must await publication elsewhere. Dr. McCoart's "coaching class" for the higher-level APP calculus examination, supplementing as it does regular high school courses, is an idea that might be applied to a number of other APP examination subjects, such as physics, chemistry, biology, and history. Meeting for just one two-hour period per week outside of school hours and serving a large geographical area, such a class can be both effective and, in the long run, economical. Students in his class paid $5 per week each, but if there had been thirty students the cost per student could have been cut. Even $150 for the year, plus some $29 for the APP examination is a bargain, however, if it provides really sound knowledge of calculus and eight college credits. We expect the students who complete this course to earn 4s or 5s on the APP level BC calculus examination and go into college advanced calculus courses in the summer or fall of 1975, while most of them are still in high school.[7]

FEASIBILITY OF WITHIN-SCHOOL PROGRAMS

Pro

1. They occur during the regular school day and therefore avoid the transportation problems and absences that classes held in the late afternoons, evenings, or on Saturdays cause.

---

[6]The standardized calculus test was administered by the writer. Dr. McCoart had not seen it; however, two weeks before the test he was given a list of the topics it would cover. This list merely set forth the major topics studied in the usual thorough high school or college course.

[7]Note added at galley proof stage: See footnote d of table 7.1 for the final test results, which were excellent.

2. They are part of the school program and therefore should make articulation with other levels of the subject easier. Also, most of the eligible students will probably enroll in the special classes. Few who do well will drop out.

3. Classes are readily available for scrutiny by school personnel.

4. Students and teachers are accessible to guidance counselors. For example, Mr. Lerner developed continuing close relationships with the students and their parents, so that counseling and arrangements for tutoring could increase the effectiveness of the teaching.

5. They permit excellent part-time outside teachers to be used inexpensively, or perhaps without cost. Often one can get free teaching by properly assisted community persons, such as engineers or housewives who majored in mathematics, either directly or by approaching, say, an engineering firm and asking its president to release a suitable employee for that purpose.

6. They set a model within school for work with gifted in other subjects.

Con

1. It may be difficult to schedule a two-hour period per week, especially across grades, and not interfere much with other classes.

2. Special programs for the intellectually talented often encounter strong overt or covert resistance from teachers, guidance counselors, principals, or parents of children not included in them. Teachers of other subjects, such as English, may resent absences from their classes, even though the students are probably superior in those subjects also. Mathematics teachers may feel threatened by "expert" outsiders who are not certified high school teachers.[8] Problems of classroom utilization may occur, because most classes meet for forty-five or fifty-minutes, not two hours. Thus, the school setting is far more complex than the university class or the other class conducted outside of school hours.

3. Someone (e.g., school, parents, and/or PTA) must pay the outside instructor, if he or she will not donate the time. Of course, the school might use one of its own teachers, if a suitable mathematics teacher can have two hours per week of time freed. In some junior high schools, however, there will not be any mathematics teacher well enough prepared to continue the program successfully into algebra II and III, geometry, trigonometry, and analytic geometry.

4. The talent base in grades 6 and 7 in the typical public school is too slight to make it possible to start with a large enough class of each sex. Also, most junior high schools do not even have a sixth grade. To find 20 upper-5 percent boys in the seventh grade of an average school, for example, one would need 400 boys in that grade! If the school has a considerably greater amount of talent than average, 200 to 300 might suffice, but that would be only for the boys. For a class

---

[8]Both Dr. Fox and Dr. Stanley began their teaching careers as mathematics teachers in public high schools.

of 20 girls, too, the enrollment in the seventh grade alone would have to be 400 to 800.

Especially if one starts with more than a single grade, as School R did, attrition from one year to the next will probably cut the class size down considerably—33 percent in the present study. Also, the number of years each student can remain in the program will vary; at School R a fourth-grader would have five or six years, whereas a seventh-grader would have only two or three. Very few fourth- or fifth-graders will be ready for such a program, so it might be wise to confine the recruiting and selection to not more than two grades, such as sixth and seventh, and to begin the classes at the start of the year rather than in the middle. (One encounters a dilemma here, because although few fourth- or fifth-graders will qualify, those who do so will tend to be the real stars eventually because of the splendid earlier preparation they get.)

Attrition occurs because students do not succeed in the special class, lose interest, transfer to other schools within the vicinity, move away, or encounter parental (and often teachers' or counselors') objections to their being accelerated in the school's mathematics program.[9]

5. As noted earlier, the two-hour period may be too long for some students' attention span. The younger or less able the student, the more likely this is to occur. But in our special countywide classes we have seen a nine- to ten-year-old boy with an IQ near 200 proceed happily and well through algebra I–III, geometry, trigonometry, and analytic geometry in sixty two-hour periods. The next year his ten-year-old friend did the same thing; he also earned the highest grade in a college course in computer science, competing with seven of our older mathematics prodigies and twelve adults, and made A in a second-level computer course. The more brilliant they are, the earlier they should be identified and helped. But there are few nine- and ten-year-olds as able as these. One fifth-grader (rank 4 in the appendix) at School R was nearly that able, however. In advance it seemed somewhat unlikely that the other two boys in the lower grades (ranks 20.5 and 26) could keep up with the rest of the McCoart class. They were admitted on trial and did quite well, considering their age and grade placement, but scored at the bottom of the twenty-one.

Some of the above five arguments against within-school homogeneously grouped fast-mathematics classes also apply to school-systemwide classes outside school hours. On balance, we prefer that classes be held in the late afternoon, evening, or on Saturday so that they can enroll a more mathematically apt, relatively homogeneous group of twenty to thirty students of the same sex. Where a school has quite a few talented youths, however, and facilities for working with them in available-size groups, it would of course be far better to do this than to wait vainly for a suitable systemwide plan.

---

[9]Year-by-year integration actions of school systems may also cause attrition because of transfers from the school.

CONCLUSION: QUALITY OF SCHOOLING CAN MAKE
A GREAT DIFFERENCE

Many interpreters of the "Coleman Report" (Coleman et al. 1966), especially Jencks et al. (1972), seem to say that quality of schooling is not very important. For high school mathematics, however, it is clear from the special classes we have conducted thus far that type of class and quality of instruction are vital for learning. In *far* fewer hours the students in these classes have learned *far* more mathematics well than they would have in a regular classroom several years later.

A well prepared, fast-pacing instructor is a key element in this instructional package. Homogeneous grouping according to mathematical and verbal reasoning ability is another. High expectations are a third. Concurrent and future opportunities are a fourth; successful students are encouraged to skip school grades, take college courses for credit while still in high school, work for advanced placement credit by examination, enter college full-time early, try mathematics competitions, and the like. Our interest in them is meant to be continuous, at least over the years from the time they are first identified until they complete graduate school and are employed. We are available for consultation on any aspect of their education.

Small class size may be another important feature, but in other programs we have had similar success when there were thirty-one students in a class (see George & Denham, chapter 6 of this volume).

Well-meaning teachers sometimes try one of three types of "enrichment": so-called busy work, irrelevant material (such as a drama class for boys whose major interests are mathematics and science), or really effective procedures that leave the student even more bored in later grades (such as a splendid modern-mathematics program in grades K–7 that leads only to conventional algebra in grade 8). Clearly, we believe that a considerable amount of acceleration in subject matter and/or grade placement must accompany enrichment, or be employed in lieu of it.

These fast-mathematics classes and other aspects of our study cater to individual differences in a persistent attempt to find, study, and develop talent. The principles and procedures we have worked out can be used in other schools and for other subjects. Until they are, intellectually gifted students—particularly those with superb mathematical reasoning ability—will for the most part continue to get little that effectively meets their real intellectual needs.

REFERENCES

Astin, H. S. 1974. Sex differences in mathematical and scientific precocity. In J. C. Stanley, D. P. Keating, and L. H. Fox (eds.), *Mathematical talent: Discovery, description, and development*. Baltimore, Md. 21218: The Johns Hopkins University Press, pp. 70–86.

Bennett, G. K., Bennett, M. G., Clendenen, D. M., Doppelt, J. E., Ricks, Jr., J. H., Seashore, H. G., and Wesman, A. G. 1962. *Academic promise tests.* New York: The Psychological Corporation.

Bennett, G. K., Seashore, H. G., and Wesman, G. A. 1972. *Differential aptitude tests.* New York: The Psychological Corporation.

Coleman, J. S., and Campbell, E. Q., Hobson, C. J., McPartland, J., Mood, A. M., Weinfeld, F. D., and York, R. L. 1966. *Equality of educational opportunity.* Washington, D.C.: U.S. Government Printing Office, OE-38001.

College Entrance Examination Board. 1973. *College Board guide for high schools and colleges, 1973-74.* Princeton, N.J.: College Entrance Examination Board.

Fox, L. H. 1974. A mathematics program for fostering precocious achievement. In J. C. Stanley, D. P. Keating, and Lynn H. Fox (eds.), *Mathematical talent: Discovery, description, and development.* Baltimore, Md. 21218: The Johns Hopkins University Press, pp. 101-25.

Jencks, C., Smith, M., Acland, H., Bane, M. J., Cohen, D., Gintis, H., Heyns, B., and Michelson, S. 1972. *Inequality: A reassessment of the effect of family and schooling in America.* New York: Basic Books.

Raven, J. C. 1958. *Standard progressive matrices: Sets A, B, C, D, and E.* New York: The Psychological Corporation.

Smith, R. R., Lankford, Jr., F. G., and Payne, J. N. 1962. *Contemporary algebra, book one.* New York: Harcourt, Brace & World.

Appendix 7.1

Table 7.A1. Academic Promise Test (APT, Bennett et al. 1962) and Raven's Standard Progressive Matrices (SPM, Raven 1958) scores of 17 preselected boys and 23 preselected girls in the fourth through seventh grades of School R, 19–20 December 1973

Rank on N	Sex	School grade Jan. 1974	Birth date	APT scores (# right) N	V	AR	LU	T	SPM score	Chosen for class?	June 1974 alg. I %iles[a]	Nov. 1974 alg. I %iles[a,q]
1	F	7	Mar. '61	54^b	55^c	37^d	57	203	56	Yes	95	95
2	M	7	Feb. '61	52	47	47	53	199	50	Yes	68	83
3	M	7	Mar. '61	51^e	54^f	48	52	205	60	Yes	99	99.8
4	M	5	Aug. '63	46	51	51	38	186	49	Yes	99.4	–
5.5	M	7	Aug. '61	45^g	44	55	51	195	57	Yes	68	83
5.5	F	7	Apr. '61	45^h	46	39	45	175	52	Yes	49	49
7.5	M	7	July '61	44^i	51^j	51	47	193	48	Yes	95	90
7.5	M	6	July '62	44	48	51	36	179	51	Yes	73	–
9.5	M	7	July '61	43	46	45	40	174	49	Yes	73	73
9.5	M	6	Oct. '62	43	36	42	41	162	49	Yes	68	–
11	F	6	Sept. '62	42	48	52	49	191	56	Yes	73	–
12	F	6	Dec. '62	41	46	50	47	184	55	Yes	90	–
13.5	F	7	July '61	39	44	50	50	183	51	Yes	95	73
13.5	F	7	Oct. '61	39^k	47	46	49	181	53	Yes	49	97
15	F	7	July '61	38^l	40^m	44	47	169	50	Yes	83	95
16.5	F	7	July '60	36^n	36	48	31	151	55	Yes	73	90
16.5	M	7	May '61	36	42	17	34	129	51	Yes^o	–	–
18	F	6	Oct. '62	35	49	45	49	178	45	Yes^p	–	–
20.5	F	6	Feb. '62	33	47	46	48	174	55	Yes	49	33
20.5	F	7	Jan. '61	33	41	49	48	171	48	Yes	49	49
20.5	M	6	July '62	33	37	52	40	162	50	Yes^p	–	–
20.5	M	4	Jan. '64	33	43	49	30	155	48	Yes	18	–
24	F	6	May '62	30	43	48	52	173	47	Yes	39	95
24	F	5	May '63	30	35	43	32	140	43	No	–	–
24	F	7	Oct. '60	30	33	37	33	133	53	No	–	–
26	M	5	Sept. '63	28	36	44	41	149	44	Yes	29	–
27	M	7	July '61	27	41	48	39	155	49	No	–	–
28	M	4	Feb. '64	25	22	36	17	100	43	No	–	–
29	M	4	Aug. '64	23	25	35	17	100	43	No	–	–
30	F	5	Jan. '63	21	26	46	29	122	49	No	–	–
31.5	F	4	Aug. '64	20	32	44	37	133	51	No	–	–
31.5	M	4	July '64	20	30	37	18	105	43	No	–	–
33	F	4	Apr. '64	17	33	45	23	118	47	No	–	–
34.5	F	4	Nov. '63	16	29	30	26	101	49	No	–	–
34.5	F	4	Mar. '64	16	19	45	19	99	46	No	–	–
36.5	M	4	July '64	15	35	42	16	108	46	No	–	–
36.5	F	4	Oct. '64	15	26	31	27	99	35	No	–	–
38	F	4	June '64	13	24	34	20	91	38	No	–	–
39	F	5	Jan. '63	12	24	32	38	106	47	No	–	–
40	F	4	July '64	5	17	25	17	64	37	No	–	–

[a] Ten of the 11 girls were tested on 5 June 1974 with Form B of Educational Testing Service's Cooperative Mathematics Test, algebra I, copyright 1962. The other girl was tested with it on June 11. The 10 boys were tested with Form A on June 7. All testing, except of the absentee girl, was done by Dr. Stanley; Mr. Lerner tested her. The percentile ranks shown here are for the national *eighth-grade* norm group, as provided in the manual for the test.

Table 7.A1 (continued)

The 14 students (9 girls and 5 boys) who continued in the class during the fall were retested on 21 November 1974 by the writer, girls with Form A and boys with Form B. The percentile ranks of their scores are shown in the last column.

[b]By comparison, she made 410 (53rd percentile of a random sample of *male* high school juniors and seniors) on the Scholastic Aptitude Test Mathematical (SAT-M), taken in our January 1974 mathematics talent search. This norm and the norms below are from page 5 of College Entrance Examination Board (1973).

[c]She made 580 (94th percentile of a random sample of high school juniors and seniors) on the Scholastic Aptitude Test Verbal (SAT-V) in the verbal talent search held at The Johns Hopkins University in February 1974.

[d]This score is curiously low, compared with the girl's other four scores. Note that she scored highest of everyone on N, V, and LU. AR was given first. It is a 60-item test with only a 20-minute time limit, so speed plays an important part. SPM, which also measures nonverbal reasoning, is untimed.

[e]SAT-M 570, 86th percentile.

[f]SAT-V 520, 85th percentile.

[g]SAT-M 450, 63rd percentile.

[h]SAT-M 390, 60th percentile.

[i] SAT-M 470, 67th percentile.

[j] SAT-V 540, 88th percentile.

[k]SAT-M 330, 41st percentile.

[l] SAT-M 380, 57th percentile.

[m]SAT-V 420, 63rd percentile.

[n]SAT-M 350, 49th percentile.

[o]See footnote 4 in the text.

[p]These two students dropped out soon after the class began. They were two of the three "Yes" students with Spanish surnames.

[q]On March 6, 1975 all but Nos. 1, 20.5F6, and 24F6 took Form B of the Cooperative Mathematics Test of second-year algebra (i.e., algebra II). Nos. 1 and 24F6 were absent, whereas No. 20.5F6 had dropped out of the class. Their percentile ranks on national norms were as follows (using the order of this table): 67, 99.2, 59, 25, 88, 79, 17, 59, 95, 79, and 48. Then on June 3, 1975 all thirteen students took Form A of the cooperative algebra II test and earned percentile ranks on national norms as follows: 88, 85, 99.7, 38, 95, 97, 75, 59, 85, 98, 79, 43, and 29. To summarize the results, one might say that the class was *highly* successful for four of the five boys and five of the eight girls who completed it. One other girl (the first 13.5) did reasonably well. Only one boy and two girls seemed to need more exposure to second-year algebra before going on to other mathematics courses, and they could get this during the summer. Despite having been taught only one two-hour period per week for one and one-half school years, even the lowest of these three scored better than 29% of high-school students do after studying algebra II for approximately 360 45- or 50-minute periods—and she was only a seventh-grader!

Appendix 7.2

DAT SCORES OF WOLFSON I CLASS

In Fox (1974[I:6]) the progress of nine boys and seven girls through SMPY's first special fast-mathematics class was detailed. Not included there were results of the 12 May 1973 testing of those sixteen highly able youths with the new version of the Differential Aptitude Tests, published by The Psychological Corporation. At that time one was a fourth-grader, ten were seventh-graders, four were eighth-graders, and one was a tenth-grader. Raw scores, percentile ranks by sex on eighth-grade norms, and other information are shown in table 7.A2. Rows are arranged in descending order of total score on DAT.

It is easy to see from the table that numerical ability ranged from five perfect scores (40) to one 33. The corresponding percentile ranks were twelve 99s and four 97s. This is especially remarkable when one considers that end-of-*eighth*-grade norms are being used, whereas only five of the sixteen students were that high in school. The extremely high scores show how well selected for quantitative aptitude the group was a year earlier and also how stimulated it had been mathematically by Mr. Wolfson, Miss Michaels, and Mr. Bates.

The verbal reasoning scores were nearly as high, ranging from two perfect 50s to a 34 and from thirteen 99th percentiles to a 90th percentile. Even the fourth-grader scored at the 95th percentile on VR.

Only one of the eight subtests, Clerical Speed and Accuracy, proved even mildly difficult for the Wolfson I class. On it, however, only four students scored below the 50th percentile of end-of-eighth-grade norms. Physical maturation probably plays a large part in CSA scores.

Only the tenth-grader (who had skipped the ninth grade) attained the 99th percentile of eighth-graders on Mechanical Reasoning, but no one scored below the 75th percentile.

The boy who ranked highest on DAT total score entered The Johns Hopkins University as a full-time student with sophomore standing in the fall of 1974 at age fourteen years nine months. During the first semester he took sophomore physics, advanced calculus, introduction to number theory, and American government, making excellent grades.

The boy who ranked only one point lower on DAT-Total also began college advanced calculus that fall, as a part-time student. He did well the first semester and continued with it during the second semester.

The person who ranked generally lowest on the DAT (a seventh-grade boy) was also the poorest achiever in the class. The person who ranked seventh on the DAT (a seventh-grade girl), was not an excellent achiever; she was next to the bottom of the group by the end of the course period. This occurred even though on APT Verbal Reasoning she earned one of the only two perfect scores. Both of these students who "underachieved" in the Wolfson I class have subsequently moved ahead well in their regular school mathematics classes. The latter skipped the ninth grade.

As of the middle of the 1974–75 school year all sixteen of these students seem to be doing well in school. Their grade placement ranges from ninth grade, with tenth-grade chemistry and eleventh-grade calculus (the former fourth-grader), to middle-of-sophomore-year status at Johns Hopkins (the former eighth-grader whose DAT scores are shown in the first row of the table). The boys have progressed much faster and better than the girls, only one of whom has

Table 7.A2. Differential Aptitude Test (Bennett, Seashore, and Wesman 1972) raw scores (RS) and percentile ranks (PR) of the 16 Wolfson I students on the 8 subtests of Form S, administered 12 May 1973

Student[a]	School grade 1972–73	Sex	Numerical ability		Verbal reasoning		Abstract reasoning		Language usage		Spelling		Space relations		Mechanical reasoning		Clerical speed and accuracy	
			RS	PR[b]	RS	PR	RS	PR	RS	PR	RS	PR	RS	PR	RS	PR	RS	PR
6	8[c]	M	40	99	50	99	47	99	49	99	99	99	59	99	58	95	52	90
1	8	M	37	99	48	99	49	99	57	99	97	99	60	99	57	90	48	85
2	10[d]	M	37	99	48	99	48	99	47	97	91	97	60	99	67	99	40	55
3	7	M	40	99	49	99	48	99	53	99	94	99	50	97	57	90	45	75
4	7	F	37	99	46	99	44	97	56	99	94	97	47	97	50	95	57	90
10	7	F	39	99	49	99	46	99	52	99	84	90	53	99	50	95	57	90
11	7	F	37	99	50	99	46	99	55	99	97	99	47	97	53	97	41	40
15	7	F	35	97	47	99	47	99	51	99	94	97	51	99	45	85	53	85
7	8[c]	M	40	99	45	99	49	99	37	90	89	97	55	99	52	80	48	85
9	8	F	40	99	42	97	50	99	43	90	89	95	55	99	55	97	39	35
12	7	M	40	99	46	99	41	90	48	97	87	95	45	95	58	95	38	50
13	7	F	36	99	47	99	45	97	48	97	95	99	41	95	43	75	46	60
5	7	M	35	97	48	99	41	90	46	97	96	99	33	75	53	80	42	65
21	7	F	38	99	45	99	47	99	47	95	94	97	31	75	43	75	36	25
8	4	M	34	97	38	95	46	97	37	90	78	90	43	95	53	80	42	65
16	7	M	33	97	34	90	44	95	39	90	54	50	45	95	55	85	35	35

[a] The code numbers used are the same as in Fox (1974[1:6]). They are the ranks on the algebra I test administered to the group in August 1972, after only 18 hours of instruction (except for nos. 1, 9, and 21, who neither took algebra I in school nor joined the class until September 1972).
[b] Percentile ranks shown are national spring-of-eighth-grade sex norms, which differ somewhat in boys and girls. For example, student no. 5 scored higher on numerical ability than 97 out of 100 male eighth-graders do in the spring.
[c] Skipped the seventh grade.
[d] Skipped the ninth grade.

even skipped a school grade. Just two of the nine boys have not skipped at least one grade, and one of those has been taking college courses for credit regularly part-time. It seems clear that this first of our special fast-mathematics classes had enormous facilitating effects on the boys, and moderate ones on some of the girls. Such success is due, we believe, to the superb teaching and stimulating ability of Mr. Wolfson with an extremely able group that with a single exception—the tenth-grader—had not yet taken even one algebra course in school.

The success of the Wolfson II, Fox, and McCoart classes (see chapters 6, 9, and 7, respectively, of this volume) indicates that the effects were not unique to the first class or to Mr. Wolfson. This out-of-school type class is a powerful way to look after mathematical needs of quantitatively highly apt youths. The concepts and techniques should be readily adaptable to other subjects. From many standpoints it would seem desirable (though not necessarily as effective) to have the classes conducted by the school system itself, rather than by an outside agency such as a university. Alternatively, the school system might contract with the outside agency to set up classes and supervise them. Such classes should enroll only unusually able students, not less than the upper few percent of the age group in that system. Even most of those probably could not progress as fast as the Wolfson I and II classes, which consisted of students extremely highly selected for mathematical aptitude from several counties.

In addition to the systemwide classes, special classes or groups within individual junior high schools located in talent-rich areas will be needed. The McCoart and Wagner classes at School R and other within-school classes in progress with SMPY's help explore how this can be done best. Of course, the less able the group the less swiftly and well it can move through the mathematics curriculum.

Even the mathematically most apt 5 or 10 percent within a school system need special opportunities, however, such as having algebra I available in the eighth or even the seventh grade. Every effort should be made to see that such students are encouraged and helped to complete courses in calculus, computer science, and finite mathematics before being graduated from high school. The most successful of them should take the Advanced Placement Program examination in calculus, offered each year (usually in May), and thereby earn college credit. As Fox points out in chapter 9 of this volume, most quantitatively able girls will probably need more special stimulation and encouragement than boys.

8
VERBALLY GIFTED YOUTH: SELECTION AND DESCRIPTION[1]

Peter V. McGinn

ABSTRACT

The Study of Verbally Gifted Youth is a five-year project designed to identify talented young people who as adults will contribute to the improvement of our society. The study also seeks to learn more about the nature of this giftedness and to develop effective methods of facilitating the education of such students.

Two hundred eighty-seven, seventh- and eighth-graders participated in the First Verbal Talent Search and earned SAT-Verbal (SAT-V) scores equivalent to those of high school juniors. Sixty-five students with SAT-V scores ≥ 570 completed additional tests of verbal ability, creativity, and social insight, earning scores similar to those of college students. Personality tests indicated that the students were socially mature and possessed a number of traits conducive to achievement, although the descriptions of boys and girls in the sample differed in a number of respects.

Thirty-one of the high SAT-V students participated in a college-level summer enrichment program—either creative writing or introductory social science. We are using student achievement in the program as a measure of the adequacy of our assessment techniques. Results are suggestive but ambiguous, and a replication of the talent search and summer program is planned.

An ideal educational system would enable each individual to develop his abilities and interests fully and, consequently, would satisfy society's needs for an array of diverse talents. Public education in America falls far short of this goal; recent educational innovations have produced mixed blessings in the light of this ideal. The emphasis in the late 1950s on mathematics, science, and engineering was both understandable and one-sided. The current interest in

[1] I thank Drs. Robert Hogan, Catherine Garvey, Roger Webb, and Julian Stanley for their helpful comments on an earlier version of this paper, and Marilyn McGinn, Mary Viernstein, Sandra Bond, and Steven Daurio for their assistance in the data collection and analyses.

disadvantaged students is quite laudable and in the spirit of the goals of education, but it is still too narrow. It is imperative that educators also recognize the needs of the verbally and humanistically gifted, and facilitate the realization of their potential. In a book entitled *Excellence*, Gardner (1961) observed that, "A society such as ours is dependent upon many kinds of achievement, many kinds of complex understanding. It requires large numbers of individuals with depth of judgment, perspective and a broad comprehension of the problems facing our world (p. 35)."

The Study of Verbally Gifted Youth is a response to this need. It is a five-year project being conducted at The Johns Hopkins University under a grant from the Spencer Foundation. In a number of respects, e.g., in terms of methods used to identify students in the first year of the study, SVGY has been modeled after the Study of Mathematically Precocious Youth (SMPY) undertaken by Professor Julian C. Stanley, also at Johns Hopkins, and also funded by the Spencer Foundation. SMPY has been extensively described elsewhere (Stanley, Keating, & Fox 1974, and the present volume).

This paper reports the results of the first talent search of the Study of Verbally Gifted Youth. First, I will review the results of a method using tests to identify verbal talent (psychometric approach). Then I will discuss in some detail two very high-scoring subsamples derived from this approach. The important questions to be examined are: What type of talent was identified by this psychometric method? What patterns emerge from the data that confirm the adequacy of this strategy or suggest the need for revision? How can the Study of Verbally Gifted Youth be improved?

The major conceptual problems of this study concern the definition and identification of verbal and humanistic giftedness in children. We hope to select young people who as adults will contribute to the improvement of our society and facilitate their education and development. The nature of the link between childhood behavior and such performance as an adult is still unclear. Terman's pioneering work in this field suggests that a high IQ is a major factor in success in later life (Terman & Oden 1947), but other interpretations of his results are possible (e.g., McClelland 1973).[2, 3]

The present study has been operating under the assumption that identification and definition can be simultaneous complementary processes. In order to avoid a possibly premature commitment to a fuller and intellectually more satisfying definition, we have used an operational definition of giftedness, i.e., a high score on a measure of verbal ability. Based on the success of Professor Stanley in using the College Entrance Examination Board's Scholastic Apti-

---

[2]McClelland's article in the *American Psychologist* has received substantial criticism. See "Comments" in January 1974 issue of the *American Psychologist*.

[3]Additional controversy involves the definitions of intelligence and success. See, for example, "The intelligence/creativity distinction" (Wallach 1971) and the exchange between Chomsky (1972) and Herrnstein (1972).

tude Test to find youngsters talented in mathematics and science, we have employed the verbal section of the Scholastic Aptitude Test (SAT-V) as an initial selection device. The SAT-V is most commonly administered to high school juniors and seniors who intend to apply to college. It is a broad test of developed verbal ability, measuring such skills as reading comprehension, verbal reasoning, and vocabulary—skills needed for successful performance in college courses.

DESCRIPTION OF TALENT SEARCH SAMPLE

Two hundred eighty-seven twelve- and thirteen-year-old students participated in the first Verbal Talent Search. Each had previously scored at or above the 98th percentile of national norms on a standardized measure of verbal achievement. All students completed the verbal and mathematical sections of the SAT, the Allport–Vernon–Lindzey Study of Values, a family background questionnaire, and a biographical inventory adapted from the one developed by Schaefer (1970).[4]

In table 8.1 the SAT scores of the talent search sample are compared with those of college-bound juniors and seniors tested in 1972–73 (Educational Testing Service 1974). Although apparently a homogeneous group (all students scored in the 98th or 99th percentile on a grade-appropriate test), the talent search students earned scores ranging from 230 to 680 on the SAT-V. Their average of 445 is comparable to the 443 earned by the norm group.

Several other features concerning the data in table 8.1 should be noted. First, on both the SAT-V and the SAT-M, eighth-grade boys and eighth-grade girls earned significantly higher ($p < .002$) scores than their seventh-grade counterparts. Although longitudinal data would be preferable and other explanations are possible, this suggests that the abilities measured by the SAT increase rapidly in bright students during the junior high school years.

Second, the eighth-grade students in this Verbal Talent Search sample scored significantly higher (boys, $p < .02$; girls, $p < .002$) than the norm group on SAT-V, but were not significantly different from the norm on SAT-M.[5]

---

[4]All instruments were administered during a single, large test session, except the Biographical Inventory which was completed at home.

[5]Three explanations are possible for this discrepancy. To quality for the Verbal Talent Search, students needed certification of high ability on a standardized measure of verbal ability but not mathematical ability. In addition, there was probably some degree of self-selection to participate in either the Verbal Talent Search or the Mathematical Talent Search of SMPY on the part of students who qualified for both, i.e., students would likely participate in the contest for which they judged their interest and ability were greater. The contests were conducted at the same university within one month of each other and qualifying students could participate in the one of their choice. Finally, the scores may have been influenced by the order of administration, SAT-V first, and the greater motivation of verbal talent search students to perform well on SAT-V. It is not likely that

Table 8.1. Comparison of SAT-V and SAT-M scores of Verbal Talent Search students with a norm group of college-bound juniors and seniors

		Boys		Girls	
		SAT-V	SAT-M	SAT-V	SAT-M
7th grade[a]	N	52	52	67	67
	Mean	410	434	393	396
	SD	77	90	86	80
8th grade[b]	N	65	65	103	103
	Mean	476	490	476	447
	SD	90	91	91	79
Norm[c]	Mean	443	503	443	460
	SD	107	116	107	105

[a]Includes two 6th-grade students.
[b]Includes four under-age 9th-grade students.
[c]N=1,349,271 juniors and seniors tested in 1972–73. Separate norms by sex are given for SAT-M, but not for SAT-V.

Third, for both seventh- and eighth-graders there was no difference between boys and girls on level of verbal ability, but boys were significantly higher on mathematical ability (seventh grade, $p < .02$; eighth grade, $p < .002$). Evidence will be presented below, however, that indicates sex differences in verbal talent or interest, despite equivalence of scores (see chapter 9 for discussion of sex differences in mathematical talent).

Demographic Data and the SAT

The relationship of SAT scores and family background was examined in several ways. Correlations of SAT-V with parental education and occupation are presented in table 8.2, along with correlations of SAT-V with student characteristics. Education and occupation of each parent were rated on a five-point scale as explained in table 8.2. Girls' scores are significantly related to both paternal and maternal variables. Only maternal variables are significant for the boys.[6] It must be remembered, however, that the present group is different from the general population in two ways. Students are far above the average in verbal ability and, as can be seen in table 8.A1 (appendix), their

---

relative strength of verbal or mathematical ability in the student population played a role. As Keating (1974 [I:2] and chapter 2 of this volume) demonstrated, mathematically talented eighth-graders are very capable of exceeding the high school average on SAT-M.

[6]Partially analyzed data from the 1974 Talent Search show weaker correlations between SAT and parental variables. Only the correlations of girls' SAT-V with fathers' educational and occupational levels are significant.

Table 8.2. Correlations between students' scores on SAT-V and demographic and biographic characteristics[a]

	Boys		Girls	
	N	r	N	r
Educational level of father[b]	115	.07	158	.42*
Occupational level of father[c]	105	.18	144	.41*
Educational level of mother	113	.35*	165	.37*
Occupational level of mother	63	.27[†]	91	.28[†]
Level of first occupational choice of student	112	.00	158	.14
Student's liking for school[d]	117	−.09	170	−.06
Number of older siblings	117	−.11	170	−.03
Number of younger siblings	117	.04	170	−.11

[†]$p < .05$ [†]$p < .01$ *$p < .001$

[a]All data were obtained from a questionnaire completed by students during the talent search test session. N's are variable because of incomplete or uncodable data and because many mothers are housewives, for which no occupational code is assigned.
[b]Education was coded on five categories: some high school, high school graduate, some college, college graduate, more than college.
[c]Occupation was coded on five categories: semiskilled and unskilled workers; skilled workers; technicians and owners of petty businesses; semiprofessionals, minor professionals, executives of medium-sized firms, and administrators of small businesses; major professionals and executives of large firms.
[d]Liking for school was coded in four categories: nonexistent, slight, fair, and strong.

parents are generally highly educated and cluster in the top occupational categories.[7]

The other biographical and demographic characteristics reported in table 8.2 are unrelated to SAT-V scores. Thus the important question appears to be not how does SAT-V relate to these characteristics, but rather what are the characteristics of this unusual sample of very bright students? Table 8.3 allows such a description.[8] Over half of the students aspire to the top occupational category—i.e., major professionals and executives of large firms. This is true for both males and females. Moreover, students in both groups report a generally favorable attitude toward school, with over 85 percent in the fair or strong liking categories. Finally, almost half of the students in this highly able sample are first-born.

[7]It would be incorrect, however, to assume that there is a sharp restriction of range in students' intellectual ability. As was noted above, students' scores ranged from 230 to 680 on SAT-V. Caution is needed in interpreting these correlational data not because of restriction of range but because the sample is so atypical.
[8]The *Equality of Educational Opportunity* report by Coleman et al. (1966) provides some comparison data collected from a national sample of 97,000 twelfth-graders. The largest single group of those students (35 percent) anticipates a professional position when they have completed their education. Another 34 percent selected categories including unskilled, semiskilled, skilled, and technical occupations.

Table 8.3.   Distribution of students' responses on selected biographic and demographic variables

	Males	Females
First occupational choice		
Unskilled, semiskilled, and skilled workers;		
technicians; owners of petty businesses	14%	13%
Semiprofessionals, minor professionals, executives of		
medium-sized firms, administrators of small businesses	20	34
Major professionals and executives of large firms	66	51
Housewives		2
Liking for school		
Slight or nonexistent	15	6
Fair	60	61
Strong	26	33
Number of older siblings		
0	42	51
1	32	25
2	15	9
3	7	11
4+	4	5
Number of younger siblings		
0	33	34
1	36	31
2	19	23
3	7	7
4+	5	4

Biographical Inventory

Most students participating in the 1973 Talent Search also completed a biographical inventory. A summary of their responses provides a general description of the interests and activities of a sample of very bright junior high school students. The data which are presented in table 8.4 also permit an examination of sex differences in such a sample.

Most of the students have several close friends in school, friends who are usually near their own age. As a group, they enjoy reading. Approximately half the students read over thirty books per year. Although few participate regularly in cultural activities, such as attending concerts, most do play musical instruments. Many students report involvement in projects to the extent of skipping meals and staying up late. Although low on some indicators of active fantasy life, such as number of imaginary childhood companions, most of the students report vivid memories and occasional or frequent daydreaming.

As noted above, there are sex differences. On the average, girls have a greater number of hobbies. In addition, the types of activities in which boys and girls participate are somewhat different. Both groups include many avid

Table 8.4.   Percentages of responses on selected biographic items

Boys—first row, N=80; Girls—second row, N=125						
	p	0	1	2	3	4
Number of present hobbies	< .05	2.5	7.5	17.5	30.0	42.5
		0.0	3.2	16.0	20.0	60.8

	p	Younger	Same	Older	Older & Younger	Other
Age of friends	NS	2.6	42.3	11.5	21.8	21.8
		0.8	42.7	9.7	23.4	23.4

	p	0	1	2	3	4
Number close friends in school	NS	3.8	8.8	21.3	11.3	55.0
		2.4	8.8	16.0	17.6	55.2

	p	Yes	No
Spend much free time reading	< .1	73.8	26.3
		85.6	14.4

	p	0–5	6–10	11–30	31–50	Over 50
Number of books read in a year	NS	6.3	25.0	31.3	20.0	17.5
		4.0	14.4	31.2	21.6	28.8

	p	Never	Seldom	Occasionally	Frequently
Frequency of writing for enjoyment	< .001	43.8	30.0	20.0	6.3
		14.4	30.4	33.6	21.6

	p	Yes	No
Art or writing hobby	< .001	25.0	75.0
		60.0	40.0

	p	No	1	2–5	6–10	10
Invented something, wrote original story, song, etc.	< .1	6.3	13.8	40.0	11.3	28.8
		6.4	6.4	28.0	12.8	46.4

	p	Yes	No
Private art lessons	< .005	7.5	92.5
		25.8	74.2

	p	Yes	No
Craft lessons	< .05	33.8	66.3
		52.0	48.0

	p	Never	Seldom	Occasionally	Frequently
Visit art museums	< .005	10.0	57.5	26.3	6.3
		8.9	32.3	50.8	8.1

Table 8.4 (continued)

		Never	Seldom	Occa-sionally	Fre-quently	
Attend plays	< .005	21.5	48.1	29.1	1.3	
		9.6	39.2	40.8	10.4	
		Never	Seldom	Occa-sionally	Fre-quently	
Attend concerts	NS	30.0	40.0	23.8	6.3	
		20.8	42.4	28.0	8.8	
		Yes	No			
Play musical instrument	< .05	55.9	44.2			
		71.0	29.0			
		Yes	No			
Role in a play	NS	43.8	56.3			
		55.2	44.8			
		Never	Seldom	Occa-sionally	Fre-quently	
Involvement in project (e.g., skipping meals)	NS	12.5	26.3	30.0	31.3	
		9.6	17.6	36.8	36.0	
		Never	Seldom	Occa-sionally	Fre-quently	
Vivid memories	< .005	2.5	11.3	46.3	40.0	
		0.0	4.8	28.8	66.4	
		0	1	2	3	
Number of imaginary friends as a child	< .01	75.0	13.8	5.0	6.3	
		52.8	21.6	7.2	18.4	
		0	1	2	3	4
Number of childhood fears	< .1	15.0	21.3	36.3	15.0	12.5
		17.6	19.2	20.0	24.8	18.4
		Never	Seldom	Occa-sionally	Fre-quently	
Daydreams	< .01	10.0	28.8	40.0	21.3	
		3.2	20.0	34.4	42.4	
		Yes	No			
Science hobby	< .005	41.3	58.8			
		19.2	80.8			

Table 8.4 (continued)

		Yes	No
Created mechanical or electronic object	< .001	42.5 5.6	57.5 94.4
		Yes	No
Membership in science club or organization outside of school	NS	51.3 44.8	48.8 55.2

readers, but the girls engage in writing to a much greater degree than the boys. They also report more interest in arts and crafts and participate slightly more often in cultural activities. Finally, as assessed by such items as tendency to daydream, the girls have a significantly greater degree of imagination. Boys display a higher level of activity than the girls, however, in science hobbies and interest in mechanical and electronic objects.

The items selected for use in the talent search questionnaire were based upon assumptions about the kinds of activities which foster or signify verbal and humanistic giftedness. Generally speaking, the typical student in the talent search is active, with a wide range of interests, imaginative, and sociable. On the basis of this inventory, however, the girls as a group seem to conform more closely to the type of student for whom the talent search was directed.

Study of Values

The Study of Values (Allport, Vernon, & Lindzey 1970) assesses the relative importance of six basic interests or motives in personality—theoretical, economic, aesthetic, social, political, and religious. Its six scales are scored in an ipsative fashion—i.e., the test is designed so that 40 is the average for any value. Scores on the various values may range from approximately 10 to approximately 70. Generally speaking, a person is characterized by how much above or below this midpoint he is on each scale. There are separate norms for each sex, however, and the test manual recommends that an examinee's scores be compared with the norms for the appropriate sex.

In table 8.5, the talent search boys are compared with a norm group composed of tenth-, eleventh-, and twelfth-grade boys (Allport, Vernon, & Lindzey 1970). As a group, SVGY boys scored highest on the theoretical and political and lowest on the religious values. They could be described as intellectual and competitive. Compared with the norm group, however, they appear less pragmatic and more considerate of others.

Table 8.5. Comparison of average Study of Values scores of Verbal Talent Search boys with those of a norm group of high school boys reported by Allport, Vernon, and Lindzey (1970)

	SVGY (N=109)		Norm (N=5320)	
	$\overline{X}$	SD	$\overline{X}$	SD
Theoretical	44.85	7.01	43.32	6.40*
Economic	40.85	6.99	42.81	6.86[†]
Aesthetic	36.71	8.00	35.14	7.75*
Social	40.67	7.92	37.05	6.25[‡]
Political	42.08	6.86	43.17	5.92
Religious	34.70	8.57	37.93	8.31[‡]

*p < .05
[†]p < .01
[‡]p < .001

In a similar manner, girls are compared with the female norm group in table 8.6. The talent search girls peak on the Social and Aesthetic scales and score lowest on the Economic scale. Social and aesthetic persons may be described as kind and sympathetic, but also individualistic. These traits appear much stronger in the SVGY girls than in the norm group. In addition their scores indicate they are more intellectual and competitive, but much less pragmatic or religiously oriented.

Using tables 8.5 and 8.6, it is also possible to compare the boys and girls in the talent search. Boys score significantly higher on the Theoretical (p < .002), Economic (p < .002), and Political scales (p < .05), and lower on the Aesthetic, Social, and Religious scales (all are p < .002). Speculating on the results of the Study of Values in conjunction with the biographical inventory, I would like to suggest that these girls may be more likely than the boys to respond

Table 8.6. Comparison of average Study of Values scores of Verbal Talent Search girls with those of a norm group of high school girls reported by Allport, Vernon, and Lindzey (1970)

	SVGY (N=15ʹ)		Norm (N=5320)	
	$\overline{X}$	SD	$\overline{X}$	SD
Theoretical	39.01	7.60	37.04	6.86*
Economic	34.50	7.06	38.17	6.33*
Aesthetic	41.58	8.47	38.23	7.14*
Social	46.21	7.26	43.27	6.93*
Political	40.19	6.35	39.05	5.92[†]
Religious	38.58	7.40	43.75	8.12*

*p < .05
[†]p < .001

imaginatively and creatively to their experience. However, they may be less likely than the boys to systematize their ideas and convince other persons of their worth.

DESCRIPTION OF THE HIGH VERBAL SAMPLE

To explore in greater detail the concomitants of verbal giftedness as measured by SAT-V, a high verbal sample was selected. Of the 287 students in the Verbal Talent Search and 667 in the Mathematical Talent Search conducted by SMPY, 65 students scored 570 or greater on the SAT-V. They were invited to return for additional testing and were administered several personality inventories and ability measures. The Study of Verbally Gifted Youth did not itself test all of these students; some were tested by the SMPY. In addition, not all students took all of the tests. Furthermore, some of the students were tested in 1972, and only 1973 data were considered in the present analyses. Therefore, I specify in table 8.7 the number of students tested with each instrument.

Results

As shown in table 8.7, this group of students is exceptionally able. The mean score on the SAT-V (615) was at approximately the 90th percentile of college-bound juniors and seniors who take the SAT; on the SAT-Mathematics the average (587) corresponded to approximately the 75th percentile. It should be noted, however, that the inclusion of "winners" from the Study of Mathematically Precocious Youth inflates this latter score.[9] This does not diminish the fact that this is a very bright group of junior high school students.

Further evidence for this conclusion can also be seen in table 8.7. The Terman Concept Mastery Test (CMT) is a high-level intelligence test. Although it would probably be inaccurate to consider it an adequate measure of intelligence in the sense of sampling broadly from the universe of intelligent behaviors, a high score reflects facility with words and good verbal reasoning. Educational, vocational, and avocational history and activities would presumably have a large influence on a score. It is impressive, therefore, that the average student in this group scored 67.5, which is roughly equivalent to the mean score (73) obtained by Air Force captains, who were college graduates (Terman 1956).

The Modern Language Aptitude Test (MLAT) was selected for use with these students because it deals with basic verbal skills, such as the ability to derive meaning from symbols, although its value for purposes other than

---

[9]Eighteen males with an average SAT-M of 701 increases the average for the total group by 44 points.

Table 8.7. Average performance on seven tests by students with SAT-V scores greater than or equal to 570

Test	Total Group N	Total Group Mean	Boys N	Boys Mean	Girls N	Girls Mean	Norm Group	Mean
SAT-V	65	615.1	37	617.8	28	611.4	College-bound jrs. & srs.	443
SAT-M	65	587.4	37	631.9	28	528.6	College-bound jrs. & srs.	482
CMT-Part 1	54	31.9	29	34.0	25	29.4		
Part 2	54	35.6	29	39.0	25	31.6		
Total	54	67.5	29	73.1	25	61.0	College-grads	73
Modern Language Aptitude Test	47	69.3	21	73.9	26	65.6	College freshmen	61.2
Chapin Social Insight Test	44	22.2	21	21.9	23	22.5	High school students	15.7
Remote Associates Test	48	16.0	22	15.6	26	16.4	UCLA freshmen	16.02
Barron-Welsh	53	22.3	30	19.9	23	25.4	Unselected adult males	13.9

Note: Very few of the high SAT-M boys who were winners of the Mathematical Talent Search of SMPY were administered all seven of these tests in 1973. This factor accounts for most of the discrepancies in the number of students for each test.

predicting second language learning has not been established. The average score obtained by the boys in our group was 73.9; for girls it was 65.6. These figures correspond to the 75th and 50th percentiles for college freshmen of the comparable sex (Carroll & Sapon 1959).

In line with the rationale for the Study of Verbally Gifted Youth, the Chapin Social Insight Test was used as a measure of social judgment. Gough (1965) characterized high scorers on the Chapin as perceptive, imaginative, and sensitive to nuances of the behavior of others. Further, he reported a positive correlation with being described as a good leader and a negative correlation with inflexibility and lack of interpersonal understanding. In our sample, the mean score was 22.2. This is slightly below the average score reported for college students, but well above the average for high school students.

Two tests designed to measure creativity were also included in the battery —the Remote Associates Test (RAT) and the Barron–Welsh Art Scale. The developers of the RAT defined the creative thinking process as "the forming of associative elements into new combinations which either meet specified require-ments or are in some way useful" (Mednick & Mednick 1967, p. 1). The test presents stimuli which are related through networks of low probability asso-ciates and for which the student must supply the missing link. For example, in the item: cookies, sixteen, heart, the answer is sweet. Students in our sample had an average score approximately equal to UCLA freshmen.

The Barron–Welsh Art Scale is a section of the Welsh Figure Preference Test. In research at the Institute of Personality Assessment and Research at Berkeley, Barron (1965) found positive correlations with originality and verbal fluency, and negative correlations with rigidity. The scores of the present sample exceed those of unselected adults but are far below the mean scores of artists and art students, which are reported to be approximately 40.

On each of the scales discussed thus far, this group of junior high school students, selected on the basis of high SAT-V scores, performs at a level comparable to college students or adults. Within the group, there are different strengths and weaknesses when individuals are considered. Nevertheless, in an analogy to golf, it is as if each student had been given a handicap of fifteen strokes. No matter how students compare to each other on various skills, most will be well above the average of his or her age-mates in the general population.

Of the three measures that were used to explore the personological characteristics of the gifted—the California Psychological Inventory, the Myers–Briggs Type Indicator, and the Holland Self-Directed Search—only the CPI was administered to a sufficiently large proportion of this high SAT-V sample to be discussed at this point.

In figures 8.1 and 8.2, the group profiles on the CPI are plotted for males and females.[10] There are several features of these profiles that are worth noting. First, as a group these students are reasonably well adjusted. In addition, they appear more mature than their age-mates, i.e., for both males and females the group profile is closer to the adult norms than is a random sample of eighth-graders tested by Lessinger and Martinson (1961). Furthermore, both sexes peaked on two significant scales—flexibility and achievement via independence—suggesting they are not only intelligent but also independent, imaginative, original, and spontaneous. They may also be somewhat lazy or careless, but they have the intellectual ability to compensate for those traits.

DESCRIPTION OF THE SUMMER ENRICHMENT SAMPLE

The last subpopulation of students I will discuss is the group that participated in our summer enrichment program. Forty-five high SAT-V students were invited to take part in either a writing course or an introductory social science course to be sponsored by the Study of Verbally Gifted Youth, and thirty-one accepted.[11] Preliminary analysis revealed no striking differences

[10]Because of the inclusion of high SAT-M boys in this high verbal sample, there is a large degree of overlap with the sample discussed by Haier and Denham (see chapter 11).

[11]High SAT-V students who were first identified by SMPY and were winners in their talent search were not invited. In addition, students whom we had previously learned would not be available during the summer were not asked to participate. This accounts for the difference between sixty-five high SAT-V students and forty-five invited students.

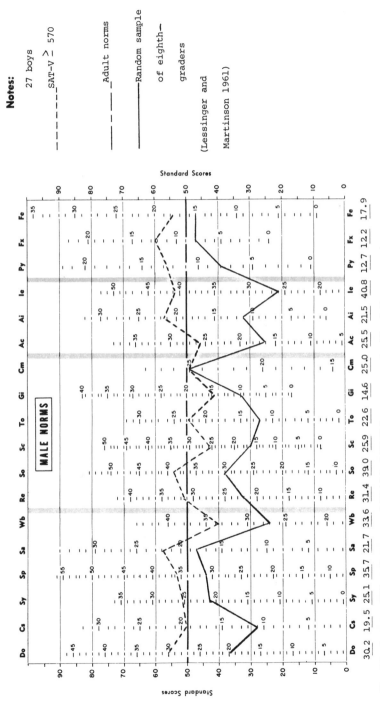

Fig. 8.1. Average CPI performance of 27 high SAT-V boys compared with adult norms and eighth-grade random group.

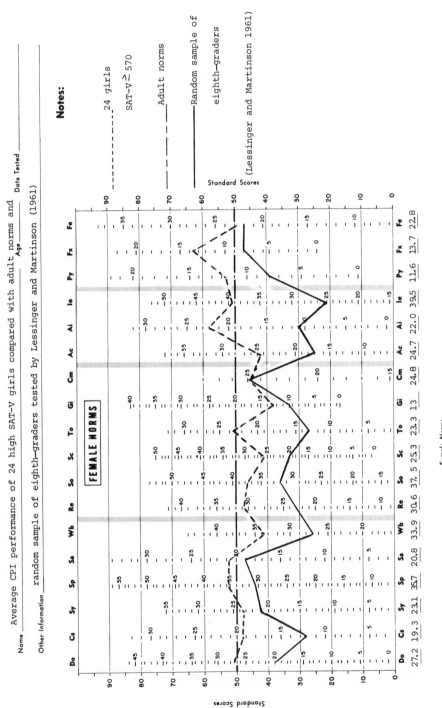

Fig. 8.2. Average CPI performance of 24 high SAT-V girls compared with adult norms and eighth-

between those who accepted and those who declined, and therefore further analyses were not carried out.

The summer program was especially designed for these students. However, it was conducted at a level that was considered appropriate for college students. The courses demanded independent work and reading and fostered sustained and objective discussions of the subject matter. Each student also participated in a productive thinking program based on the course developed by Covington, Crutchfield, Davies, and Olton (1972).

We have profiles for twenty-nine of the thirty-one students in the summer program on the Myers–Briggs Type Indicator and twenty-seven on the Holland Self-Directed Search. The Myers–Briggs is derived from Jungian theory wherein types are defined in terms of how people use their minds, e.g., is more attention devoted to the outside world or to the world of inner experience? There are four pairs of scales in table 8.8—Extraversion-Introversion, Sensing-Intuition, Thinking-Feeling, and Judgment-Perception. For each pair, the individual receives a letter score that indicates direction of preference along with a number score showing its reported strength. It is not possible to reconstruct individual profiles from table 8.8, but it is clear that no single profile could characterize all of the individuals in the group. Nevertheless, considered all together, the males appear to be analytical, insightful, and intellectually curious. The females share this insightfulness and intellectual curiosity. They will probably be less concerned with abstract analyses, however, and more with interpersonal understanding. Data presented by Myers (1962) suggest that the boys resemble scientists and architects, while the girls are more similar to writers. In both groups the preference for intuition over sensing is high. This is generally found in creative groups, although certainly it is not a sufficient condition for creativity.

Table 8.8. Percent and mean strength of preferences on the Myers–Briggs Type Indicator by boys and girls in the 1973 summer program

Scale	Code	Boys (N = 12)		Girls (N = 17)	
		%	Mean	%	Mean
Extraversion	E	25	17.7	47	21
Introversion	I	75	14.1	53	22
Sensing	S	08	5	0	–
Intuition	N	92	30.3	100	34.2
Thinking	T	58	21.9	12*	9
Feeling	F	42	15.8	88	27.4
Judgment	J	33	28	29	20.6
Perception	P	67	25	71	33.5

*$\chi^2 = 5.1178$, p < .025

The second instrument, the Self-Directed Search (SDS—Holland 1973), finds its origins in the world of vocational counseling. The rationale is that environmental opportunities and a child's special heredity lead to preferences for certain types of activities. With age there is increasing differentiation of preferred activities, competencies, and values, which in turn constitute a personality type. Using the SDS, the individual checks his activities, competencies, and occupational preferences. A score, 0–15, is derived for each of the six occupational categories listed in table 8.9 (i.e., Artistic, Social, Enterprising, Conventional, Realistic, and Investigative). A person's profile (three-lettered code) consists of the three categories with the highest scores, e.g., AIS. Results for the summer enrichment sample are shown in table 8.9.

Table 8.9. Average scores of summer participants on Holland's Self-Directed Search

Scale	Code	Boys (N=12)	Girls (N=15)
Realistic	R	3.9	1.9
Investigative	I	12.6	9.1
Artistic	A	4.3	11.5
Social	S	5.3	7.3
Enterprising	E	5.2	2.4
Conventional	C	1.5	0.9

Using Holland's SDS terminology, the boys as a group can best be described as investigative.[12] This is the type characteristic of a scientist or mathematician. Such a type may be described as analytical, curious, introspective, and precise. The girls also scored highly on the investigative type, but even more highly on the artistic type.[13] Such a person would be more at ease dealing with ambiguity, more idealistic, and more imaginative. Certainly these descriptions do not apply uniformly to all the individuals in the sample. Nevertheless, the descriptions of the group which they yield are provocative. They suggest that a group selected on the basis of high verbal ability also has characteristics that are conducive to achievement. Males and females with equivalent ability, however, reveal different preferences and traits. Using only these tests as a guide the sexes would be expected to seek different vocations and make contributions that are qualitatively dissimilar.

[12]Ten of twelve boys had their highest score on I, but the remainder of the three letter codes were quite variable.

[13]All fifteen girls had A in their three letter profile. For eleven of them it was their highest score. I was the first letter for three girls, and was included in thirteen three-letter profiles altogether. S was also the highest score in three cases, and was included in eleven profiles altogether. (Ties are possible, which accounts for having seventeen "highest" scores for only fifteen students.)

SUMMER PERFORMANCE AS A CRITERION

At the end of the summer program each student was rated on a scale from zero to three by the project director, the instructor of the social science or writing course, and the instructor of the creative thinking course. These were personal judgments of each student's ability to profit from the summer enrichment courses. As such, the ratings probably had two components: an estimation of the student's promise and a prediction of the likelihood that he would make use of this talent. The interrater correlations are presented in table 8.10. All are significant, $p < .02$. Although the ratings were made independently, these individuals had discussed students during the course of the program, so complete independence cannot be guaranteed. In addition, the raters had access to the students' scores on the various tests and inventories prior to the time they made their ratings, but they did not refer to these when making their ratings.[14]

Table 8.10. Interrater correlations for rating of performance in summer program

	Writing instructor		Social science instructor		Creative thinking instructor	
	r	(N)	r	(N)	r	(N)
Creative thinking instructor	.72	(14)	.58	(17)	—	
Director	.90	(14)	.82	(17)	.52	(31)

Despite these limitations, the summer rating, which is the average of the three ratings, is the most reasonable criterion of verbal and humanistic giftedness we have presently available. It is a rough index of a student's promise as evidenced by imagination and maturity of thought, that is, by his or her interest and ability in working with complex ideas in a fashion which is both disciplined and creative.

In a sense, the present study is a heuristic exercise. Selection, description, and evaluation are mutually interdependent, and the results of each process are useful in modifying the others. We have used the summer rating to provide additional insight into the nature of giftedness as displayed by our present sample. To learn more about the predictors of outstanding performance in the summer program (and to learn indirectly about the selection of verbally and humanistically gifted students), we compared students' scores on tests with

[14]There is the possibility of criterion contamination. With the small number of students, bias in favor of a few well-known high-scorers could have a marked effect. This does not appear to have occurred, however. The results of our research using the summer ratings which will be discussed below are sensible but were not predicted. It is unlikely, for example, that the observed sex differences would have been found if the summer ratings were biased in favor of high-scorers.

their summer ratings. With such a small N, statistical significance is hard to achieve. The results to be discussed in this section are not significant and must be considered as tentative. We plan a replication of the summer program, after which a reanalysis of these data will be made.

The correlations between test scores and summer ratings are presented in table 8.11. The correlations are small or moderate and statistically non-significant. Nevertheless, there is a pattern that suggests a difference in achievement for males and females. In agreement with the findings of Seashore (1962), women are more predictable than men on the basis of aptitude measures. However, the present data indicate that other types of scales, e.g., creativity measures, are more predictive for men.

Table 8.11. Correlations between rating of performance in summer enrichment program and scores on eight tests of creativity and mental ability

Tests	Boys		Girls	
	N	r	N	r
SAT-V	14	.23	17	.44
SAT-M	14	−.29	17	−.09
CMT	13	.09	17	.50
MLAT	12	−.31	17	.24
RAT	13	.17	17	.20
Chapin	12	.32	17	.17
Guilford-type Consequences	14	.34	17	.09
Barron–Welsh	12	.50	17	−.10

In addition, data from the Study of Values and the CPI follow a similar pattern. Scores of these tests are not predictive for girls, but several moderate correlations—i.e., $.4 < r < .7$—indicate that the highest-rated boys were self-confident, independent, and socially concerned.[15]

The biographical inventory data do not seem to add much at this point. For the boys, evidence of independent and continued interest in solitary hobbies, such as writing or music, seem to be more characteristic of those rated highly in the summer program, although this interpretation is advanced with caution. It would be difficult to proffer even as tentative a description on this for the girls.

CONCLUSION

Summarizing the data that have been presented, it is clear that the first Verbal Talent Search attracted a sample of bright youngsters from relatively small, relatively well-educated, middle-class homes.

[15]For boys, summer rating correlated +.72 with the Social scale and −.61 with the Economic scale on the Study of Values, and +.44 with Capacity for Status, +.44 with Self-acceptance, +.53 with Empathy, and −.62 with Achievement via Conformance on the CPI.

The extensive testing that was done with the brightest of these students reveals them to be equal in ability to students several years older. Moreover, they score well on tests of creativity and social judgment. As a group they are well adjusted and intellectually motivated. As with ability tests, their results seem more characteristic of young adults than young adolescents. Boys and girls scored equally well on these tests. However, personality and interest measures showed fairly consistent sex differences. The tests suggest that the boys are mildly withdrawn or introverted, analytical, rational, theoretical, and pragmatically oriented. On the other hand, the girls seem to be imaginative, intuitive, and interpersonally oriented. In addition, the data imply that although the girls may have more of the qualities for which we were looking, they may not be as likely as the boys to present and defend their ideas vigorously.

Are the results that show the students to be superior to their age-mates in terms of ability and personal adjustment confounded by a generalized, superior test-taking ability on the part of these students? Are they really more creative and more mature than their age-mates, or do they merely perform exceptionally well on any kind of paper and pencil test? I do not have data that can directly answer this question. However, the summer rating, which was a global measure of students' ability and effectiveness in participating in class, is suggestive. Of thirty-one students who participated in our summer courses, one-third were judged to show exceptional promise, but another one-third were considered to have profited little from the experience. As reported, girls' ratings correlated most highly with their ability scores, while boys' ratings seemed to be more related to performance on other types of measures. A second talent search has been conducted, and another enrichment program was offered in the summer of 1974. One major purpose is to see if a replication will yield similar results.[16]

Based on the experience of our first year, we have made or are planning several revisions in our procedures. In the 1974 Talent Search (see footnote 16 for results), we expanded our eligibility requirements. Students could qualify either by being certified as having a standardized verbal test score in the 98th or 99th percentile or by submitting creative written work. In addition, we are becoming actively involved in seeking out minority students and other types of youth, such as lower-class students, who may be extremely talented but are unlikely to participate in the talent search as it is presently conducted.

Another line of investigation that is being pursued involves closer study of the nonwinners of the talent search. A small, randomly selected group of the lower-scorers in the 1973 Talent Search was invited back with the very high-

---

[16]Preliminary results of the 1974 program are included in *Study of verbally gifted youth: Second annual report to the Spencer Foundation 1 September 1973–1 September 1974,* by Robert Hogan et al., available from ERIC Document Reproduction Service, P.O. Box 190, Arlington, Va. 22210. $0.75 for microfiche or $5.40 for hardbound copy.

scorers for further study. In 1974 we invited over forty-five nonwinners to participate in additional testing. Using these data, we will be able to expand our comparison between bright students and very bright students.

Lastly, there is the question of the development of these children. Aside from the scanty demographic information presented in this paper, little is known about the students. The greater emphasis of the program has been on identification of verbally gifted students along with trial efforts at helping them develop to their potential. Such an approach can be justified in the short-run. However, it seems of great importance to learn more about the family and social conditions that are probably at least partially responsible for producing these children. As the size of the subject pool becomes greater, it is anticipated that such research will assume a larger role in the study.

The first year of the study has been quite productive. We have demonstrated that psychometric approaches have some utility and that tests designed for older persons can be used successfully with a very bright but younger group. It is clear from our summer enrichment program that the very brightest junior high school students are capable of performing well above their grade level.[17]

On the other hand, we cannot claim to have discovered who or what the verbally and humanistically talented are. It is apparent that the SAT, although an appropriate ability test for this group, is too narrow in scope to serve as the sole selection device. The abilities to abstract and to analyze are central to superior academic performance and can be measured by tests such as the SAT-V. Many human talents may be left out, however, including some that may be necessary for innovative thinking and problem solving (Wallach 1971). For example, skills such as idea generation and question asking may be required in combination with traits such as tolerance for ambiguity, persistence, and a propensity for reflection (Covington 1970). Based upon our results, using measures of personality, interest, and creativity, and the success of other researchers, such as Holland (1961), using biographical inventories, we will place increasing emphasis in the future upon systematically exploring the utility of these other approaches to selection.[18]

[17]During the first academic year following the program, five of the 1973 participants took courses for credit in local colleges: Introduction to Psychology (2), Freshman Composition (2), American Literature (1), Elements of Writing (1), and Introduction to Computer Science (1). The average grade earned was approximately B+.

[18]In the 1975 Talent Search, both the initial screening and selection of finalists relied heavily on demonstrated nonacademic achievements in addition to test scores. Analysis of the test results and observation of students' performance in our summer program should enable us to compare the relative advantages of alternative selection strategies.

REFERENCES

Allport, G., Vernon, P. E., and Lindzey, G. 1970. *Manual for the Study of Values*, 3rd ed. Boston: Houghton Mifflin.

Barron, F. 1965. The psychology of creativity. In T. M. Newcomb (ed.), *New directions in psychology, II.* New York: Holt, Rinehart and Winston, pp. 1–134.

Carroll, J. B., and Sapon, S. M. 1959. *Modern language aptitude test manual.* New York: The Psychological Corporation.

Chomsky, N. 1972. Psychology and ideology. *Cognition* 1: 11–46.

Coleman, J. S., Campbell, E. Q., McPartland, J., Mood, A. M. Weinfeld, F. D., and York, R. L. 1966. *Equality of educational opportunity.* Washington D.C.: U.S. Government Printing Office.

Covington, M. V. 1970. The cognitive curriculum: A process-oriented approach to education. In J. Hellmuth (ed.), *Cognitive studies,* vol. 1. New York: Brunner/Mazel.

Covington, M. V., Crutchfield, R. S., Davies, L., and Olton, R. M. 1972. *The productive thinking program.* Columbus, Ohio: Charles E. Merrill.

Educational Testing Service. 1974. *Guide for high schools and colleges 1974–1975.* Princeton: College Entrance Examination Board.

Gardner, J. W. 1961. *Excellence, can we be equal and excellent too?* New York: Harper.

Gough, H. G. 1965. A validation study of the Chapin Social Insight Test. *Psychological Reports* 17: 355–68.

Herrnstein, R. J. 1972. Whatever happened to vaudeville? A reply to Professor Chomsky. *Cognition* 1: 301–09.

Holland, J. L. 1961. Creative and academic performance among talented adolescents. *Journal of Educational Psychology* 52: 136–47.

———. 1973. *Making vocational choices: A theory of careers.* Englewood Cliffs, N.J.: Prentice-Hall.

Keating, D. P. 1974. The study of mathematically precocious youth. In J. C. Stanley, D. P. Keating, and L. H. Fox (eds.), *Mathematical talent: Discovery, description, and development.* Baltimore: The Johns Hopkins Press, pp. 23–46.

Lessinger, L. M., and Martinson, R. A. 1961. The use of the California Psychological Inventory with gifted pupils. *Personnel and Guidance Journal* 39: 572–75.

McClelland, D. C. 1973. Testing for competence rather than for intelligence. *American Psychologist* 28: 1–14.

Mednick, S. A., and Mednick, M. T. 1967. *Examiner's manual: remote associates test.* Boston: Houghton Mifflin.

Myers, I. B. 1962. *The Myers–Briggs Type Indicator manual.* Princeton, N.J.: Educational Testing Service.

Schaefer, C. E. 1970. *Biographical inventory creativity.* San Diego: Educational and Industrial Testing Service.

Seashore, H. G. 1962. Women are more predictable than men. *Journal of Counseling Psychology* 9: 261–70.

Stanley, J. C., Keating, D. P., and Fox, L. H. (eds.) 1974. *Mathematical talent: Discovery, description, and development.* Baltimore: The Johns Hopkins Press.

Terman, L. M. 1956. *Concept Mastery Test manual.* New York: The Psychological Corporation.

Terman, L. M., and Oden, M. H. 1947. The gifted child grows up. *Genetic studies of genius,* vol. 4. Stanford, Calif.: Stanford University Press.

Wallach, M. A. 1971. *The intelligence/creativity distinction.* Morristown, N.J.: General Learning Press.

Appendix 8.1

Appendix Table 8.A1.   SAT-V scores of students at each level of parental education and occupation

Parents' education	Fathers			Mothers		
	N	Mean	SD	N	Mean	SD
Some high school	22	417	99.6	20	409	95.2
High school graduate	58	409	93.8	88	403	85.9
Some college	29	437	82.6	47	454	75.9
College graduate	81	459	86.4	93	478	90.1
More than college	83	479	93.7	30	494	100.6
Parents' occupation						
Semiskilled and unskilled workers	10	345	99.8	6	382	83.3
Skilled workers	28	409	85.8	4	418	47.2
Technicians and owners of petty businesses	57	446	80.9	54	446	88.9
Semiprofessionals, minor professionals, executives of medium-sized firms, administrators of small businesses	76	460	94.7	75	467	88.1
Major professionals and executives of large firms	78	480	79.9	15	515	118.6
Housewives				133	427	93.0

9

SEX DIFFERENCES IN MATHEMATICAL PRECOCITY: BRIDGING THE GAP[1]

Lynn H. Fox

ABSTRACT

A special summer accelerated algebra I program for seventh-grade girls was designed to improve their competence in mathematics, accelerate their progress in mathematics, and increase their awareness of career opportunities in science and mathematics. The class was designed to appeal to the girls' social interests. Not all the girls enjoyed the class or benefited from it. This class, however, did appear to be more successful for girls than either of two coeducational classes conducted by SMPY. The impact of participation in an accelerated class on the girls was compared with the effect of taking algebra I in a traditional class on girls and boys of similar ability. The major finding was that failure to attend to the social interests of girls in planning special educational experiences in mathematics could lead to a widening of the gap between the sexes with respect to high-level mathematical achievement.

It is generally agreed that sex differences exist in average mathematical aptitude and achievement among adolescent and adult populations. It has recently been found that the gap between the sexes in mathematical ability among very bright seventh- and eighth-graders is quite large. In a 1972 Talent Search in the greater Baltimore area conducted by the Study of Mathematically Precocious Youth (SMPY), two precollege-level tests, the College Entrance Examination Board's Scholastic Aptitude Test—Mathematics (SAT-M) and Mathematics Achievement I, were used to test 396 seventh-, eighth-, and accelerated ninth-graders who had scored at the 95th percentile or above on

[1]This paper is based on a doctoral dissertation (Fox 1974a). A preliminary report of the research was presented at the 1974 annual meeting of the American Educational Research Association in Chicago, Illinois. The author appreciates the cooperation of Baltimore County school officials in the study.

183

grade-level tests of mathematical ability. The results were startling. Twenty-two male contestants scored 660–790 on the SAT-M, which is slightly above the mean for entering freshmen at The Johns Hopkins University. Clearly there was a sizable number of very mathematically talented boys. The highest score for a girl was 600. Although 44 percent of the contestants were girls, 19 percent of the boys scored higher than the *highest* scoring girl. The difference in points between the highest scoring girl and boy was 190 points (Keating 1974 [I:2] and chapter 2 of this volume).[2]

Table 9.1. Mean scores on SAT-M for students, by grade and sex, in the 1972, 1973, and 1974 Talent Searches

		1972		1973		1974	
		Number	Mean	Number	Mean	Number	Mean
8th-grade[a]	Boys	133	524	350	540	556	541
	Girls	96	456	261	485	369	503
7th-grade	Boys	90	460	187	478	372	473
	Girls	77	423	155	421	222	440

[a]Students in the ninth and tenth grades who had not reached their fourteenth birthday were eligible for the contest. Since the number of young students in the ninth and tenth grades was small their scores are reported with those of the eighth-graders.

In 1973 SMPY, in cooperation with the Study of Verbally Gifted Youth (SVGY),[3] conducted a talent search in the greater Baltimore area and suburbs of Washington, D.C. Nine hundred fifty-three junior high school age boys and girls who scored at or above the 98th percentile on subtests of standardized achievement tests, such as the Iowa Tests of Basic Skills, were tested on SAT-M and Verbal. The highest SAT-M score of any girl was 650; 7 percent of the boys scored 660–800 (Stanley 1973). The mean scores on SAT-M for contestants in 1972 to 1974, by grade and sex, are shown in table 9.1. The mean scores for boys are higher (as much as 68 points for eighth-graders in 1972) than for girls in each grade group both years.

Thus, as early as grade seven gifted boys out-perform gifted girls on difficult precollege-level tests of mathematical ability, and the differences in performance are particularly striking at the upper ends of the distributions.[4] Since

---

[2]In addition to the usual references, citations of chapters in volume I of *Studies of Intellectual Precocity* will be as follows [I:2]. The I indicates volume I, and the 2 is the chapter number [Editor].

[3]The Study of Verbally Gifted Youth (SVGY) was begun at The Johns Hopkins University in 1972 by Drs. Robert T. Hogan, Catherine J. Garvey, and Roger A. Webb. Details of this study and the results of their 1973 contest are reported in chapter 8.

[4]The sex differences on the SAT-M found for these gifted students is similar to those found for students in regular administrations of this test to high school students. Far more boys than girls score 800, the highest possible score. In the 1973–74 academic year, 802 boys and 70 girls scored 800, of the 682,870 boys and 670,044 girls tested. This is roughly twelve times as many boys as girls.

bright girls tend to self-select themselves out of advanced mathematics courses in high school and college (Haven 1972), the gap between the sexes in mathematical achievement at the higher levels of ability widens with age. At present, very few women pursue the study of mathematics and science at the graduate level. In 1969 only 7 percent of the doctorates awarded in mathematics and 16 percent of those in the physical sciences went to women (Bisanti & Astin 1973).

Although it is possible that there are biological causes for differential mathematical aptitude between the sexes, there is, at the present time, no strong evidence to support any such hypothesis (Maccoby & Jacklin 1973; Astin 1974 [I:4]). Many researchers do feel that there is a substantial amount of data that indicate important relationships among personality, masculine interests, scientific career interests, and achievement in mathematics that account for some, if not all, of the performance differences between the sexes (Aiken 1970; Astin 1974 [I:4]; Carey 1958; Milton 1957).

SMPY's study of gifted adolescents lends some support for educational and social explanations of the sex differences at high levels of mathematical ability and achievement (Stanley, Keating, & Fox 1974). Interviews with the high-scoring males indicated that they had acquired more mathematical knowledge than their bright but less precocious peers in one of two ways. Either they had learned considerable amounts of advanced mathematics through independent study in a systematic way with the help of a teacher or parent, or they had worked informally with mathematical games, puzzles, and books, thus developing their problem-solving skills and mathematical reasoning abilities in a less systematic way (Fox 1974b [I:3]).

It appears that very few girls study mathematics independently in a systematic way, nor do many girls frequently read mathematical books or play with mathematical puzzles and games in their leisure time. Thus, some of the differences between the sexes in mathematical achievement seem to be a result of differential exposure to mathematical experiences. While girls may be very good students in school, the boys who learn mathematics beyond their grade level outside of school would seem to have an advantage. Sheehan (1968) argues that, because of superior reasoning and problem-solving ability, boys also learn more algebra in school. What motivates young students to study mathematics and science in their leisure time seems closely related to values and career interests.

In the 1972 Talent Search, Holland's (1965) Vocational Preference Inventory (VPI) was administered to all contestants. This had 84 different occupations, 14 in each of the following six categories: investigative (I), artistic (A),

---

In November 1974 the ratio of boys to girls scoring 800 was about 13 to 1. One hundred forty-three boys but only 12 girls scored 800, of the 190,057 boys and 209,546 girls tested. The mean scores for boys on the SAT-M are also higher than for girls.

realistic (R), conventional (C), social (S), and enterprising (E). More boys than girls preferred the investigative occupations, and highly precocious boys preferred them even more than less precocious boys. For girls there was a significant relationship between investigative preference and scores on the mathematics test (Fox & Denham 1974 [I:8]).

In the 1973 Talent Search the Allport–Vernon–Lindzey Study of Values was administered to all the students. Boys and girls showed typical sex differences on the six values. Boys scored higher on theoretical, economic, and political values, while girls scored higher on social, aesthetic, and religious values. The theoretical value was the highest value for 57 percent of the boys, who scored 640 or above, but for only 34 percent of the remaining male contestants, and for only 14.6 percent of all girls in the contest (Fox 1973).

Thus, investigative career interests and theoretical values appear to be correlates of mathematical precocity. Boys who have these scientific values and interests tend to seek out stimulation in these areas. Since girls value these pursuits less than boys do, it is not so surprising that they fill their leisure time with more social than scientific activities.

As long as the data remain inconclusive as to the biological basis of differences in mathematical competence, it seems worthwhile to concentrate on social and situational factors to increase women's talents and interests in mathematical and scientific careers. Even if some of the difference is a result of biological factors, it is still possible that environmental factors could be manipulated to decrease the differences in performance (Anastasi 1973). There is nothing to date which indicates that we should abandon hope for the development by women of greater achievement in the sciences. It would seem that the present data on sex differences in mathematics suggest some possible lines of attack for improving women's chances for development in these areas. If people are to succeed in mathematics-related fields, it would seem that at some early age they must recognize the possibility of career success in that area and begin to aspire positively toward developing their talents. However, if cultural biases have been operating which have led girls less than boys to consider the possibility of careers in mathematics and related areas, one must study to what extent and how these biases can be counteracted.

It is possible that some girls are better potential candidates for mathematical and scientific enrichment than others. How can these girls be identified? How could one intervene, to say, "Wait, think again. A career in mathematics or science may be a realistic goal for you"? What forms should the intervention take and what effects can we expect it to have? How receptive are bright girls to attempts to increase their mathematical skills?

Not only do girls on their own fail to seek out stimulation in science and mathematics but also they appear to be far less interested than boys in taking advantage of the special educational opportunities that SMPY has offered.

Girls, much more than boys, are reluctant to accelerate their education by grade-skipping, taking college courses, or participating rigorously in special accelerated mathematics programs. These girls seem to be afraid to try things that might make them appear different in relationship to their peers (Fox 1974c [I:6]).

FACILITATING THE DEVELOPMENT OF MATHEMATICAL TALENT FOR BOYS AND GIRLS

In the summer of 1972 a special program (SMPY I) in mathematics was initiated for the purpose of fostering precocious achievement in bright end-of-the-year sixth-grade boys and girls. The details of this program are reported in depth elsewhere (Fox 1974c [I:6]). Fewer girls than boys enrolled for the program. The girls who attended did not make the same great strides that most of the boys did, and reported enjoying the class far less than the boys did. In fact, several girls who were making satisfactory progress in the accelerated program actually wanted to drop the course because they did not like competing with the boys.

Although the groups of girls and boys were chosen primarily on the basis of in-grade percentiles on an arithmetic computation and reasoning test, their success with the program was quite different. This may be partially a result of the fact that the boys in the program seemed to be more theoretical and enjoyed the challenge of independent study, while all but one of the girls seemed to have more social values and orientation and not to enjoy studying on their own. Although both the girls and the boys in the special class had the same opportunities to learn advanced mathematics at a rapid rate, they did not benefit equally from the experience.

In the course of one year's time, meeting only two hours a week, seven boys were able to learn approximately four and one-half years of mathematics: this included algebra I, II, and III, trigonometry, and plane and analytic geometry. Six of these boys went on to study calculus in high school or college the next year; the other boy took trigonometry and analytic geometry in high school. Only one girl completed the entire program and she chose to repeat plane geometry by individual study the following fall. Most of the girls completed "only" two years of mathematics in one: algebra I and II, in the course of a year of two-hour classes on Saturday mornings.

In the summer of 1973 a second class (SMPY II) was started for end-of-the-year eighth-graders (and a few seventh-graders) who in the 1973 Talent Search had scored 500 or more on SAT-M and 400 or more on SAT-V and had already mastered the study of algebra I. Details of this program are reported in chapter

6. This program, like SMPY I, was far more successful in accelerating the mathematical progress of boys than girls.[5]

One must wonder why this attempt to foster mathematical achievement was so successful for boys, but far less so for most of the girls. The numbers of girls in each of these special programs was small, so it is difficult to generalize to the large population of talented young women from the results of these efforts.

Interviews with these girls, observations of their behavior in the classroom, and reports of parents and the teacher suggest that at least two factors operated to reduce their success in the program. The first was that the course, taught by a male ex-physicist, was very theoretical in orientation, but the girls were social by nature—they did not find the atmosphere of the classroom or the requirements of considerable independent study to their liking. Second, there was no attempt in the program to emphasize the relevance of mathematical study to their educational and career goals—most of the girls simply did not see the value of becoming accelerated in their mathematics education.

CREATING AN EXPERIMENTAL MATHEMATICS PROGRAM FOR GIRLS TO BRIDGE THE GAP

In trying to lessen the gap between the sexes in mathematics achievement at the higher levels of ability, it appears that some attention must be paid to the social motivation and interests of the girls. In the spring of 1973 an attempt was made to create a special accelerated mathematics program for bright seventh-grade girls that would work with and not against their social interests. The program was designed to accelerate their mathematics progress in school by one year by having them study algebra I for three months in a special class outside of school during the late spring and early summer, so that they could take algebra II as eighth-graders in their schools. It was hoped that moderate acceleration would increase their level of achievement and encourage them to pursue their mathematics education with greater interest.

This class was designed to provide greater social stimulation than had been provided by SMPY I. It was for girls only. There were three women teachers to serve as role models. The class was organized around small-group and individualized instruction, being conducted very informally. Cooperative rather than competitive activities were stressed. Whenever possible and appropriate, the teachers emphasized the ways in which mathematics could be used to solve social problems. Sometimes story problems and games were used which were designed to be socially appealing. In addition to the classes, there was a

[5]SMPY I and SMPY II are elsewhere referred to as "Wolfson I" and "Wolfson II" (see chapter 7) [Editor].

series of speakers, both men and women, who met with the girls to talk about interesting careers in mathematics and science, such as psychologist, chemist, computer scientist, operations researcher, and biomedical statistician.

Besides the attempts to socialize the atmosphere of the classroom and to emphasize the social values of mathematical training, efforts were made to develop the girls' study habits and skills. They were strongly encouraged to learn to read their mathematics textbook well and to use it as a resource and a teacher. The girls were encouraged to view themselves as capable of setting homework goals and time schedules and meeting their self-imposed deadlines. At the beginning of the course basic concepts were taught in a somewhat traditional manner. As the course progressed, greater emphasis was placed on individual study, and the girls were encouraged to seek the help of an instructor only after they had read a chapter or section and attempted to solve problems on their own. The ultimate goal was that the girls would become more self-sufficient in studying mathematics and would find the experience challenging and get satisfaction from it.

SELECTION OF THE GIRLS FOR THE EXPERIMENTAL PROGRAM AND THEIR CONTROL GROUPS

Thirty-two seventh-grade girls who were enrolled in schools in Baltimore County, who participated in the 1973 Talent Search conducted by SMPY and SVGY, and who scored above 370 on SAT-M (the mean score for high school junior girls) were invited to participate in the special class. On the basis of outside referrals, two additional girls were invited.[6] Letters were sent to these girls and their parents to explain the nature of the program and to make the summer class sound as socially appealing as possible. Twenty-six girls enrolled for the class.

For each experimental girl who accepted the invitation to the class a control girl and a control boy were selected from the remaining group of seventh-graders in the 1973 contest. The control girls and boys were matched with the experimental girls on the basis of mathematical ability (scores on the SAT-M), verbal ability (scores on the SAT-V), education of mother, and education and occupation of father.

---

[6]One girl was invited because she had been eligible for the first special mathematics class conducted by SMPY in 1972, but had not attended. She was tested on the premeasures prior to starting the class. Although her score on the SAT-M was only 350, she was still included in the program. The second girl attended an all-girl private school. She had planned to study algebra on her own during the summer. When her mother heard about the special class at Hopkins, she called to see if her daughter might attend. Her score on the SAT-M was 370.

SAT-M

The scores on SAT-M for each of the experimental girls and her control girl and boy are shown in table 9.2. The mean score for the experimental girls was 436. The mean score for the control girls was 433. The mean score for the control boys was 443.

Although the differences between the three groups were small, they were statistically significant. An analysis of variance is shown in table 9.3 ($F = 5.70$, $p < .01$). Control boys scored significantly higher than either group of girls. Experimental girls did not differ significantly from the control girls. Tukey comparisons of the differences between the means for the three groups are shown in table 9.4 (Scheffé 1959).

The median scores for the experimental girls, the control girls, and the control boys were 440, 435, and 440, respectively. Since the median scores were the same for experimental girls and control boys, the decision was made to

Table 9.2.   Scores on SAT-M for the three groups

| Triad number | Girls | | Control boys |
	Experimental	Control	
1	550	560	550
2	530	520	550
3	500	490	490
4	490	480	510
5	490	460	470
6	470	490	490
7	470	460	460
8	460	480	480
9	460	460	470
10	450	450	460
11	440	450	430
12	440	430	460
13	440	430	440
14	440	420	430
15	430	460	440
16	430	430	430
17	420	440	440
18	410	420	420
19	410	390	420
20	390	380	410
21	390	360	370
22	370	370	410
23	370	370	380
24	370	350	370
25	370	330	380
26	350	370	370
Mean	436.15	432.69	443.46

Table 9.3. Analysis of variance of SAT-M scores for the three groups

Sources of variation	df	MS	F
Group (G)	2	785.897	5.699*
Triad (T)	25	8016.820	
GT	50	137.897	
TOTAL	77		

*p < .01

Table 9.4. Tukey comparison of mean scores on the SAT-M for the three groups

Comparison	Difference	Level of significance
Experimental girls vs. control girls	3	not significant
Experimental girls vs. control boys	−7	p < .05
Control girls vs. control boys	−10	p < .05

accept the control boys as the best control group available. Selection of alternate control boys from the remaining population of seventh-grade boys in the contest would have actually increased the differences. This slight bias in favor of the boys was disregarded, since it would not bias the results in favor of the experimental girls.[7] Also, the post-treatment results were analyzed by an analysis of covariance design, which adjusted somewhat for these initial differences.

SAT-V

The mean SAT-V score for girls in the experimental group was 399. The mean score for the control girls was 390. These scores are slightly higher than the mean for female high school juniors, 378. The mean score for the boy controls fell between the two groups of girls, 393. It is higher than the mean of seventh-grade boys in the talent search, 382, and above the average for male high school juniors, 371. The analysis of variance for verbal scores for the three groups yielded no significant difference. The three groups were very similar on verbal ability as measured by SAT-V (Fox 1974a).

[7]Sixteen of the boys selected scored above their matched experimental girl by ten or more points, whereas only eight of the control girls scored above their matched experimental girl. It was particularly difficult to match boys with girls on the SAT-M in the range of 350 to 400. Although there were more boys than girls in the 1973 contest, relatively fewer boys than girls scored between 350 and 400.

Education of Mothers

Mothers who had college educations might conceivably have different expectations and aspirations for their children than mothers who did not. The education of mothers was rated on a five-point scale, from 1 to 5 as follows: 1 for less than high school diploma, 2 for high school diploma, 3 for some college but less than a degree, 4 for bachelor's degree, and 5 for education beyond the bachelor's level. Seven of the mothers of the experimental girls, eight of the mothers of control girls, and six of the mothers of control boys had earned a college degree. A percentage distribution of mothers by educational level is shown in table 9.5. An analysis of variance of the education of mothers for the three groups was not significant.

Education of Fathers

Fathers were expected to be better educated than mothers and this was true. Twelve of the fathers of experimental girls, seventeen of the fathers of control girls, and fifteen fathers of control boys had a college degree. A distribution of fathers by level of education is shown in table 9.6. Using the same five-point scale for the education of the fathers as was used for the mothers, an analysis of variance was not significant.

Occupation of Fathers

The majority of the fathers of students in all three groups were employed in business or the professions. By applying the Holland code to occupations (Viernstein 1971) it is possible to classify occupations into one of six general categories: investigative, enterprising, artistic, social, conventional, or realistic. A distribution of the fathers of these students by that code is shown in table 9.7.

Table 9.5.   Percent of mothers by level of education for the three groups

Five-point scale	Girls		Control boys
	Experimental	Control	
	(%)	(%)	(%)
1 Less than high school	4	15	4
2 High school diploma	50	27	50
3 Some college	19	27	23
4 Bachelor's degree	8	15	19
5 More than bachelor's degree	19	15	4
TOTAL	100	99[a]	100

[a]Does not total 100 percent due to rounding.

Table 9.6.   Percent of fathers by level of education for the three groups

| Five-point scale | Girls | | Control boys |
	Experimental	Control	
	(%)	(%)	(%)
1 Less than high school	8	0	11
2 High school diploma	23	19	15
3 Some college	23	15	15
4 Bachelor's degree	19	39	27
5 More than bachelor's degree	27	27	32
TOTAL	100	100	100

Table 9.7.   Percent of fathers by Holland occupational type for the three groups

| Holland Type | Girls | | Control boys |
	Experimental	Control	
	(%)	(%)	(%)
Enterprising	50	38	32
Investigative	27	32	27
Realistic	19	15	27
Social	4	8	4
Conventional	0	4	11
Artistic	0	4	0
TOTAL	100	101[a]	101[a]

[a]Does not total 100 percent due to rounding.

A chi-square analysis[8] of the number of fathers who were employed in occupations of an investigative nature was not significant.

Thus, on the selection measures of mathematical and verbal aptitude and education level of parents, the three groups appear to be reasonably well equated.

Knowledge of Algebra I

None of the students in any of the three groups had taken algebra I in the seventh grade. All students were pretested on knowledge of algebra on Form A of the Algebra I Test of the Cooperative Mathematics Series (published by the

[8]For a discussion of the use of chi square to test the equality of three proportions for correlated observations, the reader is referred to Berger and Gold (1973).

Educational Testing Service) before the experimental class was started. The scores and percentile ranks on national ninth-grade norms are shown in table 9.8.

The scores on the algebra test were well below the ceiling of the test (40 correct) for all but one control boy. The mean for control boys was slightly higher than the mean for either group of girls. However, these differences were not significant. The analysis of variance is shown in table 9.9.

One interesting and puzzling result was found. There was a significant correlation between the algebra I scores and SAT-M scores for girls but not for boys. The correlation for experimental girls was highly significant, $r = .57$, $p < .01$. For control girls the correlation was somewhat smaller, $r = .41$, $p < .05$. However, the correlation for control boys was about zero, $r = -.07$.

Table 9.8. The number-correct score and percentile rank on ninth-grade national norms and the corrected-for-chance (C.C.) score on the algebra I pretest for the three groups

	Girls						Control boys		
	Experimental			Control					
Triad	No. correct	%ile gr. 9	C.C. score	No. correct	%ile gr. 9	C.C. score	No. correct	%ile gr. 9	C.C. score
1	22	48	18	23	60	22	18	27	13
2	20	42	19	22	48	19	13	13	11
3	20	42	19	22	48	18	18	27	14
4	14	13	8	19	36	14	16	23	12
5	20	42	17	18	27	14	19	36	14
6	12	8	10	8	2	5	16	23	10
7	22	48	18	19	36	14	14	13	8
8	15	15	9	12	8	5	19	36	14
9	15	15	11	22	48	18	23	60	19
10	20	42	15	15	15	11	15	15	11
11	14	13	12	19	36	13	13	13	6
12	18	27	14	15	15	9	21	42	17
13	13	13	6	13	13	8	21	42	18
14	20	42	15	16	23	10	28	79	25
15	11	6	8	17	27	14	16	23	13
16	14	13	8	13	13	6	17	27	11
17	17	27	11	16	23	10	18	27	15
18	14	13	13	15	15	9	21	42	16
19	12	8	9	11	6	5	36	99.2	35
20	21	42	16	16	23	13	11	6	4
21	20	42	17	8	2	0	16	23	11
22	8	2	5	21	42	16	16	23	11
23	5	0.6	3	16	23	14	15	15	14
24	9	4	3	14	13	11	18	27	13
25	14	13	11	18	27	13	20	42	16
26	16	23	10	13	13	10	17	27	12
Mean	15.62		11.73	16.19		11.57	18.27		13.96

Table 9.9. Analysis of variance of algebra I pretest scores for the three groups

Sources of variation	df	MS	F
Group (G)	2	45.474	1.519
Triad (T)	25	24.474	
GT	50	29.928	
TOTAL	77		

The correlations of algebra knowledge and verbal aptitude were about zero for all three groups. The correlations between verbal and mathematical aptitude were also near zero for all three groups. These correlations are shown in table 9.10.

Table 9.10 also shows the correlations between the groups on SAT-M and SAT-V. The correlations between the experimental girls and control girls on SAT-M and SAT-V were $r = .95$ and $r = .90$, respectively. The correlations between experimental girls and control boys were $r = .96$ and $r = .92$, respectively. The correlations between the control girls and control boys were $r = .95$ and $r = .94$, respectively. This is further indication of the closeness of matching on the two selection variables.

Apparently there is some relationship between performance on the test of algebra and performance on the SAT-M for girls, but not for boys. What this suggests is that for students within a somewhat restricted range of high mathematical reasoning ability (350 to 550 on SAT-M as seventh-graders) achievement in mathematics is influenced more for boys than girls by factors other than aptitude. This result is difficult to interpret. Several researchers have noted the fact that women are more predictable than men (Seashore 1962; Stanley 1967).

EVALUATING THE EXPERIMENTAL PROGRAM FOR GIRLS

The evaluation of the success of this endeavor to create a successful mathematics experience for girls was complex. The first aspect of the evaluation procedure was concerned with the question of whether or not an emphasis upon social interests would be effective in recruiting girls to at least participate in an accelerated program in mathematics. The second question was the degree to which girls succeeded in mastering the study of algebra I in an accelerated program. The third and final question was whether or not a compensatory approach to the mathematics education of bright girls was effective in actually accelerating the progress of girls in their study of mathematics in school.

Table 9.10. Correlations between scores on SAT-M, SAT-V, and the algebra I test for each of the three groups and correlations between groups on the three tests

	Girls						Control boys		
	Experimental			Control					
	SAT-M	SAT-V	Algebra I	SAT-M	SAT-V	Algebra I	SAT-M	SAT-V	Algebra I
Experimental girls									
SAT-M		.04	.57*	.95*			.96*		
SAT-V			-.06		.90*			.92*	
Algebra I						.24			-.16
Control girls									
SAT-M					.25	.41†	.95*		
SAT-V						.21		.94*	
Algebra I									-.22
Control boys									
SAT-M								.18	-.07
SAT-V									-.09
Algebra I									

†$p < .05$
*$p < .01$

Acceptance and Dropout Rates

The first evaluation of the program was a comparison of the effects of social considerations upon recruiting girls to attempt acceleration in mathematics. The acceptance and dropout rates for girls in the all-girl class were compared with those for girls in two other accelerated programs conducted by SMPY which were not sex segregated. The first SMPY comparison program was discussed in the introduction and is named SMPY I. The second program, SMPY II, was begun in the summer of 1973 and continued through the summer of 1974. This program selected students from the 1973 contest who scored above 500 on SAT-M and above 400 on SAT-V and already had learned algebra I. This class began with the study of algebra II and is discussed in detail by George and Denham in chapter 6. The selection criteria for the three groups differed. The girls invited to the all-girl class were somewhat less talented than the girls in the other two programs. Mean scores on SAT-V and SAT-M for the girls in the three classes are shown in table 9.11. Since the goals for the three programs were based on ability level it is possible to make some comparisons among the three groups.

Table 9.11. Mean scores on SAT-V and SAT-M for the girls in each of the three accelerated mathematics programs

	SMPY I[a]			SMPY II			All-girl class		
	No.	SAT-V	SAT-M	No.	SAT-V	SAT-M	No.	SAT-V	SAT-M
Accepted	6	460	512	9	510	548	26	399	436
Dropped the course	2	395	435	4	490	550	8	399	414
Completed the course	4	493	550	5	526	546	18	399	445

[a]Data were not available for one girl who completed the course.

The acceptance and dropout rates for girls in all three programs are shown in table 9.12. The acceptance rate for girls in the all-girl class was considerably higher than that for the two mixed-sex programs. Seventy-six percent of the girls invited to the all-girl class accepted the invitation, whereas only 58 percent and 26 percent of the girls invited to SMPY I and II, respectively, accepted.

The dropout rate for the girls in the all-girl class was about the same as for SMPY I and lower than that for SMPY II.[9] Eighteen of the twenty-six girls who started the program completed the course. The reasons for dropping the course varied. Some found it very difficult, while others dropped out because

[9]At the end of the first twelve weeks of the SMPY I special class, two girls and one boy joined the class. For purposes of acceptance and completion rate comparisons, they are not included. The boy, but neither of the girls, completed the full course.

Table 9.12. Acceptance and completion rates for girls in each of the three accelerated mathematics programs

	Invited number	Enrolled number (%)		Dropped number (%)		Completed number (%)	
SMPY I	12	7	58	2[a]	29	5	71
SMPY II	34	9	26	4	44	5	56
All-girl class	34	26	76	8	31	18	69

[a]Two additional girls wanted to drop out of the program, but were finally persuaded to stay. They were taken out of the special class and given a tutor. If no special arrangements had been made, the number of dropouts in SMPY I would have been four, and the dropout and completion rates would have been 57 percent and 43 percent, respectively.

they had other summer commitments, such as vacations or camp activities, which were more appealing or more pressing. Girls who completed the course were more interested in investigative careers than were girls who dropped out. Thus, the social orientation of the classroom may not have been as potent in creating a social atmosphere as it was hoped. Comparisons of the eight dropouts and the remaining eighteen girls on selected characteristics are shown in table 9.13.

The girls who dropped out of the class tended to be the girls with weak interests in mathematics and investigative careers as assessed on self-report measures. They also tended to come from homes where one or more parent was a college graduate.

Table 9.13. Comparisons of girls who dropped out of the all-girl program with those who remained, on selected characteristics

Selected characteristics	Dropped the course N=8	Completed the course N=18
Percentage preferring an investigative occupation on questionnaire	0.0	44
Percentage expressing strong liking for mathematics	25	56
Mean rating of liking for mathematics[a]	2	1.55
Percentage whose mothers had a college degree	50	17
Mean educational level of mothers on a five-point scale[b]	3.25	2.71
Percentage whose fathers had a college degree	63	39
Mean educational level of fathers on a five-point scale[b]	3.87	3.11

[a]The liking for mathematics was rated from "very strong" to "dislike" on a four-point scale. The lower number means stronger liking.
[b]1 = less than high school, 2 = high school diploma, 3 = some college, 4 = college degree, 5 = college beyond the bachelor's degree.

Mastery of Algebra in the Accelerated Program

The eighteen girls who did complete the program were successful in learning algebra at a high level. Their scores and percentile ranks on ninth-grade norms for form A of the algebra I test taken at the end of the course (July, 1973) are shown in table 9.14. The mean score for these girls was 30.6, which was at the 89th percentile on national ninth-grade norms. The mean score for eleven girls invited to SMPY II who scored 500 or above on SAT-M and who had studied algebra I in school for a full year was 30.4.[10] Thus, it appeared that the girls in the all-girl class did indeed learn a considerable amount of algebra in only three months, meeting for four hours or less per week.

Table 9.14. Posttest algebra I test scores and percentile ranks on ninth-grade national norms for 18 girls who completed algebra I

Score[a]	Percentile rank
39	99.9
37	99.6
35	97
34	96
34	96
32	93
31	89
31	89
31	89
31	89
30	89
29	87
28	79
28	79
27	79
25	66
25	66
23[b]	60

[a]Test form A. Highest possible score was 40.
[b]This girl completed the course on her own and was accepted into algebra II, where she was successful.

To further test this hypothesis, experimental girls and two control groups were retested on algebra I, form B, on 26 January 1974, as part of the 1974 Talent Search. Three of the experimental girls, four of the control girls, and two of the control boys who were either unable or unwilling to participate in the talent search were tested either prior to or following the contest. Two experimental girls and one control girl were unwilling to be tested on algebra

[10]Most of the girls who were invited to SMPY II had already studied algebra I for a full year in the eighth grade. Like all those invited, they had scored at least 500 on SAT-M and above 400 on SAT-V in the 1973 contest. Eleven of these girls were tested on algebra I prior to entering the SMPY II class.

knowledge, mathematical aptitude, or measures of interest. Therefore, post-treatment measures are available on twenty-four experimental girls, twenty-five control girls, and twenty-six control boys. Thus, final analysis is possible on twenty-three intact matched triads.

The post-test scores and percentile ranks on eighth- and ninth-grade national norms on form B of the Algebra I test of the Cooperative Mathematics Test Series for the students in each of the three groups are shown in table 9.15. The experimental girls, especially those who completed the course, scored appreciably better on the test than either of the control groups. The mean score for twenty-four experimental girls was 29, which is at the 87th and 89th

Table 9.15. Posttest algebra I scores and percentile ranks on eighth- and ninth-grade national norms for the three groups

| | Girls | | | | | | Control boys | | |
| | Experimental | | | Control | | | | | |
Triad	Raw score	Percentile gr. 8	gr. 9	Raw score	Percentile gr. 8	gr. 9	Raw score	Percentile gr. 8	gr. 9
1	40	99.9[+]	99.9[+]	34	97	97	32	95	95
2	32	95	96	37	99.4	99.9[+]	26	73	79
3	32	95	96	37	99.4	99.6	27	73	79
4	33	95	96	31	90	93	19	33	42
5	36	99	99.2	30	87	89	19	33	42
6	30	87	89	25	68	75	19	33	42
7	37	99.4	99.6	18	29	36	22	49	60
8	a, b			22	49	60	27	73	79
9	30[a]	87	89	24	56	66	33	95	95
10	26	73	79	22	49	60	20	33	42
11	38	99.8	99.9[+]	25	68	75	22	49	60
12	23[a]	49	60	31	90	93	29	87	89
13	27	73	79	27	73	79	25	68	75
14	34	97	97	21	39	48	30	87	89
15	31	90	93	20	33	42	24	56	66
16	30[a]	87	89	20	33	42	26	73	79
17	27	73	79	21	39	48	26	73	79
18	27	73	79	16	18	27	23	73	79
19	16[a]	18	27	b			32	95	96
20	b			26	73	79	18	29	36
21	33	95	96	13	8	15	28	83	87
22	15[a]	14	23	19	33	42	21	39	48
23	13[a]	8	15	20	33	42	15	14	23
24	21[a]	39	48	20	33	42	20	33	42
25	31	90	93	27	73	79	20	33	42
26	34	97	97	29	87	89	19	33	42
Mean	29.00			23.96			23.92		

[a]Girls who did not complete the program.
[b]Girls who were unwilling to take the retest.

percentiles on eighth- and ninth-grade norms, respectively. The mean scores of the twenty-five control girls and twenty-six control boys were 23.96 and 23.92, which are at the 56th and 66th percentiles on eighth- and ninth-grade national norms, respectively. The mean scores for the twenty-three matched triads were 29.57 for the experimental girls, 23.96 for the control girls, and 23.70 for the control boys. The mean score of the seventeen girls who completed the experimental program was 32.24, which is at the 95th and 96th percentile ranks on eighth- and ninth-grade national norms, respectively. The mean score for their seventeen female controls was 24.53, which is at the 68th and 75th percentiles on eighth- and ninth-grade national norms, respectively. The mean for their seventeen male controls was 23.59, which is at the 56th and 66th percentiles on eighth- and ninth-grade national norms, respectively.

An analysis of covariance design was used to determine the significance of these differences. Three covariates were used: a premeasure on verbal aptitude, SAT-V; a premeasure on mathematical aptitude, SAT-M; and a premeasure on knowledge of algebra, form A of the Algebra Test I of the Cooperative Mathematics Series.

The analysis of covariance for the 23 triads is shown in table 9.16. The differences in performance among the three groups on the test of algebra knowledge was highly significant, $F = 14.63$, $p < .001$.

The means for the three groups and the Tukey test of significance of difference between the means are shown in table 9.17. The mean score of the experimental girls was significantly higher than that of either control group. The control groups were not significantly different. The experimental girls were

Table 9.16. Analysis of covariance of scores on posttest algebra I for the three groups[a]

Sources of variation	df	MS	F
Group (G)	2	285.386	14.629*
Triad (T)	22	22.650	
GT	41	19.507	

*$p < .001$

Mean scores on the three covariates for the three groups[a]

	Girls		Control boys
Pretests	Experimental	Control	
SAT-V	404.78	393.91	396.96
SAT-M	439.13	434.78	444.35
Algebra I	11.78	12.13	13.48

[a]N = 23 for each group.

Table 9.17. Tukey comparison of mean differences on posttest algebra I for the three groups[a]

Comparison	Difference	Levels of significance
Experimental girls vs. control girls	5.61	p < .005
Experimental girls vs. control boys	5.87	p < .005
Control girls vs. control boys	.26	Not significant

[a]N = 23 for each group.

clearly more accelerated in their knowledge of algebra than the control girls and boys. (Control girls and boys were taking algebra I in regular classes at school.)

Thus, a major contribution of this study is the finding that bright girls can learn algebra I at a very high level in considerably less time than they typically would spend in a regular algebra I class. Thus, accelerated mathematics programs can indeed be effective in increasing rates of achievements. This study also suggests that attention to the social nature of girls will be an important factor in recruiting girls for the program, but may have only small effects on increasing the success rate of girls who do elect to participate.

Success in Algebra II

The letters to the experimental girls, their parents, and their schools before the start of the program had explained that girls who were successful in learning the algebra during the summer would be allowed to take an algebra II course in the fall. By the end of the summer eighteen experimental girls were considered to be ready to begin the study of algebra II.

Baltimore County public school officials had agreed to the program and had determined the criterion for success to be the 65th percentile on ninth-grade national norms. They sent a letter to the principals of schools in which the girls were enrolled, informing them of the program. However, not all principals and guidance counselors were enthusiastic about the project. Some principals may have resented not being contacted in advance of the initiation of the program; however, the major objection raised was the fact that it would be difficult to make the necessary scheduling adjustments for the girls.

During the late summer and early fall, nine girls found their principal or guidance counselor reluctant to place them in algebra II. Three girls were finally persuaded to repeat algebra I, and one girl (the one in a private school) was placed on one-month probation in algebra II. The remaining fourteen girls were officially enrolled for algebra II by the third week of school. In a number of cases, however, they were told that they were not expected to perform well, and they would be put back into algebra I if they did not succeed quickly in the course. Several counselors and teachers expressed negative feelings toward the program and told the girls not to come to them for help because they were "Hopkins' problem."

These negative reactions to the program were unexpected. Attempts to talk with principals and teachers were only moderately successful in relieving the tension in some schools. Fortunately, not all school personnel reacted so unfavorably to the girls. The major flaw in this study was the failure of the principal investigator to anticipate these reactions and devise a plan during the summer to gain greater support from the schools. However, it should be noted that the investigator was asked by top school system officials not to communicate directly with the schools but to work through the school system in relaying reports to the schools. The results of this study indicate a need for greater teacher and school involvement in the planning process of accelerated programs, particularly in light of the evidence of some teachers' negative stereotypes of bright students (see Haier & Solano, chapter 10 in this volume).

Negative reactions from the schools appeared to have had a detrimental effect upon the progress of quite a few of the girls in mathematics. Three girls, as was mentioned before, quickly gave in to the wishes of their school and repeated algebra I. Of the fifteen girls who began algebra II in the fall, two were transferred into algebra I by the end of the first six weeks of school. One girl was put back because she missed two weeks of school and earned a failing grade for the first six weeks. She had been placed in algebra II, but because of scheduling problems could meet with the class for only three of the five class sessions. This, combined with her absence and the negative feelings of her teacher, was too much to overcome. Her mother expressed the feeling that the teacher had been unnecessarily unavailable to help her daughter make up the work she missed during her illness.

The second girl who was transferred to algebra I after the first six weeks was the one in the private school. The teacher decided to make her take the final examination for algebra I that she had constructed for the year before to determine whether or not she could stay in the algebra II class. The teacher decided that her performance on that test was not satisfactory. This girl was then placed in an algebra I class with a different teacher. The teacher in the second class appeared to view the situation somewhat differently and is making special arrangements for her to continue an accelerated approach to the study of mathematics.

At the end of the first semester, two more girls were put back into algebra I. These girls attended the same school. They were the two girls who did not meet the 65th percentile criterion on the algebra test at the end of the program, but were later retested and allowed to enter algebra II. Both of these girls met with unfavorable reactions from their teacher or guidance counselor concerning their acceleration. It does appear that they were less well prepared to undertake algebra II than the other girls who completed the program. It also seems likely that they were unsuccessful in algebra II at least partly because of the lack of support and enthusiasm in their school. Two other girls from the program were enrolled in the same school. They also reported having difficulty in algebra II, but they were determined to prove that they could succeed.

Thus, by the beginning of the second semester only eleven of the eighteen girls were still enrolled in algebra II. Three of the girls were having some problems, but eight were doing very well. Three girls, all enrolled in the same school, were considered to be the very best students in their algebra II class. The teacher, counselor, and principal in their school were highly enthusiastic about the program and were pleased with the success of these girls.

Thus, out of eighteen girls who completed the program only eleven girls (61 percent) were able to accelerate their progress in school. This is 42 percent of the twenty-six girls initially enrolled for the course. Of the fifteen girls who were at least initially placed in algebra II, eleven girls (77 percent) have succeeded in staying in algebra II, and eight girls (53 percent) made excellent progress. One girl failed algebra II. A flow chart of the progression of the girls from the thirty-four initially invited through successful completion of algebra II is shown in table 9.18.

Of the eleven girls who completed algebra II, four earned final grades of A, five earned B, one a C, and one a D. Ten of these girls took geometry the following year (1974–75), and nine of them reported grades of A for the first grading period. The tenth girl did not report her grade. Thirteen of the control girls and fourteen of the control boys took geometry in the 1974–75 school year, although none have completed algebra II. (A few took algebra II concurrently with geometry.) Only five of the control girls and four of the control boys reported grades of A for the first grading period.

Students in the experimental and control groups who scored above 420 on the SAT-M were sent the same information about opportunities for college courses in the summer of 1974. Three of the experimental girls and none of the control girls or boys took courses in mathematics, computer science, psychology, or Russian.

The data at present suggest that some of the girls who participated in the experimental algebra I program and were highly successful are achieving more than their cohorts. Their interest in special educational opportunities appears to be somewhat stronger than that of the control students. Whether or not they will stay ahead in high school remains to be seen.

CORRELATES TO SUCCESS IN ALGEBRA II

It is important to consider what variables were related to success in algebra II for the eighteen girls who were able to complete the algebra I program. To the extent that success was related to cognitive variables, it is possible to

Table 9.18. Flow chart of the all-girl algebra I class

Invited to class April 1974	Enrolled May 1974	Completed program July 1974	Began algebra II Sept. 1974	Remained in algebra II	Very successful in algebra II	Passed algebra II
34	26	18	15	11	8	10
	8	3	4	3	1	
Did not enroll	Did not complete program	Did not take algebra II	Placed in algebra I	Having some problems in algebra II	Failed algebra II	

improve success rates by adjusting selection and success criteria. If the differences related more to social factors than cognitive variables, then it may be necessary to modify the entire approach to the program.

Cognitive Factors

For the eighteen girls who completed the program, the mean scores on SAT-V, SAT-M, and algebra I at the end of the course, by degree of success in the program, are shown in table 9.19. The scores of the three girls who were not enrolled for algebra II were lower than those of any other group on SAT-V and SAT-M, but not on algebra I. These girls had been successful in learning the algebra, but were simply dissuaded from taking algebra II. (Two of these girls reported being very bored in their algebra I class and were trying to study algebra II on their own.)

Of the fifteen girls who did enroll in algebra II, four were not successful and were put back into algebra I. These four girls scored slightly below the more successful girls on all three cognitive measures, especially algebra I. Thus, they were somewhat less able in terms of aptitude and had not mastered the algebra to quite as high a level as had the eleven girls who remained in algebra II. Two of these girls probably should not have attempted the algebra II, because they were the two lowest scorers on the algebra I test. The third girl missed two weeks of school during the first six weeks; probably under different circumstances she could have succeeded.

Table 9.19. Scores on cognitive tests for 18 girls who completed the special program, by degree of success in algebra II

		Number	SAT-V	SAT-M	Algebra I
Girls who completed algebra I	Not placed in algebra II	3	363	427	32
	Placed in algebra II	15	413	450	30
Girls placed in algebra II	Sent back to algebra I	4	402	440	28
	Remained in algebra II	11	417	454	31
Girls who continued in algebra II for a full year	Very successful	8	433	445	31
	Had difficulty	3	377	475	30

The eleven girls who remained in algebra II scored higher on all three cognitive measures than the seven less successful girls. It is interesting to note that the three girls who were having the most difficulty in algebra II scored higher on mathematical aptitude but considerably lower on verbal aptitude and somewhat lower on algebra I knowledge than the eight most successful girls. The mean difference in verbal aptitude resulted from the fact that one girl scored extremely low on the SAT-V, 290. It is quite likely that her difficulties in mathematics class were increased by her low verbal ability, which is one predictor of rate of learning.

Social and Motivational Factors

Selected characteristics of the eighteen girls, by degree of success in algebra II, are shown in table 9.20. There were no apparent differences in liking for mathematics between very successful girls and girls who had difficulties with algebra II. Half of the most successful girls rated their liking for mathematics as very strong. Three of the seven less successful girls expressed a strong liking for mathematics.

The educational level of the parents of the eight most successful girls was lower than that of the girls who were put back into algebra I or who were having difficulties in their schools. This trend is exactly opposite from the results of analysis of success of students (both boys and girls) in SMPY I (Fox 1974c [I:6]). In that study, students whose parents were college educated were much more likely to be successful than were students whose parents were not.

Of the eight girls who had an investigative career interest on the questionnaire, five (63 percent) were successful in algebra II. Of the ten girls who did not list an investigative career on their questionnaire, only three (30 percent) were highly successful in algebra II. If the three girls who did not enroll for algebra II are excluded from consideration, 71 percent of the girls with investigative career interests were successful in algebra II, while only 38 percent of the girls with noninvestigative interests were successful in algebra II.

Situational Factors

One other interesting difference is found between the eight girls who were successful and the seven girls who had difficulties. Only one of the eight successful girls reported having problems with her teacher and guidance counselor. All of the seven girls who were less successful reported problems with the school. Many of the problems began before school started. Parents as well as girls called to say that they were having problems with the schools. Although several parents had series of conferences with teachers, counselors, and principals, not all situations were resolved to the satisfaction of the parents. In several situations the parents felt the schools were determined to get the girls out of algebra II because they were unwilling to provide special mathematics arrangements for them in the ninth grade. (Girls who completed the study of

Table 9.20. Selected characteristics of girls who completed algebra I in the all-girl program, by degree of success in algebra II

Selected characteristics	Completed algebra I		Began algebra II		Remained in algebra II		
	Total N=18	Did not take algebra II N=3	Total N=15	Returned to algebra I N=4	Total N=11	Highly successful N=8	Had difficulty[c] N=3
Percentage preferring an investigative occupation on questionnaire	44	33	47	24	54	63	33
Percentage expressing strong liking for mathematics	56	100	47	50	45	50	33
Mean rating of liking for mathematics[a]	1.6	1.0	1.7	1.5	1.7	1.6	2.0
Percentage whose mothers had a college degree	17	33	13	0	18	0	67
Mean educational level of mothers on a five-point scale[b]	2.7	2.7	2.7	2.5	2.8	2.4	4.0
Percentage whose fathers had a college degree	39	33	40	50	36	25	67
Mean educational level of fathers on a five-point scale[c]	3.1	2.7	3.2	4.0	2.9	2.6	3.7

[a] The liking for mathematics was rated from "very strong" to "dislike" on a four-point scale.
[b] 1 = less than high school, 2 = high school diploma, 3 = some college, 4 = college degree, 5 = college beyond the bachelor's degree.
[c] One of these three girls did not pass algebra II.

algebra II as eighth-graders would need to take geometry. Geometry, however, is not available as a regular course in their junior high schools.)

School officials in some schools felt that the girls simply did not know algebra I well enough to succeed in algebra II. This may well have been true, at least for two girls who barely met the criteria for successful completion of the course.

It is difficult to believe that teachers would deliberately try to fail some of the girls. More than one parent or student reported, however, that the teacher told the student that she didn't think the girl could possibly know algebra well enough after only three months of study to do well in algebra II. Whether or not teachers or counselors did indeed intentionally fail some girls, it seems likely that such negative attitudes worked against the girls.

What does seem clear is that programs to accelerate the achievement of bright students will be far more effective if they have the cooperation of teachers and other school officials. Certainly some of the failure of the all-girl class to succeed in accelerating the girls at their schools seemed to result from the lack of involvement prior to the program of the individual schools in which the girls were enrolled.

Thus, there were two probable factors that related to the failure of the program to accelerate effectively 39 percent of the eighteen girls who completed the special program. The first was that the standard for success (scores on a standardized test of algebra above the 65th percentile on ninth-grade national norms) was not set high enough. Had the qualifying score been somewhat greater, the success rate in algebra II would have been higher. This factor, however, did not appear to account for all the failures.

The second factor is school involvement. Programs for gifted students are apt to be more successful if they do not create many articulation problems with the schools. Scheduling and class offerings are a major concern to school administrators. Programs that interfere radically with the traditional system are apt to meet with great resistance. This program might have been much more effective had it not required that the girls would need special arrangements to take geometry in the ninth grade. A few schools are flexible enough to handle this type of problem, but most are not. Baltimore County officials were cognizant of this problem when they agreed to the program. Unfortunately, they encountered more resistance to this innovation at the school level than they had anticipated.

Many of the problems with the schools could be avoided if the girls who successfully complete algebra II could be accelerated to the tenth grade the next year. Alas, this idea has met with opposition, not from the schools but from the girls and their parents. Several of the girls say they find the school work easy and think they could handle tenth-grade work next year, but they don't want to leave their friends.

Thus, a major barrier to accelerating the progress of girls academically is their resistance to grade skipping. This is becoming increasingly more evident in all phases of work with gifted students conducted by SMPY. In the 1974 Talent Search a survey was taken of seventy-two girls who had not previously been involved with SMPY. They were asked about their feelings toward grade skipping and toward participating in special fast-paced mathematics programs. Many of the seventy-two girls said that grade skipping was good for others, but that they would not want to skip a grade. A sizable number of girls said they would be interested in special acceleration within mathematics if it did not require them to skip a grade. Thus, attempts to accelerate the mathematics development of gifted girls may have to suffer under a special restraint that will not be needed for gifted boys, many of whom are eager to skip one or more grades.

It is possible that some of these negative attitudes toward grade skipping can be changed over time. A parallel situation existed in relation to taking college courses. Less than 10 percent of the girls offered opportunities by SMPY to take college courses in computer science or mathematics accepted them. Some of the girls, however, in the all-girl class have become very excited by the possibility of taking college courses. As noted above, three of the girls took college courses by the end of the 1974–75 school year. This is almost surely a positive result of their summer program experience.

CONCLUSION

Comparisons of the all-girl class with previous efforts to encourage girls to accelerate their progress in mathematics suggest that attention to both cognitive and social variables is crucial to the success of such endeavors. It is possible to motivate girls to come to a special accelerated program when social aspects of the program are emphasized. It is also possible to teach these girls algebra I in far less time than is typically required in school. However, it is still difficult to accelerate their progress in school. Failure to successfully place a considerable number of the girls into more advanced mathematics classes resulted from a complex interaction of cognitive and social variables. There is a great need for accelerated programs to be well integrated into the larger framework of the school in order to be highly effective for girls. Ideally, the schools themselves should plan and conduct them.

Applied research is in many ways more challenging and more complex than laboratory experimentation. There are numerous variables that may contribute to the outcomes, but that cannot be controlled or quantified by the experimenter. Although this makes research at times more difficult to undertake or to interpret, these efforts should be continued. Hypotheses concerning the possible causative factors for apparent differences in achievement of select populations can be effectively tested only in the real world settings in which they apply.

The end result of this study lends support to the hypothesis that some differences in mathematical achievement between the sexes, at least at the higher levels of ability, are a result of social factors. The fact that attempts to maximize the likelihood of achievement in mathematics for bright girls by manipulation of social situational variables was successful in accelerating ten of the experimental girls in school (and twenty-three of the experimental girls as a group, in comparison with their matched control girls and boys, in terms of knowledge of algebra) is indeed evidence that educational intervention which includes an emphasis on social interests of girls can make a difference. The fact that this intervention attempt failed to effectively accelerate the progress of all twenty-six girls who initially enrolled for the class suggests that cognitive as well as other social variables which were not manipulated in the present study need to be considered.

Attempts to foster greater mathematical achievement among bright girls that ignore the social aspects of the situation are likely to lead to an increase rather than a decrease in the apparent gap between the sexes at the higher level of achievement in mathematics. On the other hand, the results of this study do not support a hypothesis that social factors alone account for most sex differences in achievement at the higher level of ability in mathematics.

The underlying question is how to develop instructional strategies and manipulate classroom environmental variables to maximize performance of a given population of students. In other words, how can the applied researcher utilize knowledge of individual differences to provide a better match between pupil characteristics and the demands of learning tasks and environments? The present research suggests that attention to expressed interests and values may be very important in planning programs to elicit high-level achievement among gifted girls who have social interests and values. The question of the impact of learner style and interests upon achievement when aptitude is relatively constant needs more serious research.

Even if some of the correlates of the apparent sex differences in mathematical achievement are shown to be differences in social interests and values, cognitive differences such as spatial ability, or interactions and combinations of several factors, one should be careful not to overgeneralize such findings to all males or all females.

Some girls who score high on theoretical values and masculine career interests may not benefit more from a socially oriented program than an investigative-theoretically oriented one. Bright boys who score high on social or aesthetic values and somewhat low on more masculine values or career interests might be more successful in mathematics programs which emphasize the social relativity of mathematical skills and use high social interest versus high theoretical content textbooks and problems.

Bright girls and boys who score relatively low on measures of spatial visualization abilities might benefit from a more verbal approach to the study of geometry, trigonometry, and calculus than other students who score higher on measures of spatial abilities. On the other hand, perhaps it is possible to teach people techniques to compensate for a deficiency in spatial ability. At present there is little evidence to suggest how important these differences in spatial ability really are for mathematical achievement.

What appears to be true at present is that many more bright girls relative to bright boys of similar ability score high on measures of social values and career interests and somewhat low on measures of theoretical values and investigative career interests. Therefore, sex segregated classes, which emphasize the social relevance of mathematics, are likely to be more effective than less socially oriented classes in raising the achievement level of girls. There may be other advantages to sex segregated classes for mathematics. First, it would be easier and more appropriate to include special career educational activities and female role models as supplements to the instructional aspects of the program. Second, it would be possible to alter the textbook content, or at least the specific problem content, to be more appealing to most girls. It has been noted by several groups that tests and textbooks in mathematics appear to be biased toward male interests. Effects of such a learning and content bias upon actual achievement within the classroom are not well documented. The work of Carey (1958) and Milton (1957) suggests that girls who have more feminine characteristics might perform better on problems with high feminine interests, and that girls who have more masculine interests are apt to perform better on general problem-solving tasks than girls with more feminine interests.

Several research questions need further attention. First, to what extent are sex differences in mathematical ability, particularly at the higher levels of achievement, a result of interest and motivational differences between the sexes? of basic cognitive differences, perhaps related to spatial ability? of different responsiveness to certain classroom characteristics? of some combination of cognitive and affective factors? Or are such sex differences only artifacts of the tests currently used with adolescent populations?

Second, and closely related to the first point, is there really a differential change taking place during the transition from late childhood to early adolescence for the sexes with respect to mathematical ability?

Third, if there are real basic cognitive processing or perceptual differences between the sexes which affect mathematical achievement, can we develop instructional strategies to compensate for such differences?

Fourth, to what extent are the apparent sex differences in mathematical ability in subjects such as algebra and geometry a result of sex-interest-aptitude interaction?

The results of this study do support the hypothesis that intervention designed to foster greater achievement in mathematics among bright girls can be successful. The impact of accelerated programs, however, still appears to be far less successful for bright girls than for bright boys. Other strategies to foster more acceleration and greater achievement among bright girls need to be developed and tested. It would be interesting to compare the results of programs which include modified and accelerated instructional procedures with programs which only supplement traditional classes with career educational components. It would also be interesting to compare the results of sex segregated classes with interest (but not sex) segregated classes, when the effect of aptitude for mathematics is controlled.

At present there appears to be a growing interest among educational researchers and practitioners in the problem of fostering talent among young women in mathematics and science. The results of the present study suggest that such a task is complex. They certainly appear to raise some interesting and researchable questions.

REFERENCES

Aiken, L. F. 1970. Nonintellective variables and mathematics achievement: Directions for research. *Journal of School Psychology* 8: 28–36.

Anastasi, A. 1973. Common fallacies about heredity, environment, and human behavior. *American College Testing Research Report* 58.

Astin, H. S. 1974. Sex differences in mathematical precocity. In J. C. Stanley, D. P. Keating, and L. H. Fox (eds.), *Mathematical talent: Discovery, description, and development*. Baltimore, Md. 21218: The Johns Hopkins University Press, pp. 70–86.

Berger, A., and Gold, R. Z. 1973. Note on Cochran's Q-Test for the comparison of correlated proportions. *Journal of the American Statistical Association* 68(344): 989–93.

Bisconti, A. S., and Astin, H. S. 1973. Undergraduate and graduate study in scientific fields. *American Council on Education Research Report* 8(3).

Carey, G. L. 1958. Sex differences in problem solving performance as a function of attitude differences. *Journal of Abnormal and Social Psychology* 56: 256–60.

Fox, L. H. 1973. Values and career interests of mathematically precocious youth. Paper presented at annual meeting of American Psychological Association, Montreal, Quebec, Canada.

_____. 1974*a*. Facilitating the development of mathematical talent in young women. Doctoral dissertation in psychology, The Johns Hopkins University.

_____. 1974*b*. Facilitating educational development of mathematically precocious youth. In J. C. Stanley, D. P. Keating, and L. H. Fox, (eds.), *Mathematical talent: Discovery, description, and development*. Baltimore, Md. 21218: The Johns Hopkins University Press.

_____. 1974*c*. A mathematics program for fostering precocious achievement. In J. C. Stanley, D. P. Keating, and L. H. Fox, (eds.), *Mathematical talent: Discovery, description, and development*. Baltimore, Md. 21218: The Johns Hopkins University Press.

Fox, L. H., and Denham, S. A. 1974. Values and career interests of mathematically and scientifically precocious youth. In J. C. Stanley, D. P. Keating, and L. H. Fox, (eds.), *Mathematical talent: Discovery, description, and development*. Baltimore, Md. 21218: The Johns Hopkins University Press.

Haven, E. W. 1972. Factors associated with the selection of advanced mathematics courses by girls in high school. *Research Bulletin*, 72-12. Educational Testing Service.

Holland, J. L. 1965. *Manual for the Vocational Preference Inventory*. Palo Alto, Calif.: Consulting Psychologists Press.

Keating, D. P. 1974. The study of mathematically precocious youth. In J. C. Stanley, D. P. Keating, and L. H. Fox, (eds.), *Mathematical talent: Discovery, description, and development*. Baltimore, Md. 21218: The Johns Hopkins University Press.

Maccoby, E. E., and Jacklin, C. N. 1973. Sex differences in intellectual functioning. In *Assessment in a pluralistic society: Proceedings of the 1972 invitational conference on testing problems*. Princeton, N.J.: Educational Testing Service.

Milton, G. A. 1957. The effects of sex role identification upon problem solving skill. *Journal of Abnormal and Social Psychology*, 55: 208-12.

Scheffé, H. 1959. *The analysis of variance*. New York: Wiley.

Seashore, H. G. 1962. Women are more predictable than men. *Journal of Counseling Psychology* 9(3): 261-70.

Sheehan, T. J. 1968. Patterns of sex differences in learning mathematical problem solving. *Journal of Experimental Education* 36: 84-87.

Stanley, J. C. 1967. Further evidence via the analysis of variance that women are more predictable academically than men. *Ontario Journal of Educational Research* 10: 49-55.

————. 1973. Accelerating the educational progress of intellectually gifted youth. *Educational Psychologist* 10(3): 133-46.

Stanley, J. C., Keating, D. P., and Fox, L. H. (eds.). 1974. *Mathematical talent: Discovery, description, and development*. Baltimore, Md. 21218: The Johns Hopkins University Press.

Viernstein, M. C. 1972. The extension of Holland's occupational classifications to all occupations in the *Dictionary of Occupational Titles*. *Journal of Vocational Behavior* 2: 107-21.

10
EDUCATORS' STEREOTYPES OF MATHEMATICALLY GIFTED BOYS[1]

Richard J. Haier and Cecilia H. Solano

ABSTRACT

The attitude or stereotype that educators hold regarding gifted students can have an important effect on the implementation of educational alternatives for talented students. This paper reports data on the prevalence and content of stereotypes of gifted students in two groups of educators. One group was personally unfamiliar with students such as found by SMPY. These educators read case descriptions of SMPY students and described their conception of the students as a group by completing Adjective Checklists (ACL). Educators personally familiar with the students also completed ACLs. Results indicate that the unfamiliar educators hold negative stereotypes more frequently than their "familiar" counterparts. The content of this negative stereotype, however, is shown to be neither extremely harsh nor arbitrary.

Since its inception in 1971 the Study of Mathematically Precocious Youth (SMPY) has advocated and undertaken several innovative programs which offer educational alternatives to exceptionally gifted students. These programs include college courses for junior high school students, fast-paced special classes, grade acceleration, subject-matter acceleration, and entering college early full-time. Ultimately, the success and continuation of these programs depend to a large extent on the approval and cooperation of principals, teachers, guidance counselors, and other school officials. In the majority of cases educators have worked actively and enthusiastically to develop the potential of the talented students identified through SMPY. In a few instances, however, there has been substantial reluctance to undertake educational intervention. There are, of course, several grounds for the resistance which some educators show in dealing with highly able students. Reasons often given

[1]The authors wish to thank Julian C. Stanley for his comments on earlier drafts, and Craig Stevens for his aid with the data analysis.

for not implementing the programs are lack of money, difficulties with bureaucratic channels, scheduling problems, and the existence of adequate programs for enrichment.

While these factors undoubtedly have an effect, at times it appears that an undertone of negativism pervades some thinking about gifted students. The attitudes or stereotypes that educators hold toward gifted students are critically important to the goals of SMPY. Unfounded negative stereotypes can needlessly impede efforts made on behalf of such students. It has been repeatedly shown that negative stereotypes of the gifted have little empirical basis (Terman 1925; Cox 1954; Oden 1968; see also chapter 11 in this volume). Some experiences of the SMPY, however, indicate that a negative stereotype of the gifted child has not been eradicated in academic circles. The nature of this stereotype and the extent to which it persists are the topics of concern in this chapter.

METHOD

Subjects and Procedures

A sample of 200 principals, teachers, and guidance counselors from 50 public junior high schools in Pennsylvania was selected to represent a population of educators having no prior contact with the SMPY. The schools were chosen by county, and the counties were selected for their similarity on several demographic variables (per capita income, percent white collar workers, percent urban population, private school enrollment, and population rank in the United States) to the counties in Maryland in which SMPY high-scorers attend school. The principal of each Pennsylvania school was contacted twice by mail. The first letter was introductory and described this study; the second contained the specific materials for the study and directions for their use. The principal was asked to disseminate these materials to a male and a female mathematics teacher, a guidance counselor, and himself. He was instructed to do this without reference to experience or contact with gifted students. Thus, four educators in each school were asked to describe mathematically gifted boys in the following manner.

Each educator received a case description sheet which briefly described four real boys identified through the SMPY as mathematically gifted (see Stanley, Keating & Fox 1974). The neutrally worded descriptions included test scores, college courses taken, and grades received (see appendix 10.1). Descriptions such as these were written by the project staff for nine boys representative of the SMPY 1973 high-scoring group, of whom all had scored 640 or better on the Scholastic Aptitude Test–Mathematical. Three additional boys described were exceptionally gifted students who had been identified by the SMPY in previous years. These twelve descriptions were randomly assigned to one of the three forms of the case description sheet (one of the three exceptionally gifted students was included on each form). These three different case study sheets were used in order to broaden the basis for stereotyping. Each form was sent to a different random third of the schools contacted.

Accompanying the case descrption sheet was a copy of the Adjective Checklist (ACL, Gough 1960; Gough & Heilbrun 1965). The ACL consists of three hundred personality-relevant adjectives arranged in alphabetical order. The checklist as an attitude measure has a number of advantages for survey use. It contains a wide range of behavioral descriptions and also provides scales for organizing these descriptions. Furthermore, it has the advantage of being easily understood by persons who have had no previous experience with the rating technique and who are following written instructions.

Each educator was instructed to read the case descriptions and then check those adjectives on the ACL which he thought applied to the group of gifted boys. After completing the ACL each educator returned it anonymously in a sealed envelope to his or her principal. The principal then returned the four sealed ACLs from his school to the SMPY. The Pennsylvania sample, therefore, represented a population of educators who described mathematically highly talented boys on the basis of little or no direct experience with such students.

In order to evaluate the configuration of adjectives indicated by the Pennsylvania educators, a comparison sample was defined from the mathematics teachers, guidance counselors, and principals of 46 SMPY high-scorers. Each of these educators (henceforth referred to as the Maryland educators) was contacted and asked to complete the ACL by checking those adjectives that were descriptive of the specific student of his or her acquaintance. Thus, for each of the mathematically gifted boys, a principal, a guidance counselor, the previous year's mathematics teacher, and the current mathematics teacher were contacted (comprising a sample of 184 educators). Since several of the boys attended the same school, some educators filled out more than one ACL. An attempt was made to contact only principals and guidance counselors who were personally familiar with the given students.

RESULTS

Seventy-six percent of both the Pennsylvania and Maryland educators returned the Adjective Checklist.[2] The ACLs were first scored for the favorable and the unfavorable scales. Each of these two scales consists of seventy-five adjec-

---

[2]In Pennsylvania all three groups of educators responded at a similar rate (principals 76 percent, teachers, 76 percent, and guidance counselors 74 percent). In Maryland there were differences (principals 43 percent, teachers 87 percent, and guidance counselors 76 percent). The low rate of response for Maryland principals is probably due to lack of familiarity with the students they were asked to rate.

tives selected on the basis of ratings of favorableness or unfavorableness (see Gough & Heilbrun 1965, pp. 5–6). These scales are listed in appendix 10.2. The number of adjectives checked by each educator on each scale was converted to a standard score derived from adult normative data in the manual. These standard scores take into account the tendency to check more favorable than unfavorable adjectives and the differential numbers of adjectives checked overall. The use of these two scales allowed each educator to be categorized as holding a positive or a negative stereotype toward gifted students in the following way. A positive stereotype was defined as a higher standard score on the favorable scale than on the unfavorable scale. Conversely, a higher standard score on the unfavorable scale than on the favorable scale defined a negative stereotype. The frequency of negative stereotypes was found to be higher among Pennsylvania educators than Maryland educators; the frequency of positive stereotypes was found to be higher among Maryland educators ($\chi^2 = 10.08$, df = 1, p < .005). Table 10.1 shows the prevalence of negative stereotypes for educators by state, type of position, and sex.

In order to ascertain the actual content of the stereotypes, the adjectives most frequently checked on the favorable and unfavorable scales were contrasted. This comparison was between Pennsylvania and Maryland educators, broken down into those having negative or positive stereotypes. Table 10.2 lists the favorable and unfavorable adjectives most frequently checked by educators holding negative stereotypes. Table 10.3 lists the adjectives from the two scales checked most often by the educators holding positive stereotypes.

Three general results are apparent from an examination of the specific adjectives and their corresponding rates of endorsement. First, for each of the eight groups defined in tables 10.2 and 10.3, there are far higher percentages of

Table 10.1. Percent of educators with negative stereotypes

	Pennsylvania educators		Maryland educators	
	Total N	% neg.	Total N	% neg.
Principals				
Male	38	53	16	38
Female	–	–	4	0
Teachers				
Male	40	75	49	37
Female	36	47	33	33
Guidance counselors				
Male	16	44	19	16
Female	21	19	16	38
	151	52%	137	32%

Table 10.2. Unfavorable and favorable adjectives most frequently checked by educators holding *negative* stereotypes (percents checking)

	Pennsylvania	N=80	Maryland	N=44
Unfavorable adjectives	Opinionated	44%	Argumentative	45%
	Argumentative	43	Immature	41
	Impatient	38	Opinionated	27
	Egotistical	36	Aloof	25
	Interests narrow	34	Impatient	25
	Faultfinding	33	Self-centered	25
	Self-centered	33	Faultfinding	23
	Conceited	33	Careless	23
Favorable adjectives	Alert	96%	Intelligent	84%
	Intelligent	95	Capable	77
	Capable	94	Confident	66
	Ambitious	89	Curious	61
	Logical	81	Alert	59
	Clear-thinking	80	Active	52
	Confident	78	Cooperative	52
	Industrious	73	Logical	50

endorsement on favorable than unfavorable adjectives. This indicates that there is more agreement on the favorable attributes of these students, even for educators holding negative stereotypes. Second, the Pennsylvania educators, whether they hold a positive or negative stereotype, have higher percentages of endorsement on both the favorable and the unfavorable adjectives than their counterparts in Maryland. This would be consistent with the Pennsylvania sample basing their judgments on a stereotype. Presumably, the Maryland sample is less uniform in its ratings, since each Maryland educator is rating a different specific individual. Third, there is a large degree of consistency in the particular adjectives selected by the educators in both states. Although the rates of endorsement are quite different, there is still considerable agreement on the specific characteristics attributed to these gifted students, whether or not the educator was familiar with such students. This suggests that the stereotype of talented students, like many stereotypes, has a certain basis in fact. The unfavorable adjectives most frequently checked overall were argumentative, opinionated, and impatient. The favorable adjectives checked most frequently were intelligent and alert.

DISCUSSION

The interpretation of the results must be tempered by the limitations of the survey method employed and the particular definition of the positive and negative stereotypes. The primary conclusion that can be drawn from these

Table 10.3.   Unfavorable and favorable adjectives most frequently checked by educators holding *positive* stereotypes (percents checking)

	Pennsylvania	N = 71	Maryland	N = 93
Unfavorable adjectives	Argumentative	27%	Opinionated	15%
	Opinionated	17	Argumentative	13
	Impatient	14	Impatient	8
	Interests narrow	14	Aloof	8
	Fussy	13	Egotistical	6
	Faultfinding	11	Self-centered	6
	Arrogant	10	Interests narrow	5
	Egotistical	10	Bossy	3
Favorable adjectives	Alert	100%	Intelligent	95%
	Capable	97	Conscientious	94
	Clear-thinking	97	Dependable	92
	Intelligent	97	Alert	91
	Logical	94	Clear-thinking	89
	Conscientious	94	Reliable	87
	Ambitious	93	Confident	86
	Independent	92	Cooperative	86

data is that a negative stereotype of mathematically gifted students is held by significantly more educators unfamiliar with such students than by educators who are familiar with them. Male mathematics teachers who are unfamiliar with these talented boys seem, in particular, to hold negative opinions. Familiarity, however, ameliorates the unfavorable feelings of educators expressed toward these students. The differential effect of familiarity for male and female guidance counselors is interesting but no explanation is apparent.

In addition to the effect of familiarity, there is an indication that the negative stereotype held by educators is not overwhelmingly adverse. Even those educators who hold negative stereotypes endorse many favorable adjectives for these students. The adjectives selected by both groups of educators provide an additional basis for interpretation. In a sense, the unfavorable adjectives most frequently selected as descriptive of these students may be understandable, considering their high ability. Adjectives like argumentative, opinionated, and impatient may reflect the fact that gifted students are poorly served and subsequently bored by the standard school curricula.

In summary, the results of this survey indicate that negative characteristics are still attributed to mathematically gifted boys by many educators. This stereotype, however, is neither extremely hostile nor derogatory and may have some basis in fact. Familiarity, moreover, appears to mitigate the negative opinions held regarding these students. These considerations suggest that the negative stereotypes are likely to be troublesome but temporary obstacles in the educational facilitation of gifted boys. The situation might be somewhat different for girls, as Fox (chapter 9) suggests.

REFERENCES

Cox, C. M. 1954. Gifted children. In Carmichael, L. (ed.), *Carmichael's Manual of Child Psychology* (2nd ed.). New York: Wiley.

Gough, H. 1960. The Adjective Checklist as a personality assessment research technique. *Psychological Reports* 6: 107–22.

Gough, H., and Heilbrun, A. 1965. *The Adjective Checklist Manual*. Palo Alto, Calif.: Consulting Psychologists Press.

Oden, M. H. 1968. The fulfillment of promise: 40-year follow-up of the Terman gifted group. *Genetic Psychology Monographs* 77: 3–93.

Stanley, J. C., Keating, D. P., and Fox, L. H. (eds.). 1974. *Mathematical talent: Discovery, description, and development*. Baltimore: The Johns Hopkins University Press.

Terman, L. M. 1925. Mental and physical traits of a thousand gifted children. *Genetic studies of genius*, vol. 1. Stanford, Calif.: Stanford University Press.

Appendix 10.1

Case Description Sheet

Each paragraph describes a real student.

1. John is ten years old and in the seventh grade. On a test of mathematical ability he scored better than 93 percent of high school juniors. On a difficult test of nonverbal reasoning he scored better than 95 percent of twenty-year-olds. This boy is taking a college calculus course at night. Last summer he took a college course in algebra and trigonometry, earning a grade of B. He learned high school algebra I, II, III, analytic geometry, trigonometry, and plane geometry in thirteen months.

2. Jerry is thirteen years old and in the tenth grade. He skipped ninth grade. On a test of mathematical ability he scored better than 98 percent of high school juniors. He has completed an evening college course in astronomy with a grade of A. He has also completed two summer college courses in mathematics I and II with grades A and B respectively.

3. Peter is fourteen years old and skipped from the eighth to the tenth grade. On a test of mathematical ability he scored better than 98 percent of high school juniors.

4. John is thirteen years old and in the eighth grade. On a test of mathematical ability he scored better than 98 percent of high school juniors. He received a grade of A in a college computer science course, making 100 percent on the mid-term and 94 percent on the final examination.

Appendix 10.2

Adjectives comprising the favorable and unfavorable scales on the ACL

Favorable

active	courageous	humorous	rational
adaptable	curious	imaginative	realistic
adventurous	dependable	independent	reasonable
affectionate	efficient	industrious	reliable
alert	energetic	insightful	resourceful
ambitious	enterprising	intelligent	responsible
appreciative	enthusiastic	interests wide	self-controlled
artistic	fair-minded	inventive	sincere
attractive	foresighted	kind	sociable
calm	forgiving	logical	stable
capable	frank	loyal	sympathetic
charming	friendly	mature	tactful
cheerful	generous	natural	thoughtful
clear-thinking	gentle	optimistic	tolerant
clever	goodlooking	organized	understanding
confident	good-natured	original	versatile
conscientious	healthy	patient	warm
considerate	helpful	pleasant	wise
cooperative	honest	poised	

Unfavorable

affected	dull	irritable	shiftless
aloof	egotistical	loud	show-off
apathetic	evasive	moody	slipshod
argumentative	faultfinding	nagging	snobbish
arrogant	fickle	obnoxious	spineless
bitter	foolish	opinionated	stingy
boastful	frivolous	prejudiced	sulky
bossy	fussy	prudish	tactless
careless	gloomy	quarrelsome	thankless
coarse	greedy	quitting	touchy
cold	hard-hearted	rattlebrained	undependable
complaining	hostile	resentful	unfriendly
conceited	immature	rigid	unintelligent
cowardly	impatient	rude	unkind
cruel	indifferent	sarcastic	unscrupulous
cynical	infantile	self-centered	vindictive
deceitful	interests narrow	self-pitying	weak
disorderly	intolerant	selfish	whiny
distrustful	irresponsible	shallow	

III
THE PSYCHOLOGY OF
INTELLECTUAL TALENT

11
A SUMMARY PROFILE OF THE NONINTELLECTUAL CORRELATES OF MATHEMATICAL PRECOCITY IN BOYS AND GIRLS[1]

Richard J. Haier and Susanne A. Denham

ABSTRACT

That intellectually gifted individuals are similarly advanced in nonintellectual realms has been well documented. It is nonetheless important to describe the personality and social characteristics of the students identified through SMPY, since these students represent a more select population than has been studied in the past, and since innovative educational programs are advocated for them. This paper draws on the results of five measures (the California Psychological Inventory, the Eysenck Personality Inventory, the Study of Values, Holland's Vocational Preference Inventory, and the Adjective Checklist) to develop a composite profile of the nonintellectual correlates of very mathematically able boys and girls. Comparisons are made between the SMPY groups and nongifted age-mates, as well as between SMPY groups and adult scientists and mathematicians. Sex differences are also discussed. Overall, it is concluded that students of exceptional mathematical ability are more interpersonally effective and socially mature than their nongifted age-mates and thus more likely to encounter successfully the social and emotional challenges presented by their unique talents.

One of the most forthright conclusions of Terman's famous longitudinal study of intellectually gifted individuals was that many aspects of well-adjusted behavior are strongly associated with superior intellectual ability. As a group, Terman's sample was more mature, more successful, healthier, and had a wider

[1]The authors wish to thank Julian C. Stanley for his helpful comments on an earlier version of this paper.

range of interests than comparable nongifted groups (see, for example, Terman 1925; Oden 1968). Several other early investigations also demonstrated the validity of this "good things go together" relationship (see review by Cox 1954). In no way has the notion that gifted children are by definition "misfits," "freaks," or "queer" been proved empirically accurate. The excellence of life success displayed by many gifted individuals is regarded, moreover, as heavily influenced by personality and social factors as well as superior cognitive ability (Oden 1968), although an exact demarcation between the affective and the cognitive domains is somewhat arbitrary.

Since the publication of these pioneering works there have been two developments in the study of psychology that have renewed interest in the nonintellectual characteristics of giftedness. First, assessment of affective and related social aspects of personality has improved considerably in the last three decades. New methods of scale construction and the availability of normative data for many interesting groups have made assessment research more productive and meaningful. Second, and very recently, major research programs have been directed at the highest levels of specific rather than general (i.e., IQ) cognitive ability. The Study of Mathematically Precocious Youth (SMPY) at The Johns Hopkins University, the most advanced study of this kind (see chapter 1 for a description), has, since the fall of 1971, worked with and collected cognitive and personality information on over ninety exceptionally able, mathematically precocious boys and girls. The cognitive abilities of this special group have been reported elsewhere (Stanley, Keating, & Fox 1974). The purpose of this chapter is to characterize these students with a composite profile of personality and social attributes based on a variety of standardized measures.

A preliminary analysis of the personological characteristics of the first thirty-two boys identified through the SMPY indicated that, based on the California Psychological Inventory (see p. 231), these boys were more interpersonally effective, socially mature, and academically motivated than their age-mates (Weiss, Haier, & Keating 1974 [I:7][2]). The present study replicates those findings on a new sample of mathematically gifted boys and, at the same time, integrates data from other measures to provide a comprehensive picture of the nonintellectual correlates of mathematical precocity for boys and for girls. We hope that an overview such as this will be a helpful extension of educational counseling services to these individuals and will also be intrinsically interesting to researchers investigating the relationships between cognitive and affective variables.

Specifically, our composite profile of these students will be drawn from results of five widely used tests: the California Psychological Inventory (CPI),

---

[2]In addition to the regular references, citations of chapters in volume I of *Studies of Intellectual Precocity* will be as follows: [I:7]. The I indicates volume I, and 7 is the chapter number [Editor].

the Eysenck Personality Inventory (EPI), the Study of Values (SV), Holland's Vocational Preference Inventory (VPI), and the Adjective Checklist (ACL). These tests will, respectively, provide the following broad perspectives on this group: interpersonal effectiveness, stability and adjustment, values, vocational interests, and self-image. The rest of this paper will be organized around these five perspectives to answer the following questions: (1) What is the group profile on each test? (2) How consistent is the group from test to test? (3) How do these students as a group compare with the profiles of creative adult scientists and mathematicians? Where appropriate, differences between the boys and girls will be examined with respect to these questions. Thus, in this chapter the consistently unique and salient nonintellectual aspects of mathematical precocity will be described and summarized.

METHOD

Subjects

A total of seventy-one seventh-, eighth-, and academically accelerated ninth-grade boys (ages twelve to fourteen) were selected on the basis of high scores on the Scholastic Aptitude Test—Mathematics (at least 640) or the STEP science test.[3] Both of these tests are normed on student samples three to five years older than these students. Similarly, twenty-five girls were selected on the basis of SAT-M scores of 600 or more.[4] These selections were conducted as part of the SMPY Talent Searches in 1972 and 1973 (see chapter 4 for details). The winners completed the standardized measures described below within three months of their initial selection.

Measures

1) *California Psychological Inventory*: The CPI is "addressed principally to personality characteristics important for social living and interactions" (Gough 1969). The eighteen scales of the CPI can be meaningfully interpreted with younger samples (Gough 1969) and particularly with younger, gifted samples (Lessinger & Martinson 1961; Weiss et al. 1974[I:7]—especially their appendix C). Its broad range and previously demonstrated utility makes the use of the CPI a central feature of the composite profile of our winners group.

2) *Eysenck Personality Inventory*: The EPI is a quick two-form forced-choice inventory that yields scores on three scales: E(xtroversion), N(euroti-

---

[3]The STEP science test was used only in 1972 as a criterion for "winners." Most of the boys in this sample achieved SAT-M ≥ 640.

[4]Two girls scoring under 600, who qualified in 1972 on the basis of STEP science test scores, are included in the sample. The lower cut-off score for girls is necessary, since fewer girls were high scorers.

cism), and L(ying) (Eysenck & Eysenck 1968). The relatively few scales of the EPI provide an economical view of overall adjustment and stability, based on the assumption that most of the variance in personality can be explained in terms of emotional stability and sociability. The EPI is a particularly useful supplement to cognitive test batteries, since it is reported to be unrelated to intelligence (Eysenck & Eysenck 1968). For this study each subject completed both forms. A combined score for each scale was obtained by summing raw scores from each form, since percentile ranks of combined scores have a greater reliability than those for either form used alone.

3) *Vocational Preference Inventory*: The winners group completed six scales from the VPI (Holland 1973). The items on these scales are occupations, fourteen per scale, which are endorsed *like or dislike* by the test-taker. Each scale corresponds to one of the following six occupational groups: R(ealistic), I(nvestigative), E(nterprising), A(rtistic), S(ocial), and C(onventional). These same groups are also interpretable as personality types. Thus the frequency of positively (like) endorsed occupations within a group indicates both vocational preference and an associated personality type. Usually the preference for the six types is rank ordered for each subject, and a three-letter code describing the first three preferences is assigned. For our purposes, only the letter of the highest ranked occupational type is used.

4) *Study of Values*: The SV (Allport, Vernon, & Lindzey 1970) consists of questions asking for preferences in relatively familiar situations. Six value scales indicating T(heoretical), E(conomic), A(esthetic), S(ocial), P(olitical), and R(eligious) value orientations are scored. Because each examinee's six scores must sum to the same constant (240 points), these scales are ipsative,[5] reflecting relative rather than absolute value levels. The value structure of these students is an important consideration in determining the most efficacious way to develop their unique mathematical ability. The inclusion of the SV, therefore, adds an important dimension to the composite profile.

5) *Adjective Checklist*: The ACL is a personality assessment device comprised of 300 descriptive adjectives (Gough & Heilbrun 1965). The winners who completed the ACL checked all the adjectives on the list which they felt were self-descriptive. Although twenty-four scales can be scored from the ACL, "the greatest value of the list may accrue from noting, pondering, and analyzing those specific words which . . . a group of individuals has checked as self-descriptive [p. 4]." Hence, we may construe the specific adjectives checked as an indication of self-image. Furthermore, the proportion of favorable to unfavorable adjectives will serve as an index of positive or negative self-image.

---

[5]"Ipsative" refers to the fact that the scales on this test are *not* independent of one another. Rather, a high score on one scale takes points from some of the other scales (see Gleser 1972).

RESULTS

All the analyses to be reported, except where otherwise indicated, were done on the combined boys or the combined girls groups of 1972 and 1973 Talent Search winners. Since the testing for each year was very similar, we assumed winners from both searches represented the same population and felt justified in pooling them. This assumption was reinforced by noting no significant differences on cognitive tests between the 1972 and the 1973 groups. Not every student was tested on each measure, so each analysis reports a somewhat different sample size. No systematic group bias, however, is evident as a result of the incomplete data.

Personal Effectiveness and Maturity: CPI Results

Following the preliminary analysis of Weiss et al. (1974[I:7]) the pooled winners group of mathematically gifted boys (N=68) was compared with eighth-grade random (EGR), eighth-grade gifted (EGG), high school normal (HSN), and high school gifted (HSG) groups (Lessinger & Martinson 1961; Gough 1969). Differences among this enlarged group of mathematically gifted (MG) boys and the four other groups are distinct and significant (see table 11.1), generally supporting the trends found in the earlier study.[6] The MG boys group most closely resembles the EGG and HSG groups and least closely resembles the EGR group. Hence, with regard to interpersonal effectiveness, the MG boys are most similar to students chronologically and academically more advanced. Thus, the CPI data indicates that these boys, when compared with their age-mates, are capable of mature social interaction.

The most significant differences in favor of the MG boys group are on the scales of Achievement via Independence and Flexibility. The interpretation of this combination denotes an innovative use of intelligence and adaptability. In view of their selection criteria and the new scholastic experiences which have been provided in many cases, these personality characteristics of flexibility and foresight form a very logical and necessary part of the group's cognitive style (see Helson & Crutchfield 1970; Capretta, Jones, Siegel, & Siegel 1963). This observation accentuates the rather arbitrary nature of the distinction between cognitive and affective characteristics.

The group CPI profile for the mathematically gifted girls (MG-F) is virtually identical to the boys' profile. Only one statistically significant difference on the femininity scale (p < .001) differentiates the two groups (see figure 11.1); as might be expected, the MG-Fs score higher on this scale than the MG-Ms.

---

[6]Because the original data of the norm groups were not available, these comparisons were made with "t" tests.

Table 11.1. Means of the pooled MG boys group compared with the male EGR, EGG, HSG, and HSN groups on the CPI Scales

CPI Scale		Math-gifted (MG)		Eighth grade random (EGR)		Eighth grade gifted (EGG)		High school norm (HSN)		High school gifted (HSG)	
		Mean	SD	Mean	SD	Mean	SD	Mean	SD	Mean	SD
1 Do	(dominance)	28.1	7.3	19.5*	4.9	27.0	5.5	23.2*	6.0	28.8	6.3
2 Cs	(capacity stat.)	17.6	3.7	11.3*	3.5	17.6	3.7	15.3*	4.4	20.7*	3.4
3 Sy	(sociability)	22.0	5.4	20.7	4.2	24.4‡	5.0	21.5	5.4	26.2*	4.7
4 Sp	(social pres.)	34.6	6.4	30.6*	6.2	32.9	5.7	32.7‡	5.7	35.6	6.7
5 Sa	(self-accept.)	20.2	3.6	17.6*	3.8	19.6	3.5	18.7‡	4.1	22.6*	3.8
6 Wb	(well-being)	31.4	6.1	27.2*	6.1	35.6*	4.8	33.5‡	5.6	35.8*	4.2
7 Re	(responsibility)	29.4	4.5	21.5*	5.8	31.7‡	4.3	26.7*	5.7	31.1†	5.1
8 So	(socialization)	37.1	5.2	29.9*	5.3	40.8*	4.9	36.3	6.0	38.1	6.4
9 Sc	(self-control)	25.1	7.3	18.0*	7.2	28.2†	8.8	25.3	8.0	25.8	8.3
10 To	(tolerance)	19.8	5.2	12.1*	4.8	22.4*	4.4	17.8‡	5.3	23.1*	4.5
11 Gi	(good impress.)	13.7	5.3	10.3*	4.7	16.9‡	6.8	15.1	6.2	15.8†	6.3
12 Cm	(communality)	24.7	2.3	23.6†	3.5	26.4*	1.8	25.2	2.8	25.4*	2.1
13 AC	(achiev. via conformance)	24.7	3.8	16.4*	4.4	26.3†	4.2	22.3*	5.3	27.2*	4.6
14 Ai	(achiev. via independence)	19.6	3.9	10.9*	3.5	18.0†	3.9	14.6*	4.1	20.8†	3.5
15 Ie	(intellectual efficiency)	37.7	5.1	26.0*	5.3	38.7	4.4	33.6‡	6.3	40.5*	4.3
16 Py	(psychological-mindedness)	11.6	3.0	7.9*	2.7	11.2	2.7	9.2*	2.6	12.0	2.6
17 Fx	(flexibility)	12.1	4.1	7.7*	2.7	9.4*	3.4	9.1*	3.4	11.0	4.0
18 Fe	(femininity)	17.5	3.6	15.1*	3.4	17.4	3.2	15.4*	3.6	16.1‡	3.4
19 EM	(empathy)[a]	20.7	3.9	—		—		—		—	
		N=68		N=82		N=94		N=3,572		N=157	

Note: Comparisons in each case are between MG and the specified group.

[a]No reference groups; this additional scale was developed by Hogan (1969).

† .01 < p < .05

‡ .001 < p < .01

* p < .001

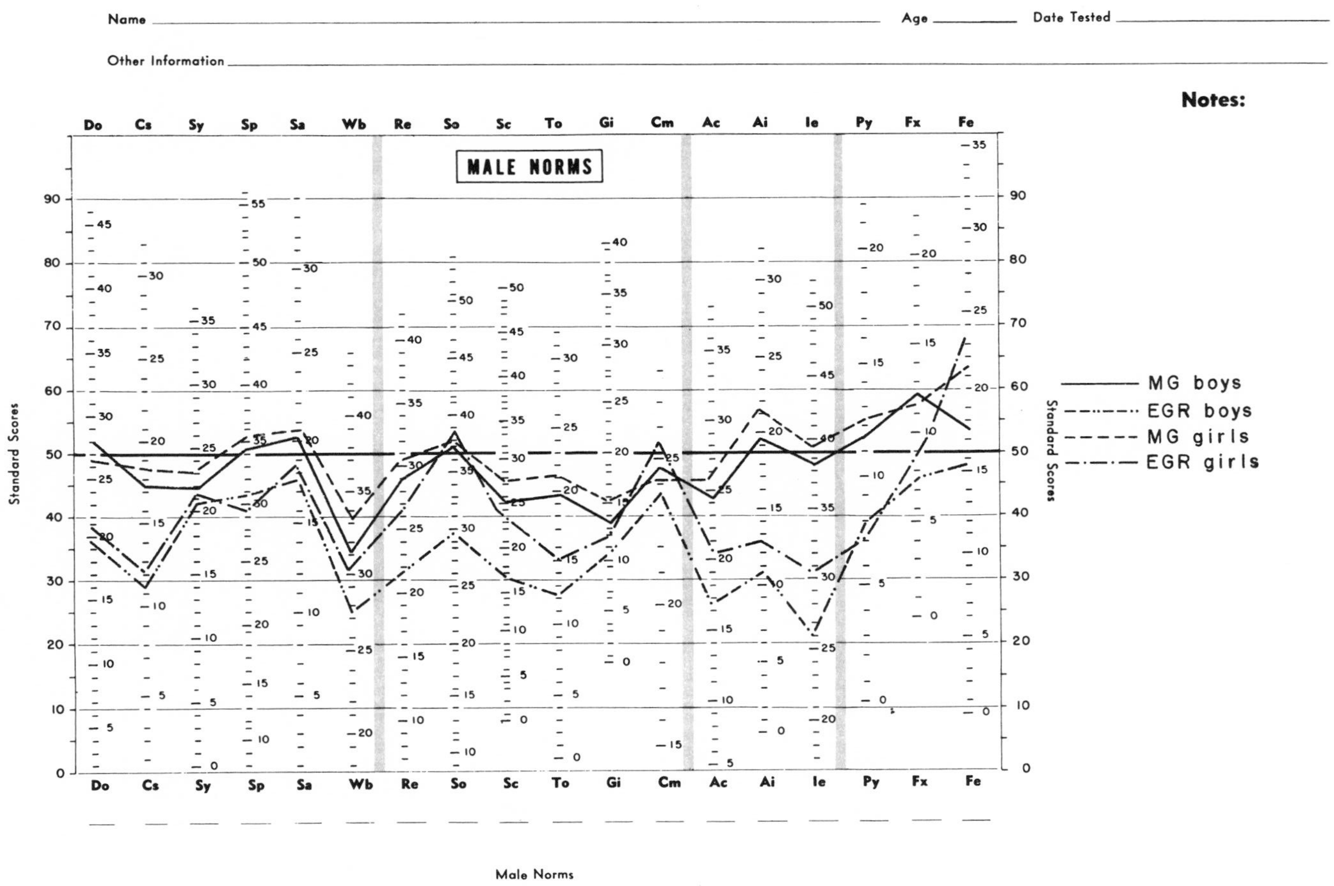

Fig. 11.1. Mathematically gifted (MG) boys and girls compared with eighth-grade random (EGR) boys and girls from Lessinger and Martinson (1961).

When compared, however, with female normative groups (Lessinger & Martinson 1961) the interpretation of the MG-F profile is somewhat different than the MG boys. The mathematically gifted girls group most closely resembles the EGG group and least closely resembles the EGR group, although, unlike the MG boys, the MG girls do not score higher than HSG on any scales (see table 11.2). Rather, the MG-F profile is distinctively characterized by the lowest femininity and communality scores of any of the comparison groups. This, together with their comparatively low score on Achievement via Conformance and high score on Achievement via Independence and their low Socialization score, depicts the MG girls as decidedly nonconforming. This complicated web of comparisons may be summarized by saying that, like the MG boys, the MG girls are more interpersonally effective than nongifted agemates and high school students, but the MG girls, unlike the MG boys, appear to be far more unconventional than their IQ-gifted counterparts. Given that the roles of mathematician and scientist typically have not been encouraged for females in our society, this finding is particularly interesting.

Personality characteristics and differences among creative male and female mathematicians were examined by Helson and Crutchfield (1970) and Helson (1971). The first of these studies indicated that, compared with "average Ph.Ds," creative adult male mathematicians showed lower scores on the CPI scale for Self-Control and higher scores on the Flexibility scale. Apparently the ability to "let go," to change mental set, and to be highly flexible are advantageous qualities for persons seeking careers in mathematics. As noted, both the MG boys and the MG girls show significantly higher Flexibility scale scores than non-IQ-gifted reference groups, and are lower on the Self-Control scale (though not necessarily significantly so) than all but one reference group (EGR). Thus the sample, both male and female, is similar to creative male mathematicians on a limited, but apparently important, set of dimensions. In Helson's (1971) sex comparison of creative mathematicians, findings showed that, relative to males, creative women were high on the Achievement via Independence, Psychological Mindedness, and Flexibility scales, while they were low on Communality and Achievement via Conformance scales. The MG girls group fits this pattern consistently. Helson (1971) also asserted that for the rebellious, somewhat introverted female Ph.D. mathematicians she studied, flexibility was a powerful determinant of creativity and success. Personal traits of independence, reflectiveness, and mental agility were found to be relatively more important for women than men. Apparently these traits are necessary for women if they are determined to contribute fully in male-oriented fields, such as mathematics and science.

On the other hand, Helson (1971) found that male mathematicians were higher than their female counterparts on several of the interpersonal effectiveness scales (Dominance, Sociability, Social Presence, and Self-Acceptance) and on the Intellectual Efficiency scale. This finding does not hold for our samples. Furthermore, Helson's sample of creative female mathematicians was intro-

Table 11.2. Means of MG girls group compared with female EGR, EGG, HSG, and HSN groups on the CPI Scales

CPI Scale		MG girls		EGR (female)		EGG (female)		HSN (female)		HSG (female)	
		Mean	SD	Mean	SD	Mean	SD	Mean	SD	Mean	SD
1 Do	(dominance)	26.9	6.2	20.7*	4.7	27.2	5.3	23.7‡	6.1	29.0	5.8
2 Cs	(capacity stat.)	18.7	4.6	12.2*	4.1	18.7	3.8	16.0‡	4.9	21.5*	3.8
3 Sy	(sociability)	23.3	6.4	21.7	4.1	25.1	5.0	21.4†	5.7	26.5‡	4.7
4 Sp	(social pres.)	35.6	7.0	29.7‡	5.6	33.3	6.3	31.1*	5.8	35.7	5.7
5 Sa	(self-accept.)	20.2	4.2	18.1†	3.8	20.6	4.3	18.9	4.4	22.3‡	3.5
6 Wb	(well-being)	33.5	6.1	30.0‡	5.6	35.3	5.5	34.6	5.7	36.0†	5.2
7 Re	(responsibility)	30.8	4.7	26.0*	4.9	33.1†	4.3	30.0	5.2	33.6*	3.8
8 So	(socialization)	36.8	6.2	37.2	5.6	42.3*	4.7	39.4†	5.6	40.4‡	5.1
9 Sc	(self-control)	27.2	10.9	23.2†	7.6	30.8	9.1	27.6	8.5	28.6	8.1
10 To	(tolerance)	21.7	5.6	15.1‡	4.9	22.9	5.2	18.7‡	5.5	24.3‡	4.3
11 Gi	(good impress.)	15.5	7.5	11.7‡	4.9	18.1	7.5	15.7	6.2	16.3	5.6
12 Cm	(communality)	24.4	2.4	25.5†	2.0	26.1*	1.7	26.1*	1.9	26.3*	1.8
13 AC	(achiev. via conformance)	25.6	6.0	20.2*	5.0	28.0†	4.6	24.1	5.3	28.2†	5.0
14 Ai	(achiev. via independence)	21.2	4.5	12.9*	3.8	19.0‡	3.8	15.5*	4.2	21.6	4.0
15 Ie	(intellectual efficiency)	39.1	4.8	30.2*	4.9	39.7	5.2	34.4*	6.5	41.6†	4.4
16 Py	(psychological-mindedness)	12.2	1.8	7.5*	2.5	10.8†	3.0	8.7*	2.6	11.3	3.0
17 Fx	(flexibility)	11.9	4.8	8.3*	3.5	10.0†	3.6	8.9*	3.2	11.0	3.6
18 Fe	(femininity)[a]	21.5	4.2	23.2†	4.0	23.5†	3.6	24.1*	3.5	23.5‡	3.4
		N = 25		N = 90		N = 77		N = 4,056		N = 107	

Note: Comparisons in each case are between MG and the specified group.
[a]Significantly greater than MG boys group, $p < .001$.
† $.01 < p < .05$
‡ $.001 < p < .01$
* $p < .001$

verted as well as rebellious. Our sample of females, although apparently as rebellious and nonconforming, is not obviously introverted. Despite these differences, which may be related at least partly to the age factor, both MG boys and MG girls appear to have the basic creative characteristics appraised by Helson.

Stability and Adjustment: EPI Results

Results of the EPI for 55 MG boys are summarized and compared with available norm groups in table 11.3. Since only four girls completed the EPI, no analysis for them is included here. The MG boys are, as a group, significantly less neurotic ($p < .05$) and less extroverted ($p < .001$) than a sample of the American college population. Thus, these winners can be classified as stable, non-neurotic, and introverted. This is very similar to the classic creative scientist pattern discussed by Roe (1953). Eysenck (1960) describes this combination of low N, low E, in terms of the following adjectives: passive, careful, thoughtful, peaceful, controlled, reliable, even-tempered, and calm. The low E is specifically described as introspective, serious, planning, fond of books, and reserved except with friends.

At first glance, the introverted classification of the EPI seems to contradict the CPI interpretation of these boys as interpersonally effective. Introversion was not a salient aspect of the winners group CPI profile. Interpreted in the classical Jungian sense, the introversion measured by the E scale indicates the preference for the intellectual rather than the social aspects of life. There is no relative or inherent advantage or disadvantage in introversion or extroversion. Introversion is seen as a matter of preference rather than ability. This point is underscored by Eysenck's descriptive phrase "reserved except with friends." It is clear from many observations of these boys over the last two years that they can be socially adroit and comfortable, although as a group they do not seek out continual social stimulation as an extrovert might. Thus, the apparent

Table 11.3. Comparison of the MG boys with a norm group on the Eysenck Personality Inventory

	Neuroticism scale			Extroversion scale		
	Mean	S.D.	P.R.[a]	Mean	S.D.	P.R.
MG boys (N=68)	18.2	12.1	39	23.2	5.8	25
American college students[b]	21.5*	8.4	50	28.2[†]	6.9	50

[a]Percentile rank.
[b]Males and females.
*$p < .01$
[†]$p < .001$

discrepancy between the MG boys' low E-scale scores and their high scores on the corresponding CPI scales seems to be less a contradiction and more a refinement.

Other available evidence suggests that the low E-scale scores and the moderate N-scale scores make sense for this group. Lynn (1959) and Lynn and Gordon (1961) found, for example, that low scores on the E scale are positively correlated with persistence and achievement. Lynn and Gordon (1961) also found a curvilinear relationship between N scores and scores on the Raven's Progressive Matrices (RPM), a test of nonverbal reasoning also given to the MG group. This curvilinear relationship indicated that persons with moderate N scores, like the MG group, tended to score higher on the RPM. This is true for this group of boys.

The results from the EPI, then, basically support the more detailed inferences drawn from the "folk concepts" of the CPI, but also add an important refinement. These boys are personally stable and effective, but tend to be serious and introspective, except when called upon to exercise their social talents.

Values: SV Results

Results for 1972 boys and girl winners on the Study of Values have been described in detail elsewhere (Fox & Denham 1974[I:8], and chapter 14 of this volume), but an examination of the pooled 1972 and 1973 winners will contribute to the complete profile of these students. These data are summarized in table 11.4. The predominant value orientation of the boys and the girls is theoretical. According to the SV authors (Allport, Vernon, & Lindzey 1970), a theoretical type denotes an "inclination to actively seek truth in a logical, often scientific manner." That these students, chosen for their excellent mathematical reasoning ability, have value structures related to science and logic is not unexpected. Certainly, ability is not the only factor leading to success, and the cultivation of precocious talent is likely to be most fruitful when an individual's values and interests are consistent with his abilities. Mathematicians and

Table 11.4. Percent of MG boys and girls scoring highest on each scale of the Study of Values

	(N)	T	P	A	S	E	R
MG boys	(71)	59.2	14.1	4.2	5.6	9.9	7.0
MG girls	(22)	31.8	20.5	20.4	13.6	6.8	6.8

T (heoretical)
P (olitical)
A (esthetic)
S (ocial)
E (conomic)
R (eligious)

creative scientists also score high on this theoretical scale (MacKinnon 1962; Hall & MacKinnon 1969).

The second most prevalent value type for the boys and for the girls is political. Political types are characterized by their concern with power. Thus, the relatively large percentage of winners scoring highest on the P scale implies that many of these students are interested in leadership and influence. Fewer boys than girls were typified by Artistic or Social value orientations.

For the purposes of the group profile the SV results may be summarized as demonstrating that both the boys and the girls have a theoretical value orientation, i.e., toward knowledge and truth. This is consistent with their actual ability and with the low E-scale scores on the EPI (for the boys) and the high achievement cluster of scales on the CPI.

Vocational Interests: VPI Results

Holland's VPI measures not only vocational interests but also ties these interests to personality types. The choices for future occupations for this group of boys and girls are predominantly Investigative (see table 11.5). Social occupations are the least preferred.

Persons who prefer Investigative activities are described by Holland as typically choosing scientific careers, and are characterized personologically as scholarly, intellectual, self-confident, independent, cautious, precise, introverted, reserved, and rational. These adjectives correspond closely to the overall view of this group from the other measures discussed thus far. The most obvious consistency is that on measures of both values and interests and on measures of personality, intellectual curiosity is very evident.

As with the SV, the results of the VPI are important for individual educational guidance and counseling. Those students who prefer activities other than Investigative may have no strong desire or interest in developing

Table 11.5.   Percent of MG boys and girls scoring highest on each scale of the Vocational Preference Inventory

	(N)	I	A	R	E	C	S
MG boys	(71)	66.9	6.3	9.9	4.0	9.6	3.3
MG girls	(11)	50.0	22.7	9.1	13.6	4.5	0

I (nvestigative)
A(rtistic)
R(ealistic)
E(nterprising)
C(onventional)
S (ocial)

their mathematical ability at the present time. Within Holland's theoretical framework it is predicted that an Investigative type person will most enjoy Investigative type work. Since the pursuit of mathematics or science as a career implies an Investigative type, those students in the group who are not Investigative types should not be chided if they are unenthusiastic about their mathematical ability. In practice, these results and their interpretations for students in SMPY programs are communicated in detail to them. Some consequently opt to pursue their interests in other areas as a result of this information.

Self-Image: ACL Results

The analysis and interpretation of the ACL is based on forty-six of the high scoring boys; not enough girls completed the ACL for meaningful group comparisons. In a way, the ACL may provide the most interesting element of the composite profile, because it asks the test-taker to evaluate or describe himself directly. Although the ACL may be analyzed in a variety of ways, only the favorable and unfavorable scale scores will be discussed. These scores, together with the specific adjectives checked most often, will provide sufficient information to assess the collective self-image of the students.

Based on ratings (Gough & Heilbrun 1965), seventy-five adjectives on the ACL are designated as favorable and another seventy-five are designated as unfavorable. The number of adjectives checked by each student on these two scales was converted into a standard score derived from a normative adult group (mean 50, s.d. 10) to take account of the tendency to check more favorable than unfavorable adjectives and differential individual tendencies for total number of adjectives checked. Our first comparison was simply of the mean differences in standard scores between the two scales within the MG group. Surprisingly, the mean standard score for the unfavorable scale was significantly higher ($p < .05$) than for the favorable scale (see table 11.6). This finding, however, requires considerable caution in its interpretation. Table 11.6 includes comparison data for creative and noncreative high school boys (Schaefer 1969). When the means of the groups are compared, it is apparent that all groups score higher on the unfavorable than on the favorable scale. Further, the MG boys, comparatively, have the lowest mean on the unfavorable scale and the highest mean on the favorable scale (although not statistically significant). Thus, it appears that the tendency toward an unfavorable self-image (as defined here) is prevalent among adolescent boys. While this finding itself deserves closer examination by researchers interested in self-image and identity development, it may be pointed out for our purposes here that the self-image of the MG boys is comparatively less unfavorable than for other adolescent groups.

Table 11.6. Standard score means and standard deviations of MG boys and creative and non-creative high school boys on the favorable and unfavorable ACL Scales[a]

		MG boys N=46	Art–Writing		Scientific	
			Creative N=100	Noncreative N=100	Creative N=100	Noncreative N=100
Favorable	X̄	46.42	43.90	45.05	44.52	44.39
	SD	8.72	9.82	9.52	10.65	9.97
Unfavorable	X̄	52.04	55.48	54.27	55.24	53.04
	SD	10.26	9.57	11.33	11.58	10.91

[a]From Schaefer (1969).

Table 11.7. The percent of the most favorable and unfavorable adjectives selected by the MG boys compared with the frequency of those adjectives selected by a control sample

		MG boys (N=46)	Control (N=40)
Favorable	Intelligent	96%	39%
	Capable	93	50
	Adaptable	89	28
	Logical	87	25
	Honest	85	50
	Clear-thinking	83	55
Unfavorable	Argumentative	67	25
	Sarcastic	52	08
	Impatient	41	33
	Opinionated	41	08
	Cynical	37	05

This point is underscored by noting the specific adjectives checked most often by the MG boys. These adjectives, favorable and unfavorable, are listed in table 11.7, where their frequency is compared with the frequency of the same adjectives selected by a nongifted control sample.[7]

In this second analysis of the ACL it is apparent that the adjectives checked by the MG boys as self-descriptive are not frequently checked by the nongifted sample. The specific favorable adjectives, moreover, depict a consistent and meaningful self-image for these boys. Likewise, the unfavorable adjectives make sense for this group. The fact that many of these boys see themselves as argumentative, sarcastic, impatient, and opinionated may indicate the degree to

[7]This control sample consisted of forty junior high school boys (matched to the MG boys on age) assigned to "average" (i.e., letter grade C) science classes.

which they are bored or dissatisfied with conventional school curricula. Not surprisingly, and providing some validity to this finding, the teachers of these students use these same adjectives to describe their gifted students (see chapter 10). In any case, these unfavorable adjectives are relatively mild (see appendix 10.2, page 222, for the full scales).

THE COMPOSITE GROUP PROFILE:
DISCUSSION AND CONCLUSIONS

Each of the five perspectives (personal effectiveness, adjustment and stability, values, interests, and self-image) may now be considered as a composite profile for these students. Considering the diversity of the measures used, the composite profile is remarkably consistent. As a group these mathematically precocious youth are interpersonally effective and socially mature, although the boys prefer intellectual and academic pursuits over social interests. While a higher percentage of girls are interested in social and artistic concerns, the girls as a group are more nonconforming with respect to sex typing. Both boys and girls are confident and well-adjusted, although some boys see themselves as argumentative and sarcastic. Thus, as a group, these students fare well. Since the patterns of their scores on the different tests are not only sensible for mathematically gifted students but also are similar to adult creative mathematicians and scientists, it is unlikely that the scores merely reflect good test-taking ability.

The "good things go together" relationship is unmistakable for this group. Yet, it is still too early to characterize how the mathematically gifted differ from other gifted students with respect to specific attributes. This analysis awaits a larger sample of mathematically gifted (particularly girls) and similar descriptive data on other talented groups.[8]

We have concentrated exclusively on group analysis and comparison. Although there are clear group trends on each measure, there is considerable variance on all measures. The temptation to discuss individual profiles is substantial, but a case study approach is beyond the scope of this summary profile. It is still somewhat premature to discuss individual cases with regard to the group profile, since a necessary and interesting part of such an examination would include outcome measures of successful education facilitation. Such measures are as yet unavailable for many students (see chapter 1, however, for a discussion of exemplary cases, and Weiss et al., 1974 [I:7, appendix C]).

Undoubtedly, it may be surprising and perhaps suspect that the group profile is so strikingly positive and without serious negative components. It is

[8]Such data are being collected by the Study of Verbally Gifted Youth at The Johns Hopkins University (see chapter 8).

well to recall the nature of selection of the mathematically gifted sample at this point: self-selection for participation in a difficult contest; high performance in that contest; and voluntary participation in the follow-up evaluations. Thus, a biasing effect in favor of the group is quite possible, and even likely.

Data such as these, moreover, are always subject to varying interpretations. It is also considerably safer to characterize a group than an individual. That all the members of the mathematically gifted sample fit the group profile exactly is, of course, unlikely. Actually, the variances on most of the personological scales are at least as large for the mathematically gifted as for the general population. There are some talented students who clearly do not demonstrate a high degree of maturity or confidence on the objective measures. These students are in the minority, and it will be particularly interesting to follow their progress. The value in these personality measures, in fact, may lie in how well they predict the future success and adjustment of these students.

Some further qualification is in order. These results, particularly of the CPI and EPI, should not be interpreted as demonstrating that these specially selected twelve to fourteen year-olds have acquired the level of sophistication of college students or adults. They are still adolescents. While their test scores may be similar (or even superior) to older persons, overt maturity and ability to interact successfully with other people have their basis in real-life experiences. The fact that these students are chronologically younger than college students and adults necessarily limits their range of experience. The significance of their advanced noncognitive profile is not that they will skip the "trials and tribulations" of youth, but rather that they are comparatively well equipped to successfully encounter life. Like all youth, they will have their special problems, but with the proper adult supervision and encouragement, the academic advancement of these talented students will not proceed at the expense of emotional or social growth.

REFERENCES

Allport, G. W., Vernon, P. E., and Lindzey, G. 1970. *Manual for the study of values: A scale for measuring the dominant interests in personality* (3rd ed.). Boston: Houghton Mifflin Co.

Capretta, P. S., Jones, R. L., Siegel, L., and Siegel, L. M. 1963. Some non-cognitive characteristics of honors program candidates. *Journal of Educational Psychology* 54: 268–76.

Cox, C. M. 1954. Gifted children. In L. Carmichael (ed.), *Manual of child psychology* (2nd ed.). New York: John Wiley & Sons.

Eysenck, H. J. 1960. *The structure of human personality* (2nd ed.). London: Methuen.

Eysenck, H. J., and Eysenck, S. B. G. 1968. *Manual for the Eysenck Personality Inventory*. San Diego, Calif.: Educational and Industrial Testing Service.

Fox, L. H., and Denham, S. A. 1974. Values and career interests of mathematically and scientifically precocious youth. In J. C. Stanley, D. P. Keating, and L. H. Fox (eds.), *Mathematical talent: Discovery, description, and development.* Baltimore: The Johns Hopkins University Press, pp. 140–75.

Gleser, L. J. 1972. On the bounds for the average correlation between subtest scores in ipsatively scored tests. *Educational and Psychological Measurement* 32(3): 759–66.

Gough, H. G. 1969. *Manual for the California Psychological Inventory* (3rd ed.). Palo Alto, Calif.: Consulting Psychologists Press.

Gough, H. G., and Heilbrun, A. B. 1965. *The adjective checklist manual.* Palo Alto, Calif.: Consulting Psychologists Press.

Hall, W. B., and MacKinnon, D. W. 1969. Personality inventories as predictors of creativity among architects. *Journal of Applied Psychology* 53(4): 322–26.

Helson, R. 1971. Women mathematicians and the creative personality. *Journal of Consulting and Clinical Psychology* 36: 210–20.

Helson, R., and Crutchfield, R. S. 1970. Creative types in mathematics. *Journal of Personality* 38: 177–97.

Hogan, R. 1969. Development of an empathy scale. *Journal of Consulting and Clinical Psychology* 33: 307–16.

Holland, J. L. 1973. *Making vocational choices: A theory of careers.* Englewood Cliffs, N.J.: Prentice–Hall.

Lessinger, L. M., and Martinson, R. A. 1961. The use of the CPI with gifted pupils. *Personnel and Guidance Journal* 39: 572–75.

Lynn, R. 1959. Two personality characteristics related to academic achievement. *British Journal of Educational Psychology* 29: 213–16.

Lynn, R., and Gordon, I. E. 1961. The relation of neuroticism and extroversion to intelligence and educational attainment. *British Journal of Educational Psychology* 31: 194–203.

MacKinnon, D. W. 1962. The nature and nurture of creative talent. *American Psychologist* 17(7): 484–95.

Oden, M. H. 1968. The fulfillment of promise: 40-year follow-up of the Terman gifted group. *Genetic Psychology Monographs* 77: 3–93.

Roe, A. 1953. *The making of a scientist.* New York: Dodd, Mead.

Schaefer, C. 1969. The self concept of creative adolescents. *Journal of Psychology* 72: 233–42.

Stanley, J. C., Keating, D. P., and Fox, L. H. (eds.). 1974. *Mathematical talent: Discovery, description, and development.* Baltimore: The Johns Hopkins University Press.

Terman, L. M. 1925–59. *Genetic studies of genius,* vols. I–V. Stanford, Calif.: Stanford University Press.

Weiss, D. S., Haier, R. J., and Keating, D. P. 1974. Personality characteristics of mathematically precocious boys. In J. C. Stanley, D. P. Keating, and L. H. Fox (eds.), *Mathematical talent: Discovery, description, and development.* Baltimore: The Johns Hopkins University Press, pp. 126–39 and 191–202.

12
CAREER-RELATED INTERESTS OF ADOLESCENT BOYS AND GIRLS

Lynn H. Fox, Sara R. Pasternak, and Nancy L. Peiser

ABSTRACT

The career-related interests of academically gifted seventh-grade boys and girls are compared with a representative sample of ninth-graders, using the twenty-three Basic Interest Scales of the Strong–Campbell Interest Inventory. The gifted boys and girls scored higher than the average ability boys and girls on investigative scales such as mathematics and science. The pattern of sex differences for both groups of students were similar, but gifted girls, unlike average girls, show strong interests on the "masculine" scales, such as mathematics. Some evidence that gifted girls may experience more conflict than gifted boys with respect to career choices in later life was found by asking students to rate eight occupations on sixteen adjective pairs on a semantic differential.

Cognitive ability and personal interests and values are important psychological factors determining an individual's career choice. It is generally agreed that men differ from women greatly with respect to interests and values and to some extent in cognitive abilities, and these differences are reflected in their varying career choices. What is not clear is how these differences between the sexes evolve during childhood and adolescence. In this chapter we shall consider the evidence of sex differences in interests and values related to eventual career choices among gifted adolescents and their implications for understanding the relationship of ability and interests, particularly in the area of science and mathematics.

Results of various studies indicate a relationship between masculine interests, scientific career choices, and achievements in mathematics (Astin 1974[I:4];[1] Carey 1958; Milton 1957). The Study of Mathematically Precocious

---

[1]In addition to the usual references, citations of chapters in volume I of *Studies of Intellectual Precocity* will be as follows [I:4]. The I indicates volume I, and the 4 is the chapter number [Editor].

Youth (SMPY) at The Johns Hopkins University has reported a relationship between extremely high cognitive ability, values, scientific interests, and career choices of young adolescents (Fox & Denham 1974[I:8]).

In the 1972 Talent Search at The Johns Hopkins University, bright seventh-, eighth-, and young ninth-grade students were administered a short form of the Vocational Preference Inventory (VPI–Holland 1965), in addition to the College Entrance Examination Board's Scholastic Aptitude Test–Mathematical (SAT-M). More boys than girls preferred the investigative careers such as science, mathematics, and medicine (Fox & Denham 1974 [I:8]). Those in the 1973 Talent Search were administered the Allport–Vernon–Lindzey Study of Values (Allport, Vernon, & Lindzey 1970). Boys scored highest on the theoretical value scale, while the girls scored highest on the social value scale (see chapter 14 of this volume). Highly precocious boys (as evidenced by scores of 640 or more on the SAT-M) showed a greater interest in investigative careers and theoretical values than less precocious boys and girls in the contest.

Many participants in those two talent searches exhibited cognitive abilities at an extremely high level. Not only did more boys than girls enter the contest but also a greater number of boys than girls had extremely high mathematical reasoning ability. A question of interest to these investigators was in what ways bright boys and girls with similar cognitive abilities differed with respect to interests.

This present study was designed to obtain more information concerning the interests and career choices of seventh-grade boys and girls of high ability (in the upper 2 percent of their grade level on the Iowa Tests of Basic Skills) who were matched on mathematical aptitude, SAT-M, and verbal aptitude, Scholastic Aptitude Test–Verbal (SAT-V), and socioeconomic level.

The gifted seventh-graders selected for this study were contestants in the 1973 Talent Search who were participating in a special study of the development of mathematical ability in young women (see chapter 9 in this volume). The criterion for selection was lower than that for the winners of the talent searches (scores of at least 640 on SAT-M). This enabled a sizable number of girls to be matched with boys on cognitive ability in order to study sex differences. Three matched groups of equal size and cognitive ability were formed: one experimental group of girls, one control group of girls, and one control group of boys. All but one of the experimental girls scored at least 370 on SAT-M.[2] Triads (one person from each group) were matched within plus or minus 20 points on both SAT-M and SAT-V whenever possible. Although not greatly so, the boys were still slightly but statistically significantly superior in mathematical aptitude.

---

[2]One of the girls in the experimental group scored 350 on the SAT-M. She was included in the study for reasons explained in chapter 9, p. 189.

The two matched control groups were selected for the present study.[3] The matched mathematical and verbal scores for each boy and girl are shown in table 12.1.

The career interests of these twenty-six boys and twenty-six girls were compared with each other and with those of seventy-five boy and seventy-five girl ninth-graders, a sample of adolescents in two junior high schools for whom summary data were available from the Strong–Campbell Vocational Interest Inventory.[4] These students were considered to be a representative sample of

[3]A few of the girls in the experimental group were not tested on the Strong–Campbell prior to the start of the experimental program, which included some career counseling. Since their scores may have been slightly influenced by the treatment, it seemed best to eliminate that group for the present comparison.

[4]Data furnished by David Campbell, formerly of the University of Minnesota, now at the Center for Creative Leadership, Greensboro, North Carolina.

Table 12.1.　Scores on SAT-M and SAT-V for the matched pairs of boys and girls in the sample of gifted students

| | Girls | | Boys | |
	Math	Verbal	Math	Verbal
	560	410	550	360
	520	490	550	490
	490	490	490	510
	490	400	490	420
	480	370	480	380
	480	290	510	290
	460	470	470	520
	460	460	470	490
	460	390	440	400
	460	350	460	350
	450	340	460	330
	450	320	430	310
	440	450	440	450
	430	430	440	430
	430	360	430	350
	430	330	460	350
	420	380	430	390
	420	380	420	380
	390	360	420	350
	380	350	410	370
	370	490	370	460
	370	430	380	460
	370	350	410	330
	360	320	370	360
	350	350	370	330
	330	380	380	370
Mean	432.69	390.00	443.46	393.46
S.D.	55.83	57.76	50.27	64.31

junior high school students and not a gifted group. They are referred to as the average adolescent group.

CAREER INTEREST SCALES

The measure of career interests used was the Strong-Campbell Vocational Interest Inventory (SCII).[5] Scores from this inventory are reported in three ways: Part One, the General Occupation Themes, which define an individual's overall occupational tendencies; Part Two, the Basic Interest Scales, which show one's consistency of interest in twenty-three specific areas; and Part Three, the Occupational Scales, which exhibit the congruency between an individual's interests and the characteristic interests of men and women in various occupations. All three intercorrelated parts are organized to provide information to help the individual define his interests and potential career choice (Campbell 1974).

The Basic Interest Scales are the main criteria used in this study, for they are the primary factor for identifying an individual's interests in relation to his vocational choice (Campbell 1974). To facilitate the discussion of the twenty-three scales, the interests were grouped into the six appropriate General Occupational Themes: Realistic (R), Investigative (I), Artistic (A), Social (S), Enterprising (E), and Conventional (C) (Holland 1966).[6] The scales included in each of the interest areas are shown in table 12.2.

According to the manual (Campbell 1974), a score of above 50 on any of the twenty-three scales indicates above-average interest for that particular theme.[7] High scores are obtained by indicating "like" for the activities pertaining to a career; low scores are obtained by indicating "dislike" for the activities pertaining to a career. An individual's interests are well differentiated if he or she earns high scores in numerous unrelated areas. This is not uncommon among adolescents. In general, the less a student's interests and career choices resemble the typical adolescent responses, the more predictive is the profile. High scores on scales such as mathematics, science, and art, which are uncommon interests for this age group, are more predictive for potential careers than are high scores on scales such as adventure, domestic arts, and religious activities, which are interests tending to decrease with maturity (Campbell 1974).

---

[5]Still in developmental stage.

[6]Scales originally devised by J. L. Holland and adapted and incorporated into the Strong–Campbell Interest Inventory by David Campbell.

[7]According to the manual a score above 50 represents greater than average interest for adults. Since adolescents typically score lower than adults on most scales (Campbell 1974) a score above 50 for adolescents can clearly be interpreted as above average interest, and a score of 55 as well above average.

Table 12.2. Scores on the 23 Strong–Campbell Basic Interest Scales for the sample of gifted students

General Occ. Scale theme	Basic Interest Scale	Girls	Boys	Difference[a]
Realistic	Adventure	55.19	56.85	−1.66
	Nature	54.58	47.58	7.00*
	Agriculture	54.50	50.73	3.77
	Military activities	52.12	55.77	−3.65
	Mechanical activities	44.58	53.35	−8.77*
Investigative	Medical service	53.77	48.92	4.85[†]
	Mathematics	53.62	58.08	−4.46
	Medical science	51.69	51.73	−0.04
	Science	50.58	59.15	−8.57*
Artistic	Writing	52.96	44.77	8.19*
	Art	52.89	41.96	10.93*
	Music/Dramatics	50.08	41.12	8.96*
Social	Domestic arts	59.58	39.04	20.54*
	Social service	52.77	43.46	9.31*
	Athletics	52.19	54.42	−2.23
	Teaching	50.62	42.04	8.58*
	Religious activities	50.15	43.96	6.19[‡]
Enterprising	Public speaking	48.92	50.23	−1.13
	Sales	47.23	45.31	1.92
	Law/Politics	46.00	48.04	−2.04
	Merchandising	45.81	44.12	1.69
	Business management	43.54	44.12	−0.58
Conventional	Office practice	52.54	45.50	7.04*

[a] Levels of significance based on Tukey test of mean comparisons.
[†] p < .05
[‡] p < .01
* p < .005

INTERESTS IN THE GIFTED GROUP

The girls in the gifted group scored above a mean of 50 for seventeen of the twenty-three interest scales; the boys in the gifted group scored above 50 for nine of the interest scales. The girls scored above 50 on every scale except mechanical activities (realistic) and the five enterprising scales (public speaking, sales, law/politics, merchandising, and business management). The boys scored above 50 on all the realistic scales except nature and all the investigative scales except medical service. The boys scored below 50 on all the artistic scales, the conventional scale, and all the social and enterprising scales except athletics (social) and public speaking (enterprising). The mean scores for the gifted seventh-grade girls and boys on each of the twenty-three scales are shown in table 12.2.

Both gifted boys and girls have well above average interest scores (above 55) on the adventure scale, and girls are high on the domestic arts scale, which Campbell (1974) says is typical of adolescents. Gifted boys, however, also have high scores on the military activities, mathematics, and science scales; the latter two are fairly uncommon for adolescents. Since gifted girls scored high (above 55) only on scales which reflect adolescent more than adult interests, while gifted boys scored high (above 55) on scales which are atypical for adolescents and more predictive of later career choices (Campbell 1974), the boys can be said to have somewhat more developed career interests than the girls.

Sex Differences in the Gifted Group

Although there are some strong similarities in interest patterns between the gifted girls and gifted boys, in that both groups score above 50 on most of the realistic and investigative scales, and below 50 on most of the enterprising scales, there are some significant differences between the two groups on a number of scales, particularly those of social and artistic interests. Campbell (1974) reports that a difference of five points or more between groups on a scale is significant. In the case of the gifted adolescents, it was possible to test these differences more precisely by analysis of variance for matched groups. (The two gifted groups had been matched on cognitive abilities and education of parents, thus eliminating bias due to socioeconomic level or ability.)

An analysis of variance of the two groups on the twenty-three scales is shown in table 12.3. The sex difference was significant, as were the difference of rating of the scales and the interaction of sex and interest scales.

Tukey tests of mean comparisons (Scheffé 1959) showed that the girls scored significantly higher than the boys on the following interest scales: domestic arts, art, social service, music/dramatics, teaching, writing, nature, office practice

Table 12.3. Analysis of variance of preferences for the 23 Basic Interest Scales for the sample of gifted students

Sources of variation	df	MS	F
Sex (S)	1	2436.32	5.14*
Pair (P)	25	349.94	
Scales (C)	22	645.81	9.15[†]
SP	25	474.41	
SC	22	614.62	8.95[†]
PC	550	70.57	
SPC	550	68.69	
TOTAL	1,195		

*$p < .05$
[†]$p < .001$

(p < .005), religious activities (p < .01), and medical service (p < .05). The boys scored significantly higher than the girls on the following scales: mechanical activities, and science (p < .005). Scales on which the sexes differed significantly are indicated in table 12.2.

There were no significant differences between the girls and boys with respect to any of the enterprising scales. Girls scored significantly higher on all three artistic scales and all of the social scales except athletics. This confirms previous findings that girls, at least very bright girls, are more interested in social and artistic pursuits than very bright boys.

The present study found somewhat less striking differences between girls and boys on realistic interests than had been indicated from the use of the VPI (Holland 1965; Fox & Denham 1974 [I:8]). For the realistic theme, girls scored significantly higher on the nature scale and significantly lower on the mechanical activities scales. There were no significant differences on the remaining three scales (agriculture, adventure, and military activities), though the boys were higher than the girls on each. For the investigative theme, girls scored significantly higher on the medical service scale, lower on the mathematics scale; significantly lower on the science scale; and there was little difference on the medical science scale. Thus, bright girls are more likely to be interested in investigative occupations which have some component of social service (perhaps as physician or applied medical researcher) than in more purely theoretical scientific pursuits. It should be noted that one investigative scale (medical service), found to be significantly different for the sexes by the Tukey test, would not have reached significance by applying the five-point "practical-importance" rule.

Twelve of the twenty-three interest scales were significantly different for girls and boys in the gifted group. On only two scales (mechanical activities and science) did girls score lower than boys, and on one of these (science) the girls scored above 50. There was only one scale, mechanical activities, on which boys scored above average and girls scored below average. Of the ten scales on which girls scored significantly higher than boys, the boys scored below 50. These were primarily on social and artistic interest scales. By far the largest absolute difference in table 12.3, which favored girls, was on domestic arts.

Thus, in the present study the major source of sex differences among highly able adolescents is that girls have stronger interests in social and artistic areas than boys. Gifted girls tend to have above average interests in both masculine and feminine interest areas, whereas gifted boys appear to have strong interests in masculine interest areas but weak interest in areas generally considered feminine, such as domestic arts, art, social service, music/dramatics, and teaching.

The two main questions of interest in the following sections of this chapter are: are these apparent sex differences in interests also found in a sample of average adolescents? Do gifted adolescents differ from a more typical group of adolescents with respect to interests, particularly those of an investigative nature?

INTERESTS OF THE AVERAGE ADOLESCENT GROUP

The students in the sample of average adolescents were almost two grades older than the gifted sample (ninth-graders during the school year versus seventh-graders at the end of the school year). The basic interest scale scores of the average group were lower than those of the gifted group on most scales, especially the scientific and artistic ones. The average ninth-grade girls scored above 50 on only nine of the twenty-three interest scales as compared with seventeen for the gifted seventh-grade girls. The ninth-grade boys scored above 50 on only five of the scales, as compared with nine for the gifted seventh-grade boys. The mean score on each of the scales are shown in table 12.4.

The ninth-grade girls scored above 55 on one social scale (domestic arts), on one investigative scale (medical service), and on the one conventional scale (office practice). They also scored above 50 on three realistic scales (agriculture, nature, and adventure), on one artistic scale (art), and on two social scales (social service and athletics).

The ninth-grade boys scored above 55 on three of the realistic scales (adventure, military activities, and agriculture) and on one social scale (athletics). The ninth-grade boys scored above 50 on one realistic scale (mechanical activities) and below 50 on the rest of the scales.

Neither ninth-grade girls nor ninth-grade boys scored above 55 on the mathematics, science, or art scales, whereas boys scored high on adventure and girls scored extremely high on domestic arts. Thus, both groups appear to have interest profiles that are typical of adolescents and less well-developed than those of gifted boys.

Sex Differences in the Average Adolescent Group

Since raw scores for the average group were not available, a study of sex differences in this group will use the five-point criterion supplied by Campbell (1974).[8] The girls scored higher on the following scales: domestic arts, office practice, social service, art, medical service, music/dramatics, and nature. The boys scored at least five points higher on the following scales: mechanical activities, adventure, military activities, and science. These differences are indicated in table 12.4.

---

[8]Individual scores for the students in the average adolescent group were not available. Therefore, as set forth in the manual, a difference greater than 5 points (one-half S.D.) was considered a difference of practical significance.

Table 12.4.   Scores on the 23 Strong–Campbell Basic Interest Scales for the sample of average ninth-grade students

General Occ. Scale theme	Basic Interest Scale	Girls	Boys	Difference
Realistic	Adventure	52.2	62.4	-10.2*
	Nature	50.7	44.2	6.5*
	Agriculture	54.2	55.6	-1.4
	Military activities	49.0	57.8	-8.8*
	Mechanical activities	39.4	52.4	-13.0*
Investigative	Medical service	57.3	46.7	10.6*
	Mathematics	43.3	45.8	-2.5
	Medical science	45.7	46.2	-0.5
	Science	40.5	46.6	-6.1*
Artistic	Writing	41.2	37.3	3.9
	Art	50.6	39.9	10.7*
	Music/Dramatics	47.5	37.4	10.1*
Social	Domestic arts	62.6	42.7	19.9*
	Social service	53.4	41.4	12.0*
	Athletics	53.3	56.4	-3.1
	Teaching	48.1	37.8	10.3*
	Religious activities	45.8	41.5	4.3
Enterprising	Public speaking	42.5	43.9	-1.4
	Sales	48.2	48.8	-0.6
	Law/Politics	40.2	44.8	-4.6
	Merchandising	46.8	44.1	2.7
	Business management	44.0	44.5	-0.5
Conventional	Office practice	56.0	44.9	11.1*

*Differences greater than five points = 1/2 S.D. and are said to have practical significance.

The pattern of sex differences for the average group was similar to that of the gifted group in that girls scored higher than boys on nature, office practice, and most of the social and artistic scales, except athletics, religious activities, and writing, and both girls and boys scored low on the enterprising scales. The sex differences between the average students as compared with the gifted students were about the same on the investigative scales and more pronounced on the realistic ones. (Average boys and girls both were low on the science, mathematics, and medical science scales. These average girls, like the gifted girls, were significantly lower than their male cohorts on the science scale and significantly higher on the medical service scale.)

The scale that showed the greatest difference between girls and boys in both groups was domestic arts (about 20 points in each group). For both groups of girls it was their highest scale score, whereas it was the lowest scale score for gifted boys. Average boys rated domestic arts low also, but not as low as the three artistic scales, the social service scale, and religious activities.

The sex differences between the average groups, like that of the more able group, are most noticeable on the scales of artistic and social interests. Average adolescent girls show less interest than gifted girls on the investigative scales. Sex differences in the average group appear to be somewhat greater on the realistic scales. Thus, male/female stereotyping of interests seems to be more typical of average girls than gifted ones. If this is true, gifted girls should score significantly higher than average girls on the realistic and investigative scales, which are more typically considered masculine areas of interest. Gifted girls in this study did score higher in these areas than the ninth-grade girls in the average sample. This is discussed in the following section.

INTEREST DIFFERENCES BETWEEN GIFTED AND AVERAGE ADOLESCENTS

Terman (1925) in his longitudinal study of highly gifted boys and girls (IQ scores of 140 and above) noted that bright girls often had interests more like those of boys than of average girls. If gifted girls do indeed have more masculine interests than average girls, the high ability girls in the present study should score considerably higher than the average girls on the realistic and investigative scales. The scales that differed by five points or more between gifted and average girls and boys, respectively, are shown in table 12.5.

Gifted girls scored higher than average girls on every realistic scale, but on only one scale, mechanical activity, was the difference greater than five points. In the investigative category the gifted girls scored at least five points higher than the average girls on the science, mathematics, and medical science scales, but not on the medical service scale. Thus, the hypothesis that gifted girls have

Table 12.5. Differences greater than five points on the 23 Strong–Campbell Basic Interest Scales between gifted and average samples by sex

Theme	Scale	Girls			Boys		
		Gifted	Average	Difference	Gifted	Average	Difference
I	Mathematics	53.62	43.3	10.32	58.08	45.8	12.28
	Medical science	51.69	45.7	5.99	51.73	46.2	5.53
	Science	50.58	40.5	10.08	59.15	46.6	12.55
A	Writing	52.96	41.2	11.76	44.77	37.3	7.47
E	Public speaking	48.92	42.5	6.42	50.23	43.9	6.33
	Law/Politics	46.00	40.2	5.80			
R	Mechanical activities	44.58	39.4	5.18			
	Adventure				56.85	62.4	5.55

stronger investigative interests than average-ability girls was confirmed. The gifted girls also scored higher than the average boys on all four of the investigative scales. For all except the science scales the difference was greater than five points.

There is one possible explanation for the fact that gifted girls differed from average girls with respect to investigative but not realistic interests. Gifted girls may not be more masculine per se in their general interests than average girls, but only more selectively masculine with respect to investigative career interests for a very pragmatic reason. Gifted girls have a greater likelihood of success-fully pursuing careers that require advanced degrees, such as those in the science, mathematics, and medical science areas, than less talented girls. Thus, aspiring to careers in these areas would be more realistic for brighter rather than average girls. Talented girls may receive more encouragement than less talented ones to actively develop their interests in these areas. There are few data to support this hypothesis at the present time. It should be noted that gifted girls scored higher than average girls on the writing, public speaking, and law and politics scales in the artistic and enterprising categories. Law and politics would clearly require more education than other enterprising areas, such as sales. (Some interest scales may be better measures of occupational aspiration level than others.)

Cognitive abilities do play a role, along with interests, in determining the level and specific nature of a career which an individual chooses. What we do not know is the extent to which cognitive abilities play a role in the early formation of career interests. If cognitive abilities are important components of the development of career interests, gifted boys should be higher on investigative scales than average boys, but not noticeably different on the other masculine interest areas, such as military and mechanical activities.

In table 12.5 the scales that differentiated between gifted and average boys are shown. Average boys scored considerably higher on the adventure scale (an indication of a less well-developed interest profile), but considerably lower on the writing, science, mathematics, public speaking, and medical science scales. Thus, gifted boys do appear to have somewhat more developed interests than average boys, and interests that are consistent with their abilities.

The result of this study suggests that sex differences in career-related interests of adolescents are largely a function of differential valuation of "female" but not "male" interest areas by the two sexes. The tendency for girls to show interest in "male" areas, particularly investigative areas, as well as "female" areas is more pronounced among gifted than among average girls. Further evidence that gifted girls employ less sex stereotyping in career valuations is provided from a study of the development of mathematical talent and interests in adolescent girls (Fox 1974, and chapter 9 of this volume) which employed a semantic differential rating of eight occupations.

SEX STEREOTYPING OF OCCUPATION

Semantic differential ratings of eight careers were available for two groups of gifted girls and one group of gifted boys. (The second group of girls and the boys are the same gifted students discussed in the previous section on the Strong–Campbell Basic Interest Scales.) These three groups were matched on cognitive abilities and socioeconomic level as described in chapter 9. The ratings were obtained prior to any special treatment for the girls in Group I (the experimental girls of chapter 9).

The students in the three groups were asked to rate eight occupations on a seven-point scale of sixteen adjective pairs in the form of a semantic differential, called a "See Myself Scale." The eight occupations were elementary school teacher, professor of English, mathematician, homemaker, physician, computer programmer, professor of science, and nurse. The adjective pairs (such as good or bad, happy or sad, and strong or weak) were selected from the evaluative domain, as described by Osgood (Osgood, Suci, & Tannenbaum 1957). One page of the See Myself Scale is shown in appendix 12.1.

The primary interest to the principal investigator at the time of construction of the semantic differential was the single occupation "mathematician." The other occupations were selected to give some comparative indices of relative valuation of that occupation with respect to other occupations, particularly those considered frequent choices of adolescent girls—homemaker, teacher, and nurse. The final selection of occupations resulted in four typically female occupations (homemaker, nurse, professor of English, and elementary school teacher) and four primarily male occupations (physician, professor of science, mathematician, and computer programmer). Although the sex typing of professor of English as female and computer programmer as male may be somewhat inaccurate in terms of the realities of employment trends in these fields, the remaining six occupations would appear to fit the typical stereotypes. In addition to the sex stereotyping the eight occupations can be classified into four which require degrees beyond the baccalaureate (mathematician, physician, professor of science, and professor of English) and four which require a bachelor's degree or less. (This dichotomy also has some limitations, e.g., quite a few computer programmers and elementary school teachers have master's degrees.)

The mean ratings of the eight occupations for each of the three groups are shown in table 12.6. A mean score of 64 indicates a neutral position with respect to that career, and a score above 64 would be considered positive. The bright seventh-grade girls, of which Group II is comprised, rated all eight of the occupations above 64. The girls in Group I rated all occupations except nurse above 64. Thus, girls tended to value male and female occupations almost equally favorably. The boys, on the other hand, were more discriminating in

Table 12.6. Mean ratings of eight careers for the three gifted groups[a]

Careers	Group I girls	Group II girls	Boys
Elementary school teacher	75.77	82.31	70.23
Professor of English	75.08	77.12	55.92
Mathematician	74.92	80.69	85.80
Homemaker	72.08	81.35	56.62
Physician	68.81	79.77	78.81
Computer programmer	68.69	66.35	77.35
Professor of science	67.69	71.23	79.81
Nurse	60.88	76.27	48.69

[a]N = 26 for each group.

their assignment of points. They rated the more typically female occupations of nurse, homemaker, and professor of English below the neutral point of 64. One female occupation, that of elementary school teacher, was rated fairly positively by the boys. Why this particular career was seen as more positive than the other female occupations by the boys is not clear. Perhaps this is a sign of changing attitudes toward the teaching profession, or perhaps some of these boys had had a male teacher in elementary school with whom they strongly identified. But still, this female occupation of elementary school teacher ranked only a poor fifth, considerably below the fourth-ranking computer programmer.

The rank orders of the eight occupations and their designations as either male or female for the three groups are shown in table 12.7. For girls the pattern of choices intersperses male and female occupations. Elementary school teacher is first for both groups, but mathematician is third and not rated much lower than elementary school teacher. For both groups of girls the spread

Table 12.7. Rank order of occupations for the three gifted groups[a]

Group I girls	Group II girls	Boys
Elementary school teacher (F)	Elementary school teacher (F)	Mathematician (M)
Professor of English (F)	Homemaker (F)	Professor of science (M)
Mathematician (M)	Mathematician (M)	Physician (M)
Homemaker (F)	Physician (M)	Computer programmer (M)
Physician (M)	Professor of English (F)	Elementary school teacher (F)
Computer programmer (M)	Nurse (F)	Homemaker (F)
Professor of science (M)	Professor of science (M)	Professor of English (F)
Nurse (F)	Computer programmer (M)	Nurse (F)

[a]N = 26 for each group.

between the highest and lowest rated occupation is less than 16 points. Boys, on the other hand, rated mathematician more than 37 points higher than nurse. For boys there was a more distinct break between the rating of the four male occupations and the four female occupations. Indeed, three of the female occupations (homemaker, professor of English, and nurse) were rated 21 points or more below the lowest male occupation.

An analysis of variance of ratings of the eight careers by the three groups is shown in table 12.8. Careers were rated significantly different, and there were significant differences between the groups. The interaction of groups and careers was also significant.

Tukey tests of multiple mean comparisons were used to determine which careers were rated significantly different by the three groups and are shown in table 12.9. The results of these comparisons are quite striking. The girls in Group I rated two of the male occupations (professor of science and mathematician) significantly lower than the boys did. Group II girls rated only one male occupations significantly higher than the boys and differed significantly from the girls in Group I on only one of these four occupations (nurse). Girls in Group I rated two of the male occupations (professor of science and mathematician) significantly lower than the boys did. Group II girls rated only one male occupation (computer programmer) significantly lower than the boys. (Group II girls rated physician significantly higher than Group I girls.)

Thus, for male careers boys are significantly higher than girls on only three of the eight comparisons, whereas, on female careers boys were significantly lower than the girls on seven of the eight comparisons.

Tukey tests of means within groups across careers were computed in order to compare the ratings of each of the four male careers with each of the four female ones. Table 12.10 indicates which of these comparisons were significant.

Table 12.8. Analysis of variance of eight careers on the semantic differential for the three gifted groups[a]

Sources of variation	df	MS	F
Group	2	3759.28	3.434*
Career	7	2267.86	8.542[†]
Triad	25	735.29	
GC	14	1869.88	7.366[†]
GT	150	1094.42	
CT	175	265.49	
GCT	350	253.86	
TOTAL	623		

[a] N=26 for each group.
*p < .05
[†] p < .001

Table 12.9. Tukey comparison of mean differences of ratings of careers among the three gifted groups[a]

Career	Group I girls minus boys	Group II girls minus boys	Group I girls minus Group II girls
Elementary school teacher	5.54	12.08[†]	−6.54
Professor of English	19.16*	21.20*	−2.04
Mathematician	−10.88[†]	−5.11	−5.77
Homemaker	15.46*	24.73*	−9.27
Physician	−10.00	0.96	−10.96[†]
Computer programmer	−8.66	−11.00[†]	2.34
Professor of science	−12.12[†]	−8.58	−3.54
Nurse	12.19[†]	27.58*	−15.39*

[a]N = 26 for each group.
[†]p < .05
*p < .005

　　Boys rated every male career significantly higher than every female career, except elementary school teacher, which they rated significantly lower than mathematician and professor of science, but not significantly lower than physician or computer programmer. Group I girls did not rate any male career significantly lower than any female career. They did rate mathematician significantly higher than nurse.

　　Group II girls did not rate mathematiciain or physician significantly different from any female occupation, but did rate professor of science significantly lower than elementary school teacher and homemaker, and rated computer programmer significantly lower than every occupation (male or female) except professor of science.

　　For Group I girls there is little evidence of sex stereotyping in their evaluation of the eight careers. Group II girls show some tendency to prefer female occupations to male ones, but it is a result largely of their strong rejection of computer programmer and partial rejection of professor of science. Boys, on the other hand, overwhelmingly prefer male occupations to female ones. Only one female occupation—elementary school teacher—was not valued significantly less than all four male careers (computer programmer and physician were not rated significantly lower).

　　The mean ratings of the four male careers and the four female careers for each of the three groups is shown in table 12.11. For boys the differences are quite large. Girls in both groups show far less sex stereotyping in their ratings.

　　Sex stereotyping of careers is linked to economic realities. At one time the occupation of bank teller was predominantly male. As more and more females entered the field the salary of bank tellers began to be relatively lower than it

Table 12.10. Tukey comparisons of mean differences of ratings of each of the four male careers with each of the four female careers for the three gifted groups[a]

Rating of male career minus rating of female career	Boys	Girls	
		Group I	Group II
Mathematician			
Nurse	37.11*	14.04*	4.42
Professor of English	29.88*	−0.16	3.49
Homemaker	29.18*	2.84	−0.66
Elementary school teacher	15.57*	−0.85	−1.62
Physician			
Nurse	30.12*	7.93	3.50
Professor of English	22.89*	−6.27	2.65
Homemaker	22.19*	−3.27	−1.58
Elementary school teacher	8.58	−6.96	−2.54
Computer programmer			
Nurse	28.66*	7.81	−9.92[†]
Professor of English	21.43*	−6.39	−10.77[†]
Homemaker	20.73*	−3.39	−15.00*
Elementary school teacher	7.12	−7.08	−15.96*
Professor of science			
Nurse	31.12*	6.81	−5.04
Professor of English	23.89*	−7.39	−5.89
Homemaker	14.19*	−4.39	−10.12[†]
Elementary school teacher	9.58[†]	−8.08	−11.08[†]

[a]N = 26 for each group.
[†]$p < .05$
*$p < .005$

had been previously. This, in turn, led to fewer men and more women being employed as tellers. It is unlikely that men lost interest in this career because it was being feminized. It is likely that the lowered salary was a more important cause of decreased male employment in the field than any fear that the job had become women's work.

It is possible that the boys in this study reacted more strongly than the girls to the financial remuneration (economic value) aspect of the careers rather than to the psychological dimension of sex appropriateness of careers. In the

Table 12.11. Mean ratings of the four male and four female careers for the three gifted groups

	Male careers	Female careers	Difference
Boys	80.44	57.86	22.58
Group II girls	74.51	79.28	−4.77
Group I girls	70.03	70.95	−0.92

selection of the eight careers this possibility was not controlled. Financial considerations, however, would not seem to account for the clearly different ratings boys assigned to professor of English and professor of science, which should be roughly comparable in salary.

What is perhaps more clearly indicated is that girls do not tend to employ either financial or sex-role criteria in their evaluation of these eight careers. (Presumably, bright girls and boys at this age could make rough distinctions among these careers on the basis of salary.)

SUMMARY

Adolescent girls and boys in both the gifted and average groups can be characterized by their above-average interest in the realistic scales of adventure and agriculture and below-average interests on the enterprising scale (except gifted boys, who were average on the public speaking scale). When one takes into account both sex and ability group, more distinctive interest patterns can be seen.

The gifted girls scored fairly high on the adventure, nature, agriculture, and domestic arts scales, which is typical of female adolescents. The gifted girls were the only one of the four groups who scored above average on the writing scale.

The gifted boys scored high on the science, mathematics, adventure, and military activities scales. They were significantly higher on the science and mathematics scales than the other three groups.[9] Although the gifted girls scored somewhat above average on these scales (and higher than ninth-grade girls and boys) they did not score as high as the gifted boys. The gifted boys had a more mature and predictive interest pattern than any other group.

Average ninth-grade girls scored high on the domestic arts, medical service, and office practice scales. Although these scales set them apart from the boys, they did not differ significantly on these scales with respect to gifted girls. Unlike the gifted girls, the more average adolescent sample scored low on most investigative and artistic scales.

Average ninth-grade boys scored high on the adventure, military activities, athletics, and agriculture scales. Their score on the adventure scale was significantly higher than for the other three groups. They were also the only group that scored above 55 (high) on the agriculture and athletics scales. Thus, average boys in this study would appear to confirm the stereotype of adolescent interest in athletics and adventure. Since they are less precocious intellectually as a group than the gifted group, it is not surprising that they, like the average girls, have less well-developed interests on the investigative interest scales.

Gifted girls and boys differed most strikingly from the average students on the investigative scales of science, mathematics, and medical science, on the artis-

---

[9]The difference between the gifted boys and gifted girls was not quite significant at $p < .05$.

tic scale of writing, and on the enterprising scale of public speaking. Gifted boys were appreciably less adventure-oriented than were the average boys. Gifted girls showed greater interest in law and politics and mechanical activities than average girls. Gifted girls scored three points lower on the domestic arts scale than average girls, but this difference was not significant. Thus, the gifted students have more developed interests in areas related to academic pursuits and somewhat less interest in the more typically adolescent interest areas than the students in the average sample.

Sex differences in the two groups were similar. Girls showed more interest in the artistic, social, and conventional scales than boys and were somewhat less interested in the investigative and realistic interest areas (except nature and medical service). Although both groups of girls showed indications of lesser science and mathematics interest than the boys, the girls in the gifted group scored above average in interest on all four investigative areas, whereas ninth-grade girls were above average on only the medical service scale. Thus, gifted girls more than average girls appear to have above average interest in traditionally masculine as well as feminine areas.

Evidence that gifted girls are interested in both masculine and feminine career areas was seen in the study of ratings of masculine and feminine careers on a semantic differential. Gifted girls in both groups showed relatively more interest in masculine careers than gifted boys do in feminine career areas. Gifted boys tended to rate feminine careers, such as homemaker and nurse, very low as compared with mathematician and physician. Gifted girls in both groups, on the other hand, tended to value most careers somewhat alike. They did not appear either to reject feminine careers, such as homemaker or elementary school teacher, nor to value them much differently than more male careers, such as mathematician or physician.

CONCLUSIONS

Intellectual ability and scientific career interests appear to be highly related. Gifted girls and boys have stronger interests in mathematics, science, medical science, writing, and public speaking than do somewhat older students of more average ability. This result would seem logically consistent with the fact that gifted students can more realistically aspire to academic careers.

Precocious cognitive ability appears to be related to a more maturely developed interest profile for gifted boys than average boys, but this result was less true for comparisons of gifted and average girls. The gifted girls are somewhat more like gifted boys than average girls with respect to interests that are fairly predictive of adult career choices. Although gifted girls do differ from average girls with respect to investigative interests, the gifted girls had somewhat less interest in these areas than gifted boys. What appears to be true is that gifted girls make fewer clear distinctions between preferences for male and female career interest areas than gifted boys and appear more drawn to male interest areas than girls of average ability. These data suggest that high cognitive ability leads to more conflict for gifted girls than gifted boys or average girls with respect to future career choices.

Thus, while superior cognitive ability may lead to precocious career interest development in boys and perhaps a faster total integration of self when interests and abilities are compatible, for girls the opposite may be true. The difficulty in interpreting these results for gifted girls is that little is known about the development of career-related interests in women who do eventually seek careers in more "traditionally" masculine areas such as science and mathematics. Clearly the gifted young women in this study are as intellectually capable as the gifted boys of pursuing these types of careers. To what extent their interest profiles will become more like their gifted male counterparts and less like those of the girls of more average ability over the high school and college years is an empirical question of great interest. More data of that type will enhance our understanding of the relationship of cognitive abilities to the development of interests and eventual career choices for both men and women.

REFERENCES

Allport, G. W., Vernon, P. E., and Lindzey, G. 1970. *Manual for the Study of Values: A scale for measuring the dominent interests in personality.* Boston, Mass.: Houghton Mifflin.

Astin, H. S. 1974. Sex differences in mathematical and scientific precocity. In J. C. Stanley, D. P. Keating, and L. H. Fox (eds.), *Mathematical talent: Discovery, description, and development.* Baltimore, Md. 21218: The Johns Hopkins University Press, pp. 70–86.

Campbell, David. 1974. Assessing vocational interests: A manual for the Strong–Campbell Interest Inventory. Unpublished manuscript, University of Minnesota.

Carey, G. L. 1958. Sex differences in problem-solving performance as a function of attitude differences. *Journal of Abnormal and Social Psychology* 56: 256–60.

Fox, L. H. 1974. *Facilitating the development of mathematical talent in young women.* A dissertation submitted to The Johns Hopkins University in conformance with the requirements for the degree of Doctor of Philosophy. Baltimore, Md.

Fox, L. H., and Denham, S. A. 1974. Values and career interests of mathematically and scientifically precocious youth. In J. C. Stanley, D. P. Keating, and L. H. Fox (eds.), *Mathematical talent: Discovery, description, and development.* Baltimore, Md. 21218: The Johns Hopkins University Press, pp. 140–75.

Holland, J. L. 1965. *Manual for the Vocational Preference Inventory.* Palo Alto, Calif.: Consulting Psychologists Press.

_____. 1966. *The psychology of vocational choice: A theory of personality types and model environments.* Waltham, Mass.: Blaisdell.

Milton, G. A. 1957. The effects of sex-role identification upon problem-solving skill. *Journal of Abnormal and Social Psychology* 55: 208–12.

Osgood, C. E., Suci, G. J., and Tannenbaum, P. H. 1957. *The measurement of meaning*. Urbana, Ill.: University of Illinois Press.

Scheffé, H. 1959. *The analysis of variance*. New York: John Wiley & Sons.

Terman, L. M. 1925. Mental and physical traits of a thousand gifted children. *Genetic studies of genius*, vol. 1. Stanford, Calif.: Stanford University Press.

Appendix 12.1

Sample Page from Semantic Differential

1. See myself as a mathematician.

1. unknown–	–	–	–	–	–	–known
2. near–	–	–	–	–	–	–far
3. passive–	–	–	–	–	–	–active
4. happy–	–	–	–	–	–	–sad
5. good–	–	–	–	–	–	–bad
6. disturbing–	–	–	–	–	–	–relaxing
7. downward–	–	–	–	–	–	–upward
8. easy–	–	–	–	–	–	–difficult
9. friendly–	–	–	–	–	–	–unfriendly
10. worthless–	–	–	–	–	–	–valuable
11. imaginary–	–	–	–	–	–	–real
12. unlikely–	–	–	–	–	–	–likely
13. interesting–	–	–	–	–	–	–boring
14. dangerous–	–	–	–	–	–	–safe
15. strong–	–	–	–	–	–	–weak
16. positive–	–	–	–	–	–	–negative

13
CREATIVE POTENTIAL OF MATHEMATICALLY PRECOCIOUS BOYS

Daniel P. Keating

ABSTRACT

The high mathematical aptitude and academic achievement of the students in the Study of Mathematically Precocious Youth (SMPY) has been well documented. A further question concerns their potential for eventual productivity or creativity. A series of measures presumed to be related to and possibly predictive of later creativity were administered to seventy-two mathematics competition winners from 1972 and 1973. These included measures of interests, values, personality characteristics, figure preference, and biographical background. The results showed that this academically high-promise group rated moderately high on these measures also, and that several individuals rated very high on three or more. Eventual longitudinal follow-up should resolve some of the questions regarding the long-term predictive validity of various measures.

The Study of Mathematically Precocious Youth (SMPY) has been primarily concerned with the seeking out and facilitating of high-level mathematical reasoning ability. That the students identified by the vigorous screening procedures used by SMPY are cognitively advanced is testified to by several converging lines of evidence: their high scores on ability tests designed for students three to five years older (chapter 2 of this volume); case studies (Keating & Stanley 1972; chapter 1 of this volume); and their precocity in cognitive development using Piagetian criteria (chapter 5 of this volume). Further, this precocity is closely related to meaningful academic achievement criteria, such as highly successful performance in college mathematics and mathematics-related courses several years ahead of age-mates and often superior to older "classmates."

The existence of such high ability and concomitant academic achievement has thus been demonstrated, if not fully explicated. A number of intriguing questions arise following such a demonstration, one of which is examined more closely in this chapter: What is the likelihood that these abilities and academic achievements will be related to more long-term and meaningful criteria, such as productivity and creativity? Since this is a remarkably "high-promise" group, the opportunity to collect and examine potential indicators of such real-life criteria, along with the high probability of eventually observing different levels on these criteria, is rare.

The next step in the process is selecting potentially useful indicators of "creativity." Several options present themselves at this point. The first is to evaluate certain cognitive processes which have been considered examples of "creative thinking." Of these, the only one that has been identified as psychometrically separate from general intelligence is associational or ideational fluency, but the validation of measures of this cognitive process against creative production has not yet been done (Wallach 1970). The second option would be to evaluate the creative products themselves of the individuals in the sample, but given the age of these students (twelve to fourteen years old) such an endeavor is likely to be misleading by virtue of insufficient evidence. Another approach, the one employed here, is to evaluate the creative *potential* of the group and of individuals within the group by using indirect measures of creativity, i.e., measures showing some relationship to adult or adolescent creative production, but are not presumed to be in themselves measures of the construct.

METHOD

Subjects

The subjects in this study were junior high school students who were the top scorers in two mathematics competitions held one year apart. To be eligible for the competition the student had to be in the seventh or the eighth grade, or less than fourteen years old if in a higher grade. The top 35 scorers of 396 contestants in the first competition were invited back for further testing, as were the top 44 scorers of 953 contestants in the second competition (see chapters 2 and 3 of this volume). Of the top 79 students who were invited back, 76 accepted the invitation.

Only four girls qualified for an invitation to be retested, and all accepted. The small number makes an analysis by sex impossible, however, and they have been dropped from the subject pool, leaving seventy-two boys for the analysis. Discussions of the sex difference in these data by Astin (1974 [I:4][1]) and Fox (chapter 9 of this volume) are of interest.

[1]In addition to the usual references, citations of chapters in volume I of *Studies of Intellectual Precocity* will be as follows: [I:4]. The I indicates volume I, and the 4 is the chapter number [Editor].

The students were administered the various paper and pencil measures described below at several retesting sessions. Not all of the students have taken all of the measures, and thus the appropriate Ns are indicated for each measure. There were fifty-seven of the seventy-two boys who did take all of the measures, and this group is used as the base group. Means on each measure for those not in the base group were calculated, and no significant differences were found between the base group and nonbase group scores. Thus the base group may be considered representative of the total group.

Measures

The Allport-Vernon-Lindzey Study of Values (SV-1970) has often been used in studies of creative artists and scientists. The "classic" value structure of the creative scientist, as reported by MacKinnon (1962) is high theoretical (T), high aesthetic (A), low religious (R). Although an empirical finding, the pattern makes psychological sense in terms of the SV value structure. The T person is concerned primarily with the seeking of knowledge, a "truth" value, and the relation of this to scientific creativity is obvious. It seems intuitively that the A value is quite different from T; its basis is in an appreciation of beauty, form, and harmony. The paradox is resolved when one recalls the importance of form and harmony to the "elegant" solution in mathematics or the parsimonious scientific theory.

It has often been asserted that the best predictor of future performance is past performance. In terms of research on creativity, it does seem that the most consistently successful method of discriminating creative from less creative groups has been reported past behavior and self-ratings (Taylor & Holland 1962). A lengthy and fairly well-normed instrument of this type is the Biographical Inventory-Creativity (BIC—Schaefer 1970; Schaefer & Anastasi 1968), which yields scores on "art and writing" and "mathematics and science."

Barron and Welsh (1952) proposed that preference for certain figures may be related to a "style" factor, which may in turn have a bearing upon creativity. Creative artists tended to like more complex and asymmetrical shapes than nonartists. Although the results of extensive research with the Barron-Welsh Art Scale (BWAS) have been inconclusive (Baird 1972), some promising possibilities are offered in its use. Helson and Crutchfield (1970) reported a significant difference on the Art Scale between creative and less creative mathematicians.

Another method that has often been used for predicting creativity is the determination of consistent personality dimensions or traits among creative people (e.g., Cattell & Drevdahl 1955; Hall & MacKinnon 1969). The California Psychological Inventory (CPI—Gough 1957, 1969) was administered to nearly all the individuals in the group. Hall and MacKinnon (1969) have published a regression equation for the prediction of creativity, using the CPI Scales.

Vocational interest inventories have also been administered to this group. Their stability over time will likely prove important in a longitudinal study. The instruments that have been used are: the Strong–Campbell Interest Inventory (SCII), which is the most recent and still experimental revision of the Strong Vocational Interest Blank (SVIB), and which unites the men's and women's forms (Campbell, personal communication); and the Holland's (1958) Vocational Preference Inventory (VPI), short form.

In addition to the above listed measures, one further evaluation of the "creative potential" of these students will be made. It rests on the idea of a "minimum IQ" level for creative attainment (e.g., Cattell & Butcher 1968). Accordingly, scores on Raven's Advanced Progressive Matrices (APM) are analyzed to assess "sufficiency" of nonverbal reasoning ability.

RESULTS

The "Study of Values" (SV)

The typical value pattern of creative scientists (MacKinnon 1962) is high theoretical (T), high aesthetic (A), low religious (R). Creative mathematicians are characterized as low R (Helson & Crutchfield 1970). This group of mathematically precocious boys clearly shows the high T scores on the SV. Table 13.1 lists the values and their frequency of occurrence as highest, second highest, or lowest. Of the seventy-two subjects, forty-two, or 58 percent, had it as their highest value. An additional 13.5 (with ties counting 0.5), or 19 percent, had it as their second highest value. Thus 52.5, or 77 percent overall, had T as their first or second highest value, much higher than the 33 percent chance level. It is not surprising that these students, who participated in a mathematics competition, would show as a high value an interest in learning per se.

These students are not as high on A as they are on T. Only 3.5, or 5 percent, have it as their highest value; an additional 2, or 3 percent, have it as their second highest value. Thus only 6.5 students overall, or 8 percent, have it as their first or second highest value. This absence of an aesthetic orientation

Table 13.1. Frequency of occurrence of the six SV[a] values as highest[b], second highest, or lowest as percent of total

	Theoretical	Political	Economic	Social	Aesthetic	Religious
1st highest	59	14	8	7	5	7
2nd highest	19	37	24	10	3	6
Lowest (6th)	0	4	12	10	30	43

[a] Allport–Vernon–Lindzey Study of Values (1970).
[b] I.e., highest, second highest, or lowest within the individual's own SV profile.

could be rationalized post hoc by ascribing it to the youthfulness of the group or to other causes, but it is disconcerting nonetheless. The college experience, however, which may be helpful in the development of an aesthetic orientation (Huntley 1965), still lies ahead for this group. R is the lowest value in the sample, occurring last 43 percent of the time.

Vocational Interest Inventories

A modified version of Holland's (1965) Vocational Preference Inventory (VPI) contains six categories of occupations with fourteen specific occupations in each. The categories are: realistic (R); conventional (C); investigative (I); social (S); artistic (A); and enterprising (E). An individual's most preferred category is determined as the one with the most occupations checked.

As anticipated, the category most frequently checked as highest was I, investigative. Most of the occupations in that category are science oriented, and typically require advanced educational degrees. Of this academically motivated, mathematics-science-oriented group, 46, or 61 percent, had I as their preferred category (or it was tied with another category as most often preferred). An additional 18 or 24 percent, had it as their second value. A total of 85 percent of the group, therefore, had I in the top two preferred categories. Although not yet empirically related to creativity, it seems more than likely that if one is to be a creative scientist or mathematician a preference for I occupations is desirable, perhaps even necessary.

This preference for investigative occupations is borne out by an analysis of the subjects' scores on the Strong–Campbell Interest Inventory (SCII). The SCII gives scores on the six Holland categories, as well as more specific occupational preference information. On the SCII, which not all of the students have taken, 78 percent of those who had taken it had I as the highest score. An additional 15 percent had it as the second highest score. Thus, 93 percent overall had I as the first or second highest category. Specific scales are not included in this analysis.

The Biographical Inventory

Scores on the Biographical Inventory-Creativity (BIC—Schaefer 1970) are separated into two scales, which for males are "Art and Writing" (AW) and "Mathematics and Science" (MS). The MS score is of more importance for this group, but the AW scores have also been analyzed. Mean scores for both BIC scales are listed in table 13.2.

Some of the items on the BIC are inappropriate for this age group. Several questions, for example, refer to accomplishments and awards during high school, since the instrument was designed for and normed on a college population (Schaefer 1970). Thus it is likely that the scores of these students on the BIC would increase over time.

Table 13.2. Mean scores of mathematically precocious boys on five measures related to creativity

Measure	N^a	Mean	S.D.
BIC–AW[b]	58	100.66	8.49
BIC–MS[c]	58	106.53	4.76
CPI[d]	67	11.21	4.48
BWAS[e]	64	17.91	11.91
APM[f]	69	29.51	3.08

[a] N for total group = 71.
[b] Biographical Inventory of Creativity, Arts and Writing (Schaefer 1970).
[c] Biographical Inventory of Creativity, Mathematics and Science (Schaefer 1970).
[d] California Psychological Inventory, creativity regression equation from Hall and MacKinnon (1969).
[e] Barron–Welsh Art Scale (Barron & Welsh 1952).
[f] Raven's Advanced Progressive Matrices (Raven 1965).

But even in comparison with a college norm group, the mathematically precocious students fare well. On the AW scale, the mean score of this group is equivalent to about the 58th percentile of the college males. On the MS scale, their mean score falls at the 68th percentile. In terms of biographical background, then, this group appears to have considerable creative potential. The BIC administered at this age may even underestimate their creative potential.

The California Psychological Inventory

At first glance, this would appear to be a quite *un*creative group on the basis of personality inventory scores. Hall and MacKinnon (1969) developed a regression equation using CPI scales that separated more creative from less creative architects. Using that regression equation, this group appears less creative than a group of randomly selected eighth-graders, as well as a high school norm group (Weiss, Haier, & Keating 1974 [I:7]).

But the deficiency is more apparent than real. The most heavily weighted scale in the Hall and MacKinnon (1969) equation is Achievement via Conformance (AC), which gets a *negative* weight in distinguishing between more and less creative architects. This may be inappropriate at this age, since the randomly selected groups are clearly less achievement oriented on most dimensions.

This also points up the difficulty of analyzing adolescent personality structure and comparing it to adult norms. Not only do the scale scores change considerably over time, but the personality of a creative adult may have been quite different when that adult was an adolescent (Parloff, Datta, Kleman, & Handlon 1968).

The Barron–Welsh Art Scale (BWAS)

The BWAS has been used to discriminate between creative artists and the general population (Barron & Welsh 1952), and in other studies of creativity (e.g., Helson & Crutchfield 1970). Although the way in which this type of design preference develops over time is not known, some idea of the creativity of this group may be gathered from this instrument.

As a group, the mathematically precocious boys do not appear to be especially creative when compared with the general population. The mean of the male nonartist group reported by Welsh (1959) is 15.06 (of a possible 62). The mean of these students is 17.91 (see table 13.2) a nonsignificant difference. Thus, as a group these students appear to be more like the general population than artists. Their scores are closer (Helson & Crutchfield 1970) to less creative adult mathematicians (18.5) than to the general population, but least like adult creative mathematicians (27.5).

The Advanced Progressive Matrices

MacKinnon (1962) reported that in most fields there is no correlation between intelligence and creativity, although within those areas where one can be creative there are rarely individuals of low intelligence. Among mathematicians, however, a low positive correlation between intelligence and creativity is observed.

As one can readily see from table 13.2, this group has little difficulty in meeting a "minimum intelligence" criterion. This is not surprising, given the method of selection of the group. The mean of the group, 29, is above the 95th percentile of adult norms (Raven 1965). All but five of the seventy-two boys score at least one standard deviation above the mean for university students.

The High Creatives

From the foregoing analysis it is not clear whether as a group these mathematically precocious boys should be considered "potentially creative" or not. The BIC indicates that they are, but the CPI results suggest that they are not, and the BWAS characterizes them as more like the less creative mathematicians. But the proper objection is raised that it is not a group but rather an individual who is creative. The important question thus revolves around which of the individuals within this group are most likely to be creative. To discern this it is necessary to look at those individuals who score above a reasonable criterion on each of the measures, and then at those who score at or above the criterion on more than one measure. This is especially applicable since the measures are uncorrelated within this group (see table 13.3).

The criterion that was used was the mean score of the group plus one standard deviation. To check on the possibility that this might be a group with

Table 13.3. Correlation matrix of five measures related to creativity for 57 mathematically precocious boys (base group)

	BIC–AW[a]	BIC–MS	CPI	BWAS	APM
BIC–AW		.611[b]	.051	.251	–.184
BIC–MS			–.121	.249	.003
CPI				–.111	.001
BWAS					.064
APM					

[a] For abbreviations of measures, see table 13.2.
[b] $p < .01$; no other r's are significant at $p < .05$ level. This correlation is between two scores on the same measure, which overlap.

low creative potential, thus invalidating within-group comparisons, the same criterion was applied, using relevant norm group means and standard deviations. Table 13.4 gives the number of students who scored above the criterion, on both within-group and norm-group comparisons, for each instrument. If each of these instruments does measure some aspect of creative potential, then a number of individuals in this group would seem to have such potential.

Those students, however, who score above the criterion on *more* than one measure should be the ones considered to have the most creative potential. In

Table 13.4. Students at or above criterion,[a] within-group and norm-group comparisons

	Measures				
	BICAW[b]	BICMS	CPI	BWAS	APM
Within group (WG) criterion	109	111	15.9	30	33
No. of students at or above WG criterion	12	10	11	12	14
Norm group[c] (NG) criterion	109	109	11.7	26	25
No. of students at or above NG criterion	12	17	28	19	64

[a] Criterion = $\overline{X} + 1\sigma$ (mean plus one standard deviation).
[b] See table 13.2 for abbreviations and N's for each test.
[c] Norm groups as follows: BICAW and BICMS– college males (Schaefer 1970).
   CPI– creative architects (Hall & MacKinnon 1969).
   BWAS– nonartists (general population)–(Welsh 1959).
   APM– university students (Raven 1965).

Table 13.5. Percent of students at or above within-group or norm-group criteria[a] on one or more creativity-related measures (N = 57)

	Percent of students at or above criterion				
	On 1 or more measures	On 2 or more measures	On 3 or more measures	On 4 or more measures	On 5 measures
Within group comparison	56	26	7	2	0
Norm group comparison	96	77	32	10	2

[a]For measures and criteria, see table 13.4.

table 13.5 are listed the numbers of individuals who scored above the criterion, for both within-group and norm-group comparisons, on at least one measure, on any two or more measures, on any three or more, and on four or more. As one can readily see, the number who score above the criteria of two or more measures on norm group comparisons is still a sizable group, and ten students, or nearly 14 percent of the total group, meet the criteria on three or more measures. Thus if each of these tests do indeed measure some aspect related to creative potential, the outlook for a good minority of the group is quite bright.

DISCUSSION

From the use, with this group of mathematically precocious boys, of several different types of measures which have been held to relate to some dimension of creativity, it appears that the creative potential of this group is high. Although as a group they do not stand out from the norm groups on any measures except the APM, where they are much above the mean for university students, and on BIC-MS, where they are slightly above the mean for college students, a number of individuals within the group are far above the mean on three or four of the five measures used (see table 13.5).

There is a strong theoretical-investigative orientation of the group, and to the extent that this is important for creativity in mathematics and science, there is little difficulty for anyone in the group, If, however, the aesthetic orientation is important, a large segment of the group may have some difficulty. This is mitigated somewhat by the expectation that this aesthetic orientation will grow during the college experience. The low religious scores reflect those of creative mathematicians and scientists.

Some of the students, who at this time using these measures do not appear to be particularly creative, may in the future come up to the criteria that were used in this investigation. Developmental data on the BWAS is scant, but it seems reasonable that the scores of these students on the BIC and the CPI creativity regression equation will increase over time.

There are at least two possible explanations for the lack of agreement of creativity-related measures in this group. First, one or more of the measures used may not bear any deep relationship to creativity. The second possibility is that there is a problem of restriction of range within this group. Since they are homogeneous to a large extent on cognitive measures (although not as much as one might expect—see Keating 1974 [I:2]), the possibility of too little variation on measures that are even slightly correlated with the selection measure is acute.

A third possibility is more intriguing. It may be that each of the measures does bear some relationship to creativity, and that each of them is measuring a different aspect of creative potential (i.e., interests, values, family background). If they are valid measures in this sense, the fact that they are uncorrelated would strongly suggest such a possibility. Creativity, as used to describe highly creative production, would have to be viewed not as a unitary construct, but rather as a situation toward which a great many factors must contribute. A longitudinal follow-up of this large group of mathematically talented youngsters, which is planned, should provide some answers to these questions.

In conclusion, the third possibility discussed above suggests a multifactor theory of creativity. Many factors and influences contribute to the development of the highly creative individual, and all or nearly all of them must contribute positively for the individual to be truly creative. If but a few of the factors are negative or even neutral, the individual may be routinely productive or erratically unproductive, but not truly creative. Such an explanation would account not only for the lack of correlation among measures of creativity but also for the observed rarity of truly creative individuals.

REFERENCES

Allport, G., Vernon, P. E., and Lindzey, G. 1970. *Manual for the Study of Values* (3rd ed.). Boston: Houghton Mifflin.

Astin, H. S. 1974. Sex differences in mathematical and scientific precocity. In J. C. Stanley, D. P. Keating, and L. H. Fox (eds.), *Mathematical talent: Discovery, description, and development*. Baltimore, Md.: The Johns Hopkins University Press, chapter 4.

Baird, L. L. 1972. A review of the Barron–Welsh Art Scale. In O. K. Buros (ed.), *The seventh mental measurements yearbook*. Highland Park, N.J.: The Gryphon Press, pp. 81–83.

Barron, F., and Welsh, G. S. 1952. Artistic perception as a possible factor in personality style: Its measurement by a figure preference test. *Journal of Psychology* 33: 199–203.

Cattell, R. B., and Butcher, H. S. 1968. *The prediction of achievement and creativity.* New York: Bobbs–Merrill.

Cattell, R. B., and Drevdahl, J. E. 1955. A comparison of the personality profile of eminent researchers with that of eminent teachers and administrators and of the general population. *British Journal of Psychology* 46: 248–61.

Gough, H. G. 1957, 1969. *Manual for the California Psychological Inventory.* Palo Alto, California: Consulting Psychologists Press.

Hall, W. F., and MacKinnon, D. W. 1969. *Journal of Applied Psychology* 53(4): 322–26.

Helson, R., and Crutchfield, R. S. 1970. Mathematicians: The creative researcher and the average Ph.D. *Journal of Consulting and Clinical Psychology* 34(2): 250–57.

Holland, J. L. 1965. *Manual for the Vocational Preference Inventory.* Palo Alto, Calif.: Consulting Psychologists Press.

Huntley, C. W. 1965. Changes in Study of Values scores during the four years of college. *Genetic Psychology Monographs* 71: 349–83.

Keating, D. P. 1974. The study of mathematically precocious youth. In J. C. Stanley, D. P. Keating, and L. H. Fox (eds.), *Mathematical talent: Discovery, description, and development.* Baltimore, Md.: The Johns Hopkins University Press, chapter 2.

Keating, D. P., and Stanley, J. C. 1972. Extreme measures for the exceptionally gifted in mathematics and science. *Educational Researcher* 1(9): 3–7.

Lessinger, L. M., and Martinson, R. A. 1961. The Use of the CPI with gifted pupils. *Personnel and Guidance Journal* 39: 572–75.

MacKinnon, D. W. 1962. The nature and nurture of creative talent. *American Psychologist* 17: 484–95.

Parloff, M. B., Datta, L., Kleman, M., and Handlon, J. H. 1968. Personality characteristics which differentiate creative male adolescents and adults. *Journal of Personality* 36: 528–52.

Raven, J. C. 1965. *Advanced progressive matrices.* London: H. K. Lewis and Co.

Schaefer, C. E. 1970. *Manual for the Biographical Inventory—Creativity.* San Diego, California: Educational and Industrial Testing Service.

Schaefer, C. E., and Anastasi, A. 1968. A biographical inventory for identifying creativity in adolescent boys. *Journal of Applied Psychology* 52(1): 42–48.

Taylor, C. W., and Holland, J. L. 1962. Development and application of tests of creativity. *Review of Educational Research* 32(1): 91–102.

Wallach, M. A. 1970. Creativity. In P. H. Mussen (ed.), *Carmichael's Manual of Child Psychology.* New York: Wiley, chapter 17.

Weiss, D. S., Haier, R. J., and Keating, D. P. 1974. Personality characteristics of mathematically precocious boys. In J. C. Stanley, D. P. Keating, and L. H. Fox (eds.), *Mathematical talent: Discovery, description, and development.* Baltimore, Md.: The Johns Hopkins University Press, chapter 7.

Welsh, G. S. 1959. *Preliminary manual for the Welsh Figure Preference Test.* Palo Alto, California: Consulting Psychologists Press.

14

THE VALUES OF GIFTED YOUTH

Lynn H. Fox

ABSTRACT

*The Allport–Vernon–Lindzey Study of Values (SV) was administered to 655
gifted boys and girls who participated in the 1973 mathematics talent search.
The SV was also given to boys who were winners or near-winners in the 1972
and 1974 contests. Over half the highly precocious boys in all three years scored
highest on the theoretical scale. Only one-third of the less precocious boys in
the 1973 contest were highest in that value. Girls in the contest were most likely
to score highest on the social scale, and only 15 percent scored highest on the
theoretical value. Thus a theoretical value orientation appears to be related to
mathematical precocity and may in part explain some of the differences found
between the sexes with respect to eagerness for acceleration in mathematics.*

The major emphasis of the Study of Mathematically Precocious Youth
(SMPY) is to identify and counsel seventh-, eighth-, and young ninth-grade[1]
students who have superior mathematical reasoning ability. To identify these
mathematically talented youngsters who could benefit from educational counseling, three contests in mathematics have been held at The Johns Hopkins
University, using the mathematics section of the Scholastic Aptitude Test
(SAT-M). Students who scored 640 or above on the SAT-M were considered
highly precocious in mathematical reasoning.

The goals of the counseling program are to enrich educational experiences,
increase opportunities, and telescope the time spent in high school when
appropriate for these students. The intervention methods that have proven
successful with these students have included: taking college courses in summer,
at night, and on released time from school, while still in high school; taking
advanced course work in mathematics and science at a high school, while
remaining in grade for other subjects; special fast-paced mathematics classes

---

[1]Ninth-graders who had not yet reached their fourteenth birthday at the time of the contest were
eligible.

two hours a week; or independent study at a rapid pace under the guidance of a teacher or tutor in place of the in-grade mathematics course work (see chapter 3).

In order to decide which methods of facilitation might be best for a given individual, SMPY felt it needed to learn a great deal about the abilities, values, and interests of each individual it counseled. Therefore, winners and near-winners of the annual competition have been tested on additional cognitive and affective measures.

This paper summarizes what has been learned about the values of gifted students and how measures of these have provided insight into the nature of mathematical precocity, the differences between the sexes in this respect, and the success of various educational intervention procedures.

In the present study, the Allport–Vernon–Lindzey Study of Values (SV) was administered to 656 contestants[2] in the second talent search conducted in 1973. These students had scored at or above the 98th percentile on national norms for the numerical subtest of the Iowa Tests of Basic Skills or a similar standardized achievement test. Students who were considered winners or near-winners in the 1972 and 1974 contests were also given the SV.

The SV yields six scores, indicating strength of preference for each of six evaluative areas: theoretical, economic, aesthetic, social, political, and religious.[3] The theoretical scale was expected to be the one most associated with scientific and mathematical interests. Other researchers (MacKinnon 1962; Hall & MacKinnon 1969; Warren & Herst 1960; Southern & Plant 1968) have reported a relationship between creativity and high scores on the theoretical and aesthetic scales.

The SV has not been widely used with adolescent populations; normative data are available for high school students, but not junior high school students (Allport, Vernon, & Lindzey 1970). Chapter 15 of this volume presents evidence that value patterns for the gifted students in this study are meaningful data and not the result of random answers.

A COMPARISON OF THE GIFTED CONTESTANTS
WITH HIGH SCHOOL STUDENTS

The mean scores and standard deviations for male and female high school students (grades ten through twelve) in the normative sample for the SV Manual are shown with the contestants' scores in table 14.1. The girls in the 1973 Talent Search scored higher than high school girls on the social, theoretical, political, and aesthetic scales, but lower on the religious and

---

[2]There were 666 students in the 1973 contest; 656 correctly completed the SV.
[3]The six values of the SV are based on Spranger's *Types of Men*. The theoretical man is the type associated with scientists and academicians.

Table 14.1. Means and standard deviations of scores on the Study of Values for 656 seventh- and eighth-grade students in the 1973 mathematics contest compared with those of high school students

1973 Mathematics contestants	Total no.	Theoretical		Economic		Aesthetic		Social		Political		Religious	
		Mean	Std. dev.	Mean	Std. dev.	Mean	Std. dev.	Mean	Std. dev.	Mean	Std. dev.	Mean	Std. dev.
7th-grade girls	85	39.18	6.22	36.61	6.12	39.10	7.70	46.31	7.57	40.56	6.02	38.24	9.71
7th-grade boys	135	47.87	5.76	41.37	6.10	32.44	6.84	39.66	5.68	44.46	6.42	34.24	8.45
8th-grade girls	155	39.94	7.46	34.66	6.56	39.53	8.11	46.02	6.51	40.00	6.21	39.90	9.53
8th-grade boys	281	46.37	7.12	41.96	7.08	32.89	7.56	40.01	7.33	43.96	6.34	34.71	9.64
All girls	240	39.67	7.04	35.35	6.46	39.38	7.95	46.12	6.89	40.20	6.14	39.31	9.60
All boys	416	46.86	6.74	41.77	6.78	32.75	7.33	39.90	6.83	44.12	6.36	34.56	9.27
High school sample													
Girls	7296	37.04	6.86	38.17	6.33	38.23	7.14	43.27	6.93	39.05	5.92	43.75	8.12
Boys	5320	43.32	6.40	42.81	6.86	35.14	7.75	37.05	6.25	43.17	5.92	37.93	8.31

economic scales. The boys on the 1973 Talent Search scored higher than the high school boys on the theoretical, social, and political scales, and lower on the remaining three scales of religious, aesthetic, and economic values.

The rank order of values for each of the four groups (gifted girls, high school girls, gifted boys, and high school boys) are shown in table 14.2. The patterns of value-orderings for the girls in the two groups are somewhat different. The religious value is the highest for senior high school girls, but ranks fifth for the gifted girls. The theoretical value ranks third for the gifted girls, but last for high school girls. Thus gifted seventh- and eighth-grade girls appear to be more theoretically oriented than high school girls and less religiously oriented. Gifted boys and high school boys differ only with respect to the order for social and religious values. For gifted boys the social value ranks fourth and the religious value fifth. This is the reverse order of those two values in the high school sample. Although the gifted and high school samples of boys both score highest on the theoretical value, the mean for the gifted boys (46.86) is significantly higher than the mean of the high school boys (43.32). Thus gifted boys appear to be more theoretical than the boys in the high school sample.

Table 14.2. Rank order of values for gifted seventh- and eighth-graders and high school students

Girls		Boys	
1973 Talent Search participants	High school students	1973 Talent Search participants	High school students
S	R	T	T
P	S	P	P
T	P	E	E
A	A	S	R
R	E	R	S
E	T	A	A

Key

T = Theoretical   S = Social
E = Economic   P = Political
A = Aesthetic   R = Religious

GRADE DIFFERENCES IN VALUES[4]

Within-sex differences across the two grade groups were small. Seventh-grade girls scored significantly higher (1.92 points) than eighth-grade girls on the economic scale ($p < .05$), but did not differ on the other five scales.

[4]Since the number of ninth-graders was small and most were one-year accelerated, they are classified as eighth-graders in all tables and discussions.

Seventh-grade boys scored significantly higher (1.56 points) than eighth-grade boys on the theoretical scale (p < .01), but did not differ significantly on the other five scales. Thus we can conclude that the seventh- and eighth-grade students of the same sex who entered the contest have very similar value profiles. There were, however, sex differences in values as early as grade seven.

SEX DIFFERENCES IN VALUES

Data reported on adults, college students, and high school students in the manual for the SV show a general pattern of sex differences on the six values. Men typically score higher than women on the theoretical, economic, and political values and lower on the aesthetic, social, and religious values. These sex differences were apparent in this sample of gifted junior high school students. The mean scores for boys on the theoretical, economic, and political values were significantly higher than the mean for girls on these scales (p < .001). The mean scores for girls on the social, aesthetic, and religious scales were significantly higher than the means for boys on these scales (p < .001).

The percentage of students in the 1973 Talent Search, by grade, sex, and highest value score is shown in table 14.3. The majority of seventh- and eighth-grade girls scored highest on the social or religious values. The majority of boys in both grade groups scored highest on the theoretical and political scales.

The extent of the differences between the sexes is seen dramatically in table 14.3. Approximately 42 percent of the seventh-grade girls and 33 percent of the

Table 14.3. Percent of students by their highest value on the Study of Values for 656 students in the 1973 mathematics contest

		No.	T	E	A	S	P	R
G	Grade 7	85	12.9	9.4	7.1	42.4	10.6	17.6
i	Grade 8	155	16.1	1.9	16.1	32.9	12.3	20.6
r								
l	All	240	15.0	4.6	12.9	36.2	11.7	19.6
s								
B	Grade 7	135	40.7	9.6	3.7	10.4	25.9	9.6
o	Grade 8	281	34.5	15.3	5.0	15.3	19.2	10.7
y								
s	All	416	36.5	13.5	4.6	13.7	21.4	10.3

Key

T = Theoretical   S = Social
E = Economic   P = Political
A = Aesthetic   R = Religious

eighth-grade girls scored highest on the social value, whereas only 10 percent of the seventh-grade boys and 15 percent of the eighth-grade boys scored highest on the social scale. Only 13 and 16 percent of the seventh- and eighth-grade girls scored highest on the theoretical scale, whereas approximately 41 and 35 percent of the seventh- and eighth-grade boys, respectively, did so.

Thus, boys far more than girls value theoretical pursuits associated with mathematics and science. Aesthetic values are also associated with creative achievement in the sciences, but neither boys nor girls scored particularly high on this scale. More girls than boys scored highest on this scale, but the percentages were not large for either group.

Further evidence of the extent of the differences in theoretical and social values between the sexes can be seen in a comparison among two groups of seventh-grade girls and one group of seventh-grade boys who were matched on cognitive ability as measured by scores on the mathematical and verbal sections of the SAT (SAT-M and SAT-V). There were twenty-six students in each group. These students had participated in either the Mathematical Talent Search conducted by SMPY in 1973 or the Verbal Talent Search conducted in 1973 by the Study of Verbally Gifted Youth (see chapter 9 of this volume for details).

The mean scores for each of the groups on the six values are shown in table 14.4. The mean scores for the girls in the first group and the girls in the second group were higher for the social value and lower for the theoretical value than the boys. Both groups of girls were lowest on the economic scale, which was the third-ranking value for the boys.

An analysis of variance of the three groups on the six values is shown in table 14.5. The differences of ratings of the values was significant, $F = 9.68$,

Table 14.4.   Means[a] on the six values of the Allport–Vernon–Lindzey Study of Values for the three groups

Values	Girls		Boys
	Group I	Group II	
Social	47.02	46.46	38.65
Aesthetic	43.31	38.88	34.67
Political	40.87	39.27	44.35
Theoretical	39.13	38.87	47.52
Religious	35.83	38.96	34.21
Economic	33.69	37.56	40.67

[a]Students were tested on the SV at both of the 1973 Talent Searches (one mathematics, one verbal). Test booklets were available for students in the mathematics contest. The individual scores, but not test booklets, were available for students in the verbal contest; two students, one girl in Group I and one boy, had errors in their profile scores of four and two points, respectively. Thus, the total for neither the Group I girls nor the boys is 240.

Table 14.5. ANOVA[a] of preferences for six values on the Allport–Vernon–Lindzey Study of Values for the three groups

Sources of variation	df	MS	F
Group (G)	0	0.060	1.429
Value (V)	5	682.672	9.682*
Triad (T)	0	0.044	
GV	10	465.549	8.398*
GT	0	0.042	
VT	125	70.507	
GVT	250	55.430	
TOTAL	390		

[a]The sum of squares and mean squares for the groups and triads should be exactly zero. The small error in each is due to the errors in scores for two subjects as explained in the footnote to table 14.4.
*p < .001

p < .001, and the interaction of ratings by groups was significant, $F = 8.40$, p < .001.

Tukey tests of mean differences (Scheffé 1959) for the three groups on the theoretical and social values are shown in table 14.6. The girls in the two groups did not differ significantly on these values. Both groups of girls were significantly lower than the boys on the theoretical value (p < .005) and significantly higher on the social value (p < .005).

Table 14.6. Tukey comparison of the mean scores on measures of theoretical and social values for the three groups

Value	Comparison	Difference	Level of significance
	Group I girls vs. Group II girls	.26	Not significant
Theoretical	Group I girls vs. boys	−8.39	p < .005
	Group II girls vs. boys	−8.65	p < .005
	Group I girls vs. Group II girls	.56	Not significant
Social	Group I girls vs. boys	8.37	p < .005
	Group II girls vs. boys	7.81	p < .005

These sex differences with respect to values were particularly interesting in light of the sex differences found in mathematical ability between boys and girls in the SMPY talent searches. Not only do gifted girls show less interest in scientific endeavors as measured by the SV but also they perform somewhat less well on difficult precollege-level tests of mathematical aptitude. The mean score for girls on the SAT-M has been found to be consistently lower than for boys in all three talent searches (Stanley 1973). In the 1972 contest 19 percent of the boys scored higher than the highest scoring girl. In 1973 and 1974 these percentages dropped, but the fact remained that far more boys than girls exhibited precocious ability in mathematics. (For a more detailed discussion of sex differences in mathematical precocity see Astin 1974 [I:4] and chapter 9 of this volume.)[5]

VALUES AND PRECOCITY

Thus, differences in values appear to be related to differences in mathematical precocity. The mean score on the SAT-M for students in the 1973 contest by grade, sex, and highest value score is shown in table 14.7. Eighth-grade boys who score highest on the theoretical value (N = 97) have the highest mean score on the SAT-M. Thus, for this group the theoretical value is closely related to performance on the SAT-M. For seventh-grade boys this result was not found. Seventh-grade boys who scored highest on the religious value had the highest mean on the SAT-M. The number of boys for whom the religious value was highest was small, N = 13. Seventh-grade girls who scored highest on the aesthetic value had the highest mean on the SAT-M, but the number of girls was small, N = 6. The three eighth-grade girls who scored highest on the economic value scale had the highest mean on the SAT-M. Eighth-grade girls who scored highest on the aesthetic value scale, N = 25, had the second highest mean score on the SAT-M.

When scores are combined across grades within sex group, the results are clearer. Boys who have the highest theoretical and religious values and girls who have the highest aesthetic values perform best on the SAT-M.

The relationship between theoretical values and mathematical precocity for boys can also be seen in table 14.8. The percentages of boys by highest value on the SV is shown for the 1973 contestants who scored below 640 on SAT-M and for those who scored at or above 640. The results are dramatic. Of the forty-seven boys considered winners in 1973, 55 percent scored highest on the theoretical value, as compared with only 34 percent of the nonwinners. Table 14.8 also shows the percentage of boys considered winners in 1972 and 1974 by highest value on the SV.

---

[5]In addition to the usual references, citations of chapters in volume I of *Studies of Intellectual Precocity* will be as follows [I:4]. The I indicates volume I, and the 4 is the chapter number [Editor].

Table 14.7.   Means and standard deviations of SAT-M scores for 656 contestants in 1973 by highest value on the Study of Values

| | Theoretical | | | Economic | | | Aesthetic | | |
	No.	Mean	Std. dev.	No.	Mean	Std. dev.	No.	Mean	Std. dev.
7th-grade girls	11	464.00	89.04	8	467.50	31.51	6	485.00	91.60
7th-grade boys	55	491.64	84.12	13	486.15	56.80	5	482.00	51.67
8th-grade girls	25	516.00	68.07	3	573.33	61.10	25	528.40	65.17
8th-grade boys	97	576.08	89.69	43	550.00	71.48	14	535.71	55.98
All girls	36	500.28	77.59	11	496.36	62.33	31	520.00	71.41
All boys	152	545.53	96.45	56	535.18	73.11	19	521.58	58.71

| | Social | | | Political | | | Religious | | |
	No.	Mean	Std. dev.	No.	Mean	Std. dev.	No.	Mean	Std. dev.
7th-grade girls	36	436.67	60.80	9	421.11	66.23	15	413.33	56.65
7th-grade boys	14	473.57	104.24	35	498.86	88.38	13	540.00	90.46
8th-grade girls	51	507.06	63.25	19	508.95	68.55	32	499.06	45.67
8th-grade boys	43	537.91	81.14	54	523.70	94.97	30	546.00	76.64
All girls	87	477.93	71.04	28	480.71	78.60	47	471.70	63.36
All boys	57	522.11	90.79	89	513.93	92.73	43	544.19	80.01

Table 14.8.   Percent of boys in the 1973 Mathematics Contest and winners from the 1972,[a] 1973, and 1974 contests by highest value on the Study of Values[b]

	Total no.	T	E	A	S	P	R
Non-winners 1973	369	34.1	14.1	5.1	14.6	22.2	9.8
All winners 1973	47	55.3	8.5	0.0	6.4	14.9	14.9
Winners 1972	35	62.9	14.3	5.7	8.6	8.6	0.0
Winners 1974	53	58.5	11.3	1.9	3.8	22.6	1.9

Key

T = Theoretical   S = Social
E = Economic   P = Political
A = Aesthetic   R = Religious

[a]The Study of Values was not administered to all of the 1972 or 1974 contestants. SV scores were available only for the winners in the 1972 and 1974 who were available at a later date.
[b]Percents do not always add to 100 due to rounding.

This difference in theoretical value orientation among the high-scoring precocious boys and the less precocious ones is more dramatic than the differences that were found on measures of investigative career interests (Fox & Denham 1974 [I:8]).[6] Thus, while many able young people who enter a mathematics competition are interested in scientific careers, a much smaller percentage of students in such a contest have the strong theoretical orientation that one would expect of the "pure" scientist. A sizable number of boys have high economic or political values; their interest in investigative occupations may reflect other motivations. One might suppose that students interested in scientific careers who have economic or political values may value scientific careers because of their power, prestige status, and economic remuneration. Students interested in investigative careers who score high on the social value scale may view these careers in terms of their possible contributions to the improvement of the quality of life.

Students who exhibit the most precocious achievement in the area of mathematics, as evidenced by high scores on the SAT-M, appear to be more strongly oriented toward mathematical and scientific careers and to value theoretical pursuits more than other contestants. It seems likely that their strong interests and orientations in these directions have contributed to their precocious development.

EDUCATIONAL FACILITATION AND VALUES

Most boys who have been identified as mathematically precocious report that they have become accelerated in their knowledge of mathematics by working on their own—sometimes systematically with the help of a teacher or parent, sometimes just by working with mathematical puzzles and games. It appears that the strong theoretical orientations of these boys have motivated them to pursue these activities.

It is rare to find a mathematically precocious boy who scores highest on the social value scale of the SV. Since more than one-third of the gifted girls in the contest scored highest on the social value, it is perhaps not surprising that so few of these girls have become radically accelerated in their mathematics knowledge. Their values and interests do not motivate them to seek special outside-of-school activities in mathematics.

Mathematically precocious boys who have high theoretical interests are far more interested in accelerating their progress in school than are the gifted girls or gifted boys who have other values. The mathematically precocious boys are eager to try difficult college courses or to participate in special accelerated mathematics classes outside of school. SMPY has repeatedly found that few of

---

[6]The measure of investigative career interests was an occupational checklist derived from the Vocational Preference Inventory (Holland 1965).

the very brightest girls tend to want to try these types of educational challenges. It seems likely that differences in values between the boys and girls contribute to this finding.

Of course, not all of the boys who have taken college courses or participated in special classes scored highest on the theoretical value scale. To date, all of the boys who have taken college courses have performed well in these classes, regardless of their values or career interests. Thus, if a talented student is eager to accelerate his educational progress he is likely to be successful, even if he does not have strong theoretical values. What is clear, however, is that those students who are very precocious in mathematics and who seek further acceleration are far more likely to be the ones who have theoretical values and investigative career interests.

CONCLUSIONS

Students who exhibit unusually high-level talent in mathematics as early as grades seven and eight and who are able to benefit from special educational facilitation, such as college courses and accelerated classes, tend to have values and interests highly consistent with their abilities. It would appear that many already have personalities which resemble those of mathematicians and scientists. Students who have similar cognitive abilities but do not have the same values and career interests are less apt to seek out or accept special advancement in the areas of mathematics and science. Since girls are more apt to have social interests, it would seem that values and interests are at least partially related to the fact that so few girls become accelerated in their mathematics education.

SMPY will work closely with the winners over the coming years to encourage their continued achievement. Among the winners, a few students are not strongly oriented toward theoretical and investigative goals. It will be interesting to see to what extent they will continue to pursue science and mathematics, as compared with the others, and to what extent their values and career interests will change over the coming years. It will be interesting to see how many of the very mathematically precocious youngsters will become the creative scientists and mathematicians of the future.

REFERENCES

Allport, G. W., Vernon, P. E., and Lindzey, G. 1970. *Manual for the Study of Values: A scale for measuring the dominant interests in personality.* Boston: Houghton Mifflin.

Astin, H. S. 1974. Sex differences in mathematical and scientific precocity. In J. C. Stanley, D. P. Keating, and L. H. Fox (eds.), *Mathematical talent: Discovery, description, and development*. Baltimore, Md. 21218: The Johns Hopkins University Press, pp. 70–86.

Fox, L. H., and Denhan, S. A. 1974. Values and career interests of mathematically and scientifically precocious youth. In J. C. Stanley, D. P. Keating, and L. H. Fox (eds.), *Mathematical talent: Discovery, description, and development*. Baltimore, Md. 21218: The Johns Hopkins University Press, pp. 140–75.

Hall, W. B., and MacKinnon, D. W. 1969. Personality inventory correlates of creativity among architects. *Journal of Applied Psychology* 53(4): 322–26.

Holland, J. L. 1965. *Manual for the Vocational Preference Inventory*. Palo Alto, Calif.: Consulting Psychologists Press.

MacKinnon, D. W. 1962. The nature and nurture of creative talent. *American Psychologist* 17(7): 484–95.

Scheffé, H. 1959. *The analysis of variance*. New York: John Wiley & Sons.

Southern, M. L., and Plant, W. T. 1968. Personality characteristics of very bright adults. *Journal of Personality and Social Psychology* 75(1): 119–26.

Spranger, E. 1966. *Types of men: The psychology and ethics of personality*. New York: Johnson Reprint, 1928.

Stanley, J. C. 1973. Accelerating the educational progress of intellectually gifted youths. *Educational Psychologist* 10: 133–46.

Warren, J. R., and Herst, P. A. 1960. Personality attributes of gifted college students. *Science* 132: 330–37.

15
RANDOM VS. NONRANDOM
STUDY OF VALUES PROFILES

Joan A. W. Linsenmeier

ABSTRACT

The Allport-Vernon-Lindzey Study of Values, an ipsative test designed primarily for use with individuals with some college education, was administered to a group of bright junior high school students. It was not obvious, a priori, that the inventory would yield better than chance results with these young students. In this chapter the profiles of the students are compared to profiles randomly generated on a computer. It is found that the profiles of the students are significantly different from those that would result from random responding to the inventory items. This increases the likelihood that the profiles will remain stable over time and indicates the appropriateness of using the scores to describe the characteristics of the students.

An ipsative test is one composed of n subtests such that the sum of an individual's scores on each subtest is equal to some fixed constant k, i.e. $\sum_{i=1}^{n} X_i = k$, where X_i is his score on the ith subtest. An increase in the score on any one subtest must be compensated for by a lowered score on at least one other subtest. Several researchers have investigated the effects of this property on the correlations between the subtests of an ipsative test. Clemans (1966) showed that the ipsative intercorrelation matrix will have a large proportion of negative values and discussed the effect on the average intercorrelation of various characteristics of the ipsative instrument. Radcliffe (1963) proved that if the subtest variances of an ipsative test were equal, then the average intercorrelation of the subtests would be $-1/(n-1)$, where n is the number of subtests. Gleser (1972) derived formulae for the maximum and minimum values which this average intercorrelation can take and determined the conditions under which each bound could be obtained. Less investigation has been devoted to the constraints placed on the variance of an individual's subtest scores by the special properties of ipsative tests and the intercorrelations of the subtests.

Ipsative tests are frequently used for intraindividual comparisons, i.e., for assessing the relative strengths of various interests or goals in a single individual. Clemans (1966) has pointed out that in the individuals-by-scores matrix for an ipsative test the magnitudes of the numbers in a row are meaningful, but those of numbers in a column are not. One may compare only the ranking and not the absolute strength of an attribute for different individuals. The relative sizes of an individual's subtest scores are the important variables. It is important, therefore, to determine how much of the variance in an individual's profile is representative of his actual interests or goals and how much of it is likely to occur just by chance.

The Allport–Vernon–Lindzey Study of Values (1970) is an ipsative test suitable for verbally able senior high school, college, and adult groups. In the Study of Mathematically Precocious Youth (SMPY) at The Johns Hopkins University it was administered to much younger students, chiefly mathematically apt seventh- and eighth-graders, twelve or thirteen years old. Most of these youths were considerably brighter than average for their grades and ages, and they were given some supplemental materials to aid in their comprehension of the test items. Nevertheless, it could not be *assumed* that they were tested well with the instrument. This study and a detailed internal analysis of the responses (in preparation) were attempts to determine the adequacy of the Study of Values for that special population. In particular, this study was undertaken to show that the profiles of the students would be unlikely to result from random responding. Of course, nonrandom responding is a necessary but not sufficient condition for stability of items over time. The more pronounced the values profile is, however, the less likely it would seem that the extreme values would change radically as the student becomes older.

METHOD

The Study of Values

The Study of Values is designed to measure the relative prominence of six basic motives in an individual, corresponding to the six "types" posited by Eduard Spranger in his *Types of Men* (1966)[1]: theoretical, economic, aesthetic, social, political, and religious. The *theoretical* man values above all else the discovery of truth. *Economic* man is practical, placing paramount value on utility. *Aesthetic* man values form and harmony highly. *Social* man values love

[1]The 1966 translation of Spranger's work follows the original 1927 German version, entitled *Lebensformen.*

of people. Power is the chief value of *political* man. And *religious* man is mystical, valuing unity, the oneness of the universe. Spranger hypothesized that the value system of an individual is a mixture of these six "ideal types."

The Study of Values is composed of two parts, each consisting of questions concerning a variety of familiar situations. In each of the thirty questions of part I, the subject must indicate his preference for one of two alternatives. He may give three points to the preferred alternative and none to the other or, if his preference is slight, two points to the former and one to the latter. Each value is compared twice with each of the other five. Part II consists of fifteen questions with four alternatives each; the subject must give four points to his first choice, three to his second choice, two to his third choice, and one point to the remaining alternative. Each possible set of four values occurs once. In both sections of the test, if the subject cannot decide which alternative(s) he prefers, he is to divide the points for that question evenly among all the alternatives. Since the subjects in this study were very rarely unable to rank order the alternatives in any question, the problems introduced by the possibility of indecision are ignored in the following analysis.

An individual's score for each value is the total number of points assigned to the alternatives representing it, plus the appropriate correction factor. (The correction factors were introduced so that the means for the six values would be equal in the population on which the test norms were based.) The sum of the scores on the various scales must equal 240. The designers of the Study of Values state in their manual (Allport, Vernon, & Lindzey 1970) that it "does not . . . measure the absolute strength of each of the six values, but only their relative strengths."

Actual Profiles

The Study of Values was given to the thirty-five top-scoring students in the 1972 Mathematics Talent Search. All thirty-five were boys between the ages of twelve and fourteen, chosen on the basis of their scores on the College Entrance Examination Board Scholastic Aptitude Test-Mathematical and the Mathematics Level I Achievement Test or the Sequential Tests of Educational Progress, Series II Science, forms 1A and 1B. It was not obvious, a priori, that the Study of Values would yield better than chance results when used with these bright young students.

Generation of Random Profiles

For comparison, three sets of 100 random profiles for the Study of Values were generated using Monte Carlo methods. The replies to questions in part II were determined in the same manner for each set. For each question a permutation of the numbers 4, 3, 2, and 1 was obtained, and the first number in the permutation was assigned to the first alternative in the question, the second number to the second alternative, and so forth. All permutations of 4, 3, 2, and 1 were equally likely to occur. The replies to part I questions were calculated differently for the three sets of profiles. For the first set (edition 1) the probabilities of assigning (1) a three and a zero, and (2) a two and a one were equal. For the second set (edition 2) only threes and zeros were assigned. For the third set (edition 3) only twos and ones were used. Thus edition 2 represents subjects whose preferences are always strong, while edition 3 represents subjects with only weak preferences, leading to relatively flat profiles. Edition 1 represents subjects whose performance is intermediate between these two extremes. In all three editions each of the two alternatives in each question was equally likely to receive the greater number of points.

RESULTS

Subtest Scores

Frequency distributions of both the scores on each of the six scales and of the individual profile standard deviations were obtained for all three sets of random profiles and for the profiles of the top-scoring students. Table 15.1 shows the means and standard deviations of the scores on each scale.

The distributions for each set of random profiles approach the normal curve, and *t*-tests show that none of the means is significantly different from the expected mean, 40 plus the correction value for that scale, at the .05 level (values of $t[999]$ ranged from 0 to 1.652). Hartley's F_{max} test for homogeneity of variance shows that for each edition there is no significant difference among its standard deviations ($F_{max}[6,999] = 1.138$ for edition 1, 1.188 for edition 2, and 1.093 for edition 3; $p > .05$ for each edition).

The differences for the actual profiles do not follow this pattern. The difference among standard deviations of scores on the scales for the six values is significant at the .05 level ($F_{max} = 1.655$). For all scales but the *political* the standard deviation of actual scores is significantly greater than that of edition 1 random profiles at the .01 level ($F[34,999]$ ranged from 2.357 for *theoretical* to 4.387 for *religious*). Since the reliability of a measure is directly related to the magnitude of the variability on the measure, this implies greater reliability of these scales across individuals.

The means on the *theoretical, economic, aesthetic,* and *religious* scales are significantly different from the expected means ($t[34] = 6.01, 2.86, 5.87,$ and $3.81; p < .01$ for each of these four scales). Table 15.2 shows the percentage of actual profiles which fall one or two edition 1 standard deviations above or below the mean edition 1 scale values. Scores on the *theoretical* scale are extremely high, and those on *aesthetic* scale extremely low. *Economic* scale scores are moderately high and *religious* scale scores moderately low. The

Table 15.1. Distributions of scale scores for random profiles and actual subjects

	Theoretical	Economic	Aesthetic	Social	Political	Religious
Random, ed. 1						
mean	41.96	39.21	43.94	37.75	42.06	35.08
standard deviation	5.10	5.09	5.04	4.79	4.78	4.87
Random, ed. 2						
mean	41.94	38.86	44.00	38.30	41.97	34.93
standard deviation	6.07	6.17	5.89	5.74	5.80	5.66
Random, ed. 3						
mean	41.92	39.16	44.02	38.00	41.89	35.02
standard deviation	3.89	3.84	3.91	3.83	3.74	3.74
Actual Ss						
mean	49.97	43.29	36.03	38.66	43.46	28.43
standard deviation	7.83	8.85	8.04	7.97	6.26	10.20
Correction factor	+2	−1	+4	−2	+2	−5
40 plus correction	42.00	39.00	44.00	38.00	42.00	35.00

implications of these deviations are discussed by Fox and Denham (1974 [I:8][2]). The present paper is concerned only with the fact that the deviations do exist.

Profile Standard Deviations

Table 15.3 shows the means and standard deviations of the profile standard deviations (P.S.D.s) for both the randomly generated and the actual profiles. The P.S.D. of a profile is the standard deviation of the six scores in that profile about the profile's mean (mean equals $240/6 = 40$ for each profile). Standard deviations, rather than variances, are shown, since the distribution of the former approximates the normal curve more closely, and properties of the normal distribution are used in the comparison of actual with randomly generated P.S.D.s.

[2]Citations of chapters in volume I of *Studies of Intellectual Precocity* are as follows: [I:8]. The I indicates volume I, and 8 is the chapter number [Editor].

Table 15.2. Deviations of scores on actual profiles about means for edition 1 random profiles (percentages)

	Theoretical	Economic	Aesthetic	Social	Political	Religious
More than two std. deviations[a] above the mean	42.86	25.71	5.71	14.29	8.57	5.71
More than one std. deviation above the mean	71.43	42.86	8.57	25.71	28.57	14.29
More than one std. deviation below the mean	11.43	14.29	62.86	20.00	17.14	54.26
More than two std. deviations below the mean	0	11.43	40.00	8.57	5.71	40.00

[a]Based on standard deviations of edition 1 random scores.

Note that, as was expected, the P.S.D.s of the profiles using only threes and zeros in part I (edition 2) are larger than those using both three-zero and two-one (edition 1), whereas those using only twos and ones (edition 3) show the least variance. The standard deviation of the scores in a profile where each score was equal to 40 plus the appropriate correction factor for that scale would be exactly 3.00. Hence the correction factors account for 29.54 percent, 22.53 percent, and 42.72 percent of the variance in the edition 1, edition 2, and edition 3 profiles.

The mean P.S.D. of the actual profiles, those of the thirty-five top-scoring students, is significantly greater than that of any of the sets of random profiles at the .01 level ($t[34] = 7.763$ for comparison to edition 1, 6.395 for edition 2, and 9.353 for edition 3). F ratios indicate significant differences in variance also

Table 15.3. Distributions of profile standard deviations

	Random, ed. 1	Random, ed. 2	Random, ed. 3	Actual subjects
Mean P.S.D.	5.52	6.32	4.59	10.06
Standard deviation of the P.S.D.s	1.78	2.09	1.53	3.46

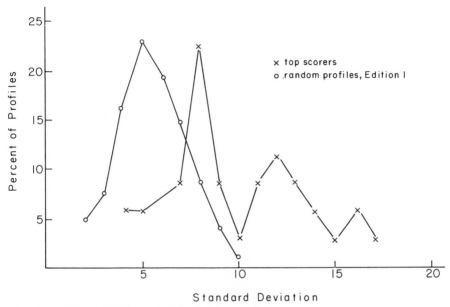

Fig. 15.1. Standard deviations of Study of Values profiles.

(F[34,999] = 3.778, 2.741, and 5.114; $p < .01$ for each comparison). Figure 15.1 shows the distributions of P.S.D.s for the actual subjects and for the edition 1 random profiles. The horizontal axis represents the P.S.D., rounded to the nearest integer, and the vertical axis indicates the percentage of profiles with that P.S.D.

The difference in profile variances is even more striking if we consider the percent of actual P.S.D.s which lie one or two edition 1 standard deviations above or below the mean P.S.D. of the edition 1 random profiles. Eighty percent of the students had P.S.D.s more than one standard deviation above this mean, as opposed to 15.87 percent expected by chance; 51.43 percent fell more than two standard deviations above the mean, as opposed to 2.28 percent expected by chance. And *none* of the students had profiles with P.S.D.s falling more than one standard deviation below the mean for random profiles. This pattern held even more strongly for the thirty-seven top-scorers (based on Scholastic Aptitude Test-Mathematical) in the 1973 SMPY contest: 83.78 percent had P.S.D.s more than one edition 1 standard deviation above the edition 1 mean, 67.57 percent had P.S.D.s more than two standard deviations above that mean, and, once again, no individual P.S.D. fell more than one standard deviation below the edition 1 mean.

CONCLUSION

The individual Study of Values profiles of the bright young students with whom this study is concerned show significantly greater variance than would be expected if the students were responding randomly to the items on the inventory. This increases the likelihood that the extreme values will remain stable over time, indicating that it is appropriate to use the profiles in describing the characteristics of the students.

The most common direct cause of the size of the individual profile standard deviations for the students being tested was high scores on the *theoretical* and *economic* scales coupled with low scores on the *aesthetic* and *religious* scales. These deviations reflect neither the design of the test nor chance factors, but true characteristics of the students.

REFERENCES

Allport, G. W., Vernon, P. E., and Lindzey, G. 1970. *Manual for the study of values: A scale for measuring dominant interests in personality.* Boston: Houghton Mifflin Co.

Clemans, W. V. 1966. An analytical and empirical examination of some properties of ipsative measures. *Psychometric Monographs*, no. 14. The Psychometric Society.

Fox, L. H., and Denham, S. A. 1974. Values and career interests of mathematically and scientifically precocious youth. In J. C. Stanley, D. P. Keating, and L. H. Fox (eds.), *Mathematical talent: Discovery, description, and development.* Baltimore, Md.: The Johns Hopkins Press, pp. 140–75.

Gleser, L. J. 1972. On bounds for the average correlation between subtest scores in ipsatively scored tests. *Educational and Psychological Measurement* 32: 759–65.

Radcliffe, J. A. 1963. Some properties of ipsative score matrices and their relevance for some current interest tests. *Australian Journal of Psychology* 15: 1–11.

Spranger, E. 1966. *Types of men: The psychology and ethics of personality.* New York: Johnson Reprint, 1928.

IV
CRITIQUE AND DISCUSSION

16
A HISTORICAL STEP BEYOND TERMAN

Ellis Batten Page

The occasion of this symposium is most valuable for me. Not only is the director of the study, Julian Stanley, a close personal friend. He is also one of my heroes in psychological measurement, and, for other reasons as well, I have watched this study with great interest.

THE UNUSUAL NATURE OF SMPY

The Study of Mathematically Precocious Youth is, in a number of ways, the most refreshing one on the current scene. It seems to have turned somewhat away from the transitory, fashionable rhetoric of the 1960s and early 1970s. Those of us in education can recall the era merely by echoing a few of the popular words: creativity, the deprived, the equality of educational opportunity, compensatory education, the open classroom, alternative education, affirmative action, performance contracting, behavior mod. I surely mean no scorn for these. They embodied the concerns and ideals of a particular time in American history. One term after another was artfully contrived, often from the best of motives, to guide the policies and to channel the national resources in some chosen direction. One after another these terms, reified in programs, have been well supported by government and foundations. One after another, they have become shopworn, and researchers disillusioned. The greatest disenchantment, for those who have looked closely at it, may have come from the performance contracting experiment conducted by the OEO (Page 1972). But in all of them, a certain message has been coming through, little by little, a signal emerging from the noise. The message has been this: We in the social sciences know far less about changing behavior than we had thought.

Throughout the time, however, the science of measurement and the technology of prediction have steadily improved, and the storm-tossed social scientist, battered and ship-wrecked on the beach, finds that he *has* something very valuable, after all. It is the power of selection. *Selection*, right now, not treatment, is where he is really best.

And the evidence of this professional ability had been around all the time. There was Binet; there was Terman; there was the military testing in both major wars; there was Flanagan's pilot screening; there was the remarkable success of the College Boards, and its duplication in the ACT Program. With all the current furor about testing, and the political suppression of it in many communities, more tests are, nevertheless, in use today than ever before: the Measurement Research Center, scoring millions of tests, reports an exponential growth; the president of a major testing company assured me that every year there is a substantial increase in sales. Most professionals do feel better able to predict and diagnose, with such information as tests provide. As Cronbach (1970) wrote: "the general mental test stands today as the most important technical contribution psychology has made to the practical guidance of human affairs" (p. 197).

Not since Terman, however, has any team used tests to pursue the very gifted, with the expert zeal of SMPY. Undaunted by the ideological wars of social half-science, SMPY has explicitly sought out "*manifest* talent" (not the sort that is "latent," i.e., uncertain of diagnosis). And it has sought out this talent in the discipline furthest from the contamination of transitory rhetoric. The edifice of mathematics remains peculiarly unstained by ideology; and those who argue that all science has a "political" orientation have to look carefully away from math while they do so. In fixing its attention so resolutely on these enduring qualities, the SMPY team has probably foregone many of the headlines bestowed in the daily papers. But they will gather more chapters in the history of science over the decades ahead, just as the Terman work survives, not only as a classic of psychology, but in the productive and valuable lives of the Terman youngsters themselves.

THE UNUSUAL NATURE OF MATH

In concentrating on mathematics, moreover, SMPY has moved an important historical step beyond Terman. It is not solely in its elevation above politics and fashion that math is especially appropriate. There are a number of other extremely important reasons for its unique suitability for such a study. Math has reached a level of unprecedented power. Historically, many have recognized its centrality to understanding other matters. Galileo described the universe as a "vast book which stands forever open before our eyes . . . but it cannot be read until we have learnt the language and become familiar with the characters in which it is written. It is written in mathematical language, and the letters are triangles, circles and other geometrical figures, without which it is humanly impossible to comprehend a single word" (Newman 1956, p. 731). And Newton apparently regarded God as a kind of cryptographer and the world about him as a kind of mathematical riddle. In science, he pursued the algebra of motion as, in his secret study, he pursued the mysteries of the occult (Keynes 1956).

But we have had so many powerful developments since the time of Galileo, both in the hard and softer sciences. George Boole (1854) may have been hyperbolic in describing his binary logic as "the laws of thought," but the current investigators of cognitive process have at least opened the law *book*, and their tools have been mathematical psychology, computer simulation, and artificial intelligence. The astonishing achievements of math in biology, which have unlocked the living cell, are so fresh as to need no reminder. Even the humanities are not far behind. Serious scholarship in history is moving steadily in a mathematical direction, and will never recover from the pioneer authorship study of the Federalist Papers (Mosteller & Wallace 1964). Linguistics is moving mathematically, with the algebra of the syntactic grammars giving way to the more useful relational calculus, and semantic grammars already functioning in startling ways (Minsky 1968; Winograd 1969). And operations research is powerfully applying math to decision-making itself (Wagner 1970).

A peculiar feature of such work is the *direction* of the influence. With the exception of mavericks like Carl Bereiter and myself (both English majors through two degrees), the direction has been from math to the softer science, not the other way around. For instance, the history of scientific psychology has many exemplars of hard scientists who moved into behavioral analysis (the SMPY founder is one distinguished example). But if any psychologist has achieved importantly after converting to physics, he is unknown to me.[1] This directional supposition (if justified) implies that, in aiding math prodigies at an early age, we are potentially aiding all those disciplines which depend on new, deep insights of mathematical applications. And we have seen that such disciplines include, in fact, *all* scholarly fields.[2]

THE YOUTH OF MATHEMATICIANS

The biographies of important mathematicians teach us that the greatest contributions commonly come early. In fact, there is a kind of ordering of disciplines by the age of greatest productivity, with an apparent loading toward

---

[1] Proof of such a negative generalization is, of course, virtually impossible. But no one so far has provided me with an exception.

[2] It is a corollary of this analysis that each discipline might be characterized as being more or less "quantitative." David Brown (1974) has characterized each department of a university by calculating, for all undergraduate majors of that department, a mean SAT-M minus the mean SAT-V. In other words, he has characterized each department by the degree to which the major students have greater mathematical than verbal ability. The technique has high face validity: the top three departments are statistics, civil engineering, and mathematics itself; the bottom is English. Both education and psychology, having a hard and soft mixture, are in the middle.

youth of certain fields, and an apparent loading toward middle age of certain others (Lehman 1954). In general, the early-peaking fields appear to be those which are not dependent on the accumulation of large data bases, of large informational stores; but are, rather, dependent on the facile manipulation of symbols, on long strings of transformations. Thus, math and chemistry, romantic poetry and sonatas, are alike in being ripe fields for youthful accomplishment: small events are turned and twisted and rephrased to conform with certain high and elegant ideals. Accomplishment does not depend so much on what is known, but on what one can do with a little. By contrast, the aging historian, the aging traditional taxonomist, depend on the processing of relatively large masses of less orderly information. The youth-peaking fields, then, might depend on the sharp, deep insights typical of Raven's matrices. The age-peaking fields might depend more, relatively, on the crystallized intelligence of vocabulary, on firm disciplinary habits of thought, and on the accumulation of varied skills. If these generalizations are correct, then it is not simply desirable, it is *crucial* that the potentially productive in such formal and elegant fields be exposed in their very formative years to the best materials available. George Polya once advised a bright but puzzled freshman that he shouldn't worry: that one doesn't *understand* the calculus; one becomes *accustomed* to the calculus. If gifted youngsters are to use the calculus with ease at eighteen, they should become *accustomed* to it as early as possible. Some provision for young prodigies, then, has a particular aptness in the field of mathematics.

THE IMPORTANCE OF INSTRUCTION

Notwithstanding the existence of math prodigies, and notwithstanding the youthful surge of math—*experience* in math is apparently essential to productivity. This is not exactly obvious. Some other fields are apparently far less dependent on tuition. And there is evidence from school testing that argues the importance of math education. For example, if one looks at age-equivalencies for seventh-grade students, one will find far more seventh-graders who can *read* three years ahead, than can solve *mathematical* problems at the tenth-grade level. Math is not commonly learned at home, beyond the most elementary level. And it is not commonly picked up on one's own. The tools must be *learned*. A college freshman can, with these tools, solve mathematical problems that baffled Galileo. Yet which freshman can write better drama than Galileo's contemporary, Shakespeare? Or, for that matter, better poetry than Horace? Even the genius of Aristotle would not be sufficient, unaided, to do routine college problems today. Beyond the difficulty, or impossibility, of inventing the needed tools, mathematical tuition is important in another respect. These tools are sequenced, more than in any other field in the wide span of school subjects. They will not be understood if encountered casually in daily life, the way one picks up some history, some poetry, some medicine. Destroy the order too far, and we have apparently destroyed the comprehension.

In general, the identification of the very gifted in any field should be to some *purpose*, and this purpose would usually be instruction. Yet other youth-peaking fields (such as poetry) do not apparently depend in the same way on tuition. And if there is a necessary sequence in some of these (such as poetry), no one knows what it is. Here again, the selection of math as the discipline was inspired.

THE USE OF ADVANCED TESTS

Once one has decided to identify the gifted, especially out of a huge population, then how may one go about it? On the one hand, all the extremely gifted will bump their heads on the ceiling of the tests designed for their age-mates. On the other hand, it is sometimes said, a bright ten-year-old is not an average fifteen; he is a bright ten. From this viewpoint, different ages are not suitably measured with the same instrument. Indeed, when this viewpoint is pushed far enough, some are led to say (truthfully but misleadingly) that "everyone is an individual." SMPY rightly pushed this objection aside and took the much sounder, historical line that intelligence is linear, and additive, and identifiable no matter at what age it is exhibited. There is a still stronger assumption, again the historical one in the measurement of intelligence: that intelligence will continue to grow, much as one's own individual rate, at least as long as physical growth continues. This sweeps aside the fiction that the prodigy will necessarily "burn out" (one definition of burning out would be to reach his asymptote earlier than his age-mates). This sounder view is rather that the asymptote will be *higher*, not earlier, and higher in some reasonable proportion to the faster early growth.

This use of advanced tests, however, leads us to some problems in exposition and in the understanding or analysis of test results. What does it mean, for instance, that Johnny, age twelve, achieved a score of 540 on the SAT-M? And that Jill, age fourteen, achieved 570? Would we expect Johnny to do better than Jill, when he is fourteen? If so, how much better? What I suggest is an explicit move toward an adapted "mental age" concept as a tentative step toward putting such information, extraordinary as it is, in more orderly form. From such a step, one may optimistically predict the discovery of some important parameters for such rare and valuable talents.

THE DEFINITION OF Q

The historical definition of intelligence was

$$IQ = 100 \frac{MA}{CA},$$ (1)

where IQ was intelligence quotient; MA was the mental age of the youngster, defined by the age-group most similar to his total score; and CA was the chronological age of the youngster. The mean of IQ is 100, and the standard deviation was traditionally found to be about 16 points. But suppose that IQ were to be calculated from raw scores on a test, as is now often the case. Then we may say that

$$IQ = 100 + 16Z,$$ (2)

where Z is the difference of a score from the mean, measured in standard deviations; that is, Z has zero mean and unit variance, and is

$$Z_i = (X_i - \bar{X})/\sigma_X.$$ (3)

From (1) above, it is obvious that

$$MA = \frac{IQ \cdot CA}{100},$$ (4)

and therefore, from (2) and (4), that

$$MA = \frac{(100 + 16Z) \cdot CA}{100}.$$ (5)

These are well-known elements. Now let us define

Q_i = the quotient (such as IQ, or MQ, etc.) for the ith individual not in the age range of the norm group;

C_n = the *mean* chronological age for the norm group; and

C_i = the chronological age for the ith individual, not in the norm group.

By analogy with the IQ, we define the quotient score as

$$Q_i = 100 \frac{MA}{C_i}, \text{ and from (5)}$$ (6)

$$Q_i = \frac{100 (100 + 16Z) C_n}{100 C_i}, \text{ and thus}$$ (7)

$$Q_i = (100 + 16Z_i) \left(\frac{C_n}{C_i}\right),$$ (8)

where Z_i is now the score in standard deviations for the ith individual, as measured around the mean of the average student of the norm-group age.

For a sample problem, let us say that the average chronological age of high school seniors, at time of testing, is seventeen years. Let us also assume that there is, for the *average* seventeen-year-old, so far as we can tell, a mean SAT-M of 460, with a standard deviation of 110. Then, if Johnny achieved 540, for him

$$Z_i = \frac{540 - 460}{110} = \frac{80}{110} = .727$$

Then for Johnny, age twelve,

$\frac{C_n}{C_i} = \frac{17}{12} = 1.42.$ And

$C_i = (100 + 16[.727])(1.42) = (111.62)(1.42)$

$\qquad = 158$, for Johnny's Q in math, or MQ.

In general, we have the extremely simple formula,

$$Q_i = \left(\frac{C_n}{C_i}\right) \cdot Q_{ns} , \qquad (9)$$

where Q_{ns} is the quotient-equivalent (e.g., MQ-equivalent) for the chronological age C_n, for the score s (that score achieved by the ith individual). Very often Q_{ns} may be easily estimated from the percentile equivalents given for the average student of the norm-group age.

USES OF THE QUOTIENT Q

These general formulas (6) and (9) may of course be modified as more accurate information is gained. For example, it may be that the constant 16 would not be appropriate for data from the SAT-M or other test of interest. If one holds to the analogy with IQ, that Q_i represents the ratio of MA (for SAT-M) to CA, then the constant may be other than 16, depending on the different degree of overlap of the various age levels. Information about age-level overlap could be gained in a number of ways, some estimated within a norm group, others from different testings of small samples. Where other information is available, it might be wiser to work directly with mental ages, rather than with the general formulas. But where such direct mental ages are not available, the use of Q appears to offer advantages.

These advantages are of the sort that generally come from standardized scores. They allow us to express simply what would otherwise be awkward;

and they allow us to compare what would otherwise be incomparable. Johnny's score would now be comparable, roughly, with Jill's (his 158 vs. her 141), and with his own later scores. Such scores further permit some summary and analysis of data, currently impossible. In the annual report, for instance, one could report the mean *precocity* of the group; surely that would be meaningful, despite some softness in the estimates. And the precocity of individuals could then be correlated with other measures. Once such an index is adopted, there may be rather rich returns of information.

THE PARAMETERS OF IMPROVEMENT

Where there are successive test occasions for the same measure, and these are across a number of years, it would also be interesting to borrow a model from mathematical learning theory. At any time t,

$$X_i(t) = \alpha_i - \beta_i e^{-\gamma_i t} , \qquad (10)$$

where $X_i(t)$ is the score made on some instrument (such as SAT-M), where α_i is the youngster's asymptote, and $\alpha_i - \beta_i$ is the initial score made, and γ_i is the rate of growth, and where e is the base of the natural logarithm (Atkinson 1972; Page 1973). Of particular interest here are the three parameters, α, β, and γ, all of which tell us important information about the youth and are estimated from a number of scores achieved. Of great interest, then, is the relationship among such parameters. For example, there has been a widespread belief that intelligence is uncorrelated with learning. For real, important cognitive measures such as SAT-M, this seems to me nonsense. But under some conditions (especially where the learning is of arbitrary and meaningless associations) data will appear to confirm this lack of relation. (For an excellent review, see Zeaman & House 1967.) A close study of such parameters for important measures of the highly gifted, and perhaps also for some average students, should illuminate this problem. Of particular interest would be the discovered correlation between α and γ, that is, between asymptote and rate of growth.

THE SOURCE OF SEX DIFFERENCE

Let us turn to a repeated discovery in SMPY, a discovery met with apparent embarrassment and dismay. I refer to the sex difference in extremely high math performance: the difficulty of locating equally gifted girls, and their relatively less stable dedication to extreme achievement. The editors of *Mathematical Talent* (Stanley, Keating, & Fox 1974) wrote that the sex differences "were both unexpected and disconcerting" (p. 70). Helen Astin was called in as a special trouble-shooter in such matters. She noted the often-found superiority of girls on some traits, and of boys on others. She apparently believed that the differential increase with age (Aiken 1970) implies that such differences are the result of "differential cultural reinforcement over time" (Astin 1974, p. 71). (But what would one say about height, which also shows increasing differentials with age?) And she dismisses "genetic components" as being "as yet inconclusive" (p. 71). In the same volume, Anne Anastasi pleaded the same agnostic view, not solely for herself but apparently for everyone: "Conceptually, I do not know what is meant by an innate or genotypic ability. And empirically, I maintain *we know nothing* about the genotypic (or biochemical or neurological) basis of the behavioral characteristics we call abilities" (p. 89, italics added). In chapter 9 of this volume, Fox speaks, understandably, of attempting to "bridge the gap." And three authors in chapter 12 seek to relate interest patterns to the cognitive differences among these precocious youngsters of both sexes. In turning away from the biological or genetic explanation of group differences, these scholars are surely consistent with most other psychologists and educators.

In fact, however, there is no need to strain so hard away from a genetic interpretation of some of these cognitive differences. Some of the data fit comfortably into what is now a fairly clear genetic model. More than thirty years ago, O'Connor (1943) suggested that spatial visualizing ability fell into a pattern typical of recessive sex-linked inheritance. And other investigators (Stafford 1961; Hartlage 1970) collected the central evidence necessary to such a hypothesis, measures of both-sexed parents and offspring. It remained for two educational psychologists, Darrell Bock and Donald Kolakowski (1973), to lay out the theory and data of such inheritance in a virtually conclusive way. Their findings bear only on spatial visualization (SV), yet the influences of such SV on mathematical ability are not trivial. Such SV abilities may be considerable. Validity results for the Differential Aptitude Tests (DAT) show positive correlations with such school subjects as geometry, quantitative thinking, drafting, and shop mechanics.[3] SV is often treated as one *component* of intelligence (as in the DAT), yet it correlates only very weakly with verbal IQ. For a long time, it has been known that SV was much higher for boys than for girls, in fact that only about one-quarter of the girls passed the boy median. And the attempted explanations of these differences have typically been (as Helen Astin put it) "differential cultural reinforcement over time," i.e., the encouragement of sex roles.

[3]Kolakowski and Malina (1974) have demonstrated how SV might have fostered selectivity through its influence in battle and in the hunt.

What destroys this explanation and leaves the environmentalist helpless is a major finding across three studies over twelve years. It is this: *girls* correlate more highly with their *fathers* than with their mothers, and *boys* correlate more highly with their *mothers* than with their fathers. Now, if one attempts to explain this cross-sex parent-child correlation as a kind of Oedipus-Elektra effect, then one is unable to explain the female decrement in mean score. If girls are simply modeling themselves on their fathers, then why are they lower than their brothers? On the other hand, if they are modeling themselves on their *mothers*, then why are they more correlated with their *fathers*? No social-expectancy model can satisfy all of the statistical findings.

In contrast, the sex-linked recessive genetic model brilliantly satisfies all requirements: Imagine that each girl gains one X chromosome from the two her mother has; and gains the *only* X chromosome of her father. In this case, she will be more correlated with her father than with her mother. Imagine, too, that the boy gains his *only* X chromosome from the two his mother has. Then he will clearly correlate more highly with her, than with his father, who had no X chromosome to give. This would explain the cross-sex parent-child correlation.

Now imagine that the valuable space gene, contributing to SV scores, is *recessive*. For the boy, then, whatever gene he received will be operative, since he has only one X chromosome. The girl, however, is at a disadvantage, since both X chromosomes must carry the recessive or she will not manifest the gene. This would explain the decrement of girls, at the same time explaining the cross-sex correlation. From such a persuasive model, the frequency of that recessive gene is estimated at about one-half, thus explaining the median overlap found between the sexes. In short, boys appear to manifest this trait half the time ($p = \frac{1}{2}$); and girls one-quarter of the time ($p^2 = \frac{1}{4}$).

The high quality of this explanation should give behavioral scientists pause. When was the last time we came up with any social explanations which had the same satisfying consistency and comprehensive power? Of course, finding such cross-sex correlations requires substantial numbers of subjects, probably beyond the reach of SMPY as now designed. Yet, hopefully, it may help us to accept sex differences, in part at least, as genetic differentiation which will be more profitably explored in a genetic way and should be better understood in the future. And such explanations need not always work against women! It would be very interesting, for example, to search for sex-linked *dominants* which might explain, in part, the apparent verbal superiority of girls.[4]

---

[4]Recent study of educational values (Page & Breen 1973) showed a high importance for "quantitative" abilities: generally third out of seven traits, preceded only by "verbal" ability and by "personality." But some differential sex expectation was shown, with quantitative slightly less emphasized for girl students and with "arts" and "social studies" assuming slightly more emphasis than for boys.

OTHER GROUP DIFFERENCES

It is part of the same zeitgeist today, in psychology and in education, that we should also feel embarrassed over the differential showing of various ethnic groups. (In these extremely talented ranges, some ethnic groups seem over-represented, and others under-represented, compared with their proportions in the population at large.) Whether the causes of these differences are entirely social, as so many social scientists appear to believe, or whether they are at least contributed to by different gene frequencies, as Jensen (1973) very powerfully argues, cannot be decided here. For whatever reason, we know that there *are* mean ethnic differences in measured ability in such mathematical areas. And in preparation for this symposium I decided to explore a simple theoretical model of such distributions.

I wondered what would happen if I set up two populations: one a "majority" population, with a mean of 100 IQ; and another as a "minority" population, with a mean of 109 IQ, but with the same standard deviation as the majority. And this "minority" would have only 4 percent of the total population. This minority group, then, is rather similar in description to Jewish Americans, as described in various studies. It seemed a fair question to ask: At what point, if ever, will the 4 percent group begin to catch up with the majority population as we move up the IQ scale? The results are seen in table 16.1.[5]

Table 16.1.   Contribution of a "minority group" to extreme high scores of a population, given that the minority has 4 percent of total group, and has a mean 0.6σ above the majority

Standard deviations above majority mean (z)	"Minority's" proportion of population above this point z	IQ equivalent, if σ of IQ = 16
1	.0830	116
2	.1287	132
3	.2081	148
4	.2967	164
5	.4284	180
6	.5730	196
7	.7073	212

It is striking the way the minority group gains on the majority as we move up the IQ scale. At one standard deviation the minority is doubly represented (8 percent instead of 4 percent). At two standard deviations it is triply represented, and at three standard deviations it is over-represented five times. At about five and one-half standard deviations, the 4 percent minority actually overtakes the

[5]This table was generated by iterative procedures on an HP-65, provided to the writer by a grant from the University of Connecticut Research Foundation.

96 percent majority in the rare frequencies found at such exalted heights. In IQ terms, this means that the majority and minority become equally frequent above 180 IQ.

This elementary model, of course, should not be taken as a picture of any real culture. Indeed, there are a number of deviations from actuality: Any real "majority" population would not be a 96 percent monolith; it would itself consist of many subgroups, with different means and standard deviations and differing percentages of the total. We know that IQ distributions, though approximately Gaussian, violate expectation at extreme ranges. And much of the empirical evidence to support this model is not solidly known.

Yet the model is, nonetheless, provocative. The higher one goes, the greater is the over-representation of talented groups. And these higher levels are extraordinarily important in their scientific, social, and cultural impact. Large numbers of our most creative scientists have come from such high ranges. And in the present study of precocity, if we wish to translate the remarkable SAT-M scores into IQ terms, then we should not be surprised at the differing numbers of youngsters, contributed by different ethnic groups. Given the known mean differences in the society at large, we should rather be surprised if they came out the same.

THE IMPORTANCE OF CONTINUITY

The particular genius of SMPY, like that of the Terman study, is that it has been interested in young individuals of exalted promise, from any segment of society. Today, such a high purpose is not necessarily in the most fashionable mode. More credit, therefore, to the researchers. And one may predict that the program will still be of scientific, human, and social interest, as part of the nurturance of such extraordinary and valuable talent, long after most contemporary psychology has been superseded. Those responsible for the work and for its funding are urged to provide long-range follow-up of these cases, and the identification of new ones, and of the careers that are here launched. Fortunately, those prepared for such longitudinal research, able and well-trained and young enough to follow their talented teen-agers across the decades, are already well represented in the personnel of the study.

REFERENCES

Aiken, L. R. 1970. Attitudes toward mathematics. *Review of Educational Research* 40(4): 551–96.

Anastasi, A. 1974. Commentary on the precocity project. In Stanley, J. C., et al, (eds.), *Mathematical Talent: Discovery, description, and development*. Baltimore, Md.: The Johns Hopkins University Press, pp. 87–100.

Astin, H. S. 1974. Sex differences in mathematical and scientific precocity. In *Mathematical talent: Discovery, description, and development*. Baltimore, Md.: The Johns Hopkins University Press, pp. 70–86.

Atkinson, R. C. 1972. Ingredients for a theory of instruction. *American Psychologist* 27(10): 921–31.

Bock, R. D., and Kolakowski, D. 1973. Further evidence of sex-linked major-gene influence on human spatial visualizing ability. *American Journal of Human Genetics* 25(1): 1–14.

Boole, G. 1854. *An investigation of the laws of thought*. London.

Brown, D. L. 1974. Faculty ratings and student grades: A large-scale multivariate analysis by course sections. Ph.D. dissertation, University of Connecticut.

Cronbach, L. J. 1970. *Essentials of psychological testing* (3rd ed.). New York: Harper and Row.

Hartlage, L. C. 1970. Sex-linked inheritance of spatial ability. *Perceptual and Motor Skills* 13: 428.

Jensen, A. R. 1973. *Educability and group differences*. New York: Harper and Row.

Keynes, J. M. 1956. In Newman, J. R., *The world of mathematics*. New York: Simon and Schuster, vol. 1, pp. 277–85.

Kolakowski, D., and Malina, R. M. 1974. Spatial abilities, throwing accuracy, and man's hunting heritage. *Nature* 251: 410.

Lehman, H. C. 1953. *Age and achievement*. Princeton, N.J.: Princeton University Press.

Minsky, M. (ed.) 1968. *Semantic information processing*. Cambridge, Mass.: M.I.T. Press.

Mosteller, F., and Wallace, D. 1964. *Inference and disputed authorship: The Federalist Papers*. Reading, Mass.: Addison Wesley.

Newman, J. R. (ed.) 1956. *The world of mathematics*. New York: Simon and Schuster, vol. 2.

O'Connor, J. 1943. *Structural visualization*. Boston: Human Engineering Laboratory.

Page, E. B. 1972. How we *all* failed in performance contracting. *Educational Psychologist* 9(3): 40–42.

———. 1973. Effects of higher education: Outcomes, values, or benefits. In Solomon, L., and Taubman, P. (eds.), *Does college matter?* New York: Academic Press.

Page, E. B., and Breen, T. F., III. 1973. Educational values for measurement technology: Some theory and data. In Coffman, W. E. (ed.), *Frontiers of educational measurement and information systems*. Boston: Houghton Mifflin, pp. 13–30.

Stafford, R. E. 1961. Sex differences in spatial visualization as evidence of sex-linked inheritance. *Perceptual and Motor Skills* 13: 428.

Wagner, H. M. 1970. *Principles of management science: With applications to executive decisions*. Englewood Cliffs, N.J.: Prentice-Hall.

Winograd, T. 1969. A computer program for the understanding of natural language. Ph.D. dissertation, M.I.T.

Zeaman, D., and House, B. J. 1967. The relation of IQ and learning. In Gagne, R. M. (ed.), *Learning and individual differences*. Columbus, Ohio: Charles E. Merrill, pp. 192–212.

17

SMPY IN SOCIAL PERSPECTIVE

Carl E. Bereiter

In addition to reading the papers included in this volume, I have had the pleasure over the last two years of reading the newsletters sent out to students participating in the SMPY program. These newsletters convey the same high regard for mathematical excellence that is found in the scholarly papers, but they convey something else—a spirit of fun, a delight in doing and learning about mathematics. There are enticing book reviews, problems that I have enjoyed wrestling with myself, and lively bits of mathematical history and biography.

I think it is important to be aware of this lighter side of the program, because it helps us to see it from the students' point of view. It is unfortunately true that for most people, including a large number of otherwise well-educated adults, learning mathematics is remembered as a grim experience. There is some danger that this negative attitude will react to the high seriousness of the scholarly papers with the impression that SMPY is an ordeal inflicted on the helpless young. The truth, of course, is that learning mathematics is a great joy to those who are favorably disposed toward it, providing it is offered at a suitable level of challenge.

My own work in mathematics education (Bereiter & Engelmann 1966) has been with younger children at the opposite extreme of aptitude from those involved in SMPY, and yet the problems of instruction have important similarities. In both cases the regular mathematics curriculum is found to be unsuitable. In one case it is unsuitable because it presumes too high a level of initial ability, it moves too rapidly, and its conceptual demands are too high. In the other case it is unsuitable for the opposite of these reasons. But in both cases the problem is to find a better match between curriculum and teaching methods on one hand and the abilities and interests of the students on the other.

The strategy that SMPY follows for high-aptitude students is rapid acceleration of learning, to bring the students' level of knowledge up to their level of aptitude, followed by regular instruction at this level, with the possibility of further acceleration. The same basic strategy applied to low-aptitude students has discouraging consequences. It means dropping back to a lower level and proceeding more slowly, with the result that students fall farther and farther behind average students. The alternative that I and my co-workers have been pursuing is to look for ways to accelerate learning even though aptitude is low. Fortunately for SMPY, this kind of alternative need not be sought for students whose aptitudes deviate above rather than below the norm. While ways to teach below-average students need to be invented, ways to teach above-average students can be found simply by looking ahead a few years in the curriculum. SMPY has exhibited admirable commonsense in making use of these available means instead of trying to innovate where no innovation is required.

In this regard, SMPY may count itself the beneficiary of the past weaknesses of school mathematics instruction. In college, years ago, I took a course expressly designed for students like myself who had come through high school without having grasped any mathematical ideas or developed any usable skills beyond simple arithmetic. It was not a dummy course, however. It moved very rapidly, covering the foundations of arithmetic and all of high school algebra in six weeks, before moving on to more advanced topics. And it was a beautiful course. Everything made sense. Courses of that kind would not exist if school mathematics instruction accomplished its objectives, but such courses do exist and they are ready-made for the highly talented young student, who can go into them directly from elementary school and thereby skip over years of unchallenging drudgery.

RAKING THE RUBBISH

In a well-known piece of legislation that was never enacted, Thomas Jefferson proposed a public school system in which each year the "boy of best genius" in each elementary school was to be chosen to go on to secondary school, and then by a further series of equally severe eliminations students would be selected for advancement through secondary school and eventually to the state university, so that, in Jefferson's words, "twenty of the best geniuses will be raked from the rubbish annually." As it has turned out, of course, almost everyone advances to secondary school and the raking is not very severe even for admission to universities.

The whole idea strikes one as quaint but vaguely appealing, and it is interesting to find Julian Stanley reporting a long career of using tests to rake out the occasional boy or girl of "best genius" for urging on to higher things. Jefferson would certainly approve, but would those who might call themselves Jeffersonian Democrats?

Testing is widely used for educational selection and placement, but the concern is almost always with minimal criteria. Will the student pass? Not surprisingly, then, criticism of educational testing turns on the incidence of false negatives—students who are denied admission because they fall below minimum cut-offs, but who might nevertheless pass if given the opportunity. A lively concern at present is with minority students who fall into this category and who might therefore be claimed to be victims of biased selection, even though the tests used in selection show no predictive bias (Thorndike 1971; Flaugher 1974).

At issue here are two quite different purposes of schooling. One we may call the "human resource development" purpose and the other the "individual development" purpose. Both purposes are evident in the SMPY literature, with no effort to distinguish between them. Yet a number of problems look different, depending on which purpose is salient.

The Jefferson–Stanley approach serves best the human resource development purpose. The goal is to discover a certain number of highly capable students who will be helped with a view to maximizing their potentially great contributions to society. From a technical standpoint the main problem is elimination of false positives, so as to ensure that those selected are indeed highly capable. There need be little concern for the possibility that some highly capable students are being missed, so long as ample numbers of capable ones are found.

It is clear from the results presented in the first two chapters, by Stanley and Keating, that the SMPY screening methods are very successful in dealing with this selection problem. The selection of extreme groups is intrinsically a risky business, because the use of extreme cut-off points on score distributions tends to select people who had errors of measurement working in their favor. The use of tests with high ceilings does not eliminate this problem; on the contrary, it can mean there are more items that people will get right only by chance. What becomes clear, however, is that by using several different selection tests with high ceilings, errors of measurement are sufficiently well cancelled out that the student who excels on all of the tests is without doubt an exceptionally competent person.

If viewed from the standpoint of the individual development purpose, however, the SMPY approach is seen as only a bit less Draconian than that proposed by Jefferson. The losers under Jefferson's scheme are those whose talents do not happen to result in creating a favorable impression on teachers and those particularly unfortunate students who happen to be the 'second best geniuses' in classes that contain more than one highly qualified student. The losers under Stanley's scheme are those whose talents do not happen to be fully reflected in test scores (and no matter how worthy and appropriate the tests may be, their validity is certainly less than perfect). Under both schemes there are bound to be losers who have been handicapped one way or another in the development of their abilities and who might well be ones who would benefit the very most from special educational opportunities.

I point this out, not to denigrate SMPY's accomplishments, but only to put them in social perspective. The relative weight given to human resource and individual development goals tends to go through cycles. During the time of the 'sputnik scare' attention was sharply focussed on society's need for high-level intellectual talent, and SMPY would no doubt have aroused much more excited interest then than it does now. For at present the concern seems to be much more with seeing to it that everyone has the most favorable possible chance, and so it is natural that a program aimed at helping those who will probably do well anyway does not generate much excitement and that, in general, concern is more with those who are screened out by selection procedures than with those who are screened in.

But SMPY is not altogether consistent in its concern for finding sure winners and ignoring the chancy cases that are eliminated in the process. This appears dramatically in the treatment of girls. The facts are that fewer girls than boys emerge as clearly gifted in mathematics, and of those girls who are identified as gifted a smaller percentage respond well to acceleration. From a strict human resources standpoint these are facts that present no problems. There are evidently plenty of mathematically gifted youths who can profit from acceleration, and if few of them turn out to be girls that is just the way it is.

Yet we find in the work of SMPY a good bit of agonizing about the poorer showing of girls and noble efforts to do something about it. It isn't obvious why similar concern is not lavished upon other 'disadvantaged' groups, such as the poor and ethnic minorities; one legitimate reason would be that females are by far the largest of these 'disadvantaged' subpopulations in respect to mathematical achievement.

It would be quite understandable if SMPY did not concern itself with 'underdog' problems at all, since to do so raises all the problems of social and biological causation, test fairness, remediation, affirmative action, and so on, that beset education in general and that a small special-focus project can hardly hope to deal with. But it is puzzling to find SMPY taking up this concern so selectively.

ATTITUDES TOWARD THE MATHEMATICALLY GIFTED

That educators have some prejudice against mathematically gifted boys seems evident from the study by Haier and Solano (chapter 10). It appears that the prejudice is quite weak and only shows up when account is taken of the general tendency of people to rate others positively—for positive evaluations seem to prevail even among those educators who are scored as having negative stereotypes. Moreover, the negative attributes they assign to mathematically gifted boys—argumentativeness and opinionation—are ones that the boys tend to assign to themselves, as shown in chapter 11.

There is no indication that these slightly negative attitudes stand seriously in the way of providing special educational opportunities for mathematically gifted boys. Educators who have had contact with SMPY show more favorable attitudes, and they seem to have cooperated well with SMPY's efforts. Lynn Fox's account of efforts to provide special educational opportunities for mathematically gifted girls, however, tells a somewhat different story. It seems that school people in several different institutions reacted quite defensively to these efforts. The reasons may have to do entirely with situational politics and have no general significance, but there may be some fundamental factors involved that are at least worth brief speculation.

One possibility is that mathematically gifted boys may be perceived as so different from other students that proposing special treatment for them implies no criticism of the regular school program. Mathematically gifted girls, on the other hand, may, apart from their special ability, appear more 'normal'. Their giftedness itself may be less conspicuous; they may simply be perceived as 'good students' rather than as persons lying far beyond the normal range. And thus to suggest that they should skip grades or that they can learn a year's worth of algebra in a summer is to say to the educator: "You're not teaching much anyway, so let them skip it."

In favor of this conjecture is Fox's observation that the gifted girls are more involved in peer social relationships than the gifted boys and more eager to remain with their age-mates—hence more drawn to what is 'normal'. Opposed to this conjecture, however, are the findings of Haier and Denham (chapter 11), which show that on a variety of nonintellectual measures mathematically gifted boys and girls are more like each other than they are like their nongifted same-sex age-mates. This is dramatically shown in figure 1 of chapter 11, where across the profile of California Psychological Inventory scores the gifted boys and girls trace close and parallel paths, while the randomly selected boys and girls tend (with much less consistency, however) to trace another path.

And so an alternative conjecture is that mathematical giftedness in girls is perceived as less normal and natural, with the result that school officials are more inclined to think that their deviations from the norm should be cured rather than encouraged. Clearly, what is called for is some more direct evidence. A rerun of the 'stereotype' study with girls as the object of reference is one possibility, but I think not a very wise one. It is possible that many educators never have seen, or been aware of seeing, a mathematically gifted girl, and so their evaluations might have little relevance to reality. Fuller descriptions might provide better anchorage in reality (as they might for boys as well)—journalistic vignettes rather than bare factual bones. Or perhaps the attitudes of educators toward actual mathematically gifted boys and girls in their experience could be explored in depth. If boys and girls could be matched on ability as well as a number of noncognitive characteristics, the differences in how they are perceived could be quite revealing.

MISCELLANEOUS OBSERVATIONS

The ages of twelve to thirteen appear to be well-chosen as a time to intervene in the mathematical education of gifted boys. The regular school curriculum is on a plateau. The boys themselves are usually on a social plateau, having accomplished the developmental tasks of childhood and not yet having got caught up in the concerns of adolescence. The same is not true of girls, however, who enter adolescence psychologically as well as physically at an earlier age. Thus it may be that many of the problems that have arisen in trying to provide accelerated teaching for girls have to do with its timing. The programs might work better if they were started a couple of years earlier or a couple of years later.

I have had a little experience myself in trying to teach advanced material to early adolescents—a summer course in creative thinking, another in mathematical investigations (where I was understudy to Professor Shmuel Avital, and more a learner than a teacher), and a year-long course in problem-solving. In all of these it appeared that girls, especially, but also the less outstanding boys, functioned best when they did their thinking in small groups rather than alone or in a whole-class setting. In small groups the motivation of leading students tended to rub off on the others instead of inhibiting them, as it otherwise often does, and the less able students would find they could make contributions even though they did not have what it took to carry the ball entirely by themselves. I mention this as a possible way of accommodating those students, especially girls, who tend to get discouraged in a situation of individual striving and competition.

The program for verbally gifted youths is clearly still groping for direction. It is noteworthy, at least, that young people can be found who are relatively as gifted verbally as others are gifted mathematically; but it is far less clear what their needs are. For one thing, the verbally gifted can probably get more out of regular instruction than their mathematically gifted counterparts. *To Kill a Mocking Bird* and *Julius Caesar* are worth reading, even by children who have already read them or comparable works, whereas there is nothing to gain by going over quadratic equations if you have already mastered them. And many of the better sort of writing assignments in English and social studies are ones that gifted students can profitably carry out, there being no definite ceiling on the level at which they can be executed. Moreover, there is less need for instruction in the humanities and social studies. Gifted students can go far by independent reading and discussion with one another. Thus there is less chance that a special course can offer something conspicuously rewarding in comparison to what the students can get for themselves.

Nonetheless, it seems to me that some wiser curricular choices could have been made for the verbally gifted than have been made. In my experience social science is a dead loss for twelve-year-olds. The concern for people outside their immediate experience, which psychologists since G. Stanley Hall have noted as an outstanding development in adolescence, has not yet taken hold. It appears that without this broadened social identity, most of what interests social scientists is seen as pointless and boring—at best of purely 'academic' interest. I believe that for children of this age more mileage could be gotten out of teaching Latin. At least it is something they can get their teeth into.

THE NEED FOR ECONOMIC JUSTIFICATION

As I suggested earlier, the preponderance of educational concern today is with the underdog, and so a project like SMPY faces problems in establishing a basis for support if it is to grow beyond demonstration and have a substantial, continuing impact on education. The kinds of things that SMPY is doing are amply justified both in terms of enriching society and in terms of enriching the lives of certain of its deserving members, but in the practical world it is not enough to be on the side of the angels. It is necessary to show cause why people should support this particular form of goodness when there are so many other forms of goodness clamoring for support.

Thus I hope I will not be thought devoid of idealism when I suggest that SMPY ought to put some effort into showing that what it is doing pays monetary and not just spiritual dividends. As a parallel case, there is a compensatory preschool program for low-IQ children that has won continuing support for years from a financially troubled state legislature on the strength of evidence that it saved the tax-payers money. In this case the demonstrable savings came from children who were able to survive in regular classes when they would otherwise have been placed in more expensive special classes for the mentally retarded. Saving tax dollars was no more the purpose of that program than it is the purpose of SMPY, but saving tax dollars proved to be its key to survival.

It seems likely that a careful analysis would show that SMPY also pays for itself. The savings in skipped grades alone would amount to thousands of public dollars per child. Then there is the somewhat more slippery accounting item of 'value added' in the form of higher levels of skill attained, plus the value of additional years of productive activity gained by reducing the number of years spent in school. What are needed to make a convincing argument, of course, are not generalized claims of this sort, but actual dollar estimates based on good economic analysis.

I think this kind of analysis is needed, because otherwise SMPY may tend to be regarded as just another kind of welfare service offered to a not very needy clientele, and it will always be vulnerable to the objection that the service is not offered equally to all who deserve or could profit from it. Its political justification has to rest, not on what it does for individual students but on what it does for society. I think a strong case can be made on that basis, but in the present social climate the case needs to be made with all the strength that reason and science can muster.

REFERENCES

Bereiter, C., and Engelmann, S. 1966. *Teaching disadvantaged children in the Pre-school.* Englewood Cliffs, N.J.: Prentice–Hall.

Flaugher, R. L. 1974. The new definitions of test fairness in selection: Developments and implications. *Educational Researcher* 3(9): 13–16.

Thorndike, R. L. 1971. Concepts of culture fairness. *Journal of Educational Measurement* 8: 63–70.

18

GENERAL DISCUSSION

ABSTRACT

During the afternoon of the symposium, a general discussion of the topics raised by the papers presented in the morning session (i.e., chapters 1 through 17) was conducted. In addition to the authors of chapters in this volume, the following individuals participated: L. Carey Bolster, associate co-ordinator of mathematics for the Baltimore County, Maryland, Board of Education; William C. Clark, supervisor of mathematics for the Montgomery County, Maryland, public schools; Jonathan Day, an undergraduate at Johns Hopkins University; Leon Lerner, a guidance counselor at the Roland Park School, a Baltimore City public school; Jean-Pierre Meyer, associate professor of mathematics at Johns Hopkins University; Merrill Kenneth Wolf, professor of neuroanatomy at the University of Massachusetts; and Joseph R. Wolfson, the teacher for several of SMPY's special classes. The topics discussed include: the use of the Q statistic; the security of tests; the development of reasoning ability; interpreting inventory data; facilitating verbal talent; reflections of M. K. Wolf; gaps in skills; methods of acceleration; educational bridging mechanisms; continuing acceleration in college; counseling for the gifted; financial support of programs; and planning for program diversity. I have tried to retain as much of the richness of a deeply interesting conversation as possible in its translation to a readable manuscript.
THE EDITOR

THE USE OF Q

STANLEY: I would like to address a point raised by Ellis Page in his discussion (chapter 16). It is highly desirable to age-standardize, somehow, the SAT-M and other scores, because we do have great disparity in the age of the youngsters we are testing. We have tested youngsters as young as nine years old. One boy scored 730 on SAT-M while he was still ten years old, but only after he had learned a great deal in the Wolfson I class. One of the problems that had occurred to me, and seems very difficult to resolve, is that we have some individuals who have been tutored and have participated in many special learning activities, including college courses in many cases, whereas other individuals have been relatively unfacilitated. From the data we have on hand, my strong suspicion is that the highly facilitated ones simply improve their SAT-M scores a great deal more at these early ages than the unfacilitated ones, but that they may not maintain that rate of improvement as time goes on. We may have changed the developmental curve by putting a "bump" in it at one particular time, but we may not have changed the asymptote much. If we use the same system for both groups, then, we might predict 900 or 1,000 for the ten-year-old with the 730. If the same boy had not done any of the special things we arranged for him, such as participation in the Wolfson I class, I doubt that he would have achieved more than 600 or so at age ten. In effect we have given him 130 more points. It's possible that this has put him on a nicer trajectory which will continue, but it's also possible that all we have done is hasten his 730 by two or three years, and that the other, unfacilitated youngster will actually asymptote at the same point. Actually, it probably would increase the asymptote score somewhat. There is sure to be some interaction of training in mathematics with the level at which the SAT-M tapers off. But it probably would not be as great as in an achievement test situation, for example, where if you don't study calculus, you don't know and can't do calculus. For SAT-M it is more basic reasoning ability. Once you get all the tools at some age, such as linear inequalities and application of the Pythagorean theorem, more mathematics training will probably not change the asymptote score greatly. So for the case I mentioned, we would mis-estimate if we use the 730 score rather than the 600 score to predict from. That would occur to me as a danger. How would you react to that?

PAGE: I don't regard that as a mis-estimate. The intention of Q, as it was proposed, was not to find innate potential necessarily, but just to give us something that's comparable across ages. I would say that Q would still be valuable even if not regarded as fixed. I would not regard it as a defeat if someone were very high in Q and then dropped across time.

STANLEY: So you're not trying to get an estimate or prediction of the point at which he asymptotes. Based as it is on an MA (mental age) kind of statistic, Q would provide an inflated estimate if the base score were inflated by training. As times goes on, it would drop off.

PAGE: As a technical matter, I suppose you have considered the possibility of using the GRE-Q (Graduate Record Examination—Quantitative) if you want to continue measuring a youngster and he begins to bump his head on the ceiling of the SAT-M.

STANLEY: Actually, the GRE-Q doesn't seem to be that much harder. We have used the difficult Doppelt Mathematical Reasoning Test. We tend in most cases, however, to begin moving into the mathematics achievement tests, such as GRE Mathematics Achievement or the Advanced Placement Program examinations. I don't think we need to worry too much anyway, because it takes an almost perfect score on SAT-M to earn an 800, 58 or so out of 60 items. That is unlike the Mathematics Achievement Level II, where 38 out of 50 items correct may earn an 800. So the SAT-M has a fairly high ceiling, even for a 730 person.

SECURITY OF THE TESTS

WOLF: I would like to raise a practical question, since I don't know these tests. How long a test is the SAT-M, and what is the possibility that a bright student might memorize it in the course of repeated testing?

STANLEY: There are sixty items to be done in 75 minutes, so it's a fast-paced, rigorous exercise. Incidentally, that's why these students are so flexible; they have to be flexible to move that rapidly among content areas and problem types. Further, there are several different forms of the test each year, so it's never necessary for a student to take the same test twice. If a youngster did that by mistake, the results might, of course, be biased.

WOLF: I ask because that in fact happened to me. By the time I was eleven I had memorized all of the Stanford–Binet test.

KEATING: It might be worth noting that one of the advantages of using the SAT for identification and screening of students with high-level reasoning ability is that it is a secure test. It has many different forms changed regularly, and is unlikely to be compromised by some students' having seen the items prior to taking the test.

STANLEY: We also have used the old version of the Academic Promise Test that is no longer available and that few schools have copies of any more. We have our own comparison norms in mind, because the published norms are out of date, but it is useful to have a test that no one has access to. Let me mention one other thing in connection with possible invalidation of test results. We heard earlier some concern as to whether the teachers in some of the special classes might be teaching to the test. We tried very hard not to let the teachers know what the test items were like, so that it would be uncontaminated. We didn't even supply a list of the topics to the teachers until after the tests were finished. One possible source of contamination is if the youngster himself had access to the test beforehand through a parent or teacher. This is, of course, quite unlikely, but we took the precaution of using Form B of the tests first, on the grounds that most schools would normally have Form A. So the results are fairly well protected against those possible sources of bias.

PAGE: I was sure they were. Teaching the test was so obvious in the first performance contracting work that now everyone is conscious of it.

STANLEY: We also checked the scores against the teacher's ratings for any major discrepancies.

DEVELOPMENT OF REASONING ABILITY

KEATING: I would like to pursue with Ellis Page for a moment the developmental implications in the use of something like the Q statistic. Using this kind of evaluation, would you see a meaningful way of gaining some understanding of the rate of development of this kind of ability, and how the rate might change across time? There have always been problems with something like the IQ score of estimating the rate of development and changes in the rate, because it is so thoroughly age-standardized. Are developmental questions like that within the realm of Q as you proposed it today?

PAGE: Only in the following sense. I should mention that my background is more in terms of artificial intelligence (A.I.) or simulation, rather than Piagetian cognitive development, and this influences my perspective. If one looks at how an applied math problem is solved, there are several obvious requirements: Does the person have the computational algorithm available? Is the person able to translate from the words into the algorithm? When he's finished, can he get back to the words again to print out the answer? There are some models of this type in the artificial intelligence field, which have been functioning for some years. At the A.I. laboratory at M.I.T., for example, there are various algebra and geometry and calculus problems that are expressed in a miniset of words. In this miniset there is a model of some small, limited world. Here the verbal problems are translated into the algorithms, solved computationally, and the answers are printed out again in English. This suggests an analysis of the problem-solving process in which there are specifiable competencies, and such an analysis should have a lot to do with understanding math ability. That's not a satisfactory answer to a straight developmental question, but I don't think in Piagetian terms.

KEATING: Relating this to my paper on the psychometric-Piagetian comparison, I was wondering if there were some way within the system you suggested to discover when specific competencies become available. A "traditional" Piagetian analysis which I have heard occasionally is that below a certain chronological age it is futile to attempt to teach certain kinds of mathematics. If the learning of calculus, for example, requires formal operational thought, then someone without such cognitive structures would not benefit from such instruction. If, further, there is a lower limit in terms of age for the acquisition of formal operational thinking, then there would also be a lower limit on the learning of certain types of mathematics. Would Q help us to answer this question of when necessary competencies emerge?

PAGE: The real question involves the stages. It is certainly clear from the SMPY evidence that if one has a high enough SAT-M, one does not have much trouble with the various college courses, including calculus. I'm sort of locked into the psychometric rather than the stages perspective.

KEATING: The question, I guess, comes down to what a high score on a psychometric test means at different ages. Does a high score on a test at a younger age indicate the presence of the same competencies which that score on the same test would indicate at a later age? That's a question we really haven't answered. In terms of practical applications, it certainly seems to indicate equivalent competencies. After selecting students by their scores on these tests, we place them in accelerated situations, such as college courses, and they are quite successful in them.

PAGE: Isn't this a beautiful empirical question? One could use a technique that's been used extensively in the research on the cultural fairness of certain tests. What one would look at would be the probability of success on various items within the tests as a function of age, in this case. That is, if the pattern of correct responses for the twelve-year olds on the SAT-M were the same as the pattern for seventeen-year olds, then one could assume similar underlying competencies or processes. If, on the other hand, there were an interaction of the probability of success across items with age, then some difference would be suspected in the underlying processes. At that point one could get a panel of judges to look at the items without knowledge of what hypotheses were involved. They could sort the items into categories of information versus process, for example, or some other dimension. This would provide a testable hypothesis about the observed difference.

STANLEY: We know by observation that these youngsters are especially good at reasoning because they don't have the substantive base for a lot of the questions. With some of them we find that they are poorer with information items and easy items and better with the hard items. That's one easier way of looking at the interaction of item difficulty and groups. If a test is scaled from easy to hard for the norm group, say seventeen-year olds, one could simply compare the item-difficulty scaling for the younger group. The younger ones might do better with the last items on the original scale, that is the harder items, and relatively poorer on the first or easy items. We saw this with our first early entrant when he took the Bennett Mechanical Comprehension Test, Form CC, at age thirteen. He missed five items on a sixty-item test, but he did not miss any of the last twenty-one items. He missed five easy items. Looking at the missed items, it seemed as if one of two things had happened. He either lacked a specific piece of information necessary to solve the problem or he used too complex a reasoning process for a simple item. Once his reasoning process became consonant with the difficulty level of the items, he got them right.

KEATING: Along these lines, I might mention some research which used the same groups discussed in chapter 5. Alfonso Caramazza and I gave them syllogistic reasoning problems of the three term series type: If John is better than Bill, and Bill is better than Sam, then who is best? If opposites, rearrangement, and negative equatives are used, there are thirty-two problems of that kind. What we found was that for the regular problems the young bright students correlated highly with college students, but were less correlated on negative equatives. The younger average students were equally correlated on both types of problems. We concluded that there might be some sort of process difference in the solution of these problems among the various samples (Keating & Caramazza, in press). This is to suggest that there are probably some item difficulty interactions across different age and ability groups, and that such studies might be quite worthwhile.

PAGE: This would be an excellent technique for studying the sex differences also. The question would be: Are the levels different but consistent in pattern? We know that the top girls didn't do as well as the top boys, but are the items the same in rank order of difficulty?

STANLEY: For many of the older students on SAT-M, the test requires perhaps less in the way of actual reasoning, because they have overlearned such things as linear inequalities and the Pythagorean theorem. They are probably operating at the lower levels of Bloom's taxonomy (1956), the comprehension and application levels. What the younger students have to do without all this input is to operate largely at the analysis level. They have to figure out the questions very quickly. This explains why persons who do well on SAT-M at an early age always have splendid scores on a completely independent nonverbal reasoning test; they have to be able to figure things out fast and well. I think, in a sense, you have a different type of person, who later, of course, will be superb on SAT-M but can be excellent even before acquiring the formal overlearned background. This explains also why they do so well in computer science at ages ten to thirteen, and can handle calculus without a hitch. They have great analytic ability. We need more evidence on this, of course.

INTERPRETING INVENTORY DATA

BEREITER: I have a few questions regarding the interpretation of some of the scales and inventories reported in various papers. On the question of educators' stereotypes (chapter 10), there seem to be two ways you could use the term stereotype here. The first is that every person could have his own stereotype of the mathematically gifted, but it wouldn't necessarily resemble someone else's stereotype. In the second case, one could think about a common stereotype that seems to be somewhere planted in the culture. As I see it, this study addresses the former kind. You want to know whether, on the whole, people are favorable or unfavorable toward the mathematically gifted, but are not really inquiring as to whether there is a common image that seems to be held. That would require a correlational study to see whether there is a pattern of response that's common to this population of educators.

HAIER: In a sense, we talked about that, because the percentages of agreement for the Pennsylvania educators were far higher than for the

Maryland educators. That seemed to indicate that there was a common basis for their judgments. They had far higher agreement on both the favorable and unfavorable adjectives that they were checking. This higher agreement wasn't attributable to a more limited number of adjectives being checked by the Pennsylvania group, since in fact they checked more adjectives on the whole.

BEREITER: That would argue for the presence of a common image. But, even at that, in order to be able to assert that there is this pattern which seems to be held in common by a number of people, correlational methods would be necessary. The indication for a common image is quite strong, but more could be done with the data to round out the picture. One could then ask how many Pennsylvanians as opposed to Marylanders held this modal stereotype. One other thing I'd like to mention. I have been taken with the fact that in the Allport-Vernon-Lindzey Study of Values (SV), "political" seemed to rank fairly high with boys in this study (chapter 14). I wouldn't have expected that, and perhaps it deserves a little further exploration. Adjective checklists of the high "political" boys might provide some clues as to what we are really getting at here. One possibility is that this is one of the features of the self-selection process, in that you may be getting more outgoing, more aggressive types of students—the kind of students who would go out for a competition, which might bear little relationship to giftedness itself. Thus if you ran a contest to pick the most average student, the ones who showed up might also be high on "political." This might hold also for some of the other personality attributes found in these students.

KEATING: I agree with your earlier comments that the real payoff for these kinds of scales is in the longitudinal follow-ups, but I'd like to pursue the question of their immediate interpretability also. I wasn't quite as convinced of the futility of trying to interpret the results that we have in order to describe the current characteristics of the group. What criteria might be used for gauging the validity of current results? Admitting and recognizing the fact that these instruments have been designed for and validated on older groups, I think some criteria are pertinent. The ones which we have used most often are whether the pattern of results makes sense across different instruments, and also whether they conform to expectations based on previous research. A specific example would be the high scores on the achievement via independence and flexibility scales of the California Psychological Inventory (CPI), which would seem to me interpretable given the nature of the selection process. I wonder how you would feel about these criteria for initial validation of the results regarding the current status of the group.

BEREITER: Those are the very kinds of scores that I would think would be the hardest to interpret—"achievement via conformity." I think it just means altogether different things when you are talking about young adolescents than when you are talking about someone who is on the borderline of adulthood. For my money, the validation would have to come through showing that those scores are valid within the group itself. Thus a youngster who has a high score on achievement via conformity should in some detectable way be more of a conforming achiever than one who has a low score, and the same distinctions would hold for all the other scales. That is, within the group these scores would have to mean something, they would have to distinguish one child from another in a meaningful way.

KEATING: But one might get into another problem with that criterion. It might be a more homogeneous group than if you had a general population, a not unlikely assumption.

BEREITER: On the other hand, if you select on a variable that doesn't have a terribly high correlation with any of these things, it shouldn't be such a serious problem.

KEATING: Some of these scales do correlate with the selection variable, though.

HAIER: True, but the variances for the mathematically gifted group on the CPI Scales approximated those in the general population, so the assumption of greater homogeneity is tenuous.

STANLEY: I'd like to make an observation along the line of Carl Bereiter's comments. The testing of the top of the top—the top 111 of 1,519 students in 1974—was done not only for descriptive purposes but also for armchair validity purposes. We were trying to find youngsters who not only score high on mathematical aptitude, but in many cases were high across the board on verbal ability, mechanical comprehension, spatial relations, concept mastery, etc. We were doing that to a considerable extent in order to program experiences for those youngsters. This involved certain assumptions about validity, but I think they were commonsense assumptions. If a youngster is very high in mathematical ability but well below the average of the college students he would be competing with in verbal ability, then he's not the best bet for taking a college course. We had better wait a little while until the verbal ability has risen. Or if a youngster is high on both mathematical and verbal ability but poor on mechanical comprehension, then he has presumably developed less physical intuition, and there may be some experiences he might not be ready for. In the retesting we developed another rather interesting criterion for special educational experiences. We figured that the student who could take a whole day of testing from nine in the morning to four in the afternoon, taking one difficult test after another, and who under those circumstances would not wilt and perform poorly toward the end, would not have any trouble taking college courses. It is a very good way of seeing if they will hold up intellectually under stress. This was only incidental to the main purpose, but it worked out nicely. The youngster who still had the bloom on the rose and at 3:30 was very eager and would ask, "But don't you have another test for me?" looked like a better bet than the one who said, "This is too much, I want to go home, I'm tired." Using all the information from these retesting sessions, we are quite successful in picking those who would do well in college courses. We have had 100 or so take a total of about 400 credits, with an overall grade point average (GPA) of approximately 3.6 (on a 4.0 scale). There were practically no Cs or Ds. Compare this to the eleventh-grade honors students who take summer courses in a different program at Hopkins. Those students are selected on teacher recommendations but without explicit testing; we do the reverse, because it would be hard for an eighth-grade teacher to know which students might do well in a college computer science course. The eleventh-grade students, who are on the average three years older, have an average GPA of 3.1. And they take somewhat easier courses. Of course we may have overdone the selection somewhat; there may be a large number of false negatives, students less able than the ones we selected but who could nevertheless do the work. The point is that all this testing provides us with a great deal of information on these students which is quite useful in selecting those able to do such advanced work.

BEREITER: My comments apply largely not to the ability and achievement tests but to the personality measures, which aren't even tests in the same sense. The interpretation of them is always chancy and remote. The available validation data on those tests are on people so different that I don't think you can automatically apply any of it. With the ability and achievement tests such as SAT-M there is some ambiguity in what a score of 560 really means, but it certainly means that a person was able to do a certain number of problems. There is no question about that.

STANLEY: But in the clinical sense, we do have some comparative benchmarks with which to look at the individual case studies. We do look at the agreement among different inventories with similar scales: the SV "theoretical" versus the Holland "investigative" for example. Those are very different inventories, one ipsative and the other not, one an occupational inventory and the other a values scale. Or if we get a high femininity score for a boy on the CPI, we look at the Strong to see if the male versus female occupational choices go in the same direction. We approximate the Campbell–Fiske (1959) multi-method validation by using these different comparisons. This isn't ideal validation, of course, since they are all paper-and-pencil instruments, but they are very different paper-and-pencil instruments. So we have a fair amount of confidence in where there is consistency. Perhaps it's misplaced confidence, but the consistency across different instruments is encouraging.

DAY: For partial within-group validation, there is the evidence of the match between descriptions of individuals not using the CPI information compared to blind descriptions using only the CPI protocols.

STANLEY: That too is a little chancy, though.

HAIER: To pursue this a little further, I wonder exactly what the role of personality assessment is in a project like this. Certainly the social and emotional development of these students is important, and such assessment might give us a handle on that. Another necessary thing would seem to be the identification of scales which would be predictive of long-term success or failure.

BEREITER: I think the predictive side is important. The most important use of it is one that you hope will never come about, and that is to look back and see what would have predicted the casualties of the system. If there are serious casualties, then you are going to want to go back and look at the data very thoroughly.

FOX: I think we should mention that we used all this information extensively in counseling with the high-scorers. We might have some one who had a 700 on SAT-M but who scored very high on social and political interests and also high on verbal ability. And we would tell him, "You don't appear to be very interested in mathematics and science. Your pattern of interests on these self-report devices suggests that your interests are in something like political science or history. Do you really want to take a math course, or is there something else you'd rather be doing with your time?" In this sense we influence a lot of outcomes, although we don't have complete evidence on the predictive validity of these scales for these students to assure us that it is definitely the right thing to do. A few of these students have gone ahead with a course in political science or economics instead of mathematics. So far they have done well. But the problem is that sometimes we contaminate our data, because we do use it to make counseling suggestions. This will lessen its value in terms of predictive outcomes.

STANLEY: I used to criticize Lewis Terman (1925–59) because he called his group "geniuses," and I said that this would affect their progress. When we started this study, I went overboard and determined that we'd affect progress as *much* as we possibly could. We wouldn't have a control group because we couldn't humanely afford to take half the people and put them aside. That would be practically impossible anyway, because they would use the information to arrange other alternatives for themselves.

FACILITATING VERBAL TALENT

MCGINN: I wanted to share a couple of impressions I had from teaching a social science seminar to the high-verbal students. There was some discussion that possibly there was less need of such courses for bright verbal students, since they would be able to do more on their own (see chapter 17). This seems to be partially true in that many of the students who took the course were avid readers and so were doing quite a lot of work on their own. But I noticed a couple of particular weaknesses when I was teaching them that might be good to work on at this age. They did not have much appreciation of the interaction of variables. I think that is the clearest way I can express it; how different things work together in different combinations. They more or less treated the effect of one variable at a time. Also, they seemed to be unable to apply what they read in books to analysis of real-life situations. An assignment that would require them to compare ideas between different authors they handled with a lot of sophistication. But when they were requested to take these ideas and discuss a social problem, they didn't have much idea about how to do it. For that reason, I think that courses and programs for these kinds of children will be helpful at this age, and wouldn't really be redundant with the kind of things that they can do on their own.

BEREITER: How interested were these students in social problems? Did they seem to have any closeness to them or were they quite removed from them? Is there any evidence that they thought about social problems by themselves?

MCGINN: Many of them were very politically interested and several of them were working on the senatorial campaign of Charles Mathias. But they didn't express much interest in social problems or poverty or things of that nature. The course centered on anthropology to a large degree, and so we talked about different groups of people. They could handle this intellectually, but when we asked, "How does this apply to groups in which you are involved?"; they were lost. I wouldn't call them a socially committed group.

BEREITER: What I'm getting at is that with children of more nearly average abilities, you don't typically find much lively social concern until adolescence. It wouldn't surprise me too much that these children don't have much of that kind of interest either. With a class of thirteen-year-olds I worked with once, who were all well above average in ability, I raised just as a speculative problem: Why are there poor people in this country? It had never occurred to them to think of such things before, and only a minority of them could develop much interest in it even then, because it was just coming out of nowhere at them. If this characterizes any appreciable number of these children, it would suggest to me that perhaps getting into social science with them at this time is not an unqualifiedly good idea. Clearly, they have a lot to learn in it, but, on the other hand, it might be premature despite their high intellectual ability. If they haven't developed any of the active concern about those things that would motivate the study and make it seem real to them, I would doubt its value. I'm doubtful about getting youngsters engaged intellectually in studies of social problems that they don't have any feeling for yet, because I think that this encourages a detached, overly intellectual approach to human problems that in the long run could be dangerous. I'd like to see them develop a concern and get very emotional about it for awhile, develop a lot of empathy and want to go out and make the world over and all of that sort of thing, *before* you start pushing too hard on their being analytical and very critical and so on.

MERRILL KENNETH WOLF

STANLEY: We are fortunate to have with us today a number of exemplars of intellectual precocity. One who was good enough to come from Massachusetts to be with us is, as far as I'm aware, the youngest college graduate in the country. He was younger than Norbert Wiener, who was fourteen years and eight months old when he got his B.A. at Tufts University. This distinguished scholar earned his bachelor's degree at Yale University at fourteen years and a few months of age. He has had a very interesting career. After graduation from Yale, he took the next seven years to study classical music, specializing in keyboard instruments. Following that, at more or less the usual age, he went off to medical school, earned his M.D., and became a distinguished neuroanatomist. He is now professor of neuroanatomy at the University of Massachusetts Medical School and a lecturer at Harvard Medical School. He is Merrill Kenneth Wolf, and I'm delighted he could be with us today. Dr. Wolf, we'd be very interested in hearing your comments and reactions to the proceedings.

WOLF: I have talked with many of you individually, but in general I would say, "Right on, SMPY!" When I received the volume on *Mathematical Talent: Discovery, Description, and Development* (1974) and glanced at it, two points struck home. One was the observation that at a typical meeting of professional educational psychologists, one might find perhaps a whole session or several sessions devoted to the special educational problems of the mentally retarded, whereas scarcely a paper or two could be found devoted to the equally severe educational problems of the people at the other end of the spectrum. Considering the human waste that is involved when the people at the high end of the spectrum drop out and are lost to the system, that struck and continues to strike me as a poor state of affairs. I'm delighted to see that "Termanism" is being revived. The second thing that struck me from that book was the observation that there may be some sort of optimum IQ level, with the people above that level having a harder time of it than people below that level, that an extremely high IQ carries some disadvantages. Without going into any psychodynamic things, I could certainly speak to the disadvantages of being unmeasurable by the Stanford–Binet test. There are some great disadvantages, and people in this situation have special problems.

STANLEY: Were you quite young when you were first tested with the Binet? There is plenty of ceiling in the test at age three, for example, with a possible IQ of 700 or so. But as you get older the IQ ceiling drops, so that an adult can have no higher than a 152. That's not enough for the kind of youngsters we're talking about.

WOLF: I don't know when formal tests of this sort were first given to me. Let me give you the main landmarks that I remember. I spoke at four months, and as I acquired a more complete vocabulary and completer sentences, my father got a set of flashcards. I believe people then subscribed to the whole word versus spelling theory of teaching reading, about which I know nothing, but it worked for me and I learned to read. At one year old my first birthday present was a first-grade reader, which I was ready for. When I was six years old, effort was made to enter me in elementary school. Based on my abilities at the time, they put me in the sixth grade. It happened to be a morning when some sort of a final examination was being given. I remember passing the final examination perfectly well, but causing such social disruption my parents were asked to please keep me home. Subsequently, they made efforts to enter me in junior high school. I remember being sent to a junior high school mathematics class. While my mathematical abilities were certainly the least strikingly precocious of my intellectual abilities, junior high school mathematics was nevertheless a stupefying bore to me. This was when I was eight or so. What was being taught was the substitution of concrete numbers for abstract symbols in an equation. I was more interested in algebra and geometry, and it was painfully boring. I lasted about two days in that class, and I asked my parents not to send me again. I don't know who got the idea of having me take the standard college entrance examination to see if I could do college work, but it was done. It was decided that I could do college work and I was sent to Western Reserve and took one course, then two, and then three. When it was clear that I was surviving, I was transferred to Yale, partly because the distinguished composer Paul Hindemith had expressed a willingness to teach me.

LERNER: What instrument did you study?

WOLF: Piano. My first teacher was a pianola, which my mother used as a babysitter. She could put me in front of the thing and simply put a record on. This was before phonograph records were terribly good. The phonograph records of the day were made by pure mechanical acoustic means. The quality of reproduction was poor, and you were limited to a three-minute piece of music. You were also limited to very eccentrically arranged orchestral groups. The problems of recording piano, for example, hadn't been adequately solved, so a lot of the best artists recorded their best music for player pianos. So that was my music teacher. In some ways it was the best teacher I've ever had: it was infinitely patient and it never made a mistake!

STANLEY: At what age did you first take a college course?

WOLF: At age ten. The course was elementary chemistry, and my preparation for it was having read chemistry textbooks by myself because I found them entertaining.

STANLEY: Did you do well in it?

WOLF: Adequately. I think the surprise was that I didn't get straight zeroes the first week.

STANLEY: Were you good in the laboratory?

WOLF: No, I was not at all good in the laboratory. When I was an adult, I went back to laboratory chemistry and proceeded to do it, but at the time my motor skills were not adequate. Actually, I don't know whether it was a question of motor skills, or attitude, or something else, but I did poorly in laboratory work.

ARE THERE GAPS IN SKILLS?

CLARK: Let me take up on Dr. Wolf's comments about skills. We're looking at the gifted at the elementary level in our county, and one of the comments that has come up in the reports is that the students may have been gifted in terms of the tests, but still lack some of the skills that are deemed to be essential for satisfactory performance.

STANLEY: Could it be that they're just interested in different things? For example, they might find the fact that $5 \times 3 = 3 \times 5$ more interesting than the fact that it equals 15. That is, they may concentrate on the commutativity principle to the exclusion of the arithmetic.

CLARK: I'm not sure. But we have had reports of specific skill deficiencies. The hypothesis was that the background they had been getting wasn't adequate for going on.

KEATING: In the courses we were running we tried in some cases to do diagnostic testing with an eye toward specific skill remediation. Our tentative conclusion from these experiences was that although some specific arithmetic skills, for example, might not be adequate, such problems could be remedied extraordinarily rapidly.

FOX: One of the things I noted in working with several of the younger children who have been involved is that their preference is for the more abstract material. The diagnostic testing would reveal a deficiency in decimals or fractions, for example, but there would be some resistance to dealing with that directly. Using the basic algebra that the child was learning, though, I was able to make the decimal or fraction problem into an equation, which he would learn very quickly and be eager to solve. Thus, in order to get them to practice or learn some of the basic skills it may be advantageous to put them into a more mathematically sophisticated format. It may then seem more interesting, and they may be more anxious to work with it.

KEATING: This brings up a general area of research that we have concentrated on less in the past but is perhaps more deserving of attention in the future, and that is the components of success in these special programs. As has been mentioned before, the group that is selected on the screening devices will still be heterogeneous on many other variables presumably relevant to success. One of those variables might be specific skills, as has been suggested. I think that we do need to look more closely at exactly what is going on in these situations in order to increase the number of successful individuals.

STANLEY: I'd like to make a plea here. It is often alleged that there are deficiencies in the skills. But if the teachers gave them a standardized test of those skills, they might find that what they have are youngsters who are bored and careless with their work. So I think that the first thing, rather than assuming the youngsters really are deficient in skills, should be to verify through a standardized test, in comparison with the appropriate class, whether they in fact are deficient. They may *never* acquire those skills if you keep them in a regular class, where they are so bored that they miss new points when they finally do come along. If you pick out the specific things they can't do and remedy them directly, as Lynn Fox did, then they can zoom through the material with an ingenious tutor and be done with it.

LERNER: I think you're being overly kind. The problem is not really with identification *or* skill deficiencies. The problem is with breaking out of the box and deciding to do something different for these children. I find, for instance, in my work in public schools that this is the hardest thing, getting teachers to approach it differently. These bright fourth- and fifth-graders are saying, "I'm bored," but nothing is done about it.

STANLEY: One of the things that would be very helpful at the county level would be the provision of excellent diagnostic tests. Not just survey tests, but real diagnostic tests that would show what it is the student doesn't know. Then the youngsters could be taught directly what they do not know, rather than being processed first through 95 percent of what they do know. In that situation, when the new material comes along, they don't recognize it—they're mentally asleep or daydreaming. The teachers often ask us what to do, and when we suggest such diagnostic testing, they say they don't have these materials. It places a heavy burden on teachers to try to do this subjectively.

CLARK: There are some aids for them. We use, for example, the SRA computational development kit, which has some diagnostic tests within it. But it seems from what I hear from the testing division that there just aren't very many good, true diagnostic measures.

STANLEY: Well I suppose we can't be purists. One could use computational tests in a diagnostic fashion, as Lynn Fox did, and just look at the items missed. Many of the teachers, particularly at the elementary level, don't know how to make use of some of these things. If they did, they could help some of these students whip through the few things they don't already know, so that they could move on to the level where they really belong.

METHODS OF ACCELERATION

STANLEY: Also with us today is another person with educational acceleration in his background. He is a serious psychology student, a sophomore at Johns Hopkins, who will probably go on to a Ph.D. in some social science area.

He is Jonathan Day. Jon, do you have anything from your special perspective that you would like to add to our discussion?

DAY: Sometimes it seems that compared to the more neglected gifted you have discussed I am at the other end of that spectrum. My experience has been somewhat similar to Dr. Wolf's: I started reading at two or so, and was tested extensively. Somehow it was a series of roads not taken. But at the end of seventh grade I began studying psychology at Notre Dame in South Bend, Indiana. I had trouble fitting into the class socially, however, and withdrew in the middle of the first semester. After that I went to Phillips Academy. This brings up something which hasn't been considered very extensively in this study, and that is the possibility of sending some of these students away to the very high-level private schools. Some of them provide almost as great an opportunity for intellectual stimulation as college, but also offer the opportunity of meeting people who are somewhat closer in age.

WOLF: And where the environment is structured to the needs of younger people. That's point I often make about my Yale experience. Perhaps one reason I survived there was because it was during the war, when every able-bodied adult was in uniform and most of them overseas. My classmates consisted of the lame, the halt, the blind, and the eccentric. I think the general dislocation of the college environment probably helped to make me look slightly less eccentric. It was pretty traumatic anyway, but that was probably the three straws off the camel's back that kept it intact.

STANLEY: At least locally, the private schools have helped us in a great number of ways. Three SMPY youngsters are in three different private schools this year. All are taking calculus along with ninth-grade subjects; two of them are eleven-years-old, and one is thirteen years old. Thus the two eleven-year-olds are three years accelerated, and the thirteen-year-old is one year accelerated. One of the major limitations of the private schools, however, is that they are usually small and, consequently, have very little scheduling flexibility. They also tend to be unalterably opposed to grade-skipping once you are there; they'll let you skip grades into them, but once there, they frown on it in most cases. Some private schools are also reluctant to let excellent and prepared students leave a year early to go to college. At some of the very top New England private schools that may not be as much of a problem, because you can get such things as advanced calculus, I presume.

DAY: Yes, the mathematics curriculum at Phillips went all the way through linear algebra. Another advantage to such a school is that it not only provides intellectual stimulation in a more socially congenial atmosphere but also permits the individual to get the experience of living away from home. One of the problems I experienced at Notre Dame was that at that time my parents moved from Indiana to Pennsylvania, and I moved into a dormitory. That was a terrible experience. But the private high school allowed for living away from home in a more acceptable atmosphere.

EDUCATIONAL BRIDGING MECHANISMS

KEATING: I would like to make two points in response to the issues which Jon has raised. One is that with the early entrants at Hopkins, we have been extremely cautious about entering them into dormitory life immediately. We recognize the potential for social disorganization in such a situation. We prefer in most cases, except when requested otherwise by the student, to have him live at home and commute for a year or so. This reduces the potential for social distress, because the family and community ties remain unbroken. The second point is that much of SMPY's more recent research has dealt with various bridging or telescoping mechanisms for educational acceleration, rather than relying on a radical three- or four-year jump all at one time. Although the model which Jon described would certainly seem very good, the unfortunate fact is that the resources for such experiences fall far short of the number who could benefit from them. We have moved toward designing for individuals wide-ranging programs which could include everything from special classes to college courses part-time to advanced placement courses and examinations. We have found that there are many ways to provide the intellectual stimulation, while not radically altering the social situation of the student in one large jump.

FOX: There are quite a number of things which can be done to accelerate in steps the educational progress of these students. Some might get to college at fifteen instead of thirteen, but with sophomore standing, and be able to finish up in just about the same time. This advanced standing could come about through advanced placement examinations, by summer or part-time college courses, or by correspondence courses. This is probably more desirable. This was really one of the goals from the beginning of SMPY, the finding of less radical alternatives for these students than simply jumping them from eighth grade to college. That was done more or less out of desperation for the first two students, and it's gratifying that it worked well in those cases. But the broader perspective of the study was to find other ways one might achieve the same goal without such big leaps.

DAY: A similar program at Phillips has been developed in the last few years by Dr. Theodore Sizer, a former dean of the Harvard Graduate School of Education. The program involved an interim period on the way to college of one or two trimesters for students who were accelerating by a year or more. The student would come to Phillips to take some advanced course work, and then use that as a springboard to move quickly into college. The residential aspects of it were thought to be helpful as well, along with greatly increased freedom in when and how to do the work and so on.

KEATING: Some of the Hopkins early entrants have used a couple of semesters here as a similar sort of experience. They get advanced work while still younger and living at home, and use that experience to go on to other high-level institutions out of state.

LERNER: Another possibility which the verbal study (SVGY) is trying at my school is to bring college-level courses into the schools, taught by college teachers. This would be the reverse of sending children to the colleges to take courses there.

STANLEY: I have strong reservations about that for several reasons. One is that the college courses are already there, and it doesn't require a major administrative move to have the child take the existing course. Second, the youngsters in the college courses have the experience of being in a real college class and of being very good compared with college students. This can change the whole outlook of a bright student who has had little but boredom for a long time. One student I think of in particular had had a very routine education, with little adjustment for his great ability. He took computer science in the day school at Hopkins at age twelve and made an A in a large class. After that experience there was no stopping him; he proceeded to seek out advanced work, including more college courses. He realized that learning could be exciting. He enrolled this fall at Hopkins at barely fifteen years old with 39 college credits, including calculus III and organic chemistry. The final advantage is that, of course, the student does get college credits on his transcript. For these reasons, we in SMPY have preferred to have these students take regular, credit college courses where feasible.

LERNER: How about the humanities?

STANLEY: I think the point extends to those courses as well. I think there are real advantages. On the other hand, if the youngsters are not competitively able to go to college and make at least a solid B, we don't think they ought to go. They get no feeling of achievement with a routine C or less. For those students who can't do the college work, it might be beneficial to have advanced work within the school.

DAY: One of the problems I have heard with the college course approach is that there are students geographically isolated from such opportunities. One could consider this another argument for establishing an intermediary educational program which could serve that population.

STANLEY: Yes, and college correspondence courses can also be useful in that situation.

CONTINUATION OF ACCELERATION IN COLLEGE

BOLSTER: A number of parents have been asking me a question that I'll pose to you. Do the area colleges allow the youngster to move more quickly through their curriculum once he has speeded up to get there?

STANLEY: Let me use the nine Hopkins early entrants as a first illustration. Three of them got credit for calculus through the Advanced Placement Program examination, and are in advanced calculus now. Some of them are also taking number theory. At ages fourteen, fifteen, or sixteen they still find advanced calculus difficult enough. They can still make As, but it's not dreadfully easy. Next year they will be in higher algebra or analysis with a very select group, so there is no real problem of skipping any more mathematics for them. They're into the right level already. At a less difficult school than Hopkins they would probably need to leap into the sophomore year right away because the freshman year competition isn't enough for them.

BOLSTER: My question was addressed more to the rate of the course they would get into, rather than what level the course was. Wouldn't these students be capable of learning advanced mathematics courses at a faster rate?

MEYER: At Hopkins relatively few students take advanced mathematics courses, and most of them are juniors or seniors. Now some very accelerated student might be able to take that course as a sophomore or even as a freshman. That course is already sufficiently hard intrinsically, plus the fact that he might be taking it several years early chronologically, that I don't think there would be any need for further acceleration within the course.

KEATING: Another thing to keep in mind is that these things tend to be arranged in units, so that some acceleration would be possible by simply doubling up on courses.

MEYER: A typical load might be four courses, for example, and one of these very ambitious and able students might very well take five or six college courses, and there would be no need for acceleration within any given course. In other words, instead of taking one course in half the time, one could easily take two courses simultaneously.

WOLF: And if I understand at all the nature of modern mathematics, I gather that it's an extremely polyphyletic discipline. As you reach a certain intellectual level, there are a great many different directions to go. I've heard it said that a physicist, for example, is likely to be conversant with at least half of what is going on in the fields of physics as a whole, whereas even a superb professional mathematician may be conversant with a quarter or less of what's going on in mathematics, because of this polyphyletic nature of the field. So I suspect that that alone means there's no problem with enrichment.

BOLSTER: One important question I'd like to ask is whether or not you are making efforts to work with other area colleges to have them go along with a self-pacing or accelerated program for these youngsters.

KEATING: We initiated direct contact with the talent search of 1974, which Bill George and Cecilia Solano detail in chapter 4. Nearly all the schools in the Baltimore and Washington areas have been highly cooperative in allowing these students to take courses.

FOX: The problem of continued acceleration within the college framework can be worked out in a number of different ways. One of the first SMPY students who ever took a course at Towson State was a very young looking seventh-grader. After the first class the teacher called him to the front of the room and told him, "You don't belong in here. This course is too *easy* for you." So she put him into her more difficult class, but, because he didn't have the credits for the prerequisite course, he continued in the first course as well. He was the best student in both sections. In other instances we have found that if a student is taking a heavier load, doubling up and so forth, and is still not challenged, the best solution is to have him move to a school where the mathematics competition is more rigorous. The better the group the faster the class will move, so this is an indirect acceleration. A very able twelve-year-old taking a course at a regular state college might have sufficient competition, but at seventeen he may need to go to a highly selective university where the competition is more on his level.

COUNSELING

BOLSTER: What I'm really trying to get at is how these experimental programs can be made to work in a large public school system with many guidance counselors, some of whom are unfamiliar with or perhaps unsympathetic to such programs. I think SMPY has done a magnificent job with the students it has worked with. But how do you transfer this experimental program to a system with a large number of students?

WOLF: I might mention in retrospect that this is something they were very concerned about for me at Yale. They worked very hard to construct an appropriate program for me there. This was not true at Western Reserve, due to the influence of one highly placed professor who didn't want to see me graduate on any terms. For example, I was prevented from taking any English courses at Western Reserve because this professor determined, "*That* shall not graduate!" At Yale there was no one with such prejudices. I was told that freshman composition was too easy, and so I was put in a sophomore English class. There was enough there to keep me busy.

KEATING: A question which we have always been concerned about but have turned more attention to lately is precisely how such experimental programs can be institutionalized. There seem to be two key ingredients. The first is the availability of flexible program scheduling that would permit all the kinds of bridging mechanisms we have discussed: subject matter acceleration, grade skipping, college courses, and others. The second ingredient is the availability of adequate guidance and counseling to draw up the right program for the right student. An enormous amount of time in the first couple of years of the study was devoted to precisely this fitting of students to various programs. That level of counseling may not be feasible from an economic point of view, but in our experience a certain degree of routinization is possible. That kind of counseling would seem more feasible.

STANLEY: In discussing the cost of identifying younsters we, of course, didn't include the cost of subsequent counseling. We do give a great deal of "Rolls-Royce" counseling to our students; they call and visit often and we work intensively with them. Once it's institutionalized you can't quite expect that much. I don't really know how much guidance these girls and boys need when they enter college. If they enter the right college with a lot of college experience already and successful advanced placement courses, they may not need very much counseling in college. They may get along pretty well on their own; I don't detect any great stresses among our early entrants.

KEATING: At the secondary school level, the initial problems are bringing the programs into existence, and then funneling the people to the right program.

FOX: A lot of the time that we spent in the beginning was on searching out or frequently creating these bridging mechanisms where they didn't exist. We had to try some things that didn't work, doors that didn't open, and then go back and try something else. If you have a countywide system, a lot of these problems are eliminated. You can have group counseling and select the groups on formal criterion scores. We used this somewhat at the Roland Park School (see chapter 7). We also use a newsletter to keep people informed about opportunities, and this could be done on a county level. This could include very specific information on college courses and times, for example. If you had just one person who had full-time responsibility for these matters, that would be sufficient. This person would need to understand psychometrics, be able to do some counseling with the students, and know the curriculum. That may seem to be asking a lot, but that is what it would require.

FINANCIAL SUPPORT FOR PROGRAMS

STANLEY: I think that if you really did this thing from a cost accounting standpoint, you would find that there's a net profit involved. When a youngster skips a whole grade or two grades, and comes to college two years early, he doesn't take that mathematics in the school system. If you add all those increments up, and count also the relief of frustration for the poor teacher who has this extremely different student and no way to handle him, then I think the net cost will be pretty small. It certainly will be far less than working with slow learners.

KEATING: Let me pursue this line of thinking, because it is a question we need to investigate more carefully. We often use an analogy to the costs and benefits of working with atypical children at the other end of the spectrum, where a great deal of money has been invested. Carl, would you give us a brief outline of how that funding came about in the special education area, and what steps one might anticipate in trying to institutionalize special education programs?

BEREITER: If you go by the historical record what you need is a President with a gifted child. That might be difficult. Actually, I think it would be very hard to make a politically viable argument on humanitarian grounds for the expenditure of funds for the gifted. It just doesn't tug at the heart strings of enough people. Look at the data SMPY has reported. I'm skeptical of what the personality measures mean, but they certainly don't indicate that these highly gifted youngsters are hurting very badly. They seem to be happy and well-adjusted and so on.

STANLEY: But they are hurting in the retardation sense. Some are unhappy, some are apathetic, and some are angry, because they have to sit through 180 periods of algebra, most of which are unnecessary for them. In that sense they are suffering terribly.

BEREITER: But they are socially well-adjusted, personally well-put-together people according to the data. In other words, it's very hard to argue that this is a population of suffering children.

LERNER: I'd like to suggest that we don't have the data on men in their forties, for example, whose life-style was affected because of their earlier experiences and who are suffering now. I'll give you an example from my counseling experience. I came across a veteran the other day who is now forty-five years old and pretty miserable. His test scores were very high. His life history indicated that he had suffered through elementary school and never got through college because of his boredom. He has a menial job and many personal problems. We may be too pat in saying these children are happy. We may be doing to these students some things that will reflect damage much later in life.

BEREITER: You could find many similar cases, and I know of some myself. But I think you would also find that the incidence of such personal disasters was lower among this group than among the average population.

STANLEY: Do you think so, Carl? We have an anecdotal report, for instance, that from a very good local high school six out of eight successive valedictorians dropped out of college. They were over-bored for so long that when they went to Harvard or Yale or Dartmouth, they just wouldn't last very long.

BEREITER: Are you suggesting that Terman's findings are out of date and that times have changed?

STANLEY: I think so partly. I think that in those days the public schools were so relatively poverty stricken that the leap from high school to Stanford, for example, was a very exhilirating experience. It could be too exhilirating, one might be so unaccustomed to studying as to flunk out. Five percent of Terman's gifted did flunk out of college. But the others at least found a quantum jump, whereas the youngsters I mentioned probably don't find that. They continue to be bored, but are now free for the first time to quit.

KEATING: If the argument can't be made on humanitarian grounds, as you're suggesting, Carl, would you then suggest that the most successful argument is likely to be on other grounds?

BEREITER: Absolutely, and I can make a fairly easy and highly convincing argument on the grounds Julian has already sketched out: savings from years not taken. We know that it costs to send a child to school for a year at the various levels. You just subtract it. At the other end of the scale, consider Dave Weikart's (1972) financing of his preschool education program for prospective mentally retarded children. He gets money from the state of Michigan every year to continue that work by showing them that children who have been through this program have a lower incidence of assignment to special education classes. Such special classes cost more, quite a bit more, and he can show that, even though he runs a fairly expensive preschool program, it pays for itself. A number of children who would otherwise be assigned to special classes, by comparison to a control group, are not assigned to them, and thus cost the taxpayer less money. It's not hard to make such arguments.

PAGE: I completely endorse Carl's idea that the social argument is a very important one indeed. The economics of the thing are important, so that legislators and others are convinced that you are genuinely saving money, getting more bang for the buck, if you move people along at a good clip. But I swear that it seems to me that there's a tremendous appeal to be made on the personal basis. For example, on the accelerated class that Julian discussed (see chapter 7), if we believe that competence is pleasant, then qualified children who are deprived of such opportunities are not exploring their abilities to the fullest. The argument that they come out all right, that is they come out ahead of the people who are behind them on the average, doesn't seem to me to be a satisfactory rejoinder.

DAY: I think that agencies that handle research projects would be willing to support funding not exclusively for the sake of the gifted youth but for the potential benefit to science and mathematics, and so on.

BEREITER: I think arguments can be made on those grounds. Maybe one thing that isn't clear in the kinds of arguments I have been giving is that I'm not arguing about what *should* be convincing, I'm suggesting what I think *will* be convincing. At the present time, an argument that shows that it will save money is the most convincing argument. Arguments on the productivity of talent used to be very convincing. They aren't any more. The whole theory supporting that seems to have collapsed and we're in a state of disorder. It's hard to argue that a dollar spent on education gets back a dollar-twenty in earnings, whereas that used to be a very persuasive argument. Right now, the old notion that a penny saved is a penny earned has tremendous appeal.

STANLEY: Three years ago I would have also given the argument that if you get your Ph.D. five years early, you would get a good job and pay taxes for five more years. But now I'm a little self-conscious about that argument, because I'm not altogether sure that you will get a better job with a Ph.D.

BEREITER: If next week everyone gets very concerned that we are falling behind the Russians, then the kind of argument that we need a lot more high level talent will become persuasive again.

PLANNING FOR DIVERSITY IN PROGRAMS

CLARK: Jon Day was saying earlier that an experience that is missing for some of these precocious youths, which isn't necessarily solved by going to a local college or university for courses, is the opportunity to get together with professionals who are outstanding in their fields, to listen and learn from them, to be stimulated and encouraged. The problem is what society is going to get out of this. The National Science Foundation has always had as one of its purposes the encouragement of our potential in science and mathematics for national purposes. Wouldn't they support a program whereby these students who are identified early can go for brief periods during the summer to interact with outstanding scientists and mathematicians? This would encourage these students to pursue such careers and, presumably, would benefit the national interest.

STANLEY: That's one approach. That's the approach used by the North Carolina Governor's School, where they have a summer school with all kinds of enriching activities. It's one way. We do it pretty directly by college courses during the summer or evenings or on released time, and you do get contact with professionals as well as other interested high-level students. I think that it is true that some youngsters, perhaps not even a majority, would like to get away from home for a time and live at a good private school. I'm sure that there are many others who would be horrified at the thought of doing that. It's not just one particular set of needs. I wouldn't want to see any one of these things as *the* panacea.

KEATING: One of the implied advantages to the kind of program that Bill Clark was proposing is the beneficial aspect of interacting with bright, able peers. We have some evidence that the impact of the special classes, for example, was more than simply rapid advancement in achievement areas. They get turned on to a lot of other things as well, and they also begin to have better feelings about being different than they had before.

STANLEY: The special fast-math classes, such as those Joe Wolfson taught, are very special situations where youngsters across a broad age range but of comparable ability have a lot of interaction in getting to know each other.

WOLFSON: Let me speak of the advantages of having them together in a special fast-paced class, rather than letting them go through the regular curriculum where they will be sure "to get everything." It's just not the same experience. A class that's geared to the 75th or even the 85th percentile is still going to be different from a class that's geared to the 99½th percentile. It will be substantially different in terms of the pacing, in terms of the interesting and challenging problems you can do. With one group we did geometry in half a year. They could, of course, just double up with another course in the regular curriculum and get it done in the same amount of time, but it just wouldn't be the same. And these students are going to be ready to do college level work before they are chronologically at the college age, whereas if they went through all the high school courses they couldn't get to the college courses. It's good that all these high school courses are available to all youngsters, but they're not always the best for specially gifted kids.

STANLEY: One thing I'd like to mention in passing is the excellent cooperation of the public schools that we have worked with. A major advantage of these schools, that has been mentioned before in comparison to the private schools, is the greater degree of scheduling flexibility and the greater number of courses that are available. More and more I have the feeling that the good public high schools are the best bet for a large proportion of these students, if this is supplemented by special classes, skipping grades, college courses, early college entrance, and so forth.

CLARK: One of the things which has to be worked out more carefully is the operation of such diversified programs in a public school system. In terms of identification of these students, for example, when is the best time to do it? And what kinds of screening devices and tests should be used? Is the pursuit of all the many courses the student could take in high school a desirable alternative to rapid pacing through one sequence and then into college courses? Should we pick up the students before they have had algebra in the regular curriculum or afterward? Which curriculum is best for them, the new unified mathematics or the more traditional curriculum? What about the summer? Should we carry on through the summer, and leave behind those who would rather not do summer course work, or have the program only during the school year? Should we have more of other kinds of mathematics as enrichment rather than concentrating on acceleration? There are many, many such questions as we try to move this into a public school system.

STANLEY: The fundamental problem to be dealt with is that for these very able youngsters the pace of *any* regular curriculum will be too slow. The decision on the curriculum is far less important from our perspective than the pacing of these students through the curriculum. And the pace will be different depending on what group level you are working with. Compare the Wolfson II class with the Roland Park class taught by Dr. McCoart (chapters 6 and 7). Thus there are two points to keep well in mind. First, there is no one program, no one curriculum which will meet all the needs. What is required is a diversity of programs, and some people will take advantage of many of them, others a few or none. The second is that acceleration is intrinsic to SMPY's perspective. Enrichment without acceleration is going to be frustrating in the long run. Let me give you an example. If the youngster graduates from Baltimore Polytechnic Institute here and comes to Johns Hopkins, he won't automatically get advanced standing or credit. He has to go from department to department and try to beg for it, and often he doesn't try. So if a youngster gets into a top-level high school program, he'd better get some college credit to avoid the misery later on of being at too low a level. At any stage of the game, good enrichment will have to be tied in with good acceleration.

KEATING: The major point seems to me to be the invariance of the principles of adequate pacing and sufficient program flexibility despite their application to a great diversity of situations.

FOX: In chapter 3 I've outlined various strategies that can be used for identifying youngsters at different ages with different ability levels. For example, identifying sixth-graders for a fast-paced algebra program might be feasible for a countywide program, but would probably not be feasible for a school-based program—there just wouldn't be enough qualified students in the latter case. There would be differences also with respect to a system with middle schools (grades 6, 7, and 8) versus one with junior high schools (grades 7, 8, and 9). Or if you set up special classes which draw from a large population base you may have one each year. With a smaller base, you might have a new one every other year or every third year.

CLARK: The optional selective testing can also present problems. This year we're going to test all the eligible students. Could the PSAT be administered by the school system for this purpose? We don't want to use the regular administration because it is on Saturday, and some of the eligible people would not take it.

STANLEY: The Educational Testing Service would probably cooperate in such a venture, if you used an older form and covered the costs. Or you could use an out-of-date form of the School and College Ability Tests (SCAT).

BOLSTER: After the testing is completed, how would students be selected? Exactly what population is being considered in these programs?

FOX: It depends; you match the selection criteria to the goals of the program. The more fast-paced the program was planned to be, the higher you would set the selection criteria. And you could have several different levels with differing selection criteria.

BOLSTER: Aren't there problems in establishing and teaching many different levels of instruction for the precocious student in a large public school system?

STANLEY: We haven't found it desirable or feasible to have a single cut-off for everything, and I don't think you'd need to do that even in a public school system. What you would need to do would be to specify the criteria for each special opportunity that was being offered.

BOLSTER: The one thing we definitely want to avoid is injuring any youngsters. We don't want to start accelerating them and then have no place for them to go.

STANLEY: We've been very concerned about that and have assumed a continuing responsibility for any youngster who started out. On the other hand, that militates against starting them out very carelessly. It means you have to be very thoughtful and careful about which students get into which programs. It is better to err in the direction of over-selectiveness and not let sympathies or parental pressures sway such decisions. If you do, there will be even more discontented parents and youngsters, as well as programs with less likelihood of success.

KEATING: The SMPY staff and I thank you for participating in this discussion. We cordially invite you to attend the Lewis M. Terman Memorial Symposium on Intellectual Talent, to be held at Johns Hopkins on November 6–7, 1975. It, too, will involve considerable discussion and a proceedings volume, No. 3 in the *Studies of Intellectual Precocity* series.

REFERENCES

Bloom, B. S. (ed.) 1956. *Taxonomy of educational objectives.* Handbook I. *The cognitive domain.* New York: David McKay.

Campbell, D. T., and Fiske, D. W. 1959. Convergent and discriminant validation by the multitrait-multimethod matrix. *Psychological Bulletin* 56, 81–105.

Keating, D. P., and Caramazza, A. In press. Effect of age and ability on syllogistic reasoning in early adolescence. *Developmental Psychology,* 1976.

Stanley, J. C., Keating, D. P., and Fox, L. H. (eds.) 1974. *Mathematical talent: Discovery, description, and development.* Baltimore, Md.: The Johns Hopkins University Press.

Terman, L. M. (ed.) 1925–59. *Genetic studies of genius.* Five volumes. Stanford, Calif.: Stanford University Press.

Weikart, D. P. 1972. Relationship of curriculum, teaching, and learning in preschool education. In J. C. Stanley (ed.), *Preschool programs for the disadvantaged.* Baltimore, Md.: The Johns Hopkins University Press.

INDEX OF NAMES

(Pages in italics denote articles in this volume.)

Acland, H., 154
Aiken, L. F., 185, 213, 303, 306
Allport, G., x, xiii, xiv, 42, 107, 112, 113, 114, 115, 116, 126, 162, 168, 169, 180, 186, 228, 235, 240, 243, 260, 264, 265, 271, 273, 274, 278, 279, 283, 285, 286, 287, 292, 322
Anastasi, A., 29, 30, 105, 109, 126, 186, 213, 264, 272, 303, 307
Aristotle, 298
Astin, H. S., 11, 22, 107, 126, 144, 153, 185, 213, 242, 260, 263, 271, 280, 284, 303, 307
Atkinson, R. C., 302, 307
Avital, S., 313

Baird, L. L., 264, 271
Bane, M. J., 154
Barron, F. X., 171, 172, 178, 181, 264, 267, 268, 271, 272
Bates, J. L., 9, 14, 157
Battermann, M. M., xviii
Beer, M., 132
Bennett, G. K., 39, 107, 154, 158, 320
Bennett, M. G., 154
Benton, G. S., xviii
Bereiter, C. E., viii, xv, xvii, xviii, 297, *308–15*, 315, 321, 322, 323, 324, 325, 326, 337, 338, 339
Berger, A., 193, 213
Bergman, L., 122
Binder, P. R., v
Binet, A., 6, 38, 58, 71, 91, 148, 296, 327
Birch, S. W., 38, 43, 53
Bisconti, A. S. 185, 213
Bloom, B. S., 321, 342
Blumberg, H., ii, iii, xvii, xviii
Bock, R. D., 303, 307
Bolster, L. C., 316, 333, 334, 335, 341, 342
Bond, S. J., 160
Boole, G., 297, 307
Booth, G. W., xviii
Breen, T. F., 304, 307

Briggs, K. C., 172, 175
Brown, D. L., 297, 307
Buros, O. K., 271
Butcher, H. S., 265, 272

Caesar, J., 313
Campbell, D. P., ix, xii, 107, 109, 110, 111, 126, 242, 244, 245, 246, 247, 250, 251, 253, 260, 265, 266
Campbell, D. T., 324, 342
Campbell, E. Q., 154, 181
Capretta, P. S., 229, 240
Caramazza, A., 320, 321, 342
Carey, G. L., 185, 212, 213, 242, 260
Carmichael, L., 99, 240
Carroll, J. B., 171, 181
Cattell, R. B., 264, 265, 272
Chapin, F. S., 171, 178, 181
Chomsky, N., 161, 181
Clark, W. C., 316, 329, 330, 339, 340, 341
Clemans, W. V., 285, 286, 292
Clendennen, D. M., 154
Cobb, M. V., 4, 22
Cochran, W. G., 213
Coffman, W. E., 307
Cohen, D., 154
Coleman, J. S., 153, 154, 164, 181
Covington, M. V., 175, 180, 181
Cox, C. M., 216, 221, 226, 240
Cronbach, L. J., 296, 307
Crutchfield, R. S., 114, 127, 175, 181, 229, 232, 241, 264, 265, 268, 272
Cyphers, R. E., xviii

Datta, L., 267, 272
Daurio, S. P., 160
Davies, L., 175, 181
Davis, F. B., 7
Day, J., 316, 324, 331, 332, 333, 338
Dearborn, W. F., 7
Denham, S. A., vii, viii, xv, 3, 37, 48, 53, 69, 72, 74, 82, 87, 88, 89, *103–31*, 109, 112,

343

114, 127, 133, 153, 172, 186, 213, *225–41*, 235, 241, 243, 248, 260, 282, 284, 289, 292, 312
DeVries, R., 91, 98, 99
Doppelt, J. E., 8, 9, 154, 317
Drevdahl, J. E., 264, 272

Edwards, J. M., 10
Elkind, D., 90, 91, 99
Engelmann, S., 308, 315
Eysenck, H. J., 225, 227, 228, 234, 240
Eysenck, S. B. G., 225, 227, 228, 240

Fiske, D. W., 324, 342
Flanagan, 296
Flaugher, R. L., 310, 315
Fox, L. H., ii, vii, viii, xv, xvii, 3, 4, 11, 12, 14, 18, 22, 28, 30, 31, *32–54*, 33, 35, 38, 53, 54, 55, 56, 63, 64, 67, 68, 69, 72, 74, 82, 83, 86, 87, 88, 103, 104, 105, 109, 112, 114, 126, 127, 129, 132, 133, 138, 139, 141, 151, 153, 154, 156, 158, 159, 161, 181, *183–214*, 185, 186, 187, 191, 207 213, 214, 216, 220, 221, 226, 235, 241, *242– 61*, 243, 248, 252, 260, 263, 271, 272, *273–84*, 282, 284, 289, 292, 303, 307, 312, 325, 329, 330, 332, 334, 336, 341, 342

Gagne, R. M., 307
Galileo, G., 296, 297, 298
Gardner, J. W., 161, 181
Garvey, C. J., xvii, 11, 35, 160, 184
Gauss, C. F., 306
George, W. C., vii, xv, xviii, 3, 35, 44, *55– 89*, 60, 69, 71, 72, 73, 74, 75, 77, 78, 82, 87, 88, 89, *103–31*, 132, 133, 135, 142, 153, 334
Gintis, H., 154
Gleser, L. J., 228, 241, 285, 292
Gold, R. Z., 193, 213
Goodenough, F., 91, 99
Gordon, I. E., 235, 241
Gough, H. G., vi, 171, 181, 216, 217, 221, 227, 228, 237, 241, 264, 272
Gowan, J. C., 38, 43, 46, 53
Gray, T., 7
Greenstein, L. K., 3
Grim, V. S., xviii
Grosshans, F., xviii
Guilford, J. P., 178
Guthrie, J. T., ii, 90

Haier, R. J., vii, viii, xv, 48, 54, 172, 203, *215–22*, *225–41*, 226, 241, 267, 272, 311, 312, 323, 324
Hall, G. S., 314
Hall, W. B., 114, 127, 236, 241, 264, 269, 272, 274, 284

Handlon, J. H., 267, 272
Hartlage, L. C., 303, 307
Hartley, H. O., 288
Haven, E. W., 185, 214
Heilbrun, A., 216, 217, 221, 228, 237, 241
Helson, R., 114, 127, 229, 232, 241, 264, 265, 268, 272
Herrnstein, R. J., 161, 181
Herst, P. A., 274, 284
Heyns, B., 154
Hindemith, P., 328
Hobson, C. J., 154
Hogan, R. T., xvii, 11, 35, 160, 179, 184, 230, 241
Holland, J. L., ix, xi, 107, 109, 110, 111, 112, 113, 115, 127, 172, 176, 180, 181, 185, 193, 214, 225, 227, 228, 236, 237, 241, 243, 245, 248, 260, 264, 265, 266, 267, 272, 282, 284, 324
Hollingworth, L. S., 4, 22
Horace, Q., 298
Horn, R. A., xviii
Horn, S. D., xviii
House, B. J., 302, 307
Huntley, C. W., 266, 272

Inhelder, B., 92, 93, 99

Jacklin, C. N., 185, 214
Jefferson, T., 309, 310
Jencks, C., 153, 154
Jensen, A. R., 305, 307
Jones, R. L., 229, 240
Jung, C., 175

Kagan, J., 91, 99
Keating, D. P., ii, iii, vii, viii, xv, xvii, xviii, 3, 4, 12, 14, 18, *23–31*, 24, 29, 30, 31, 35, 38, 48, 53, 54, 55, 67, 68, 69, 74, 82, 83, 86, 87, 88, *90–99*, 91, 97, 99, 107, 126, 127, 132, 141, 153, 154, 161, 163, 181, 184, 185, 213, 214, 216, 221, 226, 241, 260, *262–72*, 267, 271, 272, 284, 292, 303, 307, 310, 318, 319, 320, 321, 322, 323, 329, 332, 334, 335, 336, 338, 339, 341, 342
Kelley, T. L., 7
Keynes, J. M., 297, 307
Kleman, M., 267, 272
Kogan, N., 91, 99
Kolakowski, D., 303, 307

Lankford, Jr., F. G., 154
Lehman, H. C., 298, 307
Lerner, L. J., 132, 134, 135, 155, 316, 328, 330, 333, 337
Lessinger, L. M., xiv, 172, 173, 174, 181, 227, 229, 231, 232, 241, 272

Lidtke, D. K., v
Lindzey, G., x, xiii, xiv, 42, 107, 112, 113, 114, 115, 116, 126, 162, 168, 169, 180, 186, 228, 235, 240, 243, 260, 264, 265, 271, 273, 274, 278, 279, 283, 285, 286, 287, 292, 321
Linsenmeier, J. A. W., viii, xv, *285–92*
Livingston, S. A., 23
Lovell, L., 98, 99
Lynn, R., 235, 241

Maccoby, E. E., 185, 214
MacKinnon, D. W., 114, 127, 236, 241, 264, 265, 267, 268, 269, 272, 274, 284
Malina, R. M., 303, 307
Martinson, R. A., xiv, 172, 173, 174, 181, 227, 229, 231, 232, 241, 272
Mathias, C. McC., 326
McCandless, S. A., xviii
McCauley, J., 90
McClelland, D. C., 161, 181
McCloskey, B., 124
McCoart, R. F., x, xviii, 128, 130, 139, 140, 141, 142, 146, 149, 150, 159, 340
McGinn, M., 160
McGinn, P. V., vii, xv, xvii, *160–82*, 325, 326
McNemar, Q., 16, 22, 93, 99
McPartland, J., 154, 181
Mednick, M. T., 171, 181
Mednick, S. A., 171, 181
Meyer, J. P., xviii, 316, 334
Meyers, P., 123
Michael, W. B., xviii
Michaels, L., 157
Michelson, S., 154
Miller, W. S., 7, 8
Milton, G. A., 185, 212, 214, 242, 260
Minsky, M., 297, 307
Mood, A. M., 154, 181
Moshin, S. M., 114, 127
Mosteller, F., 297, 307
Mussen, P. H., 99, 272
Myers, I. B., 172, 175, 181

Newcomb, T. M., 181
Newman, J. R., 296, 307
Newton, I., 296

O'Connor, J., 303, 307
Oden, M., 161, 181, 216, 221, 226, 241
Olton, R. M., 175, 181
Osgood, C. E., 253, 261
Otis, A. S., 6, 58

Page, E. B., viii, xv, xvii, xviii, 3, *295–307*, 302, 304, 307, 316, 317, 318, 319, 320, 321, 338

Parloff, M. B., 267, 272
Pasternak, S. R., viii, xv, *242–61*
Payne, J. N., 154
Pegnato, C. C., 38, 43, 53
Peiser, N. L., viii, xv, *242–61*
Piaget, J., 90, 91, 92, 93, 96, 97, 98, 99, 262, 319
Pierce, J. A., xviii
Plant, W. T., 274, 284
Polya, G., 298
Pythagoras, 317, 321

Radcliffe, J. A., 285, 292
Raven, J. C., ix, x, 16, 39, 42, 92, 99, 107, 127, 135, 154, 155, 235, 265, 267, 268, 269, 272, 298
Ricks, Jr., J. H., 154
Roe, A., 234, 241
Rottman, J. N., 10
Rulon, P. J., 7

Sandhofer, L. S., xviii
Sapon, S. M., 171, 181
Schaefer, C. E., 162, 181, 237, 238, 241, 264, 266, 267, 269, 272
Schaefer, R. A., 90, 91, 99
Scheffe, H., 93, 190, 247, 261, 284
Schmidt, J., 75
Seashore, H. G., 154, 158, 181, 195, 214
Shakespeare, W., 298
Shalika, J., xviii
Sheehan, T. J., 185, 214
Siegel, L., 229, 240
Siegel, L. M., 229, 240
Silverstone, H. J., 132
Simon, T., 6
Sizer, T., 332
Smith, M., 154
Smith, R. R., 154
Solano, C. H., vii, xv, 3, 44, *55–89*, 60, 72, 74, 77, 82, 87, 88, 89, 203, *215–22*, 311, 334
Solomon, L., 307
Southern, M. L., 274, 284
Spearman, C., 92, 127
Spranger, E., 113, 274, 284, 286, 287, 292
Stafford, R. E., 303, 307
Stanley, J. C., ii, vii, xv, xvii, *3–22*, 4, 12, 22, 23, 24, 27, 29, 30, 31, 32, 38, 53, 54, 55, 57, 67, 68, 70, 72, 73, 74, 75, 76, 77, 86, 90, 97, 99, 103, 119, 123, 126, 127, *132–59*, 141, 151, 153, 154, 155, 160, 161, 181, 184, 185, 195, 213, 214, 215, 216, 221, 225, 226, 241, 260, 262, 271, 272, 280, 284, 292, 295, 303, 307, 309, 310, 316, 317, 318, 320, 323, 324, 325, 327, 328, 329, 330, 331, 333, 336, 337, 338, 339, 340, 341, 342
Stevens, C., 215

Stoll, F., 90
Strong, E. K., ix, xii, 107, 109, 110, 111, 242, 244, 245, 246, 250, 251, 253, 265, 266, 324
Suci, G. J., 253, 261

Tannenbaum, P. H., 253, 261
Taubman, P., 307
Taylor, C. W., 264, 272
Terman, L. M., 6, 8, 21, 23, 31, 38, 43, 54, 91, 99, 161, 170, 181, 216, 221, 225, 226, 241, 251, 261, 296, 306, 325, 327, 337, 342
Thorndike, R. L., 31, 99, 310, 315
Tiegs, E. W., 6, 22
Torrance, E. P., 38, 53, 54
Tukey, J. W., xi, xiii, 202, 246, 255, 256, 257, 279

Vernon, P. E., x, xiii, xiv, 42, 107, 112, 113, 114, 115, 116, 126, 162, 168, 169, 180, 186, 228, 235, 240, 243, 260, 264, 265, 271, 273, 274, 278, 279, 283, 285, 286, 287, 292, 322
Viernstein, M. C., 160, 192, 214

Wagner, A. L., xviii, 139, 140, 141, 142, 145, 159

Wagner, H. M., 297, 307
Wallace, D., 297, 307
Wallach, M. A., 23, 31, 161, 180, 181, 263, 272
Warren, J. R., 274, 284
Webb, R. A., ii, 35, 90, 98, 99, 160, 184
Wechsler, D., 71
Weikart, D. P., 338, 342
Weinfield, F. D., 154, 181
Weiss, D. S., 48, 54, 226, 227, 229, 239, 241, 267, 272
Welsh, G. S., 171, 172, 178, 264, 267, 269, 271, 272
Wesman, G. A., 154, 158
Wiener, N., 327
Winograd, T., 297, 307
Witty, P. A., 38, 54
Wolf, M. K., 316, 318, 327, 328, 329, 331, 334, 335
Wolfson, J. R., v, ix, x, 14, 17, 18, 105, 106, 114, 115, 116, 121, 125, 126, 127, 128, 129, 130, 132, 133, 139, 144, 147, 148, 156, 157, 159, 188, 316, 317, 339, 340

York, R. L., 154, 181

Zeaman, D., 302, 307